SURVIVING 7TH AVENUE

One Woman's Story About the Perils of the Fashion Industry

KATE LIEGEY

ISBN: 979-8-9941507-3-3

DEDICATION

This book targets those hopeful dreamers who encountered doubt on their path to a career in fashion. It pays tribute to those who steadfastly chased their ambitions, exemplifying the determination to hold onto their values amid numerous challenges.

I would also like to dedicate this book to my dear friend Trish, who endured countless iterations of my stories and offered invaluable and constructive feedback—though it wasn't always easy to hear, it was essential for accurately in conveying my narrative. She is the most courageous woman I have ever met, and her unwavering support and undying faith in God has been a source of strength for me throughout the challenges I've faced in both the fashion industry and in my life.

To my lovely niece Serena, who has my strength and determination to make her own path in life. From the time that she was a little girl, until now, as a beautiful woman, we end our conversations with:

I am strong.

I am beautiful.

I am smart.

I am valuable.

I am loved.

I *am* a strong woman. Everything that's hit me in my life I've dealt with on my own. I've cried myself to sleep and wiped my own tears. I've emerged stronger from experiences intended to defeat me, gaining resilience every day thanks to my faith in God, who guided me through the bleakest moments of my life.

My faith is a living, daring confidence in God's grace. It isn't about asking God to stop the storm, it's about trusting him to help me through it.

TABLE OF CONTENTS

PRELUDE

If most people knew about the wild, sometimes devastating, occasionally thrilling forty-year ride I've had through the fashion industry—and why I'm finally ready to spill all the secrets—would they be shocked?

Maybe it would reveal the opportunities I overlooked or hint at where I'm headed next. It might expose just how naive I was, or perhaps how stubborn and foolish I could be. But it might also show that I had the guts to stand up to the bullies, predators, and power-hungry executives who tried to crush me at every turn.

You decide.

This story isn't some sanitized fairy tale—it's raw, messy, and absolutely true. I lived through every humiliating, exhilarating, heartbreaking moment of it, from the cocaine-fueled garment center of the 1980s to the celebrity brand circus of today. I've worked with A-list stars, country music royalty, reality TV personalities, chart-topping rappers, and some of the most notorious sexual predators you've never heard of—the garment center bosses who ruled their empires through fear, intimidation, and worse.

In the end, it wasn't my career that defined who I became as a person—it was surviving a career in fashion. I'm sharing this story for everyone who's ever worked in the apparel industry and endured the same kind of hardships and experiences I did. In this business, it doesn't matter if you fought back or gave up, as long as you stayed true to yourself.

These past forty years have flown by like a fever dream. I was lucky enough to start when talent was scarce and money flowed freely—before fast fashion, before social media influencers, before algorithms decided what was trendy. Those were different times, and in many ways, better times because you had to rely on your talents and instincts.

This career took me everywhere: exotic factories in remote corners of the world, backstage at fashion shows in Paris, celebrity mansions in Los Angeles, underground markets in Istanbul. I got paid to shop for trends in the world's greatest stores, to dig through vintage treasures at Parisian flea markets, to discover new fabrics in Milan. Who wouldn't love a job like that?

But here's what they don't tell you in fashion school: for every glamorous moment, there were a dozen moments of pure hell. Sexual harassment wasn't just common—it was expected. Wage theft wasn't an accident—it was a business model. Backstabbing and cheating wasn't unfortunate—it was survival.

I didn't get rich, but the experiences? Priceless. The lessons? Brutal but invaluable. Looking back, I honestly don't know how I survived it all, except that I am an eternal optimist and I loved to design clothing. Maybe I'm tougher than I thought, or maybe I'm just too stubborn to know when to quit.

The fashion industry today isn't the same beast I wrestled with for four decades. It's younger, faster, more ruthless. In a world built on the illusion of youth and beauty, now dominated by TikTok influencers and overnight Instagram sensations, where does that leave someone like me?

I'm not sure what happens next. I don't have all the answers, and

I'm not pretending I do. But I owe a debt of gratitude to everyone who laughed and cried with me, who picked me up when I was down, who never stopped believing that somehow—against all odds and way too many times—I'd rise from the ashes of whatever disaster had just exploded in my face, ready for the next adventure or hard-learned lesson.

Maybe my story will help you understand why I had to write this book. Maybe it will save some bright-eyed kid from making the same mistakes I did. Or maybe I just needed to look this industry in the eye one last time and say, "Enough is enough."

I wrote this for every young person who dreams of working in fashion but has no idea what they're walking into. The choice of what to do with this information is yours.

But don't say I didn't warn you.

INTRODUCTION:
You'll Never Work
in This Business Again!

This phrase has become so familiar in my career that I've grown numb to hearing it. Why am I writing this book? When I shared my story with a literary agent a few years ago, she compared it to the woman who wrote that explosive tell-all about Hollywood, the one that exposed the dirty underbelly of the movie industry. Her book revealed the lies, cheating, stealing, sexual harassment, and countless other scandals that made Hollywood the magnet it is today for people seeking power, fame, money, and attention.

That's when I realized my book would follow the same path, only it would expose a different industry: the apparel industry, or as we insiders call it, "the garment center."

Throughout my professional journey, I've experienced situations that brought feelings of horror and shame, often leaving me disenchanted with the world of fashion. Yet there were also inspiring and exciting moments that challenged me and helped shape me into the fighter and survivor I am today.

By writing my story, I hope to steer young men and women away from the challenges I've faced while clearing my mind and finally detaching from this tumultuous journey. My intention is to expose both the positive and negative aspects of the fashion industry, realities rarely discussed by those within it.

Many industry insiders who have bravely shared their insights now face career destruction or damaged reputations at the hands of the business leaders who run this industry.

The Glamorous Facade

The fashion industry did have its advantages once I reached a certain level of expertise. I traveled the world, shopped in exotic cities, flew first class, worked in Asia, stayed in five-star hotels, and enjoyed fabulous food. It was filled with thrills, innovation, and journeys to places that would have been financially out of reach had I not entered this field.

When I got into fashion, I had dreams similar to those hoping to break into the movie business. I wanted fame, money, power, and adventures. But more than that, I wanted to create something beautiful from nothing, to transform a piece of fabric into something truly exceptional that would be appreciated by everyone who wore it.

This isn't meant to sound arrogant; I simply wanted to design beautiful clothing that merged quality with artistic value. Everything else was just incidental rewards that came with success in the fashion industry.

The Warning

The literary agent who discussed my book delivered a stark warning: if I wrote my story and exposed all the names and events I'd encountered, I would probably never work in the industry again. Ever.

After thinking about it for exactly two seconds, I realized I didn't care anymore about ruffling a few "Gucci" feathers. I refused to let bullies deter me from telling my truth.

Don't misunderstand me, I loved this crazy business for many years and would fight to the end to stay in it, or at least die trying. But it was clear that by writing this book and revealing the "dirty little secrets" that arise daily in my interactions with celebrities and tyrants in the garment center, I would jeopardize my chances of future employment, especially in New York City.

That was okay with me. I would simply have to start another adventure or write a sequel to this insane story. If this is what it takes to name names and expose the truth about my experiences in the fashion industry, so be it.

Why I'm Really Writing This Book

I'm writing this as a cautionary tale for men and women who want to enter the fashion business. If I can help some misguided young souls who have stars in their eyes, thinking this industry will never take advantage of their gender, race, religion, or design talent, then that's worthwhile.

Am I writing this to clear the air and my conscience? Absolutely.

Do I want justice for even the smallest wrongs done to me and others in this business? Hell yes, and I can say that without a tinge of guilt.

Many characters in my book continue to flourish, and as the saying goes, a leopard doesn't change its spots, particularly when it's the leader of a fashion company.

The Reckoning

This moment feels like a reckoning—a statement settling the score with an invoice marked "PAID."

Take my story for what it's worth: a wild and unimaginable account of one woman's tumultuous journey through the hidden corners of the fashion industry. My goal is to inspire others to rethink the glamorous narratives that media and tabloids portray about fashion careers.

While some aspects of the industry may seem appealing, I can assure you there are many unsavory characters out there, and I've encountered more than my fair share.

So, pour yourself a cocktail, keep some tissues handy, and dive into the wild journey of my unpredictable career in fashion.

CHAPTER 1:
And God Created Retail

In the late 1980s, I stepped into the fashion world as a complete newcomer. I can still picture the defining trends of that era: bell-bottom pants swishing as people walked, frayed jeans that looked artfully worn, midi and maxi skirts in flowing fabrics, tie-dye peasant blouses in vibrant colors, and ponchos that seemed to be everywhere. I embraced every single trend with enthusiasm.

Looking back, my naive decision to stay in the fashion industry after my first encounter with sexual harassment reveals just how blindly optimistic I was about what lay ahead. That moment would mark the beginning of a lifelong battle to fight for my rights as a woman in business. I was determined to be judged on my talents and abilities, not on my appearance or body.

Fashion had captured my heart from my earliest memories. The moment my mother handed me my first Tammy doll, I fell completely in love with her and her adorable pink polyester polka dot dress. Barbie was strictly forbidden in our household. Growing up in a devout Catholic family, my parents worried that Barbie's exaggerated figure might plant inappropriate ideas in my impressionable young mind.

The instant I got my hands on that wholesome, girl-next-door doll, I went straight to work with a pair of scissors, cutting off the hemlines of her dresses. My mother watched in dismay as I "improved" Tammy's wardrobe. In my young mind, I reasoned that Tammy deserved to show off her best feature, her legs, which would help her compete with Barbie's obvious advantages. From that first snip of the scissors on Tammy's hemline, I knew with absolute certainty that the fashion industry was my calling.

I possessed an instinctive understanding that I could transform the ordinary into something extraordinary. Of course, I had no idea what treacherous journey awaited me on the path known as "Seventh Avenue"—the fashion industry, what insiders sometimes called "the dark side of the garment center."

Since I've already begun at the beginning with Tammy and my childhood fascination, I won't dwell extensively on my upbringing. What you need to know is this: I was raised in a middle-class family that was decent but dysfunctional in typical ways. I attended Catholic school from kindergarten through college, absorbing what felt like an excessive dose of Catholic guilt along the way. Despite the guilt, it was a genuinely enriching education that included healthy discipline and traditional values. This experience awakened a rebellious streak in my personality that has stayed with me throughout my entire life.

I majored in merchandising in college, and immediately after graduation, I packed my bags for the big, exciting city of New York to launch my fashion career. For an entire year, I slept on a friend's couch until I secured a small one bedroom apartment on the upper east side. I hunted for treasures in thrift shops to build a stylish wardrobe on practically no budget, while I waitressed at some very dubious establishments. When I finally secured my first job at a major department store, I was absolutely thrilled. The excitement was even greater because I had been selected as one of the rare women accepted into their prestigious "executive training program." In those days, this was truly an honor, and I felt elated to be chosen for such a distinguished opportunity.

On the first day of the program, I immediately sensed the intimidating presence of male dominance ready to assert itself at every opportunity. The class composition told the whole story: twenty men and just three women. It became clear within minutes that the men controlled everything and viewed women as both sexual objects and inferior beings. At times, I wondered if they even saw us as human at all, perhaps we were simply eye candy, perks that came with being in the training program. The overwhelming male energy filled every corner of that classroom, and all three of us women felt it immediately.

The training program operated on a harsh pass/fail system over three months. Pass, and you could advance to become an assistant buyer in a fashion division; fail, and you were no longer "invited to stay" in the program. It was strictly win or lose with no middle ground. Those three months tested me severely, but I thrived on the challenge and was absolutely determined to finish at the top of my class.

Sam Randolph, the son of a wealthy suit manufacturer, claimed the seat next to me on that very first day. He leaned over to my desk in an unsettling way and informed me that he planned to get me kicked out of the program. He also intended to get the other two "chicks" sitting across from me thrown out as well. I leaned back toward him with a sweet smile and politely responded, "Go to hell."

Sam constantly bragged about having inside connections. After all, his father and the president of this department store were supposedly "best friends," If it was true, I assumed Sam's success in the training program was virtually guaranteed. Despite this supposed advantage, he broke into nervous sweats whenever instructors asked him questions because he never knew any of the answers.

Even though Sam was only twenty-one, his appearance was thoroughly unappealing. His hair was already thinning and receding, his complexion was sallow and unhealthy, and his upper lip was perpetually dotted with beads of sweat and pimples. Standing at just five feet five inches, he wore cheap, poorly fitted suits that did nothing to enhance his skinny, underdeveloped frame. I couldn't understand why someone whose father owned warehouses full of designer suits would dress like he shopped at discount stores. He had terrible breath and a foul mouth, using curse words as if they were normal vocabulary. Back then, I was genuinely shocked to hear such language spewing from his lips, words I would never dare repeat. Simply put, the guy was slimy and made my skin crawl.

"Hey Blondie," he whispered in my ear one morning, "do you want to feel what it's like to be with a real man?"

"Sure," I replied without missing a beat. "Do you know one? You creep."

And with that exchange, the war between the sexes officially began.

Sam made it his mission to get all the women kicked out of the program, recruiting the other men to join his revenge campaign. The blatant sexual comments became a daily ritual: "Nice boobs," "I'd like to spank that ass," and worse. After enduring two weeks of sleepless nights and tears, I decided it was time to take matters into my own hands.

Mrs. McAllister served as the head of Human Resources at this large department store and was highly respected by the entire upper management team. I sat in the quiet reception area outside her office, ankles crossed and hands folded neatly in my lap, good Catholic school habits die hard. After fifteen minutes, her secretary, Mrs. Adams, a petite woman in her seventies, ushered me into Mrs. McAllister's office. As I described the verbal abuse from the male trainees, tears began streaming down my face. She sympathetically offered me a tissue, came around from behind her desk, and sat beside me. Then she looked directly into my eyes and spoke quietly but firmly.

"Dear Katie, I have worked in this department for forty years. I have watched them come and go. I tell you girls the same thing every year: 'Honey, it is a man's world.'" She leaned over to take my hand. "Katie, I suggest you go home, get married, have a few babies, and forget all this nonsense." She sat back in her chair and glanced at the clock, remembering it was lunchtime and she never deviated from her strict schedule or a meal. She jumped up and escorted me toward the door.

I stared at her in complete shock before gasping, "Are you kidding me?" I snarled through my sniffles. "A man's world? Oh, hell no, ma'am!"

"What if I don't want to get married right away? Or ever? Maybe I want to work. Maybe I need to work, it's not like my name is Rockefeller and I have a trust fund!" My voice rose with each word.

"Now calm down, dear," she said with a patronizing smile.

She stood very still and delivered her final verdict: "Look sweetie, the first-floor perfume counter is for girls like you. That's where your place is here at Macy's, if you insist on working in this industry."

I stared at her, completely stunned and speechless.

Then I carefully smoothed my designer thrift-store Chanel skirt, looked her straight in the eye, and declared, "Ma'am, I don't think so.

I will finish this training program if it kills me, and I will become a successful designer!"

As I rose from my chair, she looked directly at me and mocked, "It just may, my dear."

"It just may what?" I asked roughly.

"It just may kill you." She laughed.

I stood up abruptly and slammed the door behind me.

I'll show her, I'll show all of them, I thought as I returned to class, feeling defeated but not broken.

She Who Laughs Last Laughs Best

When I returned from Mrs. McAllister's office, my new friends Lauren and Kelly were waiting excitedly for me. They rushed over, demanding to hear everything she had said.

"Well, what did she say? What is she planning to do about the guys?"

"She said we should be strong and show all these men that we are not quitters!" I lied smoothly.

"Yes, we are strong!" they shouted in unison as we embraced.

"We knew she would be on our side! She's a woman, for God's sake!" Kelly exclaimed.

I took both their hands, squeezed them tightly, and said, "Okay girls, now let's teach these little bastards who's boss!"

That night, I lay in bed trying to devise a plan to stop the harassment. What if I failed? What if I was asked to leave the program or, worse yet, got caught perpetrating a decisive scheme to take these men down? Would I end up selling perfume at that first-floor counter like Mrs. McAllister predicted? *Oh God, please help me... I need a plan!*

I woke up the next morning at 6:00 a.m. feeling energized and ready to face the world with a plan in place. More importantly, I felt ready to take on Sam Randolph, the evil incarnation of Satan's tailor.

If I was going to risk everything, I decided I better look absolutely fabulous. After all, I was in fashion! I curled my long blonde hair, fastened my faux pearls around my neck, and put on my newly purchased push-up bra. I pulled out my dark gray thrift-store Christian Dior suit and cinched a thin alligator belt around my waist. I slipped into painfully high black pumps and applied pink lipstick with just a hint of shimmer as the finishing touch.

After giving myself a complete once-over, I turned to my pug and announced, "Wish me luck! If I succeed, it's burgers tonight, girl! But if I fail, it's back to ramen noodles, my friend."

I swear my little pug winked as I closed the door behind me.

I hurried down the street and found a seat on the Fifth Avenue bus. During the ride to Macy's, a wave of emotion washed over me. I felt empowered with inner strength and a fierce determination to fight for our rights as women. This was about more than just staying in the training program, it was about breaking the tradition of "a man's world," as Mrs. McAllister had so bluntly put it. This powerful drive was what I later called my "Oprah aha moment": Be empowered as a strong, smart, confident woman, and own it! That was my plan.

I wobbled slightly on my stiletto heels as I entered Macy's classroom. Kelly and Lauren sat across from me, saving the seat next to me for Sam. As predicted, he slithered over and leaned uncomfortably close.

"You look sexy today, Blondie," he said, drooling as he rubbed my shoulder. Every fiber of my being recoiled.

I leaned toward him and whispered breathlessly, "Thank you, handsome. You look pretty sharp today too."

Ugh! Disgusting! I cannot believe I just said that, I thought to myself, but I couldn't let anything deter me from my plan.

"Hey, you want to go to lunch with me?" he asked, still drooling while staring directly at my chest.

"Hey Sam, my eyes are up here," I snapped at him.

"Okay, sure. I'd love to have lunch with you," I whispered.

Oh God, please help me get through this day, I prayed silently. I actually have to eat with this creep. I promise to make it to Mass Sunday, I'll even go to Confession. Please help me get through lunch today without throwing up!

When the clock struck twelve, I knew I had to give the performance of my lifetime to win this battle of "men versus women."

Sam treated me to lunch at a cheap diner with two-for-one specials. We ate mediocre tuna sandwiches, drank flat Coke, and munched on stale chips, all while surrounded by a musty, mildew odor. I flirted playfully, holding my breath, batting my eyelashes, and hanging on his every self-important comment, and there were many. Midway through our meal, he remarked, "This is great, beautiful. You're not too shabby for a dumb blonde and I can't wait to get you into my bed." He chuckled as a crumb from his sandwich flew out of his mouth and landed on my vintage Christian Dior lapel.

Great, I thought, now I have to get my suit dry-cleaned.

It took every ounce of my inner strength not to slap his disgusting face. Instead, I tossed my hair back and laughed coyly, nearly hitting him with my curls. As we prepared to leave, he rested his hand on the curve of my back and slowly lowered it to brush against my backside.

I pulled away deliberately, as if to convey that I was a "good Catholic girl."

We crossed the street back to class. I knew this was survival of the fittest, and it was my duty to right this wrong for all the women who might encounter Sam Randolph in the future world of fashion.

His hand kept brushing against mine as we walked, so I quickened my pace to almost a run.

"Wait up," he panted behind me. I ignored him but turned to blow him a kiss just as we stepped onto the Macy's escalator. When we took our seats back in the classroom, I knew it would be a victorious week because now I had a plan in motion to destroy this little weasel.

After class, Kelly and Lauren rushed over to me. "Okay, what happened at lunch? How are we going to get that jerk?"

"Patience, girls, patience," I smiled mysteriously. "I have a plan."

Just then, Sam sauntered over and leaned close to me. I could smell the mustiness of his old suit and the lingering onions from lunch on his breath.

"Hey Blondie, do you want to get a 'cock-tail' after class?" He laughed and spat simultaneously.

"Love to, Sam," I exclaimed while recoiling, trying to prevent any more stains on my suit.

After class, Kelly, Lauren, and I walked into the crisp fall air. I knew I needed to eliminate him quickly because if he touched my rear end one more time, the New York Post's morning edition would feature the headline: "Garmentos" Sleazy Son Skewered by Stylishly Sensational Stilettos!"

Having drinks with Sam after work was painful beyond description and gave me new appreciation for the term "Artful Dodger." Every time he fondled my knee or touched my hair, I jerked away until I thought I might fall off the banquette. Sam rambled on endlessly about how wonderful he was in bed, how wealthy his father was, and how he was engaged to a plain, unremarkable girl. She had been promised to him at a very young age for marriage, according to his religious traditions, but that didn't stop him from perusing other women.

He made it crystal clear that a blonde Catholic girl like me would never be the fortunate wife or girlfriend of a "decent" religious boy like himself. *Thank you, God!* I thought, pitying the poor girl who would be stuck marrying this jerk.

"Then why ask me for a drink?" I asked curiously.

"Oh, I can sleep with as many attractive girls as I want, just not marry them," he laughed. "Get it, Blondie?" I can have anything I want, I am the son of a very powerful man. He sneered and punched my arm.

"Ouch! Absolutely, I get it," I replied. *But you won't get anything from me,* I thought angrily.

His arrogance in thinking I would even sit next to him on a bus, let alone sleep with him, infuriated me even more. For a moment, I considered abandoning the entire plan, but I couldn't let down my new friends who were counting on me to rewrite the rules of the training program.

But I needed to take one for the team and show this creep that I wasn't going to let him win, no matter what.

After several interminable hours of listening to his inappropriate, disgusting commentary, it became crystal clear how my plan would work to get this jerk thrown out of the training program.

The next day, I met with my fellow female trainees and co-conspirators to outline my plan of attack. As they shrieked with laughter and approval, I gave them specific instructions on how we would annihilate this slimy character and show the other men on the training program that we were not to be messed with.

We decided that tomorrow would be "slimy Sam day," and we all prepared for battle by going home and getting a good night's sleep.

Later that evening, I took a walk through Central Park, and I could sense my impending liberation. Soon, I would no longer be subjected to Sam's blatant sexual innuendos and unwanted touching. I would show him just how determined I was to succeed on my own.

I wondered why this double standard existed in business, or was it specific to the fashion industry? Where were the employee manuals stating that men couldn't treat women as sexual objects in the workplace, much less grope them? Where did it say that degrading women in public was acceptable behavior? Why was it considered normal, even praiseworthy, for men to show such complete disregard for women?

Every Friday, Mrs. McAllister conducted a mandatory senior staff meeting with all twenty division heads in one conference room. The meeting lasted an hour, during which she reviewed new policies and addressed outstanding issues. Since the training program director was required to attend, we trainees were given a free period to study, explore the sales floor, or—in today's case, "set up a big jerk."

Mrs. Adams, Mrs. McAllister's secretary, always left during this hour to have lunch with her husband, and this Friday was no different (or so she thought). With Mrs. McAllister's office unguarded, I needed to move quickly since time was crucial. I leaned over to Sam and gently touched his scrawny knee, caressing it slightly. With a feverish look in my eyes, I said in my breathless "Marilyn Monroe" voice, "Hey handsome, I have a really exciting idea that involves just you and me, baby," I whispered into his ear.

Oh my God! I've never seen so much hair in anyone's ears! I nearly gagged, thinking I might faint.

Stop! Stay focused on the big picture, I told myself. Oh God, I'm going to throw up, there's a jungle in there! Focus, girl!

"Really, Katie? Do you want to get 'freaky'?" He drooled with excitement as his saliva hit me in the eye.

Can I get an eye infection? Stop it, I thought. This is serious.

"Absolutely. Right here and now!" I lied and giggled. "Let's get freaky." He grinned like a lecher.

In another breathless voice, I whispered, "Oh Sam, ever since we had drinks, I haven't stopped thinking about you. If I have to wait any longer to hold you in my arms, I'll go insane." *I should be nominated for an Academy Award,* I thought.

"Here? Now? Are you serious?" he said, looking shocked yet excited.

"No, not here, silly," I winked. "We can use Mrs. McAllister's office. She's at that meeting and her secretary is out for lunch." I smiled coyly. "We have one hour, handsome. One long, hot, and steamy hour," I whispered longingly into his hairy ear.

"Oh, it won't take that long, Blondie," he giggled with excitement as sweat poured down his pimpled face. *You got that right,* I thought to myself. *Three minutes should do it.*

I instructed Sam to go into Mrs. McAllister's office and wait for me on her couch. "Oh, and take off your pants," I said sweetly. "I just need to go to the ladies' room to freshen up, then I'll meet you there in five minutes." I winked. His assumption that he could waltz into an executive's office at will was astonishing.

"Hey Blondie, do you have protection?"

"Of course," I smiled. You bet I do! You idiot, every woman here is my protection, I laughed to myself.

Naturally, Sam had to stop and brag to the other guys about how I was going to "put out" just for buying me drinks. As they exchanged arm punches and high-fives, Lauren snuck into the training director's office to steal a piece of official letterhead. Kelly stood guard to ensure Sam went into Mrs. McAllister's office and did exactly as instructed.

As planned, Sam boldly walked into Mrs. McAllister's office, leaving the door slightly open. When Kelly peeked inside, she watched him quickly remove his polyester pants and toss them on the floor. At first barely able to control her laughter, she gasped when Sam pulled off what appeared to be "Underoos" underwear to reveal what we later described to our friends as "the Monster."

She composed herself and ran back to inform us that Sam was lying naked on Mrs. McAllister's couch, waiting for the deflowering of a blonde "Catholic girl."

Meanwhile, Lauren had written the message and set our plan in motion. She wrote it on the official letterhead she had stolen from the training director's office and delivered it to Macy's president's office. I walked into Mrs. McAllister's meeting, leaned over her desk, and quietly told her that Macy's president was waiting to speak with her in her office. She jumped up, flustered, and told everyone to continue discussing among themselves until she returned. She smiled at me and hurried down the long hallway to meet with the president. She must have wondered why the president would leave his "executive tower" to meet with her, perhaps a promotion for all her years of loyal service to the company?

She rushed into her office beaming with excited anticipation. "Hello Bob!" she called out as she entered, then came to a complete, crashing halt.

At that exact moment, Macy's president was reading the note his secretary had handed him. "Please come quickly to Mrs. McAllister's office now," it read. "We have a situation." The note was signed by the executive training program director.

I joined Kelly and Lauren at the end of the hallway, watching as Mrs. McAllister opened her office door expecting to see the president. We could barely contain ourselves, we were laughing so hard. Anticipating what was about to happen next felt both hilarious and thrilling.

"Shhhhh. You'll ruin it!" Kelly whispered to me.

"Oh, I don't think so!" I replied, still laughing.

Suddenly, we heard the loudest, most blood-curdling, gut-wrenching scream from Mrs. McAllister. A moment later, Sam Randolph scrambled out of her office, embarrassed and completely naked, running down the hallway. With his pants and "Underoos" clutched in his hands, he ran directly into Macy's president, his father's best friend!

"Oh my God," Sam moaned. "It's not what you think, sir!"

Mrs. McAllister then ran out of her office with her arms flailing as she caught another glimpse of Sam's nakedness and promptly fainted on the floor in front of the president and everyone who had emerged from their offices and conference rooms to see what was happening.

"Someone get Mrs. McAllister some water immediately!" the president screamed.

"What the hell is going on here, Sam?" the president yelled. "Why are you naked? Are you some kind of sick pervert?" His face turned blood red as he screamed.

Sam stood there frozen and speechless for the first time in his life.

A crowd of twenty directors and the entire training program gathered in the hallway. "Oh my God!" everyone exclaimed simultaneously. One director leaned over to me and asked in shock, "Good Lord, is that Sam Randolph?"

"Why yes, it is, ma'am," I replied, feigning shock while trying not to laugh.

"Oh my God, he's completely naked!" the director exclaimed, causing everyone to gasp and laugh.

"No, he certainly isn't wearing any clothes!" I said, giggling.

Just then, four security guards arrived, demanding to know what the problem was and why everyone was screaming. As soon as they got a full view of Sam's naked body and "the Monster" standing at attention, plus Mrs. McAllister lying unconscious on the floor, they roughly grabbed Sam by the arms and quickly escorted him to the security office, his naked body in full view for everyone to see.

A very flustered Mrs. McAllister sat on the floor, still in shock, as the president tried to help her up while remaining flustered himself. Mrs. McAllister, weighing approximately 250 pounds, struggled to move. The president, a tall, thin man, attempted to lift her alone but lost his balance and landed right on top of her.

We all gasped and then burst into uncontrollable laughter again.

"Show's over, people!" he yelled as he jumped to his feet. Two additional security guards pulled Mrs. McAllister off the floor and helped her stand. She smoothed back her hair bun and pulled down her skirt, which had ended up around her waist, revealing her bright red girdle to everyone present.

"Pretty stylish!" I laughed, and then everyone joined in the laughter again.

"The staff meeting is over," she whispered meekly, flushed and embarrassed as she waddled back to her desk. "Trainees, return to class immediately!" she demanded. "This show is finished!"

She turned and walked into her office, her skirt still caught in her girdle. We all laughed again as she slammed the door behind her.

I returned to my seat in the training room and looked around to see every male trainee's head turned downward, avoiding eye contact with me and my friends. It was a surreal moment that all us women secretly cherish to this day.

Victory—oh, the sweet smell of success! I thought.

"That will teach these boys not to mess with us," Kelly laughed. The guys remained silent, still in shock.

Later that day, we learned that Sam Randolph would not be "invited" to continue in the training program. Furthermore, if any other young man attempted a similar stunt, he would also be asked to leave. All the male trainees were then required to attend "sexual harassment training."

"Well, girls, we won the battle, but not the war," I smiled. "That, my friends, might take a lifetime."

That evening, as I put on my coat to leave, I passed by Mrs. McAllister's office.

"Katie," she called out. "Come into my office."

I stepped inside, still pretending to be upset about the day's events.

"You didn't have anything to do with that young man's behavior today, did you, Katie?" she asked sternly.

"Why no, Mrs. McAllister, of course not," I replied, affecting a shocked expression.

"Very well. Just remember that men can act like animals, and you always need to stay on guard in this business," she stated, still visibly shaken.

"Good night, my dear," she smiled.

"Good night, Mrs. McAllister," I said sweetly, trying not to laugh.

As I turned to leave, I heard her let out a hearty laugh.

Secretly, Mrs. McAllister knew she would never see me working at Macy's first-floor perfume counter. She recognized that a woman like me had bigger plans, and God help the fashion industry.

One thing was certain: Mary Frances McAllister would never forget the sight of "the Monster" for as long as she lived. Over time, this story evolved into legend, recounted to everyone fortunate enough to be selected for the training program!

As for Sam Randolph's fate? He eventually took over his father's business, ran it into the ground, and was sued for sexual harassment by several female employees. He left many people unemployed and owed millions to the manufacturers he had cheated. However, I can say with absolute certainty that this "Catholic girl" is one he will never, ever forget.

CHAPTER 2:
The White Elephant

After enduring the challenging experience at Macy's training program and two years as an assistant buyer for women's sportswear, I knew I needed a fresh start somewhere that wouldn't constantly remind me of how undervalued I felt as a woman in the fashion industry. The memory of that humiliating encounter with the training program boys and Mrs. McAllister's dismissive advice still stung, but I refused to let it define my early career path.

In 1982, I set my sights on JCPenney's corporate offices in New York. Despite my growing awareness of the fashion industry's harsh realities through shared stories with other women, who had experienced the hardships of sexual harassment, I remained surprisingly naive about what lay ahead. JCPenney had earned the unfortunate nickname "white elephant" among fashion insiders, a term that perfectly captured how most people viewed the struggling retailer. In those days, their sales were disappointing, their reputation was lackluster, and frankly, most fashion professionals wouldn't dream of working there.

But that's exactly why I wanted it. While others saw a sinking ship, I saw opportunity. This wasn't just about finding any job; it was about proving I could make a real impact and showcase my design abilities where they were desperately needed. The challenge excited me more than intimidated me, which probably says something about both my determination and my inexperience.

A Bold Strategy Pays Off

Rather than follow the conventional route of sending resumes and waiting for callbacks, I devised what I thought was a brilliant strategy. Every day at lunchtime, I would march into JCPenney's Human Resources department, wearing my most eye-catching outfits, and simply wait. I'd unwrap my humble peanut butter and jelly sandwich from its wax paper covering and sit there for exactly one hour, hoping someone would notice me and give me a chance to apply for a position in the buying office.

Looking back, it was either incredibly bold or completely foolish, probably both. But desperation can breed creativity, and I was determined to stand out in a sea of forgettable applicants. Day after day, I showed up like clockwork, treating the HR waiting area like my personal networking lounge and fashion runway.

On the fifth day, my persistence finally paid off. A large, jovial man with a perfectly groomed mustache approached me with curiosity rather than annoyance.

"Are you waiting for somebody?" he asked, his voice carrying a warmth that immediately put me at ease. "I've seen you here every day for the past week."

"Why yes," I replied, unable to contain my enthusiasm. "I'm waiting for a job in the buying office!"

His eyebrows raised in amusement. "Oh really? With whom?"

"I'm not sure yet," I admitted with complete honesty. "I'll just stay here until someone notices me and is available in Human Resources to interview me."

Something sparkled in his eyes, perhaps he appreciated my unconventional approach, or maybe he admired my sheer determination. "They've definitely noticed you and your eye-catching outfits," he said with a chuckle, "and it seems luck is on your side today. I could use an assistant in men's shirts. What's your name?"

"Katie," I said, practically bouncing out of my chair with excitement.

"Do you know anything about men's shirts?" he asked, clearly testing me.

Without missing a beat, I replied, "Yes, of course. My dad wears them!"

It wasn't exactly the most professional answer, but it was honest, and something about my earnestness must have charmed him. He laughed not at me, but with genuine amusement at my refreshing directness.

Welcome to JCPenney

The man introduced himself as Ron Donaldson, the men's buyer at JCPenny's and within minutes, he had marched into the Human Resources director's office, instructed her to prepare the necessary paperwork, and returned to officially welcome me to his team. I squealed with excitement like I'd just won the lottery, which probably wasn't the most dignified response, but I couldn't help myself. After facing numerous rejections this year while applying for fashion jobs without much experience, someone finally recognized my potential.

"Thank you, Mr. Donaldson! You won't regret it!" I gushed.

"I better not," he replied with a wink that suggested he was already invested in my success.

As he started to walk away, he paused and turned back with a more serious expression. "Katie, can you do one favor for me when you start working here on Monday?"

"Yes, anything, Mr. Donaldson!"

"Tone the outfits down, please. We're very conservative here, this isn't Macy's."

I glanced down at my stunning plaid kilt, warm red cashmere sweater, and eye-catching purple knee-high boots. Suddenly, I understood why I'd been getting so many stares in the elevator. My outfit screamed "fashionista" rather than "conservative corporate employee." I couldn't help but laugh at myself, no wonder they'd noticed me.

That evening, I rushed home and conducted a ruthless wardrobe purge, removing anything that might be considered too flashy for my new role at JCPenney.

The First Day

Monday morning arrived with all the nervous energy of a first date. I woke up extra early and carefully selected my most conservative blue Calvin Klein pantsuit, accessorizing it with a thin black designer belt. The company's requirement that I wear nude stockings, a policy I found rather antiquated, completed my transformation from fashion rebel to corporate conformist. I slipped into my YSL black low-heeled pumps, purchased on sale during better financial times, and caught the 5th Avenue bus to begin my new chapter at JCPenny's.

At the time, in order to save some money, I moved into a spacious two-bedroom apartment owned by Christie, a wild college friend whose lifestyle was as chaotic as her schedule. By day, she worked as an accountant; by night, she performed as a stripper. Her stage name, "Boom-Boom," perfectly captured her larger-than-life personality. She was a striking red head with an hourglass figure that would make Barbie jealous, and she had an unfortunate weakness for married men and cocaine. While her sense of humor could be infectious, her messy lifestyle and the parade of questionable characters she brought home made her far from ideal roommate material. The silver lining was that she rarely came home before 3:00 a.m., which meant I usually had the apartment to myself during normal hours.

Walking into the JCPenney building on 6th Avenue at exactly 9:00 a.m., I felt a mixture of excitement and terror. The security guard directed me to Ron Donaldson's office, and I was given a company badge, my first tangible proof that I actually belonged here. As the elevator climbed to the 10th floor, my heart pounded with anticipation.

The elevator doors opened to reveal Ron waiting for me, his face lit up with a welcoming smile. Beside him stood an impeccably dressed older African American woman whose presence commanded immediate respect.

"Katie, your suit looks great! Ron smiled. Please meet Yvonne, she's my invaluable assistant here in the men's department and the real force that keeps our office functioning smoothly."

Yvonne offered a polite but reserved smile, her cautious demeanor clearly reflecting years of experience with eager new trainees who might not last the month. Her wariness was understandable; in her position, she'd probably seen countless bright-eyed newcomers flame out within weeks.

A Lesson in Industry Reality

Before diving into my new role, I should mention something

that troubled me about the fashion industry during this era. Prior to the 1980s, the garment center was shockingly non-inclusive, particularly when it came to people of color. Throughout my career, I would witness firsthand the obstacles and systemic biases that African Americans faced when seeking employment in fashion.

I remember one particularly disturbing conversation with a previous employer who bluntly told me that hiring African American candidates "wasn't an option" for his company. I chose to ignore such backward thinking and, as I advanced in my career, made it a personal mission to recruit and mentor talented individuals regardless of their race, sexual orientation or background. It was a small act of rebellion, but an important one.

Ron Donaldson: An Unlikely Mentor

Ron invited me to the company cafeteria for coffee and breakfast, where he outlined my future role on his team. Despite his considerable size, he was a man who clearly enjoyed his food—he carried himself with dignity and dressed impeccably. Every day, he explained, suppliers would treat him to lavish lunches at five-star restaurants, a perk of being the person who wrote the big orders that could make or break their businesses.

"The suppliers would rather I not bring Yvonne to these lunches," he confessed, "but I don't care what they prefer. Having a big order book gives you the power to do the right thing." His grin revealed both his enjoyment of fine dining and his principled approach to business.

After a few months of proving myself, I would be invited to join these weekly lunch excursions—an invitation that thrilled me not just professionally, but personally. My paycheck was modest, and I was constantly struggling to make ends meet. The men I dated weren't exactly the type to wine and dine me at establishments like Le Cirque, Balthazar, 21, or Delmonico's, where Ron seemed to know every maître d' by name.

These lunches became a masterclass in both fine dining and business relationships. Ron had a peculiar ritual with his meals that fascinated me. He would always order a "chopped" salad, orchestrating its preparation like a conductor leading a symphony. He'd instruct the waiter to lay out all the ingredients on a chopping board and cut them into tiny, uniform pieces before serving.

"My mustache," he explained one day when I finally worked up the courage to ask. "I can't stand getting food caught in it, so this is the best way to enjoy a salad without creating a disaster." He also mentioned that he'd promised his wife to eat more greens daily, a commitment he took seriously despite his obvious preference for steak and potatoes.

Despite his substantial build, Ron was impeccably dressed, always wearing custom shirts with elegant cufflinks and suits that were so perfectly tailored they looked like they came from a Savile Row shop. He was one of the most stylish men I'd ever encountered, proving that good taste had nothing to do with conventional body types.

During these lunches, while the men would excuse themselves for the restroom, I developed a rather embarrassing habit of wrapping up leftover rolls and slipping them into my purse for dinner. It wasn't exactly dignified, but when you're struggling to pay rent, pride becomes a luxury you can't afford.

A Friendship That Would Change My Life

Over time, Yvonne began to warm up to me, and we developed a genuine friendship that would profoundly impact my understanding of both the industry and myself. Sadly, several months into our relationship, I discovered that she had been battling a serious illness for some time. The news devastated me.

For six months, I made daily visits to her hospital room after work, bringing stories of my adventures with Ron and the latest office gossip. These visits became precious to both of us. She cherished hearing about the world she was missing, while I gained wisdom from someone who had navigated the industry's challenges with grace and integrity.

One September evening, as I held her increasingly frail hand, she shared advice that would guide me throughout my career.

"Never take a kickback, Katie," she said, her voice weak but determined.

"I won't, I promise," I replied, fighting back tears.

"Listen to me carefully," she continued, managing a faint smile. "If you take even one kickback, you'll never be able to make a truthful decision again. That choice will weigh on your conscience forever."

Yvonne became more than a colleague; she became a role model and mentor whose influence would shape every major decision I made in the years to come. When I faced difficult situations later in my career, I would always ask myself: "What would Yvonne do?" Her example of maintaining integrity in an industry rife with corruption became my North Star.

This conversation established the one inviolable rule I followed throughout my time in the garment center. Despite numerous offers and opportunities over the years, I never accepted kickbacks from supplier's eager to get their products into our stores. This decision sometimes put me at a disadvantage financially, but it allowed me to sleep well at night knowing my recommendations were based on merit, not monetary gain.

Unfortunately, I couldn't say the same for many of my colleagues. I witnessed several people I knew engage in systematic theft from their employers, accumulating enough illicit profits to retire comfortably. One manufacturer made Friday rounds through a specific garment center building, distributing payoff envelopes to buyers who showed him special favor. At Christmas, he would casually hand out genuine Rolex watches to the people he had "in his pocket," as he called them.

The corruption was so normalized that it barely registered as scandalous to most people in the industry. But Yvonne's words echoed in my mind whenever I was tempted to compromise my values for financial gain.

A Devastating Loss

On one bleak December day, Ron entered my office with tears streaming down his face. I knew immediately, without him saying a word, that Yvonne had passed away. In a quite whisper, he told me to grab my coat, and we walked silently through the falling snow to her favorite restaurant.

He ordered Yvonne's favorite meal for both of us, and we spent hours alternately laughing and crying as we shared memories of her incredible strength, sharp wit, and wicked sense of humor. The stories flowed as freely as our tears, tales of her quick comebacks, her protective instincts toward younger employees, and her ability to manage Ron's sometimes scattered approach to business.

Years later, I learned that Ron had quietly picked up all of Yvonne's funeral expenses for her family, a gesture that perfectly captured his character. Despite his occasional gruffness and his position in an often-cutthroat male dominated industry, he possessed a fundamental decency that showed itself in moments like these.

Yvonne had shared many stories with me about the discrimination she faced in the fashion industry, until she started working for Ron. She adored him, and we both felt fortunate to work for someone who valued character over connections, integrity over profit. At the time, I believed he would always support me, no matter what challenges arose.

I was about to learn how naive that assumption was.

China Beckoning

By spring, JCPenney had begun exploring the possibility of importing products from China, a relatively new concept in the early 1980s. Eager to position myself as an expert in this emerging field, I enrolled in two evening classes each week focused on Chinese import regulations and duty rates. The coursework was challenging and complex, requiring me to master tariff codes and understand the intricate legalities of international manufacturing.

Many nights found me working late at the office, poring over research materials about China and dreaming of the day I might actually visit this mysterious country that seemed poised to revolutionize the fashion industry. The idea of being among the first Americans to establish manufacturing relationships there both thrilled and terrified me.

Little did I know that my dream was about to become reality in the most unexpected way.

It was a rainy Monday morning in May when I heard Ron shouting from his office, something that rarely happened and always meant serious trouble. I jumped up from my chair and hurried to investigate, finding him in a heated discussion with Jim, his immediate supervisor.

"No way!" Ron was saying sternly. "I am absolutely NOT traveling to China!"

"But Ron," Jim insisted, "someone has to go from my division. This is your department, and you're spearheading this China initiative."

"No, Jim! I have a family, and nobody knows what's really happening over there!" Ron's voice carried a note of panic I'd never heard before. "I refuse to be some guinea pig for this company!"

Jim stormed out of Ron's office, clearly frustrated with his refusal to make the trip. Ron remained at his desk, obviously wrestling with the possibility that he might be forced to travel halfway around the world at his age, leaving his family behind for weeks.

Seeing an opportunity that might never come again, I took a deep breath and knocked on his door.

"Ron, excuse me," I said, poking my head into his office.

"Yes, Katie," he replied without looking up from his paperwork.

"I'll go."

"Go where?" He finally raised his eyes to meet mine.

"To China."

"Are you crazy? China is no place for a young woman to travel alone. It's not appropriate or safe."

Without hesitation, I launched into the biggest lie of my professional life. "I've traveled all over the world with my dad. China, India, you name it, I've been there."

"Really?" His skepticism was evident.

"Absolutely. I've been everywhere," I said, smiling while lying through my teeth.

"Where in China have you been?" he pressed.

"Oh, everywhere, the north and south." I replied with false confidence, praying he wouldn't ask for specifics.

"Really?"

"Really," I said, maintaining my composure despite my racing heart.

"I'll think about it," he said, returning his attention to his paperwork.

A week later, I found myself on an overnight coach flight to Shanghai, carrying nothing but a backpack filled with underwear, 2 pairs of jeans, 3 T-shirts, and enough snacks to survive what I hoped wouldn't be my final adventure.

The Journey to the Unknown

The truth was, I had never ventured beyond America's borders. This trip represented everything I had dreamed of since childhood—adventure, independence, and the chance to be a part of something groundbreaking in the fashion industry. At this point in the 1980s, very few Westerners were doing business in China, and even fewer were brave (or foolish) enough to travel there alone.

The journey itself was grueling: New York to Los Angeles, Los Angeles to Hawaii, Hawaii to Hong Kong, and finally to Shanghai. Each leg of the trip felt longer than the last, and by the time I reached my destination, I was exhausted, disoriented, and more than a little overwhelmed by what I had gotten myself into.

When I landed in Shanghai, I had sent Ron a telegram confirming my safe arrival, remember this was long before cell phones or the internet, so I was truly on my own in this foreign land. I had also told my parents I was taking a business trip to London, knowing they would have tried to stop me if they knew I was traveling halfway around the world to a country that seemed as mysterious as Mars to most Americans.

I could practically hear my father's voice: "You're going to be sold into slavery or worse!" His protective instincts would have kicked into overdrive if he'd known the truth.

First Impressions of China

At the Shanghai airport, a tiny Chinese man held up a handwritten sign with "KATIE" scrawled across it. I waved enthusiastically, excited to meet my first contact in this fascinating new world.

"Xièxiè," I called out in my terrible attempt at Mandarin, earning a patient smile from my greeter.

Walking outside into the crushing 110-degree heat felt like being slapped in the face with a wet towel. My driver pointed to a beat-up green Volkswagen van that looked like it had seen better days sometime in the previous decade. Despite hearing my father's voice warning me not to get in, I threw caution to the wind and climbed into the front seat, ready to embrace whatever adventure awaited.

The van had no air conditioning, and the back was filled with about a hundred cages of live chickens that created a symphony of squawking and an aroma that made my eyes water. As we drove through the sweltering heat, I began to feel nauseous from the combination of jet lag, hunger, and the overwhelming smell of our poultry passengers.

"Food?" I asked desperately, pointing to my mouth and stomach while making eating gestures that probably looked ridiculous.

My driver, who clearly spoke no English, watched my charades with amusement before understanding dawned on his face.

"Ah! Chīfàn," he said with a smile.

"Yes, chīfàn," I repeated, having no idea what it meant but hoping it involved something edible.

He made a sudden turn and stopped at a gas station, disappearing for twenty minutes before returning with chopsticks, a white Styrofoam container, and a water bottle. Inside the container, I found rice, vegetables, and some mysterious items that might have been alive not too long before being prepared. Starving after more than twenty-four hours without a proper meal, I devoured everything with enthusiasm, discovering that it tasted remarkably similar to the Chinese food I'd eaten in New York, only better, probably because I was so hungry.

After expressing my gratitude with more terrible Mandarin, I settled back for what would prove to be a four-hour journey through an increasingly rural landscape. As darkness fell, I felt completely isolated from everything familiar, listening to music on my Walkman and trying not to think about how far I was from home.

Welcome to the Factory

Eventually, we turned onto a dirt road that led to a complex of buildings lit up in the distance. The bumpy ride made me feel queasy again, but the sensation disappeared as soon as we stopped and I stepped out into the cool evening air.

To my amazement and delight, about a hundred factory workers and their manager were holding up a huge banner that read "Welcome Miss Katie!" It was such an unexpected and touching gesture that I nearly cried. Here I was, thousands of miles from home, being welcomed by people who had never met me but were treating me like an honored guest.

"Hello," said Henry, the factory owner, bowing respectfully. Only then did I realize that my chicken-accompanied chauffeur had already departed with his van, leaving me truly alone in this foreign land.

Just as I was preparing to deliver my rehearsed speech about how JCPenney and this factory were going to change the world together, I was struck by terrible stomach cramps that doubled me over in pain.

"Could you please tell me where the bathroom is?" I gasped, overwhelmed by urgent digestive distress.

A young woman quickly led me to an office with a small bathroom, where Henry proudly pointed out what he called an "American toilet" that had been specially installed for my visit. His pride in this accommodation would have been touching under different circumstances, but at that moment, I was focused on more pressing concerns.

What followed was one of the most humiliating experiences of my young life. I spent over an hour alternately vomiting and dealing with severe diarrhea, feeling like I was experiencing what death might feel like at twenty-four years old. The smell in that small bathroom was indescribable, like something had died and been left to rot in the heat.

Eventually, the same young woman knocked gently on the door and entered with a cup of warm water. "For your stomach," she said softly in perfect English. I would later learn that warm water was a traditional Chinese remedy for various ailments, though at the time it seemed like an odd prescription for my condition.

I was amazed that she didn't gag or run away. Her kindness in that moment of vulnerability would stay with me forever.

As I sat there contemplating my mortality on Henry's specially installed "American toilet," I remembered reading about traditional Chinese toilets in library books before my trip. Most facilities in China featured porcelain bowls set into the floor that required users to squat, a technique I never mastered in my many subsequent trips to China. The installation of a Western-style toilet specifically for my visit was an incredibly thoughtful gesture that I truly appreciated, especially given my current predicament.

Recovery and Discovery

After what felt like hours in the bathroom, I finally emerged to find the entire factory workforce still standing outside in the darkness, exactly where I had last seen them. When they saw me appear, they burst into enthusiastic applause, apparently relieved that I had survived my first encounter with Chinese cuisine.

Henry immediately provided me with a large bowl of plain rice, chopsticks, and tea. Still feeling weak and queasy, I managed to eat slowly, hoping the rice would settle my troubled stomach.

"Please show me to a bed," I asked weakly. The young woman led me to the women's dormitory, where I would spend the next four weeks sleeping on a bamboo mat with a clean blanket. Despite the simple accommodations, I found the experience oddly peaceful. The sound of leaves rustling in the evening breeze and the gentle hum of a small fan at my feet created a surprisingly soothing environment.

As I drifted off to sleep in this unknown but beautiful new world, I felt a sense of accomplishment mixed with anticipation for what the coming weeks would bring.

Life in the Factory

The next morning, I was gently awakened by the same young woman who had helped me through my digestive crisis. Looking at my watch, I realized I had slept for ten straight hours, the deepest sleep I'd had in months.

The factory's bathing facilities consisted of a bathroom lined with traditional squat toilets and one communal shower. Most factories didn't have hot water or heating, so my morning shower was shockingly cold. But I didn't mind, I felt reenergized and excited about the work ahead.

I dressed in jean, an American flag T-shirt, and sneakers, then headed down to meet Henry for what would become my daily routine. A hearty bowl of rice and steaming tea awaited me, which I consumed as if it were the most delicious meal I'd ever tasted.

For the next four weeks, I lived and worked alongside the factory employees, sleeping on my mat in the dormitory and learning every aspect of shirt production from cutting to finishing. The work was intensive, but I was fascinated by the skill and dedication of the Chinese workers. They taught me techniques I had never seen before and showed patience with my clumsy attempts to master their craft.

When I finally packed the last box of samples for Ron, I realized that my trip to China was about to push the apparel industry into uncharted territory. Very few Western companies were manufacturing in China at this time, and I felt like a pioneer exploring unknown lands.

Communication with the home office was limited to telegrams or unreliable international phone calls that often dropped mid-conversation. Unlike today's instant global connectivity through Skype, email, WeChat, and mobile phones, that era felt like the "Wild East"—a place where business rules were still being written and anything seemed possible.

The experience was both exhilarating and isolating. I felt like Robinson Crusoe on a grand adventure, but I also couldn't wait to return to familiar American comforts like hot showers, cheeseburgers, and reliable telecommunications.

The Triumphant Return

A day and a half later of travel, I arrived back in New York with a suitcase full of perfectly crafted shirt samples, eager to show Ron and the JCPenney team what we had accomplished. But first, I needed rest, a hot shower, and some real American food in that order.

I spent the weekend recovering from jet lag and culture shock, then headed to the office on Monday morning to present the fruits of my Chinese adventure.

The entire department was waiting for me, buzzing with curiosity about my mysterious journey to the other side of the world. I was bombarded with questions that revealed how little Americans knew about China at the time: "Were you scared?" "How are the hotels?" "Was the food terrible?" "Did you see any ninjas?"

"No hotels, terrible food sometimes, and definitely no ninjas!" I replied, laughing at their misconceptions.

I was then escorted into Ron's boss's office, where the entire executive team had gathered. Everyone from our department and several other floors had crowded outside the door, creating an atmosphere that made me feel like either a conquering hero or a condemned prisoner, I wasn't sure which.

Opening my suitcase full of shirt samples felt like unveiling treasure from a far-off land. Each cotton shirt was crafted with meticulous attention to detail, and I could hear the crowd's delighted "oohs and ahhs" as I displayed the array of beautiful fabrics in plaids, stripes, and solid colors.

The moment of truth came when Ron tried on the azure-blue striped shirt I had specifically designed with his eye coloring in mind. The fit was perfect, as good as the custom shirts he had made by London's finest tailors.

"You did very well, kid," Ron said with genuine pride, examining the shirt's soft cuffs and real shell buttons. "I think we're about to change the entire retail industry."

Sharing the Success

The president of our department was equally impressed. "Great job, Katie," he said. "Now go home and get some rest, because tomorrow we're flying to Dallas to present your achievements to the entire JCPenney corporate team."

I made a quick stop at my friend Kelly's apartment to retrieve my pug, who had been staying with her during my absence. Holding my beloved pet again after four weeks apart reminded me just how much I had missed the familiar comforts of home, even as I was excited about the professional opportunities my China experience had created.

JCPenney was a massive corporation with over a thousand employees and stores across the United States. Dallas represented their biggest market, so I was both nervous and thrilled at the prospect of sharing my experiences and insights with the company's top leadership.

That night, I repacked for Dallas and fell asleep cuddling my pug, already missing her again as I prepared for another separation. I also called my parents to check in, carefully maintaining the fiction that I had been in London. They were relieved to hear from me and glad I was home safely, completely unaware of the true adventure their daughter had just completed.

The Dallas Presentation

On the morning flight to Dallas, Ron and I discussed my remarkable journey to China. His pride in my accomplishment was evident, but so was his amazement that I had survived the experience with only a stomach ache.

"I'm incredibly proud of you, Katie. You did a wonderful job," he said sincerely. "Frankly, none of us were sure you'd make it home in one piece."

"Thanks," I replied, chuckling to myself as I reflected on how foolish I had been to embark solo on a journey, as a young woman, halfway around the world with no real international experience. The fact that everything had worked out felt like a minor miracle.

When we reached our Dallas hotel, I immediately headed downstairs upon learning about a lavish lunch buffet. After four weeks of rice, vegetables, and mysterious Chinese delicacies, the sight of familiar American food was almost overwhelming.

"Bacon!" I shouted with perhaps too much enthusiasm, startling the woman in front of me who looked at me as if I had never seen food before. I loaded my plate with eggs, rolls, bacon, fruit, and everything else I had missed during my Chinese adventure.

Sitting alone at a table, I ate with the enthusiasm of someone who had been stranded on a desert island. Everyone watching me probably thought I had some sort of eating disorder, but I didn't care. I had lost about fifteen pounds during my trip, and since I was already quite slim, I needed to regain some weight to fit properly back into my favorite designer clothes.

Ron sat across from me, smiling with amusement at my obvious joy in American cuisine.

"Hungry?" he asked with a laugh.

"Not anymore," I replied with my mouth still full of food, finally satisfied.

I spent the rest of the day presenting my China experiences to the JCPenney team, painting a vivid picture of the wonderful people I had met, the incredible factory facilities, and the vast opportunities that awaited American companies brave enough to venture into this new market.

The country that had once seemed impossibly foreign and mysterious had captivated me completely. I had become a true believer in the potential of Chinese manufacturing and was eager to return as soon as possible.

The Dark Side of Success

That evening, I prepared for the CEO's cocktail party in the hotel's banquet hall. My black Diane von Furstenberg wrap dress had become too large after my weight loss, so I cinched it with a silver snake belt and added black knee-high boots to create a memorable look. Despite still adjusting to the time change and feeling exhausted, I was determined to make a good impression.

Ron had given me permission to skip the party and rest in my room, but I decided this was too important an opportunity to miss. I made my way to the bar, ordered a club soda, and observed the executive dynamics playing out around me.

The scene was dominated by what was known as the "good old boys club"—an informal but powerful network where gender trumped talent every single time. No matter how smart, capable, or accomplished you were as a woman, without a penis, you would never gain entry into their inner circle.

I felt like I was staring through a window into a world where I didn't belong, watching the men engage in animated discussions about the stock market, politics, and global economics while the women were relegated to small talk on the periphery. After a couple of hours of feeling increasingly isolated, I decided to call it a night.

As I headed toward the elevator, I heard soft moaning coming from behind some potted ferns near the elevator bank.

"Help me," a man's voice pleaded weakly.

I bent down to investigate and discovered one of Ron's largest suppliers lying on the floor, extremely intoxicated and in obvious distress.

"Are you alright, sir?" I asked, fighting back inappropriate laughter while trying to assess whether he needed medical attention.

Suddenly, he grabbed my ankle and pulled me down, causing me to land on top of him. As I struggled to get back on my feet, he began making increasingly inappropriate comments and advances.

"Nice breasts," he slurred with a lewd grin, trying to grab me. "Do you want to have sex with me? I've had my eye on you, China girl."

"Stop it, sir!" I demanded, scrambling to my feet and backing away from his groping hands.

"I need you to come to my room and give me a massage," he continued, leering at me while pointing to his obvious arousal. He actually unzipped his pants to show me what I'd be "missing" if I didn't comply with his request.

"I'm going to get you some help," I said, stunned by his behavior but determined to handle the situation professionally.

Part of me wanted to leave him there, exposed and humiliated, for everyone to see what kind of person he really was. Instead, I hurried back to the bar to find Ron and discreetly inform him about his supplier's condition.

"Understood," Ron replied quietly, quickly rallying two other colleagues to help with the situation. "We'll take care of this, Katie. You can go back to your room now."

The supplier was a large, obnoxious man who stood about six feet four inches tall and held a position of considerable influence in Ron's eyes. Yet I couldn't shake the feeling of being completely disrespected and objectified by someone who was supposed to be a professional colleague.

This incident fundamentally changed how I viewed the supplier, and I felt disgusted by his behavior, especially given everything he had said to me. Ron and the two other men helped get him to his feet and discreetly escorted him to the elevator, while I stood there trying to process what had just happened.

Ron looked at me sternly and said, "Not a word of this to anyone, Katie. Understood?"

"Understood," I mumbled, watching the elevator doors close as the men tried to prop up their inebriated colleague.

As I headed to my room to pack for our departure the next day, I couldn't stop thinking about the supplier's behavior and what it might mean for my future interactions with him. The incident left me deeply unsettled and wondering if this was the kind of treatment I could expect as I advanced in my career in the fashion industry.

The Crushing Blow

Monday morning brought what should have been a celebration of my successful China and Dallas mission. Instead, Ron called me into his office and quietly asked me to close the door.

"Katie, I truly admire your courage and hard work, but I have to tell you that your time in this department is coming to an end. I need to transfer you to another area."

"Why?" I shouted, feeling completely blindsided. "I didn't do anything wrong!" I remained seated, struggling to understand what was happening.

Ron put his head down and spoke quietly, unable to meet my eyes. "Our supplier feels uncomfortable about you working on the same floor where he conducts business with us. He spoke to my boss, and management has decided you should move to the children's shoe department on the second floor, far away from this office. This way, he won't have to see you and feel embarrassed about what happened in Dallas."

The words hit me like a physical blow. "I'm sorry, Katie, but he's invaluable to us."

"Are you kidding me, Ron?" I couldn't contain my outrage. "I went to China for you! I did an amazing job, you said so yourself. I would never tell anyone what happened with him."

Ron couldn't meet my eyes as he repeated, "I'm sorry. Please pack up your desk now so you can move immediately."

The hurt and anger I felt was overwhelming. Here I was, being punished for someone else's inappropriate behavior. I had traveled halfway around the world, lived in conditions most Americans couldn't imagine, and delivered exactly what the company needed and dreamed of. Yet I was being banished to the children's shoe department because a drunken supplier couldn't handle his own embarrassing behavior.

As I packed my belongings into a cardboard box, Ron's new secretary, a buxom woman who clearly enjoyed other people's misfortune appeared to escort me to the elevator.

"What a shame," she said with barely concealed glee. "You must have done something really terrible to end up in children's shoes. It's a dead-end department down there."

"I did nothing wrong!" I snapped, my anger finally boiling over.

"Sweetheart, this industry is run by men," she replied with a condescending tone. "Since you're not part of their club, they've decided you need to leave."

I pressed my hand against the elevator door to keep it from closing and turned to face her directly.

"Sweetheart," I said, matching her patronizing tone exactly, "there's no way I'm going to let any man dictate my place in this industry, especially since I did nothing wrong!"

The door closed on her shocked expression, leaving me alone with my thoughts and my resolve.

A Painful Exit

Instead of reporting to the children's shoe department, I walked straight through the lobby and out the front door of the JCPenney building, determined not to look back.

Ron disappeared from my life after that day, leaving me heartbroken that someone I had respected and trusted couldn't find the courage to stand up for what was right. Despite knowing I was innocent and had dedicated myself completely to improving his department and pioneering the company's import program, he had chosen the path of least resistance.

This was my brutal reminder that the "good old boys club", was an invisible but impermeable barrier that would challenge me throughout my career. In the years that followed, I would discover just how difficult it would be to break through this network of mutual protection and shared interests that consistently favored men over talent and merit.

Reflection and Resolution

That Saturday afternoon, I met my friend Kelly for brunch at our favorite spot, needing to process what had happened and figure out my next move.

"I'm really starting to think the fashion industry might be more than I can handle," I confided over mimosas that I couldn't really afford. "Maybe it's going to wear me down before I can make any real impact."

"You have to stay strong, Katie," Kelly replied with characteristic determination. "This isn't just about you, it's about all of us trying to make it in a man's world."

"I thought fashion was supposed to be creative and exciting," I said, feeling defeated. "Instead, I'm discovering that succeeding as a woman in this business means fighting an uphill battle every single day."

"More drinks!" I called to our waiter, deciding that if I was going to contemplate my professional mortality, I might as well do it properly.

As we shared the story of the supplier found face-first in the hotel lobby's potted plants, we couldn't help but laugh at the absurdity of it all.

"Can you imagine if the situation were reversed?" Kelly asked. "If a woman had been found in that condition, she'd be fired immediately and blacklisted from the industry."

"Absolutely," I agreed. "But because he's a man with money and connections, I'm the one who gets punished."

"Maybe I should have listened to my parents and gone into nursing," I mused.

"Are you kidding?" Kelly laughed. "Dealing with bedpans and hospital bureaucracy? No thanks! At least in fashion, when you get screwed over, you can look fabulous doing it."

"That's true," I admitted with a smile. "We'll always have great clothes, even if we can't always count on fair treatment."

As we raised our glasses in a toast to better days ahead, I made a silent promise to myself. I wouldn't let the Ron Donaldson's and corrupt suppliers of the world drive me out of an industry I was passionate about. If anything, their behavior had shown me exactly why the fashion world needed more women who were willing to fight for integrity and fairness.

The road ahead would be challenging, but I was determined to travel it on my own terms, with my principles intact and my head held high. After all, I had survived four weeks in a Chinese factory, mastered the art of eating with chopsticks, and proven that I could deliver results under the most challenging circumstances.

If I could handle all of that, I could certainly handle whatever the fashion industry threw at me next.

The "white elephant" of JCPenney had taught me valuable lessons about both the possibilities and limitations of corporate America. More importantly, it showed me that my real strength lay not in conforming to other people's expectations, but in staying true to my own values, no matter what the cost.

As I prepared for whatever came next, I knew one thing for certain: I would never again let someone else's moral failings become my professional downfall.

CHAPTER 3:
The Darkest Side of 7th Avenue

Looking back at one of my earliest positions on Seventh Avenue in the late 1980s, I still feel the weight of an experience that fundamentally changed how I viewed the fashion industry. What started as an exciting opportunity quickly became one of the most disturbing chapters of my career, a harsh introduction to the predatory underbelly that existed in many garment center companies.

I discovered the job opportunity through a classified ad in the *New York Times*, a merchandiser position at a sportswear company that supplied major retail outlets. The salary was exceptionally high for a merchandising role, which immediately caught my attention. When the owners responded to my résumé the very next day, I was thrilled. Finally, I thought, my big break had arrived.

The Deceptive Interview

Determined to make the best impression possible, I carefully selected my outfit: a silk Balenciaga floral dress with a linen blazer, paired with hot pink strappy sandals I'd found on sale at a small boutique on the Upper East Side. The ensemble felt perfect, professional yet fashionable, exactly what someone in the fashion industry should wear to an interview.

Walking into their stunning Seventh Avenue showroom, I felt a surge of excitement about what lay ahead. The space was impressive, filled with racks of beautiful clothing and the energy of a successful business. I settled into my chair, eager to meet Barney, one of the owners, along with his partner Tim.

My first red flag came immediately. Barney, a wirily little man with a receding hairline, sat uncomfortably close to me and launched into inappropriately personal questions. "Are you single?" he asked without any preamble. Caught off guard but trying to maintain professionalism, I lied and said I had a boyfriend, hoping to shut down whatever direction this conversation was heading.

His response made my skin crawl. He winked and said, "Too bad. I like single girls working for me," while his hand moved to caress my knee. The combination of his leering expression and unwanted touch made me question whether I should simply get up and leave right then and there.

Just as I was contemplating my exit strategy, salvation appeared in the form of a short, attractive well-dressed man who practically ran across the showroom to greet me. "So, fabulous to meet you, Katie!" he said with genuine warmth and an infectious smile. "Just ignore Barney. Everyone else does!"

"Screw you," Barney shot back at his partner, before he moved to the other side of the conference table, giving me space to breathe again.

The man introduced himself as Tim, Barney's business partner, and I immediately sensed he was gay—which, in that moment, felt like a blessing. Finally, I thought, someone who wouldn't be trying to get into my pants while I was just striving to do my job. Tim's enthusiasm was infectious, and we talked for over an hour while Barney sat in sullen silence, occasionally staring at me in a way that made me deeply uncomfortable.

Despite the rocky start with Barney, I left the interview feeling optimistic about working with Tim. When he called the next day to offer me the position and asked if I could start immediately, I didn't hesitate. "Yes, I can start tomorrow," I said, barely containing my excitement.

As I hung up the phone, I couldn't believe my luck. Here I was, landing one of my first real jobs in the apparel industry, working in what appeared to be a beautiful office, for what seemed like a great boss-Tim, earning more money than I'd ever made so far in the fashion industry. It felt like fate was finally smiling on me.

The Bait and Switch

The next morning, I woke up early and dressed carefully in a crisp white linen pantsuit—professional, clean, and appropriate for my new role. I took the bus to 34th Street and Seventh Avenue, filled with anticipation about beginning this new chapter of my career.

The moment I entered their office, however, everything changed. Barney immediately grabbed my arm—not gently, but with a firm grip that left no room for argument and announced he was taking me to see my "office." When I asked why we were leaving the beautiful showroom I'd interviewed in, his response was swift and brutal.

"Oh, you're a talker?" he barked. "Well, shut the fuck up and just follow me!"

His grip tightened as he practically dragged me down into the elevator, out the front door of the showroom building and down the street. I struggled to keep pace in my heels, and when I asked where he was taking me, his answer came with that same self-satisfied grin I'd seen during the interview: "To your office, sweetheart."

His commentary about my footwear was equally degrading. "Heels are only for the bedroom," he sneered, "so don't wear them again unless you want me to think you're planning to fuck me after work." The crude language and sexual innuendo made me feel sick, but I was trapped in this situation, at least until I could figure out what was really going on.

We stopped in front of a dingy building that looked nothing like the polished showroom where I'd interviewed. The windows were broken, and the only entrance was a freight elevator. "Welcome to your new office, sweetie," Barney said, laughing in a way that sounded almost sadistic, as if he was enjoying some private joke at my expense.

Descent into Hell

The freight elevator took us to the sixth floor, where the doors opened onto what could only be described as a sweatshop. Racks of clothing stretched as far as I could see, and the space was filled with sewers, cutters, and shelves stacked high with fabrics in every conceivable color and pattern. The working conditions were immediately apparent, this was not the glamorous fashion industry job I'd been anticipating.

But even this warehouse setting wasn't my final destination. Barney grabbed my arm again and led me to the darkest, most remote corner of the space. "Here it is, honey," he said with sarcasm dripping from every word as he patted me on the bottom. "Welcome to your new glamorous office!"

What I saw made my stomach turn. The space was filthy beyond description, cluttered with old fabrics, garbage piled in every corner, and a smell so foul I had to cover my mouth to keep from vomiting immediately. The stench was overwhelming, a combination of mustiness, decay, and something I couldn't quite identify but that made my eyes water.

"What is that smell?" I managed to ask before Barney started walking away.

"Rat shit or a dead rat, honey," he called back with obvious amusement. "Get used to it—it will grow on you." His laughter echoed through the warehouse as he walked away, shouting at the sewers who had paused their work to witness my humiliation. "Get back to work you lazy ingrates!" He yelled at them.

"The phone should work," he shouted back at me, as if that small mercy was supposed to make up for the deplorable conditions.

I called after him, "Wait!" but when he turned around, his face was filled with such contempt that I almost took a step backward.

"What the fuck do you want?" he snarled. "I'm busy and don't have time for some snotty little princess's emotional breakdown."

Fighting back tears, I asked the most basic question: "What would you like me to do?"

"You said you're a fucking designer!" he screamed. "So, fucking design!"

The Wall of Shame

Before abandoning me completely, Barney had one more humiliation to deliver. He grabbed my arm again—his grip leaving marks I'd discover later and dragged me to a wall covered in writing. Women's names were scrawled in permanent black marker, one after another in a long, damning list.

"Do you see those names, cupcake?" he asked with mock sweetness.

"Yes," I managed to whisper, though my voice was shaking.

"Those are the cunts that worked here before you, that I fired," he said with obvious pride. "So, do your fucking job, or your name will be up there too!"

With that final threat, he walked away, leaving me alone in that hellhole. I could see the sewers and patternmakers through the grimy window of my "office," whispering among themselves and occasionally glancing at me. Their expressions told me everything I needed to know, I was just the latest in a long line of victims who had been subjected to Barney 's cruel game of sexual abuse.

Sitting in the creaky office chair behind a desk covered in papers, fabric swatches, and what appeared to be a moldy sandwich left behind by my predecessor, I tried to process what had just happened to me. The reality was starting to sink in: I had been completely deceived. The beautiful showroom, the professional atmosphere, the impressive salary, it had all been a lie designed to lure me into this nightmare.

The Decision to Stay

My first instinct was to run. Every fiber of my being wanted to grab my purse and get out of that building as quickly as possible. But as I reached for my phone to call Kelly, my best friend, reality set in. I desperately needed this job. The money was still good, there had to be a reason they could afford to pay so much and I had responsibilities. My father was ill, and my mother might need financial support. Walking away wasn't really an option, no matter how degrading the situation had become.

When Kelly answered the phone and I tried to explain where I was, her reaction was immediate and passionate.

"Oh my God," she gasped after hearing my tear-filled description. "Get the hell out of there now, Katie!"

"I can't leave," I sobbed. "I need this job. I desperately need the money."

To her credit, Kelly shifted from panic to support mode. "Okay, Katie," she said more calmly, "try to make the best of a bad situation. If anyone can do this, you can."

After hanging up, I sat alone in that disgusting office, overwhelmed by emotions I could barely process. Was this really what it took to work in fashion on Seventh Avenue? Was this the price of admission to the industry I'd dreamed of joining?

I gave myself what I now recognize was a necessary pep talk: "Katie, you can do it. Honestly, it's not that bad at all." Even as I said the words, I knew I was lying to myself, but sometimes self-deception is the only thing that keeps you moving forward.

Meeting Maria

My salvation came in the form of a small, kind woman named Maria who appeared in my office doorway like an angel. "Hi, I am Maria," she said with a shy smile. When I asked her about cleaning supplies, she directed me to the bathroom next to my office.

The moment she mentioned the bathroom, I understood the source of at least part of that overwhelming stench. When I pushed open the door, the wave of nausea that hit me was so strong I nearly collapsed. The space was beyond disgusting, feces and urine covered not just the floor but extended up the walls to the ceiling. It was clear that no one had cleaned this bathroom in months, possibly years.

I made a mental note that would become a firm rule: never, ever use this bathroom. I grabbed the cleaning supplies and ran out as quickly as possible, gasping for fresh air.

But Maria's kindness gave me something to hold onto. When she returned with rubber gloves and matter-of-factly explained that the dark spots on my desk were rat droppings, I realized I wasn't completely alone in this nightmare. "Wear these gloves so you don't get sick," she said with genuine concern.

That simple act of kindness from a stranger gave me the strength to continue, so I removed my white linen blazer and rolled up my sleeves.

The Long Road to Survival

What followed were some of the most difficult days of my early career. I spent the next eight hours cleaning that office from top to bottom, scrubbing away years of accumulated filth, sorting through abandoned papers and sketches, and trying to make the space habitable. I found a face mask in one of the desk drawers, left behind by my predecessor, no doubt and put it on to help me breathe while I worked.

The physical labor was exhausting, but the emotional toll was even worse. Every surface I cleaned, every piece of garbage I threw away, every rat dropping I scraped off the desk reminded me of how far my dreams had fallen from reality. This wasn't the glamorous fashion career I'd imagined. This was survival.

When I finally left that night at 11:00 p.m., exhausted and covered in grime and my once pristine white linen pants dirty beyond salvation, I encountered José, the patternmaker who had brought me a large garbage can earlier. As a large rat scurried over my feet in the elevator, causing me to shriek and jump, he offered the first genuine encouragement I'd received all day.

"Most people would just walk out," he said with obvious respect. "You've got guts lady. I wouldn't clean out that office if you paid me!"

His words meant more to me than he could have known. In a

day filled with humiliation and degradation, someone had recognized that I was fighting for something important, my place in the fashion industry.

Small Acts of Defiance

The next morning, I made a decision that would set the tone for my survival strategy. I stopped at a street vendor and bought some pink tulips for two dollars, a small expense, but one that felt like an act of rebellion. I found a discarded glass jar in my office, arranged the flowers in it, and placed them prominently on my newly cleaned desk where everyone could see them.

It was a small gesture, but it served multiple purposes. The flowers brought a touch of beauty and life into that grim space. They also sent a message to Barney, to the other workers, and to myself: I wasn't going to be broken by this place. I was going to find ways to maintain my dignity and humanity, no matter what they threw at me.

I changed into the jeans, T-shirt, and sneakers I'd packed and continued the cleaning process. It took me three full days to make that office remotely habitable, but when I was finished, I felt a genuine sense of pride. I had taken their worst shot and not only survived it but had actually improved the situation.

"Not bad," I thought as I turned off the lights at the end of that first week. " Barney is not going to write my name on his wall of shame after all." I said to myself, determined to be the exception.

Finding Unexpected Allies

Despite the horrible introduction, I gradually discovered that not everyone in that warehouse was part of Barney 's system of abuse. The sewers, patternmakers, and other workers were, for the most part, kind and supportive people who had been trapped in this situation just like me.

José, who had encouraged me that first night, became a genuine friend. "I honestly bet everyone that you'd be out of here two days ago," he told me at the end of my first week, but his smile was warm and approving.

"Not me," I replied, fighting back tears but managing to smile back. "I'm tough, just like my dad."

The workers appreciated small gestures like the homemade chocolate chip cookies I brought in one morning, in ways that reminded me of their humanity. They were gone within minutes, and the surprise on their faces told me that acts of simple kindness were rare in this place.

As we worked together through long nights and weekends, I came to understand that this diverse group of people shared more than just a workplace. We shared food, stories about our families, and dreams of something better. The sewers helped me develop my technical skills while I contributed my design knowledge to our collaborative efforts.

Most importantly, I learned that I felt more comfortable and genuine in that warehouse, surrounded by people who understood hard work and mutual support, than I ever had in traditional office environments.

The Unveiling of Tim's True Nature

When Tim finally reappeared, the same Tim who had seemed like my savior during the interview, his reaction to my cleaned and organized office was telling.

"Oh, my fucking God, you cleaned this shithole out?" he said, genuinely shocked.

He went on to explain that this had all been a test orchestrated by Barney to see "what I was made of," and that I had apparently passed "with flying colors." But when I asked if this meant I could move to the beautiful showroom where I'd interviewed, his answer revealed the real truth about my situation.

"No, sorry, sweetie," he said without any real regret. "I need you here with the sewers, patternmakers, and fabric salesmen so you can learn the business from the ground up."

Even the company name itself was revealing: Deena Pignoli, named after Barney's favorite stripper and his love of Italy and pignoli cookies. Everything about this place reflected Barney's crude, exploitative nature.

Tim gave me my first real assignment: design twenty pieces for the Clothing Barrel, their biggest account, with samples finished by the end of the following week. When I expressed concern about the timeline, his response revealed another disturbing aspect of this operation.

"Oh, don't worry," he said with a smirk. "We keep the warehouse open on weekends and all night for deadlines."

"You mean these people work seven days a week?" I asked, unable to hide my shock.

"Of course," he replied as if it were the most natural thing in the world. "This is 7th Avenue honey, everybody stays open, especially when you hire illegal workers."

The callousness of that statement, the casual acknowledgement that they were exploiting undocumented workers who had no recourse or protection was my first real insight into just how deep the corruption ran in this company and industry.

Life in the Sweatshop

Working in that warehouse taught me lessons I never could have learned in a traditional fashion job. I discovered that the people working there, despite being underpaid and overworked, took genuine pride in their craft. The sewers helped me develop my technical skills to a professional level, while the patternmakers taught me about construction techniques that no design school covers.

But the working conditions were deplorable. During a blazing hot summer week when temperatures outside reached over 100 degrees, the warehouse felt like an oven at 115 degrees. When I tried to turn on the air conditioner, one of the workers immediately stopped me.

"This is a definite termination," she said, shutting off the unit I'd just turned on.

"Don't be ridiculous," I laughed. "It's one hundred and fifteen degrees."

Everyone stopped what they were doing and stared at me. The look in their eyes told me this was no joke.

"I'm dead serious!" she said, sweat pouring down her face.

That's when I truly understood the level of Barney's cruelty. He was willing to let his workers suffer in dangerous heat because running the air conditioning would cost him money. These were human beings, many with families to support, and he treated them as disposable resources.

The First Collection

Despite the impossible working conditions, I threw myself into designing the twenty-piece collection for the Clothing Barrel, a discount clothing chain. I sourced beautiful fabrics in bold florals and bright-colored linens, working with the patternmakers to translate my sketches into actual garment. My inexperience showed, when something couldn't be done or was too expensive, the workers patiently explained alternatives and suggested better approaches.

Their willingness to help me succeed, despite their own exploitation, was both humbling and inspiring. I brought in a small radio so we could listen to music while we worked, and slowly the atmosphere became more collaborative and even enjoyable, except when Barney appeared to terrorize us.

The female workers and I also tackled the disgusting bathroom together, which required multiple people and several hours of the most unpleasant cleaning I've ever done. Maria, our head seamstress, actually vomited several times during the process. But when we were finished, we had turned an uninhabitable space into something functional, and we'd done it together.

When it came time to present my finished collection to Tim and Barney, the fear was overwhelming. Everything I'd worked for over the past weeks came down to this moment. As they examined each piece, whispering intently to each other, I felt my heart pounding.

Barney's reaction was typically cruel, he walked away without a single word of praise or criticism, leaving me and the workers in suspense. But Tim's enthusiasm made up for his partner's coldness.

"Beautiful, Katie! I am impressed with your work," he said with genuine appreciation. "It's just what we need to get the buyer up here from the Clothing Barrel."

The workers cheered when Tim gave them a thumbs-up, and we all exchanged high-fives and laughter. For a brief moment, despite everything we'd endured, we felt like a real team that had accomplished something meaningful together.

"I couldn't have done this without you guys!" I cried.

The Corruption Revealed

The presentation to the Clothing Barrel buyer opened my eyes to another level of corruption in the garment center and one the Yvonne had warned me about. I wore one of my own designs, a floral straight-leg pant in citrus orange with a matching double-breasted linen blazer and waited nervously for the buyer's arrival.

She was a large, tired-looking woman who appeared to be in her late forties. Despite her compliment about my outfit ("Nice pants and what a gorgeous print"), what happened next was deeply disturbing.

When Barney introduced the collection, he deliberately gave Tim credit for the designs that were clearly mine. "Tim, show the buyer the samples *you* made," he said, staring directly at me to gauge my reaction.

I sat there in silence, smiling on the outside but seething internally. Barney knew perfectly well that these were my designs, and I had put enormous effort into creating an impressive collection. This seemed like yet another deliberate attempt to humiliate and diminish me.

The buyer's response was positive, "I will definitely purchase the entire group!" But what happened next revealed the true nature of business in this company. As she prepared to leave, Barney ran after her and handed her a thick white envelope.

When I quietly asked Tim what was in the envelope, his response was chilling: "Shhhh. Don't ever say anything to Barney about it. This is the garment center, Katie. Nothing is free, and don't you ever forget that."

I had just witnessed my first kickback given to a buyer, a bribe to ensure that the orders kept coming. It was a stark reminder that success in this environment often had nothing to do with the quality of the work and everything to do with corruption and payoffs.

The Darkest Revelation

Returning to the warehouse to share the good news about the buyer's reaction, I immediately sensed that something was terribly wrong. The usual energy and chatter had been replaced by an ominous silence. Workers had their heads down, and several people were clearly crying.

When I approached Maria, Salma, and Maria's teenage daughter, it became clear that something devastating had happened. It took some coaxing, but eventually, they revealed the truth that would change everything for me.

Barney had been sexually harassing Maria's sixteen-year-old daughter, touching her inappropriately and asking her about sexual acts he wanted her to perform on him. The girl was terrified, but the family felt trapped. When I suggested calling the police, their reaction was immediate and desperate.

"No way, are you crazy?" Maria cried. "We will all lose our jobs and be arrested."

"Why?" I asked, not understanding the full scope of their vulnerability.

"All of us are illegal," Salma whispered, making sure no one could overhear. "We need these jobs to feed our families, and if anyone speaks up, we all will get fired. Worse, Barney will call immigration and have us deported."

The revelation hit me like a physical blow. These weren't just exploited workers, they were undocumented immigrants who had no legal recourse against Barney's abuse. Barney had deliberately created a workforce of people who couldn't fight back, couldn't report him, couldn't seek help from authorities without risking deportation. I wondered how many other apparel companies were doing the same thing?

Maria then revealed that she too had been subjected to sexual harassment by one of Barney's factory manager friend years earlier, and when her husband had threatened to retaliate, Barney had threatened to have the entire family deported.

"Holy shit!" I said, the full scope of Barney's evil finally becoming clear. "That filthy pig!"

The Impossible Choice

At twenty-something years old, I had never faced a situation like this. I wanted to call the police, to report Barney, to find some way to protect these vulnerable people. But I was also beginning to understand the complexity of the situation and my own limitations.

I arranged to meet Tim privately, hoping that he might be different from his partner, that he might help me address this crisis head on. We met at the deli across the street from the factory, and I explained everything to him, the sexual harassment, the threats, the exploitation of undocumented workers.

His response destroyed any remaining faith I had left in him.

"Yes, Katie, Barney is a horrible man. I know it. Everyone who works or does business with him knows it, and there is nothing we can do because he doesn't care what anyone thinks of him," he said with shocking casualness. "He's rich, and I have made a lot of money with him. Furthermore, they are illegal immigrants, and nobody cares about them."

"Really? You are just as terrible as him!" I yelled, no longer caring who heard me. "You are staying quiet at the expense of these women being assaulted!"

Tim's response was to offer me a bribe disguised as a raise, and when I refused, he made it clear that opposing Barney was futile. "Okay," he said bluntly, "it's your funeral."

The Descent Continues

Despite my moral outrage, the practical reality of my situation forced me into an impossible compromise. I needed the job to support myself, and I convinced myself that staying would at least allow me to protect Maria's daughter by keeping her close to my office where I could supervise her.

I accepted the raise, knowing it was a bribe to keep me quiet, and the guilt of that decision ate at me every day. I tried to rationalize it by telling myself that my presence was the only protection these workers had, but I knew I was also protecting my own financial interests.

The following months became a living hell. Barney, knowing that Tim had told him about our conversation, targeted me for special abuse. He cursed at me daily, calling me a "cunt," a "whore," and a "bitch" in front of everyone. He knew I was protecting Maria's daughter, so his verbal assaults became even more vicious and personal.

Every Thursday, like clockwork, Barney would visit a strip club on 34th Street, have Polaroid photos taken of himself with the dancers in compromising positions, and return to proudly display these filthy images to the entire staff. He would throw the photos on my desk and make crude comments about my appearance, comparing me unfavorably to the women he'd been with.

"You need much larger breasts," he would sneer. "That's what men want, not some skinny bitch like you." He'd say, completely inebriated from his alcohol-infused strip club lunch.

The workers were forced to smile and pretend to be interested in his disgusting photos, knowing that any negative reaction could cost them their jobs. It was psychological torture designed to degrade all of us and reinforce his power over our lives.

The Breaking Point

As months passed, I reached my limit. The combination of overwork, constant verbal abuse, and the moral compromise of staying silent about the sexual harassment was destroying me physically and emotionally. I began looking for other opportunities, and when I finally found a temporary position elsewhere, I gave Tim notice that I was leaving.

His response was telling: "That's unfortunate! You're the most skilled designer we've ever had, and now Barney has sent you packing too!"

"I'm sorry, Tim, Barney's a vile pig and I can't take the stress and sexual harassment and long hours anymore."

Even in my departure, Tim made it clear that this pattern had repeated many times before. I was just the latest in a long line of talented women who had been driven away by Barney's abuse.

Barney's reaction to my resignation was swift and violent. He burst into my office, his face flushed and sweating, looking like a man who had completely lost control.

"You're a filthy cunt and you are fired!" he screamed, pounding his fist on my desk so hard that papers scattered everywhere.

"You think you're getting last week's paycheck? He yelled again, as he leaned over my desk and got right in my face. He had just returned inebriated from another strip club lunch.

"Oh, you *will* pay me!" I yelled back at him.

"You are a repulsive, and I will no longer tolerate this mistreatment and your constant groping me and the other women here."

When I stood up to continue to defend myself, his response crossed a line that still haunts me today. He unzipped his pants and exposed himself to me. He started masturbating in front of me while

I sat trapped behind my desk, too shocked and terrified to move. I could smell the alcohol on his breath.

I got up and grabbed my purse to leave, but he blocked me at the door.

"Do you think I want to fuck you?" He laughed. Well I don't, you're a skinny bitch and not my type. As for the 'illegals you are defending,' I own them!" He smirked. "Now I want your name on my wall with the rest of the cunts I fired." He yelled.

He picked up a black marker from my desk and began scrawling my name below that of his most recent victim.

"Oh my God!" I screamed back at him. "I would rather have my eyes poked out with a red-hot dagger than let you fire me. You are a disgusting animal! I quit!" I yelled at him.

"You dare yell at me? You rotten, ungrateful, fucking whore," he screamed still blocking my exit with all of his body weight. At that moment, I realized how dangerous he really was.

But he continued his assault, growing more excited as I became more distressed. He took a piece of fabric off of my shelf and rubbed himself with it. When he ejaculated on my desk, I grabbed a metal trash bin and threw it at him while the entire warehouse looked on in horror.

"Get out of my warehouse! You cunt," he yelled, zipping up his pants and walking past the workers as if nothing had happened.

I stood there, trembling and traumatized, while everyone else kept their heads down, too frightened to acknowledge what they had all just witnessed. Walking out into the summer heat, I felt a combination of relief, fear, rage, and overwhelming guilt for abandoning the workers who had no choice but to stay.

Fighting Back

That night, I went home and took the longest, hottest shower of my life, scrubbing my skin until it was raw, trying to wash away the contamination of what had happened. But by the next day, surrounded by the supportive women at my gym, I found the strength to fight back.

Irene, who ran the bodybuilding gym, handed me a business card for Eleanor, a prominent Madison Avenue attorney. "She's the most qualified lawyer in New York, and she will get your paycheck for you," Irene said with conviction.

When I protested that I couldn't afford such a high-powered lawyer, the gym manager insisted I at least make an appointment to meet with her. "Tell her you are a friend of mine," she said.

That phone call changed everything.

The Long Fight for Justice

The following day, I slipped into my grey Giorgio Armani single-breasted suit for my meeting with Eleanor. I paired it with a cream-colored silk bow blouse and took the bus to the Madison Avenue law firm. As I ascended to the twentieth floor in the elevator, I was filled with a sense of empowerment in anticipation of meeting this distinguished female lawyer.

I informed the receptionist about my appointment with Eleanor. She led me into an impressive law library and asked me to wait for her arrival to discuss matters with me. The fragrant aroma of old leather books, stacked from floor to ceiling, enveloped the room, creating a comforting and inviting environment.

A few minutes later, a petite, attractive woman walked in and extended her hand to me.

"My name is Eleanor," she stated, holding my hand tightly.

"Please sit down and make yourself comfortable." She smiled.

She was dressed in a black-and-white tweed suit and her shoes were made of the same fabric. I thought that was spectacular and realized she took pride in her appearance and must have had her clothing made for her diminutive frame. Her pristine blonde hair was in a bob and pulled behind her ears to expose two carat diamond earrings. She had a simple strand of pearls around her neck.

"So," she said, handing me a box of Kleenex, "tell me your story, Katie.

I shared with her the details of Barney's sexual harassment and the verbal abuse directed at me and my colleagues. I also recounted his repulsive and belittling remarks to the entire warehouse team, particularly targeting the women.

I described his sexual encounters with strippers and how he made advances toward all of us.

Additionally, I revealed the incident where he masturbated on my desk. She was completely taken aback and gasped in disbelief. I further informed her about the list of women on his so-called "wall of shame," who he proudly dismissed from their jobs. I also mentioned how Barney coerced Maria's daughter and threatened them all with deportation. I also told her that Tim, his business partner was complicit.

Did he ever give you an employee handbook?" she asked.

"A what? No," I said, not even knowing what that was at the time.

"Did he give you his company policies on sexual harassment in the workplace or any policies for that matter?" she asked.

"No, nothing except that if I was late for work, he would dock my pay," I said.

"Well, he is supposed to give you all that information," she told me. "That's the law, Katie, and these men in the garment center don't play by the rules and need to be held accountable.

I told her that Barney grasped my waist and arms with a strong grip, reached for my breasts, and patted my butt multiple times. He made several attempts to wrap his arms around me as well. I spoke these words calmly.

"What did *you* do?" She posed the question and waited for me to reply.

"Oh my God, I pulled away from him every time and told him to stop," I cried. "He is disgusting."

"Good," she said. "Very good."

She abruptly got up and escorted me to the elevator.

Eleanor agreed to take my case on contingency, warning me that it would be difficult and could take years. But she also promised that if we won, Barney would never hurt another woman again.

What followed was two years of legal warfare that tested everyone involved. Eleanor managed to locate fourteen other women who had worked for Barney, and most agreed to testify about similar experiences of sexual harassment and abuse. Some had been fired, others had quit, one had left the industry entirely, and one had suffered a nervous breakdown from the trauma of Barney.

Barney's legal strategy was predictable and vicious. Through his lawyers, he accused all of us of being "whores, drug addicts, and crazy liars." But Eleanor's skills as an attorney were formidable. By the time we reached the courtroom, her legal fees had approached one million dollars, while Barney had cycled through more than six different attorneys, three resigned from his case, and he fired two others.

Tim, recognizing that his association with Barney was destroying his reputation, ended their partnership and distanced himself from the case. As far as I was concerned, he was just as guilty as Barney but lacked the courage to face the consequences of his complicity.

The trial itself was emotionally devastating. Day after day, I sat in court with the other women, listening to Barney's lawyers attack our credibility and our character. Some days Barney didn't even show up, apparently just to frustrate the judge. Near the end of the trial, his arrogance reached such levels that he cursed at the judge and was fined for contempt of court.

When it came time for us to testify, each woman's story was more disturbing than the last. Barney's final attorney, a young man in his twenties, looked visibly shocked by what he was hearing. It was clear he had not been prepared for the scope and severity of the abuse we described.

After requesting a recess to consult with his client, Barney's lawyer returned looking defeated. He struggled to cross-examine any of us effectively and appeared genuinely intimidated by Eleanor's expertise. By the end of the day, Barney agreed to pay damages to all of us and cover our legal expenses. He knew he was beaten, and both his business and his reputation were beyond repair.

Justice and Redemption

Walking out of that courtroom with the other women was one of the most triumphant moments of my life. We had done something that no one thought was possible, we had taken on a wealthy, powerful predator and won.

"We won!" I screamed to anyone who would listen. "That horrible man will never abuse another woman in the workplace again!"

Eleanor quietly got into her waiting car, her job complete, while the rest of us hugged and exchanged phone numbers. We all understood that what we had shared was more than just a legal victory—it was a bond forged in the fire of shared trauma and collective courage.

After Barney finished paying everyone, he filed for bankruptcy. No one in the industry wanted to do business with him anymore, and his company closed permanently. Maria and the other workers found jobs with Tim's new company, where they could work without fear of harassment or abuse.

Years later, I encountered Maria on Seventh Avenue. She told me with tears in her eyes that her daughter had graduated from nursing school and was getting married. We embraced on that busy street, two women who had been brought together by tragedy but had found strength in each other.

The Lasting Impact

The legal precedent set by our lawsuit against Barney became a landmark case for sexual harassment law in New York State. It continues to be cited today in harassment cases throughout the fashion industry, providing legal protection for other women who find themselves in similar situations.

Eleanor's words before the trial have stayed with me throughout my career: "Men like Barney could take away our jobs and our dignity, but only if we give them the power to do so."

The settlement provided enough money for me to take time off to care for my father during his illness, and thankfully, he recovered. But it also gave me something more valuable—the knowledge that I had the strength to stand up to powerful men who thought they could abuse women with impunity.

Looking back, I can see that this experience was both devastating and transformative. It showed me the darkest side of the fashion industry but also revealed the power of women supporting each other in the face of injustice.

My passion for fashion remained strong, and I knew that as long as I had the strength to fight, I would continue creating and working in an industry I loved, despite its flaws. The experience with Barney had taught me that change comes from those brave enough to speak out, and I was determined to be part of that change.

The courage it took to fight Barney was perhaps the most important lesson I learned in those early years of my career. Maybe I was naïve when I walked out of that warehouse, but I made a promise to myself that day: I would never again allow men like Barney to define the terms of my professional life or subject me to any kind of sexual harassment again.

Unfortunately, I would soon learn that the apparel industry was filled with men like Barney, and that the fight for dignity and respect in the fashion industry was far from over. But I had proven to myself that I had the strength to fight back, and that knowledge would serve me well in the battles that lay ahead.

CHAPTER 4:
Hell Hath No Fury like Ronda

Returning Home to New York

The plane's rough landing at LaGuardia Airport jolted me back to reality, but I couldn't contain my excitement about returning to New York City. After spending a rejuvenating two months at my friend's parents' beach house in Nantucket, my personal sanctuary and the place I retreated to during difficult times, I was ready to face whatever challenges awaited me in the city. The turbulent landing made me wonder if it was a sign of the bumpy road ahead, but I pushed that thought aside as I spotted my pug's sleepy face peering at me from her travel carrier.

"We're back home!" I announced to her, my voice filled with genuine enthusiasm. She had been my constant companion through all the ups and downs of my career, and I could tell she was as happy as I was to be back on familiar ground. The moment we stepped off the plane, I called Kelly to let her know we had arrived safely and were heading to her apartment. As I flagged down a yellow taxi, my mind raced with the logistics of finding a new apartment within just a few days. My previous roommate had relocated to Los Angeles, which meant it was finally time for me to establish my own independent living space in the city I loved.

When our cab pulled up to Kelly's building, I practically

bounced out of the vehicle, nearly dropping my poor pug onto the sidewalk in my excitement. "Sorry, girl," I said, giving her sweet face a kiss. She had endured so much with me throughout my career journey, and I knew she was relieved to be back on her home turf. She immediately perked up, bounding up the stairs to the front door and barking with excitement as I buzzed Kelly's apartment to announce our arrival.

Climbing the four flights of stairs to Kelly's apartment reminded me just how out of shape I had become during my relaxing month's in Nantucket. I was completely winded by the time I reached her door, which made me realize I needed to get back to a gym routine quickly especially if I planned to wear the fitted designs of my new employer, Ronda Couture.

The Opportunity at Ronda Couture

During my stay in Nantucket, I had received and accepted a job offer that I had interviewed for prior to my leaving New York. It was from one of New York's most prestigious design companies, Ronda Couture, not it's real name, but highly successful. It was renowned throughout the fashion industry for exceptional tailoring and body-conscious clothing that demanded peak physical fitness from anyone who wore the designs. Ronda herself had built a reputation for insisting that her employees maintain a specific physique to properly showcase her clothing line. This meant that returning to a strict fitness regimen wasn't just about personal health—it was a professional necessity. Not like today where diversity is expectable, back then you had to maintain a very slender figure in order to work in a big fashion company.

Kelly greeted me with a warm embrace and immediately handed me a generous glass of white wine, her face lighting up with genuine joy. "You're finally here!" she exclaimed graciously, as we hugged.

"Let me take your bags." Her apartment on the Upper West Side was truly spectacular—a spacious two-bedroom unit complete with a wood-burning fireplace and an eat-in kitchen that was practically unheard of in New York City. Most New Yorkers our age lived in tiny spaces with kitchens barely large enough to heat up takeout, so Kelly's apartment felt like a palace.

"Wow!" I gasped as I took in the beautiful space. "This is absolutely spectacular."

"Thank you to my rich parents!" Kelly laughed, acknowledging the privilege that had afforded her such luxury. I couldn't help but feel a twinge of envy because having wealthy parents certainly made life in New York much more manageable.

"Lucky you!" I sighed, though I was genuinely happy for my friend's good fortune.

"I made dinner reservations at a local Italian restaurant around the corner," she announced, already planning our evening. I downed my wine quickly, suddenly realizing how hungry I was after the long travel day. "I'm starving!" I declared enthusiastically. Kelly efficiently gathered my bags and placed them in her guest room before addressing my next concern.

"What about my dog?" I asked, worried about leaving her alone after the long journey.

"Oh, you can bring her," Kelly assured me. "We'll eat outside." This was perfect, outdoor dining would allow my pug to join us for our reunion celebration.

"Fabulous! I am so happy to be here!" I said, throwing my arms around my best friend again, in a moment of pure gratitude and excitement.

"Me too!" Kelly smiled warmly. "We're going to have such a blast now that you're finally home!"

The Charm of New York City Dining

Eating outdoors in New York City has always been one of my favorite experiences, and that evening reminded me why. There's something magical about dining on a bustling, noisy sidewalk where people from all walks of life feel comfortable approaching your table to strike up conversations about everything imaginable, your personal story, the quality of the food, the restaurant's atmosphere, current fashion trends, and even political views. The sidewalks of "Gotham" feel like neutral territory where normal social boundaries don't apply, creating unexpected connections and encounters.

Strangers frequently approached to ask about my meal or comment on the designer clothes I was wearing. This openness is part of what makes New York so unique, the city attracts people who aren't afraid to put themselves out there, whether they're charming or completely inappropriate. Over the years, I had actually ended up romantically involved with several of these sidewalk charmers who had the confidence to approach me and strike up a conversation.

My pug also seemed to possess this New York charm, effortlessly flirting with other dogs she encountered during our street-side dining experience. She was remarkably successful at it too, which made me laugh as I told a dashing stockbroker named Matt, "Like mother, like daughter." He was quite charming himself and asked for my phone number, which I excitedly gave him without hesitation. Remember there were no dating apps or social media back then, so we actually had to talk to each other in order to form a connection.

Two bottles of wine, one shared plate of pasta, and several exchanged phone numbers later, Kelly and I walked the two blocks back to her apartment in high spirits. As we strolled through the familiar streets, I became overwhelmed with emotion about being back in the city that had always felt like my home. In a moment of pure joy and perhaps influenced by the wine, I did my best "Mary Tyler Moore" impersonation, twirling around in the middle of the street and nearly getting hit by a car in the process.

I threw my headband high into the air with dramatic flair, while Kelly, who was also slightly tipsy, laughed uncontrollably. My pug, caught up in the excitement, howled at the moon as my headband landed unceremoniously in the gutter.

"Damn!" I yelled, suddenly realizing I had lost my favorite accessory.

"I think you need a beret like Mary Tyler Moore, you idiot!" Kelly shouted through her laughter.

"Oh no! My headband!" I lamented dramatically.

"That's okay, I have plenty more at home," Kelly reassured me as she fumbled with her keys at the front door, both of us still giggling from our impromptu street performance.

The Apartment Hunt Begins

The next morning, my pug served as my alarm clock, nudging me awake at 6:00 a.m. with her eager desire to go outside on what promised to be a beautiful Saturday. I quickly dressed in my designer jeans, a Valentino tank top, and comfortable sneakers, ready to start the day with enthusiasm. My pug was right behind me as I dashed down the four flights of stairs and burst through the front door into the crisp morning air. Honestly, I couldn't tell who was more excited about the day ahead, me or her.

"Hi there!" I called out cheerfully to every person I encountered as we made our way down the street. "Good morning, what a beautiful day!" I shouted to a woman across the street. New

Yorkers typically raise an eyebrow when someone enthusiastically shouts compliments at them on a Saturday morning, but I didn't care. I simply flashed a big smile and continued our morning adventure.

Our first stop was the corner bodega for a copy of the New York Times, followed by a trip to H&H Bagels for two everything bagels loaded with cream cheese. Then my dog and I crossed the street to a coffee shop where I ordered two lattes, one for myself and another for Kelly. As I waited for our order, I couldn't help but chuckle, remembering that just days earlier in Nantucket, I had driven twenty minutes for mediocre coffee and a subpar bagel.

"Kelly! Wake up!" I announced loudly as I burst into her apartment, immediately plopping down on the couch with the New York Times real estate section spread before me. "I brought you bagels and a latte!"

Kelly emerged from her bedroom wearing fabulous Burberry pajamas with a matching eye mask perched on her head, looking like she had stepped out of a luxury lifestyle magazine. "Oh God," she moaned, clearly suffering from the previous night's wine consumption. "I have such a headache."

"Take two aspirin and eat your bagel," I instructed with the authority of someone who had consumed just as much wine but somehow felt perfectly fine. "We have an apartment to find for me today."

"What's the hurry?" Kelly yawned, still not fully awake. "You and your pug can stay here as long as you like."

While I appreciated her generosity, I explained the practical limitations: "Kelly, you know dogs aren't allowed in your building. Besides, I need a terrace for her, or at least something close to Central Park."

Finding the Perfect Apartment

Fortune seemed to be on my side that morning as I circled five promising apartment listings in the newspaper and successfully scheduled appointments for each one. "Okay Kelly," I announced after finishing my calls, "two sound reasonable, one seems questionable, the fourth sounded too good to be true, and the last one appears to be a complete dump."

"Fabulous, let's get started," Kelly laughed, finally catching some of my enthusiasm.

I decided to change into what I considered my apartment-hunting uniform, flower-adorned bell-bottom jeans paired with a pink tweed crop jacket and matching pink sneakers. I was convinced that the right outfit would somehow help me attract the perfect apartment, as if my fashion choices could influence real estate destiny.

After feeding my dog and asking her to wish me luck, a ritual that had become important to both of us, Kelly and I set out with determination to find my ideal New York home.

Our first stop was a complete disaster. "Oh God, this is absolutely miserable," I complained as we climbed six flights of stairs in an old, dilapidated building on the Upper East Side. The building looked like it hadn't been maintained since the 1950s, and I was already having serious doubts.

"Have faith," Kelly encouraged, though she looked equally skeptical about our surroundings.

The broker, a seedy-looking man with a terrible overbite, announced proudly, "So, this is a one-bedroom with ample outdoor space, or what we like to call a 'double wide fire escape.'" His enthusiasm for what was clearly a safety hazard masquerading as a selling point should have been our first warning.

The moment he opened the apartment door, a rat the size of a small cat ran directly across the kitchen floor, over my sneakers, and down the stairs. I had seen New York City rats before, but this one was particularly bold and enormous.

"Oh my God!" I screamed, jumping into the air and running as fast as my legs could carry me.

"A rat!" Kelly screamed, following close behind as we both fled down the six flights of stairs and onto the street.

Standing in the middle of the street, still shaken by our encounter with the massive rodent, we listened as the broker irritatingly insisted that "mice" were a common sight in New York City apartments, apparently trying to minimize what we had just witnessed.

"First of all, that was not a mouse!" Kelly corrected him loudly. "That was a rat the size of her dog!"

"And second, I am absolutely not living in a rat-infested dump!" I added emphatically. We have other appointments so if this is all you have then we need to leave now.

The broker, clearly bored by our reaction and probably accustomed to similar responses, sighed and said, "I only have one more apartment that I represent, and it's spectacular, but it's definitely out of your price range." Do you want to see it?

"Yes, just show us the apartment!" Kelly demanded, not willing to give up on our search just yet.

The Perfect Apartment to Call Home

As we walked to 57th Street and 6th Avenue, my excitement began to build again. This location was only two blocks from Central Park, which would be perfect for my dog's daily exercise needs.

"My dog would absolutely love this," I said, admiring the beautiful building. "And it's such a lovely location."

"You have a dog?" the broker asked, as if this was the first time the subject had come up.

"Yes, I told you that over the phone," I replied, slightly irritated. "Is there a problem?"

"No, as long as it's a small dog," he answered.

Kelly looked at me and rolled her eyes knowingly.

"Small dog?" Kelly laughed. "I hope they allow that little fatty pug of yours!"

"She's not fat, she's just a little plump," I said defensively, though I knew Kelly was right.

"Plump? No, she's the size of a butterball turkey!" Kelly whispered, enjoying my discomfort.

She had struggled with the heat in Nantucket, which meant I could only walk her at night, and her love of snacks combined with my tendency to spoil her had resulted in some weight gain.

"We're going to go jogging every day if we get this apartment," I declared with the confidence of someone making a New Year's resolution.

"Right!" Kelly laughed, clearly not believing my exercise commitment for a second.

Despite my dog's weight issues, luck was definitely on my side. The apartment was absolutely beautiful—located on the top floor of an elevator building with a doorman, offering a lovely view of Central Park. It featured hardwood floors, abundant natural light from large windows, and a small stone terrace where I could enjoy my morning coffee. The most appealing aspect was that it was rent-stabilized, which is incredibly rare and valuable in New York City.

"I love it! How much is the rent?" I asked, holding my breath in anticipation.

The broker wrote down a figure on a piece of paper and handed it to me. Before I could even look at it, Kelly grabbed the paper and immediately yelled, "She'll take it!"

"Good," the broker responded efficiently. "I'll get you the paperwork, and I'll need a check from you immediately."

When I finally saw the rental amount, I gasped at the number. "How am I going to afford this?"

Kelly smiled confidently and said, "You'll make it work. Call your dad!"

Financial Independence and Family Support

The suggestion to call my parents for financial help went against everything I believed about independence and self-reliance. I had never sought financial assistance from my parents, especially since my father had been dealing with health issues. I took tremendous pride in my ability to support myself, which sometimes frustrated my parents because they genuinely wanted to help when they could.

"Honestly, if I cut back on food expenses, walk to work instead of taking the subway, and refrain from buying new clothes, I can manage to pay this rent," I told Kelly with complete sincerity, already calculating the sacrifices I would need to make.

"Call your parents, Katie. They want to help you," Kelly insisted, understanding my situation better than I wanted to admit.

I still had a significant portion of the settlement money from my lawsuit against Barney, which I could use for the security deposit and first month's rent. Additionally, I needed to purchase some furniture and update my wardrobe for the new job. Ronda insisted that all her employees wear her clothing designs, and while we received a substantial employee discount, the pieces were still quite expensive.

That evening, I finally called my parents to tell them about the apartment I had found. The conversation went better than I had expected.

"Dad and I will help you until you get established in your new job," my mother said warmly.

"No, that's okay. I'll be fine on my own," I replied, still reluctant to accept help.

"Don't be silly, we want to help!" my father interjected gruffly, using the tone that meant the discussion was over.

"Okay, it's settled then," my mother concluded. "We'll send you a check tomorrow."

"I have an apartment!" I announced to Kelly, unable to contain my excitement any longer.

Settling into New York Life

As I updated my address with the storage company and handled the logistics of the move, it suddenly hit me how perfectly everything was falling into place. I had secured an amazing new job at a prestigious fashion house, found a gorgeous apartment in an ideal location, had my best friend Kelly nearby for support, and my beloved pug by my side in the city I adored most.

What more could any aspiring fashion professional ask for? Well, perhaps a new boyfriend, but I was confident that would come naturally after all, I was living in New York City, where opportunities for romance seemed endless.

My furniture arrived from storage a week later, giving me just two days to unpack and transform the empty space into a livable home. I was thrilled to discover that my new apartment had five spacious closets, a fashion lover's dream, especially since I would need ample space for Ronda's clothing designs.

Starting at Ronda Couture

Monday morning arrived with surprising speed, and I found myself extremely nervous about beginning my new position. I spent an extra hour getting ready, carefully selecting my new "Ronda" black dress and styling my hair in a sleek ponytail that would meet her exacting standards. This particular dress was identical to the one Ronda wore in all her press photographs for her latest collection, a strategic choice that demonstrated my understanding of the company's aesthetic and my commitment to representing the brand properly.

Ronda was notoriously particular about her hiring practices. Every woman in her office had to be a size small to properly wear and showcase her clothing designs. There were absolutely no exceptions to this rule, which meant I would need to maintain a strict diet of lettuce and carrot sticks for the foreseeable future.

Understanding Ronda's Empire

Ronda had established herself as the leading women's clothing designer in the United States through what appeared to be hard work, though industry whispers suggested she had fought ruthlessly to reach the pinnacle of her career. Standing at five feet nine inches, she commanded attention wherever she went, though her physical appearance was more imposing than elegant. Despite creating clothing for size small women, Ronda herself was not thin, she had a lumpy, uneven figure and certainly was not a size small. As she entered her fifties, the effects of aging had become increasingly apparent, leading her to undergo an intensive facelift that unfortunately resulted in a noticeably lopsided smile.

Her most prized physical feature was her long blonde hair, an obsession that consumed enormous amounts of time and energy. She went to extraordinary lengths to keep it perfectly styled and would regularly ask anyone standing nearby if her hair looked fabulous. Smart employees quickly learned that the only acceptable answer was an enthusiastic "yes"—your job and possibly your life depended on it.

Any hesitation, confusion, or failure to respond would result in Ronda complaining about your complete incompetence and stupidity to everyone in the office. She had no tolerance for anything less than constant admiration and validation.

The First Day Experience

On that crucial Monday morning, I arrived at Ronda's prestigious 7th Avenue office wearing my carefully chosen black wool long-sleeve shawl dress with its distinctive wide gold half-moon belt. Despite arriving twenty minutes early, demonstrating the punctuality and professionalism I hoped would make a good first impression, I found myself waiting in the reception area for what felt like an eternity for my new boss's secretary to acknowledge my presence.

As I sat observing the array of very thin and attractive individuals moving through the office space, a growing sense of unease settled over me. What if I didn't meet Ronda's impossibly high expectations? What if she decided I wasn't the right fit and let me go? At this relatively early stage in my fashion career, which had already been quite turbulent, I wasn't sure I could emotionally handle another professional setback.

The office itself was designed to intimidate and impress in equal measure. Ronda's sleek workspace was truly spectacular, featuring rich white leather furnishings that gleamed with an almost surgical cleanliness. The floors were covered with striking black-and-white cowhide rugs that probably cost more than most people's monthly rent, and the pristine white walls displayed gold-framed photographs of Ronda alongside numerous high-profile celebrities. Every side table featured a perfectly arranged white orchid, and the deep espresso hardwood floors created a sophisticated contrast with the marble black and white reception desk. Golden lamps provided warm lighting throughout the space, while background music reminiscent of new-age meditation tracks created an oddly unsettling atmosphere at 9:00 in the morning.

I informed the receptionist that I was starting my new position as design director for Ronda's sportswear division. She looked thoroughly unimpressed and instructed me to sit down and wait while she contacted Ronda's personal secretary. I sat quietly for the next thirty minutes, observing the office dynamics and trying to understand the hierarchy and culture I was entering.

Finally, a very thin, hyperactive, red-haired young woman dressed entirely in Ronda's designs approached me with an air of superior authority.

"I am Yvette," she announced in a pronounced French accent. "Follow me, you're late!" she barked accusingly.

"No, I've been here for thirty minutes," I replied defensively, confused by her hostile attitude.

"That attitude will get you nowhere," she snarled, her French accent making her words sound even more condescending.

I silently followed her down the long white hallway, feeling like a condemned prisoner being led to execution, and into a small waiting area outside what I assumed was Ronda's personal office.

"Sit here and wait for Ronda," she commanded brusquely before disappearing again.

Meeting the Queen

I waited outside Ronda's office for another thirty minutes, my anxiety building with each passing moment. When Yvette finally beckoned me to enter Ronda's inner sanctum, I was completely unprepared for what I encountered. The size and opulent beauty of her personal space was breathtaking, everything was completely white, from the walls and furniture to the silk pillows and luxurious area rugs. Gold-gilded picture frames lined the walls, similar to those in the reception area, but these photographs showed Ronda in completely naked and highly provocative poses. The overwhelming scent of jasmine candles filled the air to such an extent that I began feeling nauseous almost immediately.

"Wow," I managed to say as I looked around the space, trying to process what I was seeing. "This is absolutely beautiful!"

"Why, thank you," Ronda replied, clearly pleased by my reaction as she gestured for me to sit in an overstuffed white chair positioned directly in front of her imposing desk. "Katie, dear," she began in a tone that was simultaneously sweet and threatening, "I painstakingly selected you to be my new design director from hundreds of applications, so I expect you to arrive on time," she said with sharp emphasis on the word "time."

I felt as though a knife had pierced straight through my heart. Should I tell her that I had actually arrived twenty minutes early and had been waiting for her for another thirty minutes, or should I simply remain quiet and accept the blame?

"Well—" I began to explain.

"Excuse me," she interrupted loudly, "don't talk back to me. My karma is extremely fragile today. It's the first time Mercury has been in retrograde in my astrological sign in over ten years, so please, please, shut the fuck up!" She delivered this outburst with a bright smile, as if she had just offered me a compliment.

"Okay," I said quietly, not wanting to further disrupt her delicate karmic balance.

"Now, you must leave and find your new office, dear, and I'll catch up with you later," she said dismissively, waving me away from her presence like an unwanted pet. "Yvette, come and get Katie and show her to her office and introduce her to everyone," Ronda shouted to her assistant.

The Office Tour and Meeting Jeff

Yvette returned to Ronda's office, tapped me impatiently on the shoulder, and instructed me to follow her once again. I felt exactly like a lamb being led to slaughter as she raced down the hallway at a pace I could barely maintain, her heels clicking aggressively against the polished floors.

"You better enroll in a spin class if you plan on keeping up with everyone here," she called over her shoulder, making it clear that physical fitness was not optional in this workplace.

"This is the cafeteria. Over there is the bathroom, the copy machine, and here's your office. See you later, bye," she said in her characteristic snotty French tone before flying down the hallway again and disappearing from view before I could ask a single question.

"God, all she needs is a broom," I muttered under my breath, thinking about how perfectly she fit the stereotype of a wicked witch.

"I heard that!" an angelic voice said, causing me to turn around in startlement.

"Hi, I'm Jeff, the women's designer," he said with genuine laughter in his voice.

"Oh God, I didn't mean that. I'm so sorry," I apologized immediately, embarrassed to have been caught making such an observation.

"Oh yes, you did, honey. She's a first-class bitch!" he giggled conspiratorially.

Jeff was tall and slender with wavy blonde hair and piercing blue eyes that sparkled with intelligence and mischief. He was thin and impeccably dressed in pieces from Ronda's men's collection and carried himself with theatrical flair, using animated hand gestures that made every conversation feel like a performance. I immediately loved everything about him, and we became fast friends within minutes of meeting.

Hans, Jeff's boyfriend, served as Ronda's personal hairdresser and had considered her most prized employee. Jeff understood that as long as Hans remained in Ronda's good graces and their relationship stayed strong, his own job security was virtually guaranteed. This unique position gave Jeff the freedom to speak openly about everyone and everything in the office, including making pointed and often hilarious observations about Ronda herself.

The Story of Allison and the Dress

"Okay, so let me give you all the juicy details," Jeff said as he settled comfortably in my newly renovated office, which maintained the same pristine all-white decorating scheme as the rest of the building.

"Ronda started working here when she was young—okay, now try to imagine when that witch was actually young!" Jeff laughed as he continued to tell me the story, his eyes twinkling with mischief.

The challenge of determining Ronda's true age was complicated by her extensive cosmetic enhancements and recent facelift, Jeff laughed. The previous owner of this fashion label had been a remarkable, talented woman who had taken Ronda under her mentorship when she was just starting out. Even though Ronda possessed only modest talent as a young designer, it was this generous owner who recognized and nurtured her potential. Jeff stated that she taught Ronda the fundamental skills of fashion design: how to sew with precision, sketch with creativity, and tailor stunning garment's that flattered the human form.

While Ronda maintained a facade of politeness and respect whenever the owner was present, Ronda's true character emerged when she thought no one was watching. Anyone who displayed exceptional talent or who attempted to develop a close relationship with the owner would inevitably face Ronda's fierce temper and vindictive behavior. Her jealousy knew absolutely no bounds and all she cared about was protecting her turf.

Jeff continued with obvious relish, "One time, the owner traveled to Europe seeking inspiration for her summer collection. Allison, a newly hired gifted designer from Paris and another young mentee, was tasked with creating a breathtaking couture evening gown for the owner to wear to the Annual Fashion Awards ceremony. This was the pinnacle social event of the year, where everyone who mattered in the fashion industry would gather to celebrate excellence and recognize outstanding achievements. The owner had complete faith in Allison's ability to create a gown that would capture everyone's attention and represent the company beautifully, and Allison was absolutely thrilled to be entrusted with such an important and visible project."

"Allison possessed immense talent," Jeff explained. "She had previously worked with the prestigious couture house of Jean Pierre."

"He's the most famous French designer in Paris," I interjected excitedly, recognizing the significance of such an experience.

"Exactly! The dress Allison created was absolutely magnificent and became the talk of the entire office for months. That level of attention and praise, of course, enraged Ronda more than anything else in the world," Jeff whispered conspiratorially, ensuring that no one passing by in the hallway could overhear our conversation.

The Masterpiece Dress

Jeff continued the story with obvious enjoyment. "It took Allison hundreds of painstaking hours to sew the gown, and every single bead was hand-applied to delicate tulle fabric that cost $2,500 per yard. The beading process was incredibly complex and required years of training to master properly, Allison was recognized as one of the most skilled seamstresses in the entire fashion industry in Paris. The finished dress was a gorgeous shade of azure blue, which happened to be the owner's favorite color. It was absolutely breathtaking in every way imaginable."

Allison understood that this gown represented the pinnacle of her artistic achievement, and she was incredibly excited for the owner to see it and try on her creation. She had no doubt whatsoever that the owner would feel immense pride when she saw the extraordinary level of craftsmanship and attention to detail that had gone into every aspect of the design.

The precious dress had been carefully wrapped in layers of tissue paper and placed reverently in the owner's office, where it waited patiently for her return from her European buying trip. However, Ronda became increasingly worried that once the owner saw this magnificent gown and appreciated all the beautiful details that Allison had incorporated into the design, she might lose interest in

Ronda's work and transfer her favor to the more talented designer.

Ronda was absolutely determined not to allow Allison to gain any advantage over her, or anyone else for that matter, so she began devising a wicked plan to sabotage the dress and destroy Allison's reputation in the process.

"Later that day, Ronda called a meeting and asked Allison to review the dress with her and her two 'lap dog' assistants, Yvette and Charles. Since the owner always left Ronda in charge when she traveled, Allison felt obligated to comply with the request, even though she sensed something wasn't right."

"What happened next Jeff?" I asked with bated breath, completely caught up in the drama of the story.

"Well, I was taking notes during that meeting," Jeff said, settling in for the climax of his story.

The Destruction

"Ronda launched into her typical tirade about the shape and color of the dress, claiming it was completely unacceptable for the owner's figure. She insisted that the dress was the wrong size entirely and that the owner would be very upset when she discovered this major error in judgment.

Allison, maintaining her characteristically sweet demeanor, explained to Ronda that she had personally customized every aspect of the dress based on the owner's exact measurements. She was absolutely certain that it would fit the owner perfectly and create a stunning silhouette.

That's when everything went completely wrong. Ronda leaped from her chair and quickly began peeling off her clothing right there in the meeting room. She revealed a shabby white bra that didn't fit properly and a pair of old white panties with visible tears. Then, without any warning, she grabbed the gorgeous dress that was still wrapped in layers of protective tissue and tugged it forcefully over her head, convinced that she was the same size as the owner, which was absolutely not the case!"

I gasped in horror, already anticipating the disaster that was about to unfold.

"The moment she tried to force the dress over her much larger body, the delicate fabric began tearing apart. Sparkling beads and rhinestones scattered across the floor like confetti, and hundreds of hours of meticulous handwork was destroyed in seconds. Allison collapsed in her chair, sobbing uncontrollably as she watched her masterpiece being obliterated."

"Oh no!" I gasped, feeling genuine grief for Allison's loss.

"Oh yes!" Jeff continued enthusiastically. "Allison was absolutely devastated, and frankly, we all were! Ronda then picked up the ruined dress and threw it directly on top of poor Allison, coldly stating, 'I told you it wouldn't fit.'

Allison, gasping for air between her tears, finally found her voice and cried out, 'The owner is a size six and you're a size twelve, you cow!'

Ronda whipped around and looked Allison straight in the eye with pure venom. 'Bullshit. I am not a twelve, I am a six,' she screamed at the top of her lungs!

That's when I couldn't help myself," Jeff chimed in with glee. "'Honey, if you're a six, then I'm Queen Elizabeth,' He said.

'Shut up, you fag, no one is talking to you!' Ronda yelled at Jeff. Then she marched out of the office in a fury, while her two 'lap dogs' trailed behind her like loyal servants.

Allison left that night, completely humiliated, and never returned to work again."

"So, what happened to her?" I asked, genuinely concerned about this talented woman's fate.

"Oh, she's now Ronda's biggest competitor and arch-enemy. You've heard of 'Bella Donna,' haven't you?"

"Oh my God, that's Allison?" I said, completely stunned by this revelation.

"Yes, and here's the real kicker, Ronda told the owner that Allison had fled to a competitor, taking the dress and stealing company designs in the process. The owner was heartbroken and never forgave Allison for what she believed was a terrible betrayal. It was completely untrue, but the owner believed every word Ronda had told her."

Ronda's Eating Habits

Just as Jeff finished his story, my office door swung open and Yvette appeared to summon me to the design studio for a meeting with Ronda and my new team. "Ronda always orders elaborate lunches for the designers during concept meetings," Jeff informed me as we prepared to join the group.

What I witnessed next was quite a spectacle. I had never seen so much food ordered for a business meeting! For someone who demanded that all her employees maintain small figures, I was shocked by the enormous variety and quantity of food she had ordered. There was an entire roasted chicken, an assortment of gourmet sandwiches, creamy potato salad, rich macaroni salad, and two full platters of decadent desserts. I couldn't spot a single carrot stick or piece of lettuce anywhere on the entire catered spread.

The situation seemed contradictory, but I was genuinely hungry after the stressful morning and Jeff's story, so I filled my plate generously. I noticed that everyone else took only half a sandwich or a single cookie, but I shrugged it off and piled my plate high, after all, in New York City, a free meal is still a free meal, regardless of the circumstances!

Ronda called everyone to gather around the food and take their seats before the meeting officially began. Then she proceeded to tear the entire roasted chicken apart with her bare hands, as if she were a wild animal. She loaded her plate with what must have been half a pound of potato salad, a handful of dinner rolls, six or seven cookies, and several brownies. I sat there with my mouth hanging open, completely bewildered by how she could maintain any kind of figure while consuming enough food for three people.

Ronda then leaned over her overflowing plate and began eating as if it were her last meal on earth, using her fingers and showing absolutely no regard for proper etiquette. The more food she shoveled into her mouth, the more disgusted everyone around the table appeared to become. Now I understood why no one else had taken much food, watching Ronda eat was genuinely nauseating and completely destroyed any appetite you might have had.

What made the situation even worse was that she would begin talking while her mouth was completely full of food, causing particles to fly across the table and land on anyone unfortunate enough to be sitting nearby. This explained why no one ever chose to sit directly across from her at meetings, everyone except me, the naive new employee who hadn't yet learned the unspoken rules of Ronda's dining behavior.

I spent the rest of the day picking bits of chicken out of my hair, a humiliating reminder of my poor seating choice.

Jeff leaned over and whispered conspiratorially, "Oh my God! Ronda is such a pig!"

"Shut up," I whispered back, trying not to laugh out loud.

"You're going to get me fired on my first day."

"Honey, the only thing Ronda sees or hears right now is that chicken," he replied with amusement. "She's completely oblivious to everything else."

Everyone else sat in uncomfortable silence while Ronda attempted to lecture us about the beauty and technical aspects of a "bias-cut gown." She continued shoving cookies into her mouth throughout her presentation, spitting crumbs all over me with each word. Soon, her speech became so garbled and incoherent that no one could understand what she was trying to communicate, and frankly, no one seemed to care anymore. I simply observed the surreal scene unfolding before me and discreetly covered my lunch with a napkin, hoping to finish it later in the privacy of my office.

Understanding Ronda's Psychology

After the disastrous lunch meeting, Jeff and I returned to my office to review our confusing notes and try to make sense of what we had just witnessed. He began explaining the psychological roots of Ronda's disturbing eating habits and erratic behavior.

"So, honey, after Allison called Ronda a 'cow' during the dress incident, Ronda completely freaked out and started an extreme crash diet that lasted for months. Unfortunately, nothing worked because the woman genuinely loved to eat and would sneak food into her office late at night when no one else was around to witness her binges," Jeff explained with obvious amusement.

"Eventually, someone suggested she start taking diet pills so she could continue eating whatever she wanted without gaining weight. For Ronda, this seemed like the perfect solution to her problem, she could maintain her public image while indulging her genuine love of food in private.

After the Allison dress disaster, Ronda's weight began fluctuating dramatically between a size six and a size twelve, depending entirely on her stress levels and emotional state. She became addicted to diet pills, diuretics, laxatives, and God knows what other substances," Jeff said, barely containing his laughter.

"That's why she has a full private bathroom in her office, complete with a shower," he added with a knowing wink. "She needs immediate access for all those pharmaceutical side effects."

"That's absolutely disgusting!" I laughed, though I felt somewhat sorry for anyone trapped in such a destructive cycle.

Ronda's Rise to Power

Jeff continued filling me in on the company's dark history. When the original owner began considering retirement at seventy-five, she made the fateful decision to trust Ronda with the leadership of the company, believing she would honor the founder's vision of classic, timeless and elegant designs. This mandate for maintaining the brand's integrity was the owner's single most important requirement for her successor.

However, Ronda had completely different ideas about the company's future direction. She began systematically lying to the board of directors behind the owner's back, convincing them that the founder's design philosophy was hopelessly outdated and that she herself was becoming senile and incompetent. Ronda was an expert manipulator and deceiver who presented her arguments so convincingly that the board members eventually made her president of the company, giving her complete creative and business control.

This corporate coup effectively stripped the original owner of all her power and influence. The founder was absolutely devastated when she realized that Ronda had betrayed her trust so completely, and she finally saw her former protégé for what she truly was, a ruthless, ambitious person who would destroy anyone who stood in her way. Even though numerous people had warned the owner not to trust Ronda over the years, she had always treated her like a beloved daughter and refused to believe the warnings.

Once the original owner was completely out of the picture, Ronda could finally run the company according to her own vision and ambitions. She immediately changed the company name to "Ronda Couture," establishing herself as the sole creative force behind the brand. Although she possessed a lack of genuine talent in many areas, she was shrewd enough to hire the most gifted designers in the industry and then systematically take credit for all their creative work.

She manipulated the board members into funding millions of dollars for elaborate new office renovations and would stop at nothing to dress celebrity clients and keep herself constantly in the media spotlight. There wasn't a single tabloid or fashion magazine that didn't regularly feature photographs of her at glamorous events wearing her own creations.

"'Celebrity whore' would be putting it mildly," Jeff observed with characteristic bluntness. "Ronda never met a camera she didn't love, as long as she was the center of attention."

The Slapping Incident

Ronda's reputation for having a terrible temper was legendary throughout the fashion industry, yet nobody possessed the courage to confront her about her abusive behavior toward employees. I was about to learn this lesson firsthand in the most shocking way possible.

On one particularly busy afternoon, Jeff and I were

conducting a fitting session for one of my new designs that would be featured in the upcoming spring collection. Ronda entered the fitting room to check the progress on the model's jacket and pants, immediately taking control of the situation with her typical authoritarian approach.

My lead seamstress was carefully pinning the corrections I had specified when Ronda abruptly interrupted, declaring that everything was being done incorrectly. She demanded that the seamstress immediately stop following my instructions and implement her completely different vision instead.

I looked at Ronda with genuine confusion because I knew my seamstress was not only correct in her approach but was also the most skilled and experienced professional we had on staff. I calmly told the seamstress to continue following my original directions, confident that my design vision was sound.

Before I could say another word, Ronda spun around with lightning speed and slapped me hard across the face! The sound echoed through the fitting room, and I stood there completely frozen, feeling the stinging sensation on my cheek while looking at her in absolute shock and disbelief.

"You just slapped me?" I yelled at her, my voice filled with outrage and confusion. "Why did you do that? You can't just hit someone in the face without any reason!"

"I hit you, dear, because you should never, ever correct me," she replied with chilling calmness, as if physical violence was a perfectly reasonable response to a professional disagreement. As she turned to leave the room, she smiled coldly and added, "Now go wash your face and then finish the fitting properly."

I remained frozen in place, completely unable to process what had just occurred.

"Did you see that?" I asked Jeff desperately, needing confirmation that this assault had actually happened.

"Well, did you?" I demanded of the seamstress, hoping for some support or solidarity.

She simply put her head down and continued working on the jacket, clearly too frightened to acknowledge what she had witnessed.

I didn't know what to do next, so I stumbled into the bathroom to splash cold water on my burning cheek and try to regain my composure.

When I returned to the fitting room, Jeff immediately embraced me in a comforting hug.

"Oh sweetie, you're definitely not the first-person Ronda has slapped, and you certainly won't be the last," he said with disturbing matter-of-factness. "That's basically her initiation ritual into 'Ronda Hell' for all the new employees. That crazy woman has slapped more designers than I can possibly count."

"You got bitch slapped," he added with inappropriate laughter. "Get it?"

"She can't get away with this kind of behavior!" I sobbed, still trying to process the assault.

"Of course, she can, darling. She's Ronda Couture!" he replied, as if this explanation made perfect sense.

"Well, she'll be a dead Ronda Couture if she ever touches me again!" I declared furiously, glaring at both Jeff and the seamstress.

Following the traumatic fitting session, I locked myself in the bathroom and sobbed for an entire hour. The red imprint of her hand remained clearly visible on my cheek, making it obvious to everyone in the office that she had struck me. Despite this humiliation and assault, I found that I hated Ronda from that day forward while simultaneously loving my job and my creative team. I made the difficult decision to endure her abusive behavior for the sake of my fashion career, and I absolutely refused to be fired again, especially by this unstable person.

The Stripping Experience

When I finally emerged from the bathroom, I could hear a significant commotion coming from down the hallway. I hurried back to the design room, expecting to discover that someone else had just been slapped by our tyrannical boss. Instead, I arrived to witness Ronda standing in the middle of the room, flailing her arms wildly in the air and screaming profanities at the top of her lungs. She was wearing nothing but a filthy pink bra held together with a safety pin and a pair of equally dingy, faded floral underwear that had seen much better days.

I would soon learn that removing her clothing during design meetings was not uncommon behavior for Ronda. At any given moment, she would strip down to her underwear and try on pieces from her various collections, using the design team as her personal fitting assistants. The irony was not lost on any of us, here was a woman with more than enough money to purchase beautiful, well-fitting lingerie, yet she consistently wore the same tattered, stained underwear that every employee in the office had been forced to see on multiple occasions.

"What seems to be the problem?" I asked as calmly as possible while she attempted to squeeze herself into one of my newly finished designs.

"The problem?" she snapped aggressively. "The 'problem' is that this stupid, fucking, no-talented designer you hired last month is a complete waste of space!" The designer in question sat silently with his head down, having learned from previous encounters with Ronda that speaking up would only make the situation worse.

At that moment, Yvette, Ronda's assistant, rushed into the room to announce that a well-known actress was on the telephone and ready to speak with Ronda immediately.

Ronda went into complete panic mode. "My God, it's her!" she screamed so loudly that everyone in the entire building could hear her excitement and terror.

"Put her through on the speakerphone immediately!" She commanded Yvette.

Ronda remained standing there in her ratty underwear while instructing all of us to remain completely silent during the important phone call.

"Sweetie, darling! Is this my favorite celebrity?" Ronda squealed like an excited pig over the speakerphone.

"Yes, Ronda, and I need a huge favor from you!" the celebrity responded in an equally saccharine tone.

"Anything for you! Absolutely anything!" Ronda purred back at her.

Behind Ronda's back, Jeff was making exaggerated gagging motions with his finger down his throat. I tried desperately to hold back my laughter while glaring at him to stop his antics, but he continued his performance throughout the entire conversation.

"I need several new gowns for the Cannes Film Festival, Ronda sweetie. Can you send me five or ten options?" the celebrity requested.

"Oh, absolutely!" Ronda gushed enthusiastically. "I will send out my very best gowns to you by the end of this week."

"I'll expect to see you at Cannes, right?" the celebrity giggled.

"Why, I wouldn't miss it for the world, darling," Ronda promised confidently.

"Perfect, Ronda. Thank you so much," the celebrity concluded.

The line went dead with an audible click.

"Did she just hang up on me?" Ronda asked us all, her voice filled with confusion and growing anger. "Did that fat bitch just hang up on me?"

"No, no," we all responded in unison, trying to prevent another explosive outburst.

"It must have been a faulty connection," I suggested diplomatically, trying not to laugh as Jeff continued mocking the celebrity's abrupt departure.

"Yes, you're absolutely right," Ronda murmured insecurely. "It was definitely a problematic connection."

She then gathered her clothes from the floor and walked down the long white hallway in her stained underwear, apparently forgetting entirely why she had been yelling at the new designer in the first place.

"A bad connection, my ass. She was probably five blocks away!" Jeff laughed as soon as Ronda was out of earshot.

"That woman is absolutely insane!" We all agreed as Jeff pretended to slam down an imaginary phone.

Celebrity Relationships and Psychology

This particular celebrity had a long-standing relationship with Ronda, who dressed her for virtually every public event she attended. The celebrity was short and significantly overweight, probably in her early sixties, and she adamantly refused to wear a bra under any of her clothing, no matter how much Ronda begged and pleaded with her to do so.

There was nothing more visually offensive than seeing this woman's sagging, unsupported breasts moving freely underneath a meticulously crafted Ronda creation. This sight infuriated Ronda more than almost anything else, celebrity status notwithstanding, so she insisted that we sew built-in bras into every single gown we created for this difficult client.

Despite all her efforts to maintain a close relationship, Ronda was consistently ignored by this celebrity at the glamorous events they attended together. The celebrity would pose for photographs and grant interviews while completely overlooking Ronda, who stood nearby desperately hoping for acknowledgment and validation.

Ronda demonstrated a clear preference for dressing older, established stars and would become visibly irritated whenever younger celebrities wore her designs. This pattern stemmed from her deep-seated yearning for her own lost youth, and her obvious envy became more apparent whenever she spotted a younger, more beautiful star wearing one of her creations. She remained perpetually dissatisfied with her life and career, and no amount of success or recognition could alter this fundamental aspect of her bitter personality.

"Ronda desperately needs some serious therapy!" Jeff observed with characteristic wit.

We all laughed and returned to our fitting session, grateful for the temporary reprieve from our boss's erratic behavior.

Surviving a Year in "Ronda Hell"

"I actually managed to survive an entire year working for Ronda," I announced with genuine excitement as Jeff, Kelly, and I celebrated this milestone achievement over multiple martinis at my favorite bar in New York, which happened to be conveniently located directly beneath my apartment building.

"So convenient!" Jeff smiled appreciatively. "You can get completely drunk and simply take the elevator right upstairs to your apartment and pass out! If I get drunk, I somehow end up lost in Brooklyn!" he laughed.

"I cannot believe you endured all of Ronda's abuse for an entire year!" Kelly chided me with sisterly concern. "For God's sake, that psychotic woman actually slapped you!"

"Yes, she certainly did, but I also received a substantial raise this year!" I laughed as we toasted each other with another round of tequila shots.

"Well, here's to hoping you'll survive the infamous Ronda Christmas Party this year," Kelly said with a knowing smile.

"And here's to you two finally meeting some attractive men!" Jeff cheered, and we all dissolved into laughter.

The Infamous Christmas Party

Ronda's annual Christmas celebration was legendary throughout New York's fashion and entertainment industries. It featured a carefully curated guest list of celebrity A-listers, and over five hundred invitations were distributed each season to the most influential people in fashion, entertainment, and high society. Ronda became a nervous wreck for three weeks before the event, obsessively checking and rechecking that every photographer from every major magazine and tabloid would be present to document her moment of triumph.

She spared no expense for this showcase, selecting the most exclusive nightclub in New York to host her party and arranging for catering by not one or two, but four world-renowned chefs. Given

Ronda's well-documented appetite, the extravagant food selection seemed entirely appropriate.

One of Ronda's most controlling traditions involved personally selecting evening gowns for all her invited employees, ensuring that no one would outshine her on her special night. Each of us would be lined up like cattle while she methodically went through racks of clothing, selecting specific gowns for individual employees. Whether the dress fit properly or flattered your coloring was irrelevant—you were expected to wear exactly what she chose, or you would find yourself permanently excluded from her inner circle.

This year's theme was slightly different, as she decided that all employees should wear black while she stood out dramatically in an emerald-green bias-cut silk gown she had designed specifically for herself. I was actually pleased with this decision since black had become my personal uniform, and I was relieved to see that she had selected a simple beaded halter gown that fit me perfectly. All the male employees were required to wear black tuxedos as well.

Jeff was particularly excited because he insisted that he looked so distinguished in his tuxedo that he might actually outshine Ronda herself, a dangerous but amusing possibility.

As the party date approached, Ronda's behavior became increasingly erratic and unpleasant. She snapped at everyone with cruel comments and seemed to take particular pleasure in tormenting newly hired employees who were still learning to navigate her mercurial moods. If you weren't fortunate enough to receive an invitation to her party, she would essentially ignore your existence for several months afterward.

She constantly ate cookies, donuts, and any other sweets she could find throughout the office, transforming into a nervous wreck whom everyone tried desperately to avoid.

Hans's Revenge

When the party day finally arrived, Ronda looked bloated and exhausted, definitely not the ideal combination for someone who styled herself as the "Queen of Mean" and the undisputed mistress of the evening. She cursed and screamed at anyone who crossed her path, including Hans, her previously devoted hairdresser.

Hans had finally reached his breaking point after years of enduring Ronda's psychological abuse and had secretly accepted a position at a trendy upscale salon. He hadn't informed Ronda of his decision yet, knowing that the revelation would trigger an explosive confrontation. As his parting gift to his tormentor, he decided to create an elaborate updo for the party that would require an attached hairpiece crowned with an emerald beaded tiara.

The hairstyling process took Hans four full hours to complete. When Jeff and I stopped by Ronda's office at the end of the workday to observe his handiwork, we both gasped in absolute horror at what we saw.

"Well, what do you think?" Ronda asked with obvious excitement. "Is it fabulous, or is it absolutely fabulous?" she squealed with delight.

"It's certainly special," I managed to say while fighting desperately to contain my laughter.

"Special doesn't even begin to describe it," Jeff added, pinching my arm to keep me from losing control.

"I knew you were a genius, Hans, and no one else will have a hairstyle like this tonight!" Ronda exclaimed with complete confidence.

"That's absolutely certain," Hans muttered under his breath with barely concealed satisfaction.

"Is she completely delusional?" I whispered to Jeff. "Doesn't she realize how ridiculous she looks?"

"It's a perfectly awful hairdo that Hans has been planning to give her for ten years of abuse," Jeff replied with obvious admiration for the hairdresser's revenge.

"Exactly!" I laughed as we quickly retreated to my office.

Several moments later, we heard blood-curdling screams emanating from Ronda's office that could be heard throughout the entire building.

"Well, Hans just told her he's quitting!" Jeff announced with glee.

"Oh my God! I'm getting out of here before she explodes!" I laughed as I sprinted down the hallway with Jeff following close behind.

The Party Preparation

Jeff and I left the office to get ready for the party, and I had managed to secure an extra invitation for Kelly, who would meet us at the nightclub. As I prepared for the evening in my apartment, I asked my pug for her opinion on my appearance.

"Well?" I said as she sat on my bed, observing my preparation ritual. "What do you think, girl? Do I look fabulous?"

She regarded me with complete disinterest and continued chewing on her stuffed "Ronda" doll that Jeff had created especially for her entertainment. I scolded her gently when I noticed that she had positioned the doll so that Ronda's posterior was in her mouth, an accidentally appropriate commentary on our boss.

I was absolutely thrilled at the prospect of seeing all the amazing celebrities who would be attending this exclusive event. I called Jeff to let him know that I planned to arrive early to secure optimal positioning for celebrity watching. Just as I finished that conversation, my phone rang with an urgent call from Ronda.

"Katie, you need to come to the office immediately! We have a major emergency that requires your immediate attention," she cried with obvious panic in her voice.

"What happened?" I asked, immediately worried. "Are you hurt?"

"Just get to the office right now!" she screamed at maximum volume before hanging up abruptly.

After ending the disturbing call, I quickly grabbed my coat and rushed out to hail a taxi, but not before calling Jeff to inform him that I needed to return to the office to handle whatever crisis Ronda was experiencing. When I arrived at my office building, I noticed that all the lights were turned off except for a soft glow coming from Ronda's office. I knocked gently on her door and waited for permission to enter, hearing the distinct sound of intense sobbing from within.

The Emergency

"Ronda, are you, all, right?" I called through the door as I entered her office.

"Katie, is that you?" she responded through her tears.

"Yes, Ronda, it's me."

"Please come in," she sobbed pitifully.

As I walked into her elaborate dressing room, she was nowhere to be seen. Moments later, she emerged from her private bathroom, and I gasped at the shocking scene that confronted me. She looked absolutely dreadful, her elaborate hairstyle was now a tangled mess, with the expensive hairpiece lying soaked on the floor. Ronda stood before me in tattered underwear, completely topless, with her emerald-green gown torn down to her knees. Her makeup was smeared dramatically across her face, and the overwhelming stench of vomit filled the air.

"What on earth happened?" I asked in shock and horror, holding my hand over my mouth to prevent myself from gagging.

Through her tears, she explained the humiliating sequence of events: "I must have eaten too much this week, so I decided to make myself throw up because my dress wouldn't fit properly. But when I bent over the toilet, my hairpiece fell into the water, and then my dress ripped completely in half." She continued sobbing while describing how she had desperately tried to contact Hans for help, but he had told her to "go to hell."

"All right," I said, taking charge of the situation. "Get in the shower immediately, and I'll find you another gown to wear."

My primary motivation was entirely selfish, I wanted to resolve this crisis as quickly as possible so I could still make it to the party in time to see the celebrities and reunite with my friends.

I rushed down the corridor to my office and retrieved a special dress I had been saving for just such an emergency. Hidden away in an old box in a closet was the azure-blue beaded gown that Allison had designed many years earlier, the same dress that Ronda had destroyed in her jealous rage. Everyone assumed that Allison had taken it with her when she left the company, but I had actually rescued it from back of a closet and spent months meticulously reattaching each individual bead and rhinestone as a form of therapy during Ronda's worst periods of abuse.

Thanks to my dedication and countless hours of painstaking work, I had managed to repair the holes in the delicate tulle fabric and restore this stunning creation to its original glory. It was only when Jeff discovered me sewing late one night in the sample room that he realized the significance of what I was working on.

"What the hell are you doing?" Jeff had asked when he found me hunched over the dress with my sewing kit.

"I found this dress in an old storage box, and repairing it has become my therapy," I had explained to him. "Whenever Ronda makes me angry or upset, I pull it out and sew on a few more beads. The repetitive work calms me down and helps me process my frustration and in turn I am bringing this masterpiece back to life."

"You're absolutely amazing! Make that dress sparkle again!" he had encouraged me with genuine admiration.

The Dress Decision

"Katie!" I could hear Ronda screaming for me from her office, snapping me back to the present crisis. "Where did you disappear to? You're such an incompetent girl!"

After retrieving the box containing Allison's restored masterpiece, I returned to Ronda's office and quickly set about repairing her makeup and pulling her hair back into her signature sleek blonde ponytail. Although the process was unpleasant and I resented missing valuable party time, it was necessary to ensure that we could both arrive at the event without further delay and that my job was secure for at least another year.

"You should have been a professional hair and makeup artist!" she said with renewed cheerfulness after examining my work in her mirror.

"Thank you," I replied, though I was increasingly irritated by the entire situation and the fact that I now smelled like vomit.

"Actually, you would make a much better makeup artist than a designer!" she added with characteristic cruelty.

Her comment was the final straw. I thought to myself: What an absolutely horrible person. I can't believe I'm helping this miserable, nasty woman after everything she's put me through. I had originally planned to give her Allison's beautifully restored dress that had taken me six months to repair, but her continued insults changed my mind completely.

"Well, where's the dress you promised to find for me?" she demanded impatiently.

While she wasn't looking, I quickly hid Allison's dress underneath her desk where she couldn't see it. Instead, I removed my evening coat, unzipped my own beaded black gown, and handed it directly to her. Thank goodness, the fabric had some stretch in it!

"Here, you can wear my dress!" I said, barely containing my fury as I stood there in my beautiful La Perla lingerie.

"Fabulous! It will look so much better on me anyway," she replied with typical self-absorption. Can I have your underwear to? She asked me seriously.

God no! I said angrily. That's just gross!

As she struggled to zip up my dress, which was clearly too small for her larger frame—she grabbed her luxurious Russian sable coat, announced how fabulous she looked, turned off the lights, and left me standing alone in my underwear in the dark office. She called for her driver to take her to "her" party, completely abandoning me after I had just rescued her from disaster. As she departed, I noticed that my gown already had a small rip in it from the strain of fitting her lumpy body. I couldn't help but laugh at the poetic justice.

I sat down at her desk, shocked once again by Ronda's complete selfishness and lack of gratitude. Finally understanding what a truly nasty, cold-hearted person she was, I made the firm decision that it was time to start looking for another job. At that moment, her phone began ringing insistently. I answered to hear Jeff and Kelly shouting at me from the party.

"Are you okay?" they yelled over the background music. "You're missing an incredible party! Get down here immediately!"

"Allison from Bella Donna is here," Kelly added excitedly. "She's absolutely gorgeous!"

"What happened with Ronda?" Jeff asked. "You sound upset. Are you still dealing with the Queen of Mean?"

"No, she left for the party already," I replied. "Oh, never mind, you'll never believe what just happened anyway!"

"Oh yes, we will!" Jeff screamed over the loud music.

"I'm on my way. Wait for me before you do any more shots," I yelled back to them.

The Transformation

I turned on the office lights and jumped into Ronda's private shower to wash off the unpleasant smell of vomit that had transferred to my clothing and hair. I reapplied my make-up and swept my hair up into a French not. Then I carefully retrieved the azure-blue beaded gown from its hiding place under her desk. I held my breath and gently lifted the restored masterpiece over my head.

Looking into Ronda's full-length mirror, I saw that the dress was absolutely breathtaking and fit my body perfectly, exactly as I had always imagined it would. For the first time in my life, I felt like a genuine princess. I found a floor-length black velvet cape in Ronda's extensive closet, called for a limousine, and boldly charged it to her company account as I prepared to make my grand entrance.

When the limousine arrived at the exclusive nightclub, camera flashes began exploding everywhere like a fireworks display. I gracefully exited the vehicle, dramatically removed my cape, and tossed it back into the car with a flourish. I stood confidently posing for the photographers before entering the nightclub with the poise of someone who belonged in this glittering world.

I navigated through the crowds of beautiful people, searching for Jeff and Kelly while taking in the incredible scene around me. The party was absolutely spectacular—every celebrity imaginable was present, and Ronda was holding court with her usual collection of admirers and hangers-on.

Across the room, I could see Allison surrounded by her own impressive entourage, staring directly at Ronda with obvious disdain.

Just then, Jeff and Kelly rushed up to me with expressions of amazement.

"Oh my God, you look absolutely incredible!" they yelled over the pounding music. "That dress is a genuine masterpiece, a true work of art!" Kelly gasped, knowing the full story of how this gown had served as my therapy during the past year of hell at Ronda's company.

I performed my most impressive twirl, and they both applauded enthusiastically as we embraced and laughed together.

The Confrontation

At that moment, I noticed both Ronda and Allison walking toward me simultaneously from opposite directions across the crowded room.

"Oh shit," Jeff laughed nervously, "you're about to become a dead woman."

"Oh shit!" Kelly echoed, "Whatever's about to happen, it's definitely not going to be good!"

Allison stood transfixed, her eyes widening as she recognized the dress she had designed twenty years earlier, now perfectly reconstructed and being worn so elegantly by me. "You found it?" she said with tears beginning to form in her eyes. "You're Katie, right? The girl everyone says is very talented?"

"Yes, that's me," I replied shyly, feeling honored to finally meet this legendary designer. "Thank you so much, Allison. It's such an honor to meet you. I hope you're not upset, but I took the liberty of repairing your beautiful gown."

"Upset? Of course not, dear! I thought that horrible woman Rhonda, had thrown it away many years ago," she smiled warmly.

"You look absolutely stunning," she continued as she stepped back to admire her own craftsmanship after all these years. "You did a beautiful job restoring my gown. I honestly thought it was beyond repair when I saw what she had done to it. You deserve to wear it tonight!" Allison smiled and embraced me warmly.

"Thank you, Allison, but this is your beautiful work of art, and I simply couldn't bear to let it be destroyed and stuffed into a box forever," I replied gratefully.

Meanwhile, Jeff and Kelly had spotted Ronda charging across the room like an angry bull, preparing to attack me. They grabbed my hands tightly, ready to provide protection and support.

Ronda seized my arm, squeezing it painfully, and pulled me away from Allison while Jeff and Kelly held on to me desperately. "What the fuck are you doing in that dress, you bitch?" she screamed with the full force of her rage. I was genuinely terrified and had no idea what violence might come next from her.

Just as she raised her hand to strike me again, a photographer captured our confrontation with a bright flash.

Suddenly remembering that she was being photographed, Ronda quickly placed her arm around me in a fake embrace, squeezing so tightly that she actually knocked Jeff and Kelly off their feet.

"Whose dress are you wearing?" the photographers shouted, eager for information about my stunning gown.

Ronda was preparing to answer their questions and claim credit for Allison's design when I interrupted her and broke free from her painful grip.

"Why, it's a vintage Bella Donna creation by Allison!" I announced loudly enough for everyone in the vicinity to hear me clearly.

The crowd erupted into enthusiastic applause and cheers.

"Beautiful!" "Magnificent!" "Congratulations, Allison!" people screamed with genuine appreciation.

"You're fired!" Ronda whispered venomously in my ear while pinching my arm hard enough to leave bruises.

"I warned you never to lay a hand on me again!" I shouted furiously at Ronda, pulling the hairpin from my elegant updo and using it to deliberately rip apart the dress she was wearing—my dress that she had stolen from me.

Suddenly, beads from her gown began flying everywhere as the fabric gave way under the assault. As Ronda spun around frantically trying to collect the scattered beads, the dress tore completely down the back, exposing her dingy white "big girl" panties to the entire crowd of sophisticated party guests.

The crowd burst into laughter as camera flashes continued exploding, documenting Ronda's humiliation for posterity. She ran toward a side exit, screaming with rage and embarrassment.

"Let's party!" Jeff laughed triumphantly as he pulled Kelly and me onto the dance floor to celebrate our victory.

"Katie," Allison called after me over the music. "I would love for you to come work for me!"

"Well, you're in luck, Allison, I was just fired by Ronda!" I laughed excitedly as I began dancing with complete freedom.

Allison joined our celebration, laughing as she stepped onto the dance floor with us.

The Aftermath

That unforgettable night, Kelly, Jeff, Hans, and I danced and consumed tequila until the sun rose over New York City. It was an absolutely amazing night for fashion and justice, though unfortunately not so wonderful for Ronda!

Several weeks later, I learned that Ronda had retreated to a yoga ashram for six months of self-imposed exile, and I began working for Allison after a well-deserved vacation. There were rumors that Ronda was planning to launch her own lingerie line, perhaps she'd finally invest in some respectable underwear.

I never wore another Ronda design after that night. I sold all my Ronda clothing and invested the money in designers whose work I truly admired and respected.

The experience taught me that once again standing up to a bully, even at great personal cost, can lead to unexpected opportunities and genuine friendships. Allison proved to be everything, Ronda was not kind, generous, and truly talented. Working for her felt like a reward for surviving my year in "Ronda Hell."

Looking back, I realize that night marked a turning point in my career. I had learned to value my own worth and refuse to accept abuse in the name of professional advancement. The restored dress became a symbol of resilience, both Allison's original vision and my determination to preserve something beautiful despite the forces trying to destroy it.

CHAPTER 5:
The Garmento and the Rapper

Leaving Corporate Fashion Behind

Working alongside Allison for several years had been one of the most rewarding experiences of my career. Her company represented everything I valued in fashion, creativity, integrity, and genuine respect for both designers and clients. Unfortunately, like so many success stories in the fashion industry, this chapter came to an abrupt end when Allison decided to sell her business for a substantial sum.

The sale meant that all of us who had built the brand's reputation were immediately replaced by a new team. This harsh reality reflects a common practice throughout the fashion industry, established companies acquire well-respected brands not to preserve their unique vision, but to strip-mine their reputation while replacing talented teams with cheaper, less inspired workers. The result is always the same: budget versions of what were once prestigious designer labels, mass-produced without the soul or craftsmanship that originally made them special.

This pattern has become the fashion industry's way of cannibalizing itself. When companies repeatedly hire the same uninspired individuals, and shuffle them between brands, innovation dies. Creativity becomes secondary to cost-cutting measures, and the industry loses the very essence that made these brands valuable in the first place.

The harsh truth is that only the wealthiest companies with massive distribution channels, those with accounts at retail giants like Walmart and Target, can survive this race to the bottom. These companies thrive because they can sell enormous volumes at low prices, generating significant profits while treating design as merely an afterthought. Quality, originality, and craftsmanship become luxuries they can't afford in their pursuit of maximum profit margins.

Returning to the Garment Center

Despite witnessing this systematic destruction of creativity, I made the decision to step away from the corporate fashion world and return to the raw, unfiltered environment of the garment center. I convinced myself that with more experience under my belt and a talented team of designers I could bring to support me, this time would be different. This time, I would be better prepared to navigate the treacherous waters and emerge victorious.

Looking back, I realize this decision was driven more by optimism than wisdom. I was eager to boost my earnings, and the garment center, despite all its flaws, offered the potential for substantial financial rewards, if you could survive its brutal culture and unethical practices. I knew the risks, having witnessed firsthand the instability that plagued anyone working on that side of the street, largely due to predators like Barney and others who treated employees as disposable commodities.

The environment in the apparel industry truly resembled the Wild West, where established norms and ethical standards were regularly discarded in favor of quick profits and personal gain. It was a place where the strong preyed upon the weak, where contracts meant little, and where your reputation could be destroyed by a single vindictive competitor.

The Reality Behind the Glamour

Most people outside the fashion industry harbor romantic notions about what it means to work in the garment center. They picture themselves strolling down Seventh Avenue, surrounded by well-dressed, joyful young men and women showcasing the latest trends while clutching leather portfolios filled with sketches and fabric swatches. In their imagination, they see themselves working for prestigious New York City apparel companies, attending glamorous fashion shows, and living the sophisticated life they've seen portrayed in movies and television.

This romantic image couldn't be further from the brutal reality of daily life in the garment center.

From the 1980s through today, the garment center has been dominated by disheveled, overweight men known as "garmentos", a term that perfectly captures both their appearance and their mentality. These men could be seen hustling from one building to another at all hours, their rumpled suits and aggressive demeanor reflecting their single-minded pursuit of quick money, regardless of the human cost.

The reality for most people working in the apparel world, particularly women, involved enduring low wages and grueling hours just to maintain their positions. While the "garmentos" enjoyed substantial compensation, justified by their claims of supporting families, single women faced a very different experience. We struggled to advance beyond entry-level positions, constantly encountering the impenetrable glass ceiling that the apparel industry's male-dominated culture maintained with religious fervor.

The prevailing attitude among these men was that single women existed solely to serve their needs and ambitions. We were expected to be available around the clock, responding to their demands regardless of the hour or the reasonableness of their requests. This created an environment where maintaining any kind of work-life balance was impossible, and where personal relationships suffered under the relentless pressure to prove our worth in a system designed to exploit us.

The Celebrity Brand Gold Rush

I returned to Seventh Avenue at the height of what I call the rapper and celebrity brand movement, a phenomenon that transformed the garment center into something resembling a gold rush. Anyone who had achieved even modest fame, whether through a hit song, tabloid coverage, or reality television appearances, suddenly believed they could translate that recognition into a successful clothing brand.

The garment center became a magnet for these celebrities, who arrived seeking financial backers among the "garmentos" who would pay them upfront money just to have their face on a brand. Rappers, celebrities, and models were wooed by the apparel companies who promised them massive amounts of success and money.

These shrewd businessmen were more than willing to pay substantial upfront fees simply to associate their companies with famous faces and household names. The promise was always the same: massive success, unlimited profits, and a piece of the American dream wrapped in designer clothing.

Rappers, in particular, were aggressively courted by garment center companies who painted vivid pictures of wealth and success that seemed almost too good to be true. The reality, as I would discover, was that these promises were indeed too good to be true.

Most celebrities who entered into these partnerships were completely unprepared for the hustlers and con artists who populated the apparel industry. They had achieved success in music, sports, or entertainment through talent and hard work, but the business skills required to navigate the garment center were entirely different. The "garmentos" positioned themselves as fashion experts, a complete fabrication, since the actual designers were the ones with expertise, and promised clothing lines that would make the celebrities wealthy beyond their wildest dreams.

What these celebrities failed to understand was that the people who would truly profit from these ventures were the garment industry owners, their families, and their extended networks of suppliers and manufacturers. The celebrities provided the name recognition and marketing appeal, but the financial benefits flowed primarily to those who controlled the company and its production and distribution channels.

Meanwhile, employees like myself would work tirelessly, pouring our creativity and expertise into designing collections that would bear someone else's name and generate profits we would never see.

Working for Paul: A Study in Exploitation

My first position after leaving Allison's company was with a particularly wealthy garment center boss named Paul. He was a man who epitomized everything wrong with the industry's approach to celebrity partnerships, and his attitude toward the artists he worked with revealed the ugly racism that lurked beneath the surface of many garment center operations.

Paul would proudly and openly proclaim that he "owned all the niggers in the clothing industry", a statement so shocking in its blatant racism that it left me speechless the first time I heard it. Unfortunately, such attitudes weren't entirely surprising to me, as I had encountered various forms of prejudice and discrimination throughout my career in fashion. I was also reminded of the stories told me by Yvonne about her encounters with racism and abuse. The garment center had always been a place where power dynamics were enforced through intimidation and dehumanization.

The irony of Paul's racism was that he had built his substantial fortune, which he claimed exceeded $500 million by financially supporting various African American celebrities, from up-and-coming rappers to established A-list stars. He understood that their talent and cultural influence could generate enormous profits, but he viewed them purely as commodities to be exploited rather than as human beings deserving of respect and fair treatment.

Paul's business model was devastatingly effective in the short term. He would court celebrities with promises of wealth and success, front them substantial amounts of money to secure their cooperation, and then systematically extract maximum value from their names and images while providing minimal compensation in return. After a few years, when his celebrity-driven ventures had served their purpose, he would allow them to go bankrupt, leaving the stars financially destitute while he moved on to new victims with his profits intact.

I felt a moral obligation to protect the celebrities I worked with by educating them about the scams and exploitation tactics commonly used in the apparel industry. However, my efforts to warn them were often futile, as Paul and others like him had become masters of manipulation who could convince their targets that any outside advice was motivated by jealousy or ignorance.

Paul took genuine pride in his ability to deceive and exploit his celebrity clients. To him, their eventual financial ruin was simply the cost of doing business, and he felt no remorse for the careers and lives he destroyed in pursuit of profit. What made this particularly frustrating was knowing that men like Paul continue to operate throughout the industry today, preying on new generations of hopeful celebrities who believe that fame automatically translates to business success.

The Celebrity Brand Experience

Despite the ethical concerns I had about the industry's treatment of celebrities, I found myself thriving in my first job after leaving Allison's company. I had joined a large garment center operation that specialized in celebrity brands, and while the work environment presented numerous challenges, I was genuinely excited by the creative opportunities and the chance to reunite with talented designers from my previous teams.

Working directly with rappers turned out to be one of the most enjoyable aspects of my new position. Contrary to the intimidating image many of them projected in their music and public personas, I found them to be wild, unpredictable, creative, and surprisingly easy to connect with on a personal level. They brought an energy and authenticity to the design process that was often missing in more traditional fashion environments.

What I appreciated most about working with rappers was their willingness to support my creative vision when my bosses tried to water down or compromise my designs for their brands. While the apparel industry executives saw only profit margins and cost-cutting opportunities, the artists themselves understood the importance of maintaining their authentic style and image. They consistently backed me up when conflicts arose between creative integrity and corporate cost-cutting measures.

Each rapper I worked with had assembled a team of business managers, family members, or close friends to oversee their clothing ventures and financial interests. While their loyalty to the artists was admirable, none of these individuals possessed any real understanding of the apparel industry's complex dynamics. This ignorance suited the apparel executives perfectly, as it made their exploitation tactics much easier to implement.

As the designer working most closely with these celebrity teams, it became my responsibility to educate them about the basics of fashion production, distribution, and marketing. I tried to provide them with the knowledge they needed to make informed decisions and protect their interests, but their lack of business sophistication made them vulnerable to the various schemes that surrounded them.

The "garmentos" found it much easier to take advantage of celebrities whose business managers were clueless about industry standards and practices. My bosses would openly laugh about how simple it was to manipulate these teams, treating their lack of knowledge as an opportunity rather than a problem to be solved through education and honest dealings.

The Financial Shell Game

The business model used by most garment companies with celebrity brands followed a predictable and ethically questionable pattern. Celebrities would receive quarterly "royalty" checks based on predetermined percentages that the "garmento" had negotiated with them during the initial contract discussions. However, these payments were calculated after deducting staff expenses, marketing costs, production overruns, and virtually anything else the "garmento" could think of to reduce the celebrity's share of the profits.

As employees of these garment center companies, we were all aware of a practice that bordered on fraud: the maintenance of two completely separate sets of financial records. One set was prepared for the "garmentos" accountants and reflected the true financial performance of the celebrity brands. The second set was created specifically for presentation to the celebrities and their management teams, showing dramatically reduced profits and inflated expenses.

When a celebrity began to suspect they were being shortchanged, usually because their royalty payments seemed disproportionately small compared to the obvious success of their products in stores, they would be invited to review "the books." These carefully crafted financial statements would show modest profits at best, with the "garmentos" explaining that high production costs, marketing expenses, and distribution fees had eaten up most of the revenue.

The celebrities and their teams rarely had the expertise to properly analyze these financial documents or question the various expense categories that had been used to minimize their apparent profits. Instead, they would be reassured by the "garmentos" that the next quarter would yield much better results, with promises of doubled earnings that never seemed to materialize. "You'll be rich!" was the constant refrain, and most celebrities continued to believe in this illusion quarter after quarter, year after year.

The King Big Daddy Rapper of All Time

On a more light-hearted note, one spring afternoon, I received an unexpected visit that would perfectly illustrate the cultural clash between the traditional garment center and the new world of hip-hop celebrity. A well-known rapper, whom I'll call the "King Big Daddy Rapper of All Time" to protect his identity, arrived at my office to discuss a potential clothing line collaboration.

Although we had held several preliminary meetings with his team over the past few months, his approach to business was refreshingly unconventional compared to the rigid scheduling and formal protocols that dominated most garment center operations. He had a habit of showing up whenever inspiration struck him, often without any advance notice or scheduled appointment, accompanied by whatever combination of friends, family members, girlfriends and business associates happened to be with him at the time.

I had built a solid reputation within the industry for my talent in urban fashion design and, perhaps more importantly, for treating celebrities with honesty and respect. Cheating anyone, regardless of how much money was involved or who was paying my salary, had never aligned with my personal values, and word of this integrity had spread throughout the hip-hop community.

It became routine for our company's receptionist to announce over the building's intercom system that the "King Big Daddy Rapper of All Time" had arrived to see me, usually accompanied by what she diplomatically referred to as his "entourage." These announcements always created a buzz of excitement throughout the office, as employees from other departments would find excuses to walk past our conference room to catch a glimpse of the famous visitor.

This particular artist was riding high at the top of the music charts and commanded a massive, devoted fan base that translated into significant profit potential for any company lucky enough to partner with him. When he arrived for meetings, he typically brought an impressive assembly of five or six relatives, multiple lawyers and business managers, a couple of professional bodyguards, and several young women whose revealing outfits seemed more appropriate for a nightclub than a corporate office environment. This would send the "garmentos" into hiding.

While many people in the industry found this rapper intimidating, and his carefully cultivated "bad boy" image and imposing physical presence could be overwhelming, I discovered that he was genuinely amusing and surprisingly sweet once you got past the public persona. Behind the tough exterior was an intelligent, creative individual who cared deeply about his artistic integrity and wanted to ensure that any clothing line bearing his name would reflect his authentic style and values.

The Wednesday That Changed Everything

On this particular Wednesday, the "King Big Daddy Rapper of All Time" and his full entourage showed up at our company's reception area without any advance warning and no appointment. This was never an ideal situation because our company's owners had developed a pattern of systematically leaving their offices whenever they knew "rappers" were scheduled to visit. They claimed to feel uncomfortable around anyone who wasn't "one of them," revealing the deep-seated prejudices that continued to shape the garment center's culture.

I had grown accustomed to these visits and actually enjoyed the opportunity to meet creative people from the music industry. My usual practice was to escort visiting artists and their teams to our main conference room, where we would discuss upcoming fashion trends and I would present my latest design concepts and completed work for them to review. After the visitors left, I would provide detailed updates to my superiors, and if we reached a preliminary agreement, our company's lawyers would take over the formal negotiation process with the celebrity.

Unfortunately, I was never included in those crucial business discussions, despite my intimate knowledge of both the creative and business aspects of any potential deal. My role was strictly limited to the design and presentation phases, I was expected to create compelling concepts, stay quiet during business negotiations, and maintain a professional smile regardless of how the deal ultimately developed. Looking back, I realize that I might have been able to prevent several disastrous partnerships if I had been allowed to participate in the business discussions and share my insights about realistic production timelines and cost projections, but as a woman that was unheard of.

On this particular Wednesday, however, our reception area was already occupied by four rabbis who had been patiently waiting for their weekly meeting with my boss. These religious leaders showed up every Wednesday at exactly the same time to receive their cash envelopes, a practice that I later learned was surprisingly common throughout the garment-center.

I had been specifically instructed to avoid scheduling any celebrity meetings on Wednesday afternoons to ensure that the rabbis and the rappers would never encounter each other in our reception area. The cultural clash between these two groups was considered too problematic for our management to handle, so they preferred to keep these two worlds completely separate.

The practice of making regular payments to religious leaders was rooted in a tradition that many garment center companies had maintained for decades. These companies allocated a small percentage of their profits to favored rabbis, believing that these contributions would secure divine favor for their business ventures. While the amounts involved were relatively modest compared to the companies' overall revenues, the weekly ritual had taken on an almost superstitious importance for many garment center executives.

However, the rabbis appeared noticeably uncomfortable and anxious today, squirming in their seats and exchanging worried glances when the "King Big Daddy Rapper of All Time" and his loud, animated entourage unexpectedly filled the reception area with their presence. The cultural tension was immediately apparent to anyone observing the scene.

The contrast couldn't have been starker: four elderly, conservatively dressed religious leaders sitting quietly with their hands folded, while across from them sat a group of young, flamboyantly dressed hip-hop artists and their entourage, engaged in the kind of rough banter and explosive laughter that made for an uncomfortable scenario.

The sense of anxiety among the rabbis was palpable as they waited to be rescued from this awkward situation. Fortunately for them, they were promptly ushered into the owner's private office, which couldn't have happened a moment too soon from their perspective. I couldn't help but chuckle at this humorous clash of cultures as I led the "King Big Daddy Rapper of All Time" and his crew toward our conference room for what I hoped would be a productive business meeting.

The Great Elevator Misunderstanding

About halfway through my presentation to the rapper and his team, I was shocked to see my company's owner, accompanied by his two brothers, the four rabbis, three cousins, and an uncle who was hobbling around with a medical boot on his injured foot, rushing past our conference room in obvious panic. They were waving their arms frantically and heading straight for the elevators with the kind of urgency usually reserved for fire drills or natural disasters.

Assuming that some kind of emergency was unfolding, perhaps a fire or security threat—I excused myself from the meeting and stepped into the hallway to find out what was happening. My concern was that if the building was truly in danger, I needed to ensure the safety of our high-profile visitors and their security team.

I rushed down the hallway to the reception area, where I found the owner and his group frantically pressing every elevator button available, their faces showing genuine terror and desperation. When I reached out and grabbed my boss's arm to ask what was wrong, he spun around with wild eyes and shouted, "We're being robbed!"

In his panic, he shoved me so hard that I lost my balance and fell to the floor of the reception area. He completely ignored my presence as I sat there in confusion and distress, continuing to frantically push elevator buttons while muttering about robberies and calling for help.

I quickly picked myself up and ran back to the conference room where the rapper and his team were still waiting for my return. "We're being robbed!" I shouted to the "King Big Daddy Rapper of All Time" and his entourage. "You need to leave immediately for your own safety!"

The entire group leaped to their feet and rushed toward the door in their haste to reach the elevators and escape whatever danger threatened the building. In their hurry to get out, several members of the entourage accidentally knocked me down again as they pushed past me toward the reception area.

I couldn't help but notice that the "King Big Daddy Rapper of

All Time" was wearing an overwhelming amount of diamond jewelry that could have rivaled the display windows of Jacob the Jeweler, and his entourage collectively wore what must have been another million dollars' worth of diamond grills, gold chains, and other expensive accessories. Once I collected myself and got back to my feet, I hurried toward the elevator area and pulled the building's fire alarm, hoping to ensure that everyone in our company could safely evacuate if we were truly facing some kind of emergency.

The Elevator Encounter

When the "King Big Daddy Rapper of All Time" and his crew reached the elevator area, they found that the owner, his two brothers, the four rabbis, three cousins, and the uncle with the injured foot were still desperately trying to cram themselves into a single elevator car. The scene was becoming increasingly chaotic as both groups competed for the same limited space.

Just as the elevator doors began to close, the rapper's professional bodyguard stepped forward and prevented the doors from shutting, ensuring that his team could also squeeze into what was rapidly becoming a very crowded elevator car. The result was a comical sight: the "King Big Daddy Rapper of All Time," his full entourage, the company owner, his two brothers, four rabbis, three cousins, and an uncle with a medical boot all packed together like sardines in a space that was never designed to hold so many people.

The two groups immediately erupted into shouting and pushing as they jostled each other in their desperate scramble for space and position within the cramped elevator. Each group was convinced that the other was somehow involved in the robbery they believed was taking place, leading to accusations and counter-accusations flying back and forth in the confined space.

Finally, the elevator doors managed to close despite the chaos inside, leaving only an unsettling quiet in the reception area as I watched the indicator lights show their descent through all thirty floors down to the building's lobby. I found myself surrounded by my fellow employees, who had emerged from their offices to see what all the commotion was about, and we all stood there feeling bewildered by the surreal scene we had just witnessed.

Without warning, the absurdity of the entire situation hit me, and I broke into uncontrollable fits of laughter. The receptionist, who had been watching the whole drama unfold, immediately understood what I was thinking and began laughing just as hysterically as I was. Within moments, the laughter had spread throughout our entire company, with employees doubling over as they tried to process what they had just seen.

The Truth Behind the Chaos

As I stood there laughing with my colleagues, I suddenly realized what had actually happened, and the truth was far more amusing than any robbery scenario we had imagined. The owner, his two brothers, four rabbis, three cousins, and uncle with the injured foot, along with the "King Big Daddy Rapper of All Time" and his entourage, had not been the victims of any robbery at all.

What had actually occurred was a perfect storm of miscommunication and cultural misunderstanding. Since the owner had not been informed on his calendar, that the "King Big Daddy Rapper of All Time" was planning to visit today, he had likely interpreted the sudden arrival of a large group of imposing strangers as the beginning of an armed robbery. My boss assumed that the "King Big Daddy Rapper of All Time" and his entourage must have had insider information on the Wednesday Rabbi cash hand-outs. In the garment center, where cash transactions were common and valuable inventory was always present, the fear of robbery was a constant concern.

Meanwhile, the rapper and his team had probably observed the strange scene of eleven frightened men huddling together while clutching what appeared to be a safety deposit box (which was actually the rabbis' weekly cash envelope and the diamond ring my boss had bought for his wife's birthday, worth thousands of dollars), and concluded that they had walked into the middle of an ongoing robbery situation.

Each group's reaction had only reinforced the other's fears, creating a spiral of panic that culminated in the elevator scene we had all witnessed. It was a perfect example of how assumptions and prejudices could transform a simple scheduling mix-up into a crisis that revealed the deep cultural divisions that continued to exist along Seventh Avenue.

The humor of the situation wasn't lost on anyone who understood the garment center's complex social dynamics. Here was a world where different communities rarely interacted with each other, creating an environment where misunderstandings like this one were almost inevitable when these separate worlds collided.

The Aftermath and Lessons Learned

I never did learn exactly what conversations took place in that overcrowded elevator during its thirty-floor descent, but I can only imagine the confusion and gradual realization that dawned on both groups as they tried to make sense of their shared panic. What I do know is that somehow, despite the chaotic circumstances of their first encounter, we managed to secure an even larger licensing deal with the "King Big Daddy Rapper of All Time" the following week than we had originally anticipated.

"Just another day on Seventh Avenue," I found myself saying as I recounted this surreal tale to my friends Jeff and Kelly over drinks that evening. They listened in amazement as I described the cultural collision that had unfolded in our reception area and elevator, shaking their heads at the absurdity of daily life in the garment center.

The story had an interesting epilogue that revealed just how much the incident had affected our company's management. The following week, our owner implemented a new policy that established a completely separate reception area specifically for the rabbis' weekly visits, complete with a Plexiglas barrier that would prevent any future encounters between the religious leaders and our celebrity clients.

This segregated solution struck me as both practical and deeply troubling. While it would certainly prevent future misunderstandings like the one we had just witnessed, it also represented a deliberate effort to maintain the separation between different communities rather than finding ways to bridge cultural divides through understanding and communication.

As I reflected on the day's events, I couldn't help but think about how this incident perfectly captured the broader challenges facing the fashion industry. The garment center had always been a place where different worlds intersected, immigrants and established Americans, traditional religious communities and cutting-edge artists, conservative business practices and revolutionary creative expression, but too often, these encounters resulted in misunderstanding and separation rather than collaboration and growth.

The fact that segregation was seen as the obvious solution to cultural conflict revealed how deeply entrenched these divisions had become, and how little progress had been made in building bridges between different communities despite decades of shared presence in the same neighborhood.

Who could claim that segregation was a thing of the past when it was being actively implemented and reinforced in the heart of New York City's fashion district? The answer was clear: segregation was very much alive and well on Seventh Avenue, maintained not by law but by comfort zones, assumptions, and the unwillingness to engage with difference in meaningful ways.

CHAPTER 6:
"Fuck Her"

The Fashion Industry's Hidden Reality

To outsiders, the fashion industry appears as a glamorous business filled with stylish and creative people. They envision us spending our days designing beautiful apparel, laughing with colleagues, and draping stunning models in luxurious fabrics while staging elaborate fashion shows for celebrity clients.

This romanticized vision may hold true in movies or television shows, but in the real world, specifically on 7th Avenue in the mid-1990s, the reality was almost completely opposite. 7th Avenue was seedy, populated with hustlers and shady characters, and all of us were fighting tooth and nail for our place in the fashion arena.

When I use the term "garment center," I'm referring to the fashion industry hub in midtown New York City, located between 5th and 9th Avenues and West 34th to West 42nd Streets. Yes, there are occasionally beautiful models in the office for fittings, and there are astonishingly exotic materials available if you're designing for a high-end brand. However, there's also a tremendous amount of dirty, grueling hard work, along with real blood, sweat, and tears that accompany every successful fashion design team.

The Culture of Harassment and Control

The fashion industry harbored a shocking level of sexual harassment, coupled with an array of egotistical business leaders who were convinced they were God's gift to the fashion world. These executives believed they possessed the absolute authority to mistreat their employees, especially their designers. Seeing themselves as infallible, they treated their choices as sacred truths. Once your boss endorsed a collection, any form of critique or alternative suggestions was dismissed outright, with immediate termination threatening anyone who dared dissent. This toxic environment left employees feeling as if they existed in an alternate reality, where designers' voices were rendered completely insignificant. It became nearly impossible to walk away, especially for those who truly loved their work and wanted to keep pushing creative boundaries within the industry.

If you were free to create and design, and the money was decent, a designer or anyone in fashion would put up with just about anything or anyone to stay employed. That was simply the way things worked. It was profoundly unfair, and even forty years later, the situation hasn't changed much.

Most people in the "real world" have no idea that in the "fashion world", which operates as its own separate universe, employee manuals, sexual harassment guidelines, and professional protocols don't just get thrown out the window. They never made it inside the door in the first place.

Meeting Belinda: The Industry's Most Feared Executive

Case in point: Belinda, the now-defunct president of one of the largest apparel companies in the world. Her reputation preceded her wherever she went; everyone in "the industry" either knew her personally or knew of her by reputation. She had built an empire on a twisted combination of affordable clothing and the sheer terror she instilled in everyone who came into contact with her. A brilliant woman, Belinda could have been a positive role model for all women in business. Instead, she gave a terrible name to the entire female gender in the fashion industry. No one would dare challenge or contradict her, or you'd lose your job, your reputation, and your self-esteem in one fell swoop. If a buyer dared not to purchase her line, Belinda would annihilate her with one piercing, deadly look that most likely resulted in that buyer getting fired.

Cold and ruthless, Belinda maintained a "take no prisoners" attitude in every interaction. She possessed the vocabulary of a seasoned longshoreman, throwing around profanity as if it were completely appropriate for any corporate environment.

Throughout the industry, she was known as Belinda "fuck her." Everyone had at least one "fuck her" story about their encounters with her, and I would soon accumulate many of my own.

Stories of Belinda's Cruelty

The first Belinda story I heard came from Michael, an elegant gay friend of mine who had worked as an executive in one of her divisions. Now I don't know if this is true, but he told me that whenever Belinda and he were in group meetings outside the office, she was always cordial to him, although sharp and direct. But behind closed doors, Michael told me that she called him a "fucking fag," an idiot, and a queer. She reminded him that she would not tolerate getting "fucked in the ass" by him or anyone else if he didn't follow her rules.

Michael was appalled, defenseless, and deeply humiliated by her vile rants. Knowing there were no witnesses to the abuse who would dare cross her, he had absolutely no recourse. His confidence began to deteriorate rapidly, and his job performance faltered as a result. He even started to physically shake whenever he was in Belinda's presence. Just as she paid people extremely well, there was also a generous severance package available when Belinda fired you. Michael eventually took the payoff and quietly left after enduring a few years of abuse from her. The last I heard, he had quit the industry entirely and moved to the West Coast. He was extremely talented, and it was a complete travesty to witness what one woman's evil behavior could do to destroy a person's self-esteem.

Another whispered legend within the company was Jarrod, the former head of one of her now-defunct divisions. A tall and handsome man, Jarrod was engaged to marry Bonnie Thompson, the heiress to the Thompson furniture fortune, though these aren't their real names. Rumor had it that their relationship was on rocky ground, and Bonnie had been seen around town with a very eligible investment banker on more than one of the many nights she was out while Jarrod was still burning the midnight oil in his office with Belinda.

During one particularly intense market week, Belinda and Jarrod were working with a buying staff from a major department store chain. Jarrod appeared distracted, so Belinda eagerly pounced on him with such vicious malice that the department store team sat there frozen and terrified.

"What's the matter, Jarrod?" Belinda laughed with cruel amusement. "Are you too busy thinking about your beautiful fiancée, Bonnie, fucking that banker, that you can't concentrate on your job?"

The department store team looked away in shock, unable to watch Jarrod's public humiliation while Belinda continued to berate him. She laughed heartily and spewed insult after insult about his fiancée's alleged infidelity with another man and how Jarrod didn't have what it took to keep her satisfied.

Unable to endure another moment of this degradation, Jarrod got up, excused himself politely, and left the room permanently. The generous severance package Belinda offered wasn't nearly enough for Jarrod, and he decided to fight her with everything he had.

This is precisely why Belinda's company carried an extraordinary amount of insurance, specifically for these kinds of situations. Jarrod eventually held the record for the largest apparel company lawsuit settlement. In the years that followed, many employees would sue Belinda and other brutal bosses' just like her.

Katie Works for Belinda

With such a well-established reputation for abuse, few industry veterans would actively pursue a position with Belinda's company. However, there were always newcomers like myself who naively thought they could handle her mistreatment. I was never so foolish as to believe it would be easy.

I was highly motivated to work for Belinda because the financial reward was genuinely tempting. If I could survive just one year by her side, I'd be able to create my own opportunities elsewhere in the industry. I believed I was resilient and experienced enough to cope with any abusive "garment center" boss, or so I thought at the time. The real challenge would be making it through that first year without any major incidents. After five intense interviews, I secured the position and immediately reached out to my friends Kelly and Jeff. They came out to celebrate with me, along with two other friends who were also facing their own challenges in the apparel industry. Once we were all gathered together, I revealed my exciting news, and their response was one of complete disbelief.

"Are you completely crazy?" Kelly yelled across the table. "Or are you on some kind of suicide mission?"

"No," I answered defensively, already second-guessing my decision. "I just want to work for the best company in the industry, and Belinda's company is exactly that."

"The best!" Jeff cackled with dark amusement. "That's a good one! There's no doubt that she's the best at being an evil, foul-mouthed, crazy bitch that makes Rhonda look like a saint!"

"Let us know when you need Kelly and me to pick up the pieces of your career," Jeff said, still laughing at the absurdity of my decision.

"We'll be waiting for your call and happy to plan your funeral," Kelly added with grim humor.

"Okay, she really isn't that terrible," I said, now genuinely terrified by their reactions.

"Only if you think Satan's evil spawn isn't 'bad'!" Kelly laughed bitterly.

"Good luck with that. It's your funeral," Jeff smiled knowingly.

"I'd like to be cremated and have my ashes sprinkled over Nantucket, please!" I laughed nervously as we all ordered another round of drinks. "Make her's a double," Jeff yelled at the waitress. "She's going to need it!"

The First Day Disaster

My alarm started buzzing at 8:00 a.m. the next morning, and I had to be at my new job with Belinda in exactly one hour.

Why did I have those extra drinks last night? Where is my new Tom Ford suit? "I cannot be late," I muttered to myself frantically.

I showered, quickly dressed, and ran out the door. As I started to hail a taxi, I realized it was raining heavily. I didn't have an umbrella, and my hair was already having a complete frizzy meltdown. I looked absolutely awful on my first day, and I started crying to myself.

As the cab pulled up to my new office building, I jumped out hastily and landed flat on my face on the sidewalk.

"Are you alright, my dear?" a very elegant, older gentleman asked me while helping me get back on my feet.

"No," I said meekly, feeling completely defeated. "It's my first day at my new job. I forgot an umbrella, my new suit is covered in mud, my hair is frizzing uncontrollably, and I'm fifteen minutes late." He smiled sympathetically, gave me a quick once-over, and said, "Oh, you look just fine." He was clearly lying. "I'm sure your boss will understand."

"Understand? No, you don't understand! My boss is Belinda!" I watched his expression change dramatically as the blood drained completely from his face.

"Quickly, come with me," he said urgently, grabbing my arm and leading me across the lobby of my new office building.

"What's your name?" I asked as he pulled me along.

"It doesn't matter right now, dear," he answered curtly as he practically threw me into the elevator.

"Where are we going? Am I going to be fired on my very first day?"

"Belinda will definitely fire you if you arrive looking like a drowned rat!" he said matter-of-factly.

"How do you know this?"

"I know because I am her chief financial officer!" he said bluntly.

"Oh God," I moaned in despair. "I am completely finished."

"What is your name?" he asked calmly.

"Katie," I whispered.

"Okay, Katie," he said with determination. "I have a plan."

The CFO's Rescue Mission

The elevator doors slid open, and we promptly exited into a breathtaking reception area. "Josie, come here immediately!" the CFO commanded, gesturing toward an attractive young woman dressed in an elegant Chanel dress. "Have they started shooting the spring collection yet?"

"No sir, not for another forty-five minutes. We're still waiting for Belinda," she said anxiously.

"Perfect. Please run and get the hair and makeup artists for me right now," he demanded.

"But Belinda is on her way up."

"Don't argue with me, Josie. Belinda is going to be late. Now get moving!"

I stood there in complete shock, unable to process what was happening.

"And get Katie a towel and a latte," the CFO ordered her. He then turned to me and said firmly, "Stay quiet!" as he dialed the receptionist's phone.

"Max [Belinda's driver], this is [the CFO]. Just answer me calmly, do you understand? Good.

"Max, is Belinda in the car yet? Damn! How far are you from the office? Okay, perfect. Tell her there's heavy traffic on Park Avenue. Please take your time getting here. I need twenty to thirty minutes before she arrives. Excellent! I owe you a bonus, Max. Thanks."

The CFO smiled with satisfaction and hung up the phone, just as Josie flew down the hall with the hair and makeup artists in tow. The CFO immediately instructed them with military precision:

"Okay everyone, this is Katie. Work your magic and don't say a single word to Belinda about this!"

"Yes sir!" They both smiled as Josie handed me a latte. I removed my turquoise Tom Ford silk blouse and matching wool jacket, and they ordered me to also remove my Tom Ford low-rise black velvet jeans and my black Gucci belt.

"Here, put this robe on," Josie ordered me urgently. "Quickly!" she barked.

I caught a glimpse of the CFO as he vanished into his grand and impressive office. While I enjoyed my latte over the next twenty minutes, the hair and makeup crew worked their magic on my disheveled appearance. Shortly after, Josie returned with my suit, looking freshly cleaned and perfectly pressed. It was a miracle.

"Take your places, everyone! She's downstairs!" Josie yelled frantically.

Everyone scattered like roaches when the lights came on, and I returned to the reception area to wait for Belinda's arrival. The CFO came out of his office and looked me over from head to toe.

"Katie, you look absolutely stunning," he said, clearly quite pleased with himself and his rescue operation.

"Thank you so much!" I whispered gratefully. At that moment, the elevator doors opened and out stepped the infamous Belinda "fuck her."

I immediately noticed her face was a deep shade of red as she marched directly up to me.

"You, new troll, follow me. NOW!" she yelled at the top of her lungs.

I picked up my designer handbag and ran after her down the hallway like a scared puppy. As I looked back, I could see the CFO smiling with satisfaction, proud that he had saved another poor victim from Belinda's wrath, even if it was just for a single day.

Life Under Belinda's Reign

By the time I arrived home twelve hours later, my poor pug was scratching desperately at the door, demanding to be taken out even though her dog walker had been there just a few hours earlier. Yawning with exhaustion, I put on sneakers, scooped her up in my arms, and headed out the door. As we walked outside in the cool evening air, I relived each moment of my crazy first day with Belinda. That woman is absolutely insane, I thought to myself. How will I possibly work for this lunatic for an entire year?

I looked down at my pug and said, "She is truly crazy."

My pug stared up at me with understanding eyes, and I knew even she grasped that it was going to be an extremely bumpy ride.

The next morning, I heard Belinda's voice calling out for me. "Troll girl, get your fucking ass in here immediately!" Belinda screamed from her office.

As I ran into her office, I saw both of her naked feet resting casually on top of her massive desk. Her desk was a complete mess, covered in piles of paper and design boards scattered everywhere. She was painting her toenails a deep shade of crimson that perfectly matched her constantly angry face.

"What are you looking at? Do you want to do this for me, troll?" she egged me on aggressively. "Do you think you're too talented to polish my toenails? I bet you're not too good to kiss my ass, are you?"

"Is that a question?" I asked, genuinely confused.

"Fuck you, smart ass. I hate smart-ass newbies!" she yelled at me as her face turned even redder with rage.

"I'm sorry, Belinda. What can I do for you?"

"'Do' for me? Are you really just another stupid girl? Did you read your job description? You can read, can't you?"

"Yes," I answered as coolly as possible.

"Go get the damn sketches for my Macy's presentation, NOW," she yelled.

I ran out of her office and sprinted to the design department without breathing.

"Sara, I need your help," I whispered breathlessly in a panicked voice to the VP of Design.

"Okay, Katie. Relax, take a deep breath, and tell me what you need," Sara said in a soothing voice.

"I need the sketches for Belinda's Macy's meeting."

"Fine. Here they are. Now don't let her get to you!" Sara smiled encouragingly.

"Thanks," I said as I grabbed the design boards and ran back down the hall toward Belinda's office. All of the designers looked up from their desks and shook their heads sympathetically as I passed them at lightning speed.

"Another Belinda victim," one of them muttered under her breath.

"No, Katie's tough," Sara stated with confidence. "She's determined to last here at least a full year."

"Yeah, we'll see about that," another designer chimed in skeptically, "but I seriously doubt it. She's pretty, and we all know Belinda absolutely hates pretty newbies."

Witnessing Belinda's Cruelty to Bob

As I approached Belinda's office, I could see that Bob, the VP of Production, had just walked in to speak with her, so I waited outside her office within earshot of the two of them. Bob was an absolutely outstanding person, and he was always the first to lend you a hand and teach you something you didn't know about production. He was also known as one of the leading production executives in the entire apparel industry. Bob was a complete workaholic, the last to leave every night and the first to arrive each morning.

Many days, when I left at 10:00 or 11:00 p.m., he would still be in his office, deep in thought, working on something important, or talking to his overseas factories.

He was close to retirement, just a year away, so you could still see a glimmer of hope in his eyes. He hated confrontation and despised Belinda even more. When his previous company declared bankruptcy eight years earlier, he lost his entire pension. Knowing that Belinda would compensate him generously, he ultimately compromised his values to take a job with her, effectively selling his soul to the devil.

With two kids attending Ivy League schools, he had absolutely no choice but to work for Satan herself.

"Hello Belinda," I heard him say nervously as he entered her office.

"Fuck you, Bob, you're a stupid moron," she said with wicked pleasure. "Do you think I was born yesterday?" she yelled. "You are two weeks behind on the production schedule, and unless you'd like me to cut off your fucking balls right now, you better have a damn compelling explanation for your fucking stupidity!"

Bob sank into a chair in front of her desk. "I didn't tell you to sit your fat ass down, did I, Bob?" she screamed.

He quickly rose and meekly answered, "No."

"No, what? You're a dumb prick?" She laughed cruelly.

"No, you didn't ask me to sit down, Belinda. I'm sorry."

"Bob, how much do I fucking pay you?"

"A lot of money, Belinda."

"How many fucking kids do you have in college?"

"Two."

"So, who the hell pays for their fucking tuition?"

"You do," he said quietly.

"Don't you forget it!" she yelled. "Now go back to your fucking office and make this production schedule work," she screamed, "or you're fired!"

"Yes, Belinda," he said, cowering as he made his way back to his office.

I was in shock as I stood outside her office holding the design boards, unable to move a muscle.

"Troll, what the fuck are you doing standing there like an idiot? Get in here now!"

"Well, give them to me, you fool!" I moved forward tentatively and handed them to her, trying desperately not to show that my hands were shaking.

"Shit, fuck, these are complete crap. What am I paying those no-talent, ass-kissing designers for? I should fire them all! Get Sara in here NOW," she demanded.

"Yes, ma'am," I said.

As I ran back down the hall to get Sara, I could hear her screaming behind me, "Ma'am! I'm not some fucking ma'am. You're a dumb-ass bitch."

Understanding the Dynamic Between Belinda and Sara

Belinda genuinely loved Sara, though it was a twisted form of admiration.

In many ways, Sara was Belinda's complete antithesis. She represented everything Belinda dreamed of becoming but would ultimately never achieve, no matter how much money she possessed. Standing at just five feet three inches, Belinda's pear-shaped silhouette was painfully obvious to everyone. She had slender shoulders and a thick midsection that rested on legs reminiscent of tree trunks, plus a sizable backside that caused her already small suits to fit even tighter than they should. Her hair was a drab brown color and remained perpetually frizzy due to years of harsh bleach treatments and repeated attempts at straightening. Although she preferred high-end fashion, her clothes never fit well, and her blouses often showed signs of food stains from her tendency to eat voraciously while arguing with people. Even though she wore expensive diamond jewelry, it appeared more like cheap costume trinkets on her.

The five-carat diamond solitaire ring she treasured most was a gift from her husband—another of her prized possessions. I had heard that he had finally decided to leave her and take up residence with his secretary instead. The ring was too snug on her swollen left ring finger, and she found herself absentmindedly toying with it during her frequent moments of agitation.

Belinda grew up in a blue-collar, working-class family, though she never spoke to or about them. With a college education, completely out of the question financially, she started working in a department store the day after her high school graduation. Rumor had it that she was ruthless from day one and clawed her way to the top, leaving many destroyed careers behind her.

In stark contrast, Sara was quite tall and strikingly slender, resembling a high-fashion model with her long, beautifully highlighted blonde hair that gently flowed down her back and over her shoulders. Always dressed to absolute perfection in the latest designer fashions, she looked as if she had just emerged from the pages of Vogue magazine. Born into a distinguished Philadelphia family, she was Ivy League educated and carried herself with undeniable class and sophistication. Sharp as a tack and possessing a clever wit, Sara's smile rarely faded, even during the few times Belinda decided to reprimand her publicly. Her smile seemed to communicate a silent message: "Belinda, you'll never achieve my level of beauty or refinement, so screw you."

"Sara dear, Katie just handed me your design boards, and, well, I sort of hate them, to say the least," Belinda smiled with false sweetness.

"But Belinda, you approved them just two weeks ago," Sara whispered with her flawless, unwavering smile.

"I did? Funny, I don't remember that at all."

"Yes, Belinda, it was right before you left for that newly opened Macy's store gala, and I must say, you looked absolutely stunning that night."

"Oh, I did? Okay, that's all, dear." Belinda smiled at Sara with genuine warmth. "Now go back to work and take this little Katie troll person with you."

Sara's Mentorship and Belinda Stories

We left Belinda's office and walked a short distance down the hall before I said, "Thanks, Sara. She's absolutely terrifying."

"Katie, you haven't seen anything yet," Sara laughed with dark humor.

She then told me about her first Belinda story over a cup of coffee.

"I knew a woman who worked for Belinda many years ago as a vice president of design," Sara said quietly, glancing around to make sure no one was listening. "Amanda was her name, and she told me that one day Belinda marched into her office and threw an old pager onto her desk." (Cell phones weren't invented yet.)

"Frightened, Amanda asked, 'What's this for, Belinda?'

"'What the fuck do you think it's for?' Belinda snapped aggressively.

"'So, you can page me?' Amanda answered meekly.

"'Bravo! You're not as dumb a bitch as I thought, now are you?'

"'No,' Amanda answered, quivering with fear.

"That night, Amanda arrived home at 11:00 p.m. She kissed her two adorable sleeping children goodnight and settled into bed with her husband.

"A major blizzard was approaching the city as she watched weather reports on television. Amanda and her husband both dozed off until a shrill, piercing ring startled them out of their sleep. Amanda jumped out of bed and hurried to her purse, reaching in to retrieve the pager Belinda had given her. Glancing at her clock, she saw it was 3:00 a.m.

"'What the hell is going on?' her startled husband mumbled sleepily.

"'Belinda is paging me,' she said, terrified of what emergency could possibly require her attention at this hour.

"'At 3:00 a.m.? Is she completely crazy?' He yawned and drifted back to sleep.

"'Yes dear, she absolutely is,' Amanda sighed.

"Amanda called Belinda to find out what was so urgent that it couldn't wait until morning.

"'Get your ass on the 6:00 a.m. flight to Dallas for a presentation,' Belinda growled into the phone. 'I booked you a flight on United.'

"'Today, in three hours?' Amanda asked, completely shocked. 'There's a major blizzard outside, and I doubt the airports will even be open.'

"'Yes, in three hours, you moron—so what's your point? I'll meet you at the airport. Don't be late!' Belinda yelled through the phone and abruptly hung up on Amanda.

"Amanda sat there in complete shock as she turned on the TV; it was becoming one of the biggest snowstorms in New York City history. How were they possibly able to get anywhere? She turned to her husband and shook him lightly.

"'Honey, wake up,' she said softly. 'I need to tell you something.' Her husband sat up in bed and looked at her frightened face.

"'I know my salary is really phenomenal, but not at the expense of my family, so I'm quitting my job with Belinda as of right now!'

"He kissed her gently on the cheek, lay back down, and said, 'It's about time!' He laughed with relief. 'I was beginning to think I had married a masochist.'

"Amanda opened the window, took a deep breath of the cold winter air, and watched the beautiful falling snow and the Christmas lights twinkling on the trees in her yard. She then threw the pager as far out the window as she could. As she shut the window, she swore she heard it still beeping frantically in the snow. For the rest of the night, she slept like a baby."

"So, what happened to Belinda?" I asked with curiosity.

"Well—" Sara laughed with satisfaction," as Belinda ran to get into her limo to go to the airport, she slipped on the ice and broke her nose."

"Oh! That explains her messed-up nose," I laughed, finally understanding Belinda's facial asymmetry.

The Final Confrontation

The year passed at lightning speed, and I had finished my time with Belinda, bruised and battered but still somehow intact.

"Well, I made it!" I screamed as the whole design team stood up to cheer for me. "A full year working for Belinda, and I couldn't have done it without all of you, especially Sara, who had my back the entire time." I began to cry with relief and exhaustion.

Sara smiled warmly. "You did it by being a strong woman and not letting her get to you. Now, let's get through our presentation today, and then we can go have drinks to celebrate my new job in Los Angeles and your promotion to my position here." Sara smiled encouragingly.

"Ah, I don't know if I can stay here anymore," I said seriously. "I think a year in hell with Lucifer is quite enough for me."

Sara had finally had her fill of Belinda too, so she had landed a cushy job at a major designer corporate fashion label. She deserved it completely, and I was truly happy for her.

"Okay," I laughed, feeling lighter already. "Let's knock her dead. I mean with the presentation." The whole team laughed with nervous energy.

Belinda hated Friday design meetings, especially during the summer. She liked to leave the office early and head out to her Hamptons estate for the weekend.

"Let's get going, you fucking morons!" Belinda yelled as everyone reluctantly piled into the conference room. She was particularly agitated today, twisting her ring rapidly around her fat finger. "Get your goddamn asses in here, everyone! I own this fucking company, and I want to get the hell out of here today early!" She kept screaming at all of us until we took our seats around her.

Sara calmly walked up to the podium, and with me by her side, she went through the brand's latest fashion collection for the following fall season. I was quite proud of all the grueling work we had put into it; it was genuinely beautiful.

"Hurry up!" Belinda barked impatiently.

As soon as Sara finished her presentation, I slipped into the seat next to Bob. While Belinda reviewed Bob's pricing and production schedule for the month, her face started twitching ominously.

Everyone knew the warning signs, and the room became eerily silent. She turned her ring from one side to the other, moved around restlessly in her seat, and then looked directly into Bob's eyes with malice.

One more year, I was sure Bob must have thought to himself, *just hang on.*

"Bob! Bob!" Belinda screamed. "Can you hear me, you bastard?"

"Yes, Belinda," he answered, looking down at his shoes in defeat.

"What the fuck do I tell you every time I see your fucking face? Stay on schedule with my production!" Belinda screamed at the top of her voice. "Then why the fuck is my production going to be late again, Bob?"

"The factory had a fire, and we lost a week," he cried meekly.

"Bullshit!" she yelled. "You should have flown to fucking China and put the fire out yourself because I pay you more than you deserve!"

"Belinda, we're really doing everything we can," the CFO chimed in, trying to defend Bob.

"Excuse me, did I ask for your moronic opinion?"

"No... but—" he tried to get a word in.

"Then shut the fuck up!" she yelled at the top of her lungs.

As she fidgeted with her ring, Belinda's face turned an intense shade of red.

"Bob, do you want to get fired?" she yelled again at him.

"No," Bob answered curtly.

The entire team was now completely silent, and you could have heard a pin drop. The expression on Belinda's face was contorted as she looked at Bob and sneered with pure hatred.

"Bob, how much do you love your fucking kids?" Belinda egged him on cruelly.

"Show me how much you want to keep your job, Bob!" she yelled.

"Now, get on your fucking hands and knees, crawl across this floor, and beg me to keep you," she screamed.

What seemed like an eternity passed in horrified silence.

"Bob, did you hear me?" she screamed again, this time standing up for emphasis.

"Yes, Belinda," he said, his voice cracking with humiliation.

"Well then, crawl!" she commanded like a twisted dictator.

At that moment, Bob started to get out of his chair to comply with her degrading demand.

I grabbed his arm to force him to sit down, and I jumped to my feet.

"Oh my God! No, Katie," Sara whispered firmly. "Sit down."

"No, I can't just sit here!" I whispered back to her with determination.

"What the fuck do you have to say, troll? Or do you want to lose your job too?" Belinda demanded.

"No, yes," I stammered, my adrenaline pumping.

"No? Yes? What are you saying, you fucking idiot?" Belinda shrieked.

Okay, I thought. Here goes a year of brutally hard work!

"Belinda, you are extremely unfair and a rotten, foul-mouthed woman. You had every chance to be a role model for all of us, but instead, you chose to be extremely nasty and give female executives a terrible name!"

I took another breath, probably my final one in this job.

"I wouldn't work another day for you, and you don't realize that incredibly talented people work here because you're too busy demeaning everyone," I said loudly and clearly.

"You are heartless to humiliate Bob and nothing but an evil ogre, and I quit," I said, exhaling with relief and hoping my distraction would keep Bob out of harm's way.

I got up and walked out of the conference room, slamming the door behind me with all my might as everyone just sat in shock. I waited outside the door to listen in on what she was saying.

I could hear Belinda announce, "Meeting's over, assholes. Someone get my car!" And I am *not* an ogre! She yelled.

"Get it yourself," someone in the crowd shouted as everyone left the room in a hurry.

"Who said that? Whoever said that is fired!" she yelled frantically.

The Aftermath and Unexpected Recognition

I walked back to my office and started packing up my belongings just as Bob walked in with tears in his eyes.

"Katie, thank you. You didn't have to do that. I am so grateful," he sighed with relief and gave me a hug.

"Yes, I did, Bob. I couldn't watch you be humiliated by her anymore."

"I don't know what to say, Katie, except you saved my job and my dignity."

"Don't say anything. Go home to your family and enjoy the weekend, Bob," I smiled warmly.

Just as he left, Sara walked into my office.

"Wow, you really have some 'big designer balls,' Katie," she laughed with admiration.

"I just had to defend him, even at my own expense," I smiled, feeling proud of myself for standing up for what was right.

"Well then, let's go and have too many martinis, and I'll charge them to Belinda!" Sara laughed with mischievous delight.

"Sounds perfect. I'll meet you downstairs," I replied.

As I carried my box of personal items down the hallway toward the elevator, a sense of freedom washed over me for making the right choice. However, I couldn't shake off the fear of being unemployed once more.

"Hey, troll," I heard Belinda call me from her office. "Get in here, you little bitch."

"Look, Belinda, I don't need to hear you berate me anymore," I said calmly to her. "I'm leaving."

"Shut up," she said dismissively. "Do you know my CFO just quit on me too after he heard your little speech?"

"I'm sorry," I said, then blurted out, "You treat everyone horrifically, Belinda, so you get what you deserve."

"He'll be back," she laughed with false confidence. "I pay people too well here! Well, good luck, Katie." She smiled with what almost seemed like genuine respect. "I'm impressed! You really do have big balls. You made me proud today, kiddo.

Now get the hell out of my company." She laughed again and winked at me as she put on her jacket to leave.

The Unexpected Celebration

After many martinis with my friends, I managed to get home and crawl into bed, only to be woken a few hours later by my doorman buzzing me urgently.

"What time is it?" I mumbled groggily.

"Twelve noon on Saturday, Miss Katie. Please come to the lobby quickly."

"Okay, I'm on my way." I stumbled to the door, threw on my sneakers, grabbed my pug, and ran for the elevator.

The elevator doors opened onto the lobby, and the aroma of all the flowers at the front desk overwhelmed my senses. The sheer number of bouquets, baskets, and long-stem roses was so overwhelming that I couldn't even make sense of them all.

"Wow," I gasped in amazement. "What is all of this?" I asked in shock. "Who are all these for? Did someone die? Did I die?"

"They are all for you!" the concierge said with a broad smile.

"What?" I screamed in disbelief. "No way!"

Each bouquet had a personal note that read variations of the following:

"Bravo Katie!"

"Katie, you will be a legend in this town."

"It's about time someone put Belinda in her place!"

"'Fuck Her' no more!"

There was heartfelt praise and thanks from many of Belinda's former victims throughout the fashion industry. However, the most touching notes were job offers from some of the biggest companies in the industry. I stood there holding my pug and laughed hysterically with joy and relief.

I realized that standing up to Belinda was something no one had ever done before in such a public way.

I was either incredibly stupid or incredibly lucky, perhaps both.

Well, just another day in the crazy, supposedly glamorous world of fashion.

I told my doorman to give the flowers away to anyone who wanted them.

I didn't need flowers to realize that I had done the right thing. I just needed those "big designer balls" I had grown to love and depend on!

I kept one bouquet of white roses from my dad, whom I had

called the night before to tell him I had been fired again.

He wrote on the card:

I am so proud of you, Katie. However, I am terrified that you are unemployed again! Maybe next time you can smile and keep your mouth shut!

Love you, Dad.

CHAPTER 7:
The Soul Train

A Fresh Start in the Sunshine State

The toxic atmosphere surrounding my departure from Belinda had left me emotionally drained and desperate for a complete change of scenery. The relentless abuse and corporate politics of New York's garment center had worn me down to the point where I questioned whether I could continue in fashion at all. After much soul-searching, I made the bold decision to sublet my beloved New York apartment—a move that felt like abandoning my anchor—and accepted a position with a catalog company in Boca Raton, Florida.

Mark, Fore, and Strike in Florida wasn't just another fashion company; it was a unique brand that perfectly captured the essence of American leisure culture. The company's name told its story immediately—three activities that defined the affluent lifestyle of their target customers. Their distinctive logo, featuring a golf club, fishing rod, and shotgun arranged in a triangular formation around the company name, spoke to a very specific demographic: wealthy Americans who viewed their recreational pursuits as integral parts of their identity.

Michael Tiernan, the company's owner and guiding force, embodied everything the brand represented. Golf wasn't merely a hobby for him—it was a passion that bordered on obsession, influencing everything from his business decisions to his personal relationships. You could often find him on the phone with suppliers while practicing his putting stance, or scheduling meetings around his tee times. This wasn't unprofessional behavior; it was simply who he was, and it authentically reflected the lifestyle his customers aspired to live.

The Heritage of American Preppy Culture

The company carried a rich history that stretched back to 1953, when Bill Tiernan first founded it as a small sporting goods retailer. What began as a modest operation grew into something much more significant when his son Michael Tiernan inherited the business in 1973. By the time I arrived, Mark, Fore, and Strike had evolved into what industry insiders affectionately called "The Tropical Abercrombie & Fitch."

The timing of the company's growth couldn't have been more perfect. The 1980s brought a massive resurgence of preppy fashion, fueled by cultural phenomena like "The Official Preppy Handbook" and the sophisticated styling promoted by Ralph Lauren. Movies like "Chariots of Fire" had romanticized the elegant world of upper-class leisure, and suddenly everyone wanted to dress like they belonged to a country club or were invited to a yacht party. Mark, Fore, and Strike rode this wave brilliantly, positioning themselves as the go-to source for authentic preppy clothing that spoke to an older, more established clientele.

Unlike many fashion companies that chased every trend and demographic, Mark, Fore, and Strike maintained laser focus on their core customer base: affluent Americans who valued quality, tradition, and timeless style over flashy trends. This philosophy served them well for decades, though like many specialty retailers, they eventually succumbed to changing market conditions and closed their doors in 2002.

Meeting Michael: A Study in Contrasts

Working for Michael proved to be one of the most rewarding experiences of my entire career, though our relationship took time to develop. He was a fascinating study in contrasts—genuinely compassionate and warm-hearted, yet sometimes paralyzed by an almost painful shyness that seemed at odds with his position as company leader. Many employees interpreted his reserved nature as pretentiousness or snobbery, but I came to understand that this was simply a byproduct of his privileged upbringing.

Michael had grown up in a world where certain behaviors and attitudes were simply assumed—where everyone shared similar backgrounds, education levels, and cultural references. He wasn't intentionally exclusive; he had simply never been exposed to perspectives outside his own sphere. This sheltered upbringing had created an unconscious barrier between him and employees from different backgrounds, though he genuinely cared about everyone who worked for him.

What made Michael special as a boss was his willingness to learn and adapt. Once he became aware of the divide between management and staff, he actively worked effortlessly to bridge it. He may have been born into privilege, but he possessed enough emotional intelligence to recognize when his assumptions were off and humble enough to change course.

Thea: The Mentor I Needed

My direct supervisor, Thea, represented everything I had hoped to find in a fashion industry leader. As vice president of design, she brought more than twenty years of experience to her role, but what set her apart was her combination of professional expertise and genuine humanity. Thea possessed what I can only describe as effortless style—not just in her clothing choices, but in how she navigated the complex dynamics of corporate fashion.

Her management methodology was revolutionary compared to what I had experienced in New York's garment district. Instead of ruling through fear and intimidation, Thea led with a firm but nurturing approach that brought out the best in everyone on our design team. She had a wicked sense of humor that could defuse tense situations, and an intuitive understanding of when to push harder and when to provide support. Most importantly, she never lost her patience with me, even when deadlines were crushing and stress levels were through the roof.

Under Thea's guidance, I rediscovered my passion for fashion design. The toxic environments I had previously endured had slowly eroded my confidence and creativity, making me question whether I had any real talent at all. Thea helped me understand that my struggles in New York weren't about lack of ability—they were about toxic work cultures that crushed creativity instead of nurturing it. She was truly a guiding light in my life.

The bright Florida sunshine seemed to amplify this positive energy. After years of working in windowless offices and dealing with perpetually angry bosses, the warm, encouraging atmosphere at Mark, Fore, and Strike felt like a revelation. I was actually enjoying my work again, looking forward to coming to the office each day, and feeling genuinely excited about the projects we were developing together.

Discovering the Great Divide

One of the most striking aspects of Mark, Fore, and Strike was the clear physical and cultural division between the corporate offices and the warehouse operations. The building's layout told the story perfectly: management occupied the front section in comfortable offices with windows and air conditioning, while the warehouse team worked in the back section under more basic conditions. The two areas might as well have been separate companies for all the interaction that typically occurred between them.

Neither Michael nor the other executives spent much time in the warehouse, viewing it as a separate operation that didn't require their direct involvement, since it ran so efficiently. This wasn't necessarily malicious—it was simply how most companies operated. The warehouse was seen as a functional space for storing and shipping products, not a place where important business relationships were built or maintained within the corporate structure.

But I found myself drawn to the warehouse from my very first week, I think because of my fond memories of my time with Maria and that team. Initially, the warehouse workers viewed my frequent visits with suspicion and confusion. Some thought I was spying on their productivity for management. Others assumed I was simply lost and too embarrassed to ask for directions back to the office area which was in another building. A few wondered if I was conducting some kind of efficiency study that might lead to job cuts or changes in their working conditions.

In reality, I was fascinated by the scale and complexity of Mark, Fore, and Strike's fulfillment operation. Having worked primarily on the design side of fashion, I had never really understood the intricate logistics involved in getting products from concept to customer. The warehouse represented a critical link in that chain, and I wanted to learn everything I could about how it functioned.

Helen: A Force of Nature

My education in warehouse operations came primarily through Helen, the warehouse manager who would become one of the kindest people in my Florida experience. Helen was a force of nature—a tall, robust Jamaican woman whose infectious laughter could be heard throughout the entire warehouse. Her personality was as colorful as her wardrobe, which featured an endless rotation of vibrant tropical prints and flowing skirts that seemed to dance as she moved through her domain.

Helen's accent was pure music, with a lilting quality that made even her scolding's sound somehow pleasant. "Kaaaateeee," she would call out when she spotted me wandering around, "you need to quit your chatting and start packing some boxes if you want to come back here!" But there was always warmth behind her words, and you could tell she genuinely enjoyed having company in what could otherwise be a monotonous work environment.

What made Helen special wasn't just her personality—it was her incredible work ethic and genuine care for her colleagues and the company. She had been with Mark, Fore, and Strike for nearly twenty-two years, building the warehouse operation from a small-scale fulfillment center into the efficient machine I encountered. Her husband Harry worked as assistant warehouse manager, and all three of their sons had found employment with the company at various times. The warehouse truly was a family affair for Helen, and she extended that same familial warmth to everyone she worked with.

Before long, I became a regular at the warehouse. My willingness to lend a hand with packing and shipping after work or at lunch time earned me the trust of my colleagues. It truly compensated for feelings of loneliness. Other than my pug, whom I'd take to the warehouse on Saturdays, I had no other friends in Florida and I think that's why the whole warehouse was so kind to me.

Despite the demanding nature of warehouse work—the physical labor, the strict deadlines, the pressure to maintain accuracy in every shipment—Helen and her team maintained a remarkably positive attitude. They found joy in their daily routines, took pride in their efficiency, and genuinely enjoyed each other's company. It was a stark contrast to the stress-filled, competitive atmosphere I had known in New York's fashion offices.

Building Bridges Through Donuts and Dancing

My Saturday visits to the warehouse began as simple curiosity but evolved into the highlight of my week. I would arrive each Saturday morning with boxes of assorted donuts from a local bakery—a small gesture that was received with enormous enthusiasm by the entire warehouse team. Along with the donuts, I brought my old boom box, a relic from my New York apartment that had been gathering dust in storage boxes.

These Saturday sessions became magical. Helen and the other workers would bring their own contributions—homemade dishes that showcased the incredible diversity of the warehouse staff, music that represented their various cultural backgrounds, and stories that gave me insights into lives and perspectives I had never encountered before. We would spend the morning fulfilling orders and organizing inventory, but we would do it while sharing food, swapping stories, and enjoying music that ranged from reggae to country to classic soul.

The work itself became secondary to the relationships we were building. I learned about Helen's childhood in Jamaica, her husband Harry's dreams of retirement, and the aspirations each warehouse worker held for their families and futures. In return, I shared stories about my experiences in New York's fashion industry, though I was careful to emphasize the positive aspects and downplay the traumatic elements that had driven me to Florida in the first place.

For the first time in years, I felt like I was part of a genuine community rather than just another employee grinding through corporate politics. The warehouse staff accepted me without reservation, treating me as a valued member of their extended family rather than a management spy or corporate interloper and the front design office, run by Thea provided me with warmth and kindness.

Soul Train Dance Contest

The idea for our "Soul Train Dance Contest" emerged organically from the joy we were already sharing during our Saturday work sessions. I noticed how the music seemed to energize everyone, how people would unconsciously move to the rhythm while packing boxes, and how laughter would bubble up whenever someone would break into an impromptu dance move.

Being the enthusiastic New Yorker that I was, I decided to formalize this into something more structured and fun. I created a makeshift dance floor using flattened cardboard boxes laid out on the warehouse floor, and declared that everyone had to participate in our Saturday dance contest. The format was simple: we would put on different songs, and people would take turns showing off their best moves while everyone else cheered them on.

The results were hilarious and heartwarming. I quickly discovered that my rhythm was somewhere between nonexistent and actively harmful to the music. I moved with all the grace and coordination of Elaine Benes from "Seinfeld," but my enthusiasm more than made up for my lack of skill. The warehouse workers found my dancing attempts endlessly entertaining, and they took great joy in trying to teach me the latest moves.

That summer became an intensive education in popular dance. I learned to "pop, lock and drop" with varying degrees of success. I attempted the "Dougie" with results that were more comedic than impressive. As a skinny, uncoordinated girl from New York, I was hardly the ideal student for urban dance moves, but my willingness to try earned me enormous respect from the warehouse crew.

The dance contests became legendary within our small group. Harry, Helen's seventy-four-year-old husband, proved to be surprisingly agile and rhythmic, often outperforming workers half his age. Helen herself was a natural performer, her flowing skirts adding dramatic flair to every movement. Even the shyest warehouse workers would eventually join in, encouraged by the supportive atmosphere and infectious energy.

After-Hours Practice Sessions

My commitment to improving my dance skills extended well beyond our Saturday sessions. Each evening, I would return to my small Florida apartment, put my pug on the bed for safekeeping, and crank up my boom box for intensive practice sessions. I was determined to show some improvement during our next warehouse gathering, even if that improvement was marginal at best.

These solo practice sessions were both amusing and pathetic. I would spend hours trying to master moves that the warehouse workers executed effortlessly, struggling with basic rhythm while my pug watched with what I can only describe as deep concern for my mental state. She would tilt her head at increasingly sharp angles, as if trying to understand why her owner had suddenly lost all sense of coordination and musical timing.

My neighbors were initially tolerant of the nightly music sessions, but as the volume and duration increased, their patience began wearing thin. I would regularly receive knocks on my door from concerned residents asking me to lower the volume, usually around the time I was hitting my stride with particularly challenging choreography.

The most embarrassing aspect of these practice sessions was my complete self-delusion about my progress. I genuinely believed I was improving, that my movements were becoming more fluid and rhythmic. I would arrive at the warehouse each Saturday convinced that I had mastered new techniques, only to discover that my dancing remained as awkward and uncoordinated as ever.

But here's the beautiful thing about the warehouse community: nobody ever told me how bad I was. They could see my enthusiasm and genuine effort, and they valued that more than technical skill. They would cheer my attempts, offer gentle suggestions for improvement, and celebrate my small victories without ever making me feel foolish or inadequate.

The Monday Morning Transformation

The contrast between Saturday warehouse Katie and Monday morning office Katie became increasingly pronounced as the weeks went on. Saturdays were about joy, community, music, and uninhibited self-expression. Mondays meant returning to the more formal world of corporate fashion, putting away my dancing shoes (literally and figuratively), and resuming my role as a design professional under Thea's guidance.

This was by no means a negative transition—I enjoyed my design work and valued my relationships with Thea and the office staff. But there was something magical about the warehouse environment that the front office couldn't quite replicate. The warehouse was pure, authentic, and free from the political complications that seemed to plague every fashion company I had ever worked for.

Monday mornings became a time of reflection, when I would think about the weekend's activities while settling back into my design responsibilities. I would replay the laughter, the music, and the genuine human connections while reviewing fabric samples or sketching new designs. The warehouse experience was feeding my creativity in unexpected ways, reminding me why I had fallen in love with fashion in the first place.

The Moment of Truth: Caught on Camera

Several months into my tenure at Mark, Fore, and Strike, I received an unexpected summons to Michael's office on a Monday morning. The atmosphere was unusually formal—executives were seated around a large conference table, and an uncomfortable silence filled the room. My heart immediately began racing as I imagined all the possible reasons for this gathering. Had I made a serious mistake in a design? Was the company facing financial difficulties? Was my position being eliminated?

The anxiety was overwhelming. I had grown to love my job and the people I worked with, and the thought of being fired from here felt devastating. I had been careful to maintain professional boundaries and avoid the conflicts that had plagued my previous positions, so I couldn't imagine what I might have done wrong.

Michael's expression was unreadable as I took my seat at the conference table. The silence stretched on uncomfortably, with every executive looking at me with expressions that could have meant anything. Finally, Michael reached for a remote control and turned on a large television monitor that dominated one wall of his office.

What appeared on the screen shocked me into complete silence. There I was, captured in full color and life-size detail, engaged in an enthusiastic dance battle with Harry, the warehouse assistant manager. The footage showed me "busting moves" with complete abandon while the entire warehouse crew cheered us on. My dancing was every bit as awkward and uncoordinated as I had feared, but what came through clearly was the joy and energy that had become the hallmark of our Saturday sessions.

The executives had been watching this footage in preparation for our meeting, which explained the strange atmosphere in the room. I felt mortified, embarrassed, and completely exposed. All my efforts to maintain professional boundaries had been rendered meaningless by this video evidence of my warehouse shenanigans.

Michael's Response: Leadership in Action

Michael's initial question—"Katie, what were you thinking?"—was delivered with stern authority, but I could detect the hint of a smile he was trying to suppress. In my mortification, I began rambling about my genuine affection for the warehouse team, my belief that their hard work deserved recognition, and my desire to build bridges between different parts of the company.

I emphasized that we always completed our work responsibilities before engaging in any dancing, and that our Saturday sessions had actually improved productivity and morale throughout the warehouse. I was desperate to deflect attention from my embarrassing dance moves and focus on the legitimate business benefits of what we had been doing.

Thea joined the questioning, pointing out the obvious: "You are all dancing. Even Harry, who is in his seventies, moves like a teenager!" Her comment was delivered with barely controlled laughter, and I could sense that the mood in the room was shifting from stern disapproval to something more positive.

My defense—that we were on break when the dancing occurred—sounded weak even to my own ears. But something about the absurdity of the situation, combined with the genuine joy visible in the warehouse footage, began to work its magic on the executive team.

Suddenly, Michael and Thea burst into laughter, and the entire room of executives erupted in laughter with them. The tension dissolved immediately, replaced by an atmosphere of warmth and genuine appreciation. Michael's comment about my "exceptional" dancing abilities was clearly sarcastic, but it was delivered with affection rather than mockery.

The Warehouse Liaison Revolution

Michael's next words changed everything: "Katie, we have all reached a decision." My heart stopped as I prepared for the inevitable termination. In my panic, I was already mentally preparing for another job search, another move, another start-over in a different city. The familiar anxiety of unemployment began creeping in as I waited for the axe to fall.

But instead of firing me, Michael announced that Helen and the warehouse employees had unanimously voted to create a new position specifically for me: the company's first "warehouse liaison for goodwill." Thea jumped up with excitement as she delivered this news, and I found myself speechless with relief and gratitude.

The role would allow me to maintain all my design responsibilities while also serving as a bridge between the front office and warehouse operations. I would be tasked with listening to employee concerns, facilitating better communication between different departments, and helping to create a more unified company culture.

This was revolutionary thinking for a company that had previously maintained strict separation between management and warehouse staff. Michael and Thea were essentially acknowledging that my unauthorized bridge-building activities had revealed some gaps in their organizational structure, and they wanted to formalize efforts to address these issues.

Creating E.A.R.s: Employee Action Reviews

My new role as "first ambassador for change" energized me in ways I hadn't experienced since my early days in fashion. I threw myself into developing programs that would give every employee a voice in company operations, regardless of their position or department.

The cornerstone of my initiative was E.A.R.s—Employee Action Reviews—a program designed to empower all workers to share suggestions, express concerns, and contribute ideas for company growth. This wasn't just a suggestion box system; it was a comprehensive approach to employee engagement that included regular meetings, follow-up actions, and recognition for contributions.

The program's success exceeded everyone's expectations. Employees who had never been asked for their opinions suddenly had forums for sharing insights about everything from workflow improvements to customer service enhancements. Helen became the first President of E.A.R.s, a role that formalized her natural leadership abilities and gave her a platform to advocate for warehouse workers throughout the company.

One of our first major initiatives was installing tables and benches in outdoor areas so employees could eat lunch in the beautiful Florida sunshine instead of being confined to cramped break rooms. We established an annual company picnic, implemented bonuses for leadership roles, and created numerous other perks that improved daily life for everyone at Mark, Fore, and Strike.

The Business Case for Human Connection

Management's initial skepticism about employee engagement programs quickly gave way to enthusiastic support when they saw the results. That year marked one of the highest sales performance in company history, and the correlation with improved employee morale was impossible to ignore. When workers feel valued and heard, they become more invested in company success, more creative in problem-solving, and more committed to delivering excellent customer service.

The transformation was particularly dramatic in the warehouse, where productivity increased significantly while quality improved and customer complaints decreased. Workers who had previously felt isolated from company decision-making suddenly understood how their roles contributed to overall success. They began suggesting improvements to packaging, shipping methods, and inventory management that saved both time and money.

For the first time in Mark, Fore, and Strike's history, the entire company truly functioned as a unified team. The artificial barriers between departments began dissolving as people recognized their shared investment in company success. Michael and Thea deserved enormous credit for having the vision and courage to embrace this cultural transformation.

Finding Family in an Unexpected Place

My experience at Mark, Fore, and Strike represented more than just professional success—it fulfilled a deep personal need for belonging that I hadn't even realized was missing from my life. The company became like a family to me, providing the stability, support, and genuine human connection that had been absent during my turbulent years in New York's fashion industry.

This sense of belonging was particularly important given my isolation as a single woman living alone in a new city. The entire company had adopted me completely, treating me as a valued relative rather than an outsider who happened to work for the same company. Their warmth and acceptance helped heal some of the emotional wounds left by previous workplace traumas.

New York Calling: The Pull of the Past

Several times each year, Thea would organize buying trips to New York, where our design team would scout the latest fashion trends and visit key suppliers. These excursions became highlights of my time at Mark, Fore, and Strike, offering opportunities to reconnect with the city I still loved despite my complicated history there.

During one particularly beautiful October trip, I found myself falling in love with New York all over again. The crisp autumn air, the energy of the streets, the excitement of discovering new trends— all of it reminded me why I had been drawn to fashion in the first place. Thea, with her natural zest for life, turned these business trips into adventures that combined serious work with genuine fun.

Our evenings were filled with dinners at restaurants I couldn't afford on my own, late nights spent dancing and drinking cocktails with my old friends, and countless laughs as we processed everything we had seen during our shopping expeditions. I often showed up to supplier appointments wearing oversized dark sunglasses to hide hangover-induced exhaustion, but these relaxed, enjoyable experiences sparked more creativity than I had felt in years.

The buying trips became a perfect synthesis of my Florida contentment and my New York roots. I was able to maintain my connection to the broader fashion world while appreciating the stability and positive relationships I had built at Mark, Fore, and Strike.

Thea's Master Plan

What I didn't realize during these New York excursions was that Thea was orchestrating a careful campaign to rebuild my confidence and reawaken my ambitions. She could see that I had been damaged by previous workplace experiences, that I had perhaps settled for less than I was capable of achieving. While she valued my contributions to Mark, Fore, and Strike, she also recognized that my talents might be better utilized in a more challenging environment back in New York.

Thea's encouragement to "get me back in the saddle" and consider returning to New York was delivered with characteristic subtlety. She never directly told me to leave Florida, but she consistently reinforced my abilities and suggested that I was ready for bigger challenges. She also shared her own love for New York, though I suspect her enthusiasm was partly designed to fuel my own rekindled interest in the city.

The combination of professional success at Mark, Fore, and Strike and renewed confidence from our New York trips began shifting my perspective on my career trajectory. The warm weather, limited social opportunities, and Christmas lights on palm trees that had initially charmed me were beginning to feel restrictive. I found myself longing for the energy and possibilities that only New York could offer.

The Job Advertisement That Changed Everything

When I spotted a job advertisement in Women's Wear Daily for a head designer position at a successful New York apparel company, my heart immediately began racing with excitement and possibility. The position represented everything I had been working toward—a leadership role with a respected company in the city that remained the center of American fashion.

My decision to send in my resume was somewhat reluctant because I genuinely loved working at Mark, Fore, and Strike. But my own rekindled ambitions made it impossible to ignore this opportunity. I figured I had nothing to lose by exploring the possibility, even if it ultimately led nowhere.

The company's quick response and invitation for a weekend interview filled me with excitement that I struggled to contain. I immediately called my friend Kelly to share the news, and her enthusiasm reinforced my sense that this could be the opportunity I had been waiting for.

The Interview Weekend

My secret weekend interview trip to New York felt like a homecoming. Reconnecting with Kelly, walking familiar streets, and experiencing the energy of the fashion industry's epicenter reminded me of everything I had missed during my Florida exile. The interview itself went extremely well, with the company expressing genuine interest in my background and vision for their design department.

Returning to Florida after that weekend, I was filled with hope and anticipation, though I tried to manage my expectations. The fashion industry had taught me that opportunities could disappear as quickly as they appeared, and I didn't want to get too emotionally invested in an outcome I couldn't control.

The Fax Machine Drama

I was told by the New York company's HR department, to expect an offer today. The waiting period for the job offer was excruciating. I spent hours camped by the office fax machine, checking and double-checking that it was functioning properly, imagining all the reasons why the offer might be delayed. When lunchtime arrived without any communication from New York, I forced myself to join my coworkers for a meal, though I could barely concentrate on conversation or food.

The discovery that Thea had intercepted my job offer created a moment of pure panic. I hadn't yet told her about the interview, and I was terrified that she would feel betrayed by my job search activities. I returned to the fax machine after lunch, to see the surprise on Thea's face as she read the offer letter that had just come through.

The Revelation: Thea's Secret

Thea's burst of laughter as she shared with me the subsequent revelation that she had also interviewed for the same position, this completely stunned me. The coincidence seemed impossible—that two employees from the same small Florida company would unknowingly compete for the same New York opportunity seemed too unlikely to be real.

Her explanation was that she had interviewed simply to tell the HR director, that she was not interested in the position because she had "a wonderful designer who would be a perfect fit for the job," left me speechless. Thea had orchestrated this entire scenario, using her industry connections to create an opportunity specifically for me.

The realization that my mentor had been working behind the scenes to advance my career back in New York was both humbling and overwhelming. She had recognized my potential before I had fully recognized it myself, and she had been willing to sacrifice her own time to help me achieve my goals.

The Farewell

The going-away party that Thea and the entire Mark, Fore, and Strike team organized was one of the most emotionally meaningful experiences of my career. The genuine affection and support from people who had become like family made leaving incredibly difficult, even as I was excited about returning to New York.

We laughed, drank, and shared memories while acknowledging that this was the end of an important chapter in my life. The tears in everyone's eyes reflected the real bonds that had been formed, relationships that transcended typical workplace interactions.

Although I was reluctant to leave the security and happiness I had found in Florida, I was also genuinely excited about the possibilities that awaited me in New York. The experience at Mark, Fore, and Strike had restored my confidence, renewed my passion for fashion, and taught me that good people did exist in the industry—I just had to be patient enough to find them.

Lessons Learned: The Power of Authentic Leadership

Although this chapter was closing, Mark, Fore, and Strike provided a masterclass in authentic leadership and organizational culture. Michael and Thea and the entire team, had created an environment where people could thrive by treating employees as complete human beings rather than just functional units. They understood that business success and human happiness weren't mutually exclusive—in fact, they were mutually reinforcing.

Looking Forward: The Hope for New Beginnings

As I prepared to return to New York, I realized the relationships I had built, the lessons I had learned, and the joy I had rediscovered in my work had prepared me for whatever challenges awaited in New York.

And if all else failed, as I jokingly told myself, I could always pursue my newly developed career as a backup dancer on "Soul Train"—though I suspected my rhythm hadn't improved quite as much as I hoped during those late-night practice sessions in my Florida apartment.

CHAPTER 8:
When in Roma

The Garment Center Shell Game

Upon returning to New York, I was surprised to learn that my new position with the fashion company, had recently changed its name. The company appeared to have a solid reputation in the apparel industry prior to the name change, and I believed I had grown wiser from my previous experiences so a name change would not be an issue for me. How wrong I was about to be proven.

Like many businesses in the garment center, this company's owners would routinely shut down operations of several of their companies just to avoid paying employees, only to reestablish under a new name within days to dodge bonus payouts and outstanding debts. This practice was alarmingly common throughout the industry. They would often enlist younger relatives to help relaunch under the new corporate identity, creating what felt like an endless cycle of deception. While I couldn't fathom how this could be legal, it was a frequent occurrence that had become almost normalized in our world.

This name change served as a convenient escape hatch, allowing owners to avoid paying sales and design commissions, as well as old bills to people they owed money to. It was the "garmentos" unique accounting system—a form of legalized theft that had worked well for them for many years. Over the course of my career, I held several jobs in the garment center where I experienced this betrayal first-hand. After bringing in a substantial deal for a previous company. Despite working tirelessly and delivering results, I never received my promised substantial bonus. If I even dared to complain my boss would bully me into submission. The devastation of such betrayal was crushing, but the salary was still competitive, so I reluctantly accepted the situation and kept my mouth shut in order to keep working.

The excuses were always identical, delivered with the same hollow sincerity: "Times are tough, Katie." "You are lucky to work here for us." "Next year will be better, I swear to you," or "Don't worry; we will give you a Holiday bonus!" The repetition was maddening—like listening to a broken record of empty promises. These platitudes weren't worth the fight that would inevitably lead to losing another job.

The most infuriating aspect was witnessing these same owners flaunting their newfound luxury cars, palatial homes, and extravagant international trips—all financed by the designers' unpaid bonuses and stolen commissions. They had absolutely no shame about displaying their ill-gotten gains, often driving up to the office in the very Mercedes-Benz that your hard work had essentially purchased. The injustice was breathtaking in its boldness.

Meet the Brothers: A Study in Contrasts

Let me provide you with an insider's perspective on how my new apparel company operated, because understanding the players was crucial to surviving in this environment.

My new company was owned by two brothers who couldn't have

been more different if they had been cast by Hollywood for maximum dramatic effect. First, there was Jacob—a gentle giant standing six feet tall but extremely overweight. Despite his imposing physical presence, he possessed a genuinely sweet disposition and treated everyone with kindness and respect. He had a volatile heart condition that seemed to worsen whenever his brother was around, and it was painfully obvious that he lived in constant fear of his older sibling's explosive temperament.

Then there was Dave, the older brother and undisputed tyrant of the operation. Short and stocky at five feet four inches, Dave was overweight, perpetually angry, and possessed the social graces of a rabid wolverine. His temper was legendary throughout the industry, his manners were nonexistent, and he was ruthlessly calculating in business dealings. Dave treated everyone with open disrespect, would lie without hesitation, and would cheat anyone out of money if it meant increasing his profit margins. He had also acquired the dastardly trait of bullying women, something he greatly and sadistically enjoyed, especially if it brought them to tears. The contrast between the brothers was striking: while Jacob always offered genuine compliments for work well done, Dave seemed incapable of expressing anything but criticism and contempt.

Both brothers were notorious womanizers, but in the garment center, this was hardly unusual—it was practically a job requirement. Their flirting and inappropriate behavior toward women was well-known throughout the industry, particularly directed at female buyers who visited their showroom to purchase products. They also consistently harassed young, attractive women in the office, especially during "fit model" days when models would parade in front of us designers in nothing but bras and panties so we could provide feedback on fit. Since we produced lingerie and sleepwear, this level of undress was standard, but it provided these men with what they clearly considered a fringe benefit of the business.

Office gossip whispered that Jacob had been romantically involved with several models over the years, while Dave's pattern of cycling through secretaries every month had become something of a running joke. I made the strategic decision to ignore their antics completely and focus solely on my work. I also learned to never cry in front of them— no matter how bad they verbally brutalized me. This approach served me well—as a result, they rarely bothered me or my design team, perhaps recognizing that I was there to work, not to provide entertainment.

The Next Generation: Spoiled Princes of the Fashion Kingdom

In the old world of "garmentos", there existed two unspoken but absolutely rigid rules: first, sons must serve their fathers without question or alternatives; and second, these sons must marry early and quickly and start families with women chosen by their parents. This expectation of procreation was considered an integral part of their family duty, as non-negotiable as breathing.

When these young men entered the family business, they typically did so without any formal education in business or genuine preparation for the fashion industry. They worked alongside their fathers in the office, supposedly to gain experience, but in reality, they were often more hindrance than help. Despite holding impressive executive titles and occupying spacious corner offices, they were completely ill-equipped to make informed critical business decisions and struggled to understand even the basic concepts of their roles.

Many of these young men had absolutely no interest in fashion or the garment center, and were deeply reluctant to work alongside their fathers, yet they felt completely trapped by circumstances beyond their control. Leaving the family business would result in immediate estrangement and financial devastation—being cut off from the family fortune was a terrifying prospect that kept them tethered to jobs they despised. As a result, they remained silent about their unhappiness and continued showing up to work each day like well-dressed prisoners.

As an observer from outside their insular world, I noticed that many of these young men had little genuine interest in marriage or having children, especially at such young ages. Instead, they often rebelled both before and after their arranged marriages, indulging in excessive partying, drinking to dangerous extremes, and engaging in casual sexual encounters with anyone willing to participate. For some, this rebellion even extended to paying for sex with prostitutes. These privileged youths lived as if every day were New Year's Eve 1999, their lives filled with illegal drugs, expensive escorts, celebrity parties, trips to Las Vegas and Miami, and countless yacht parties—all funded entirely by their fathers' seemingly limitless bank accounts.

The Art of Spending Daddy's Money

The pressure from family tradition to conform often led these young men into positions that required minimal effort or actual contribution—as long as they showed up, pretended to look busy, and occasionally barked orders at employees like myself. Most of us seasoned workers learned to either ignore them completely or politely ask them to leave us alone, so we could actually accomplish something productive. These boys were generally between sixteen and eighteen years old, which meant we were essentially being managed by teenagers with unlimited expense accounts and no accountability.

They truly excelled at only one skill: systematically depleting their fathers' fortunes with breathtaking efficiency. Their spending sprees included the finest clothes money could buy, expensive women, and globe-trotting adventures to anywhere that promised excitement—anything to escape their fathers' watchful eyes and avoid the suffocating atmosphere of the office. They also worked diligently to keep their young wives at arm's length, as their own selfish desires consistently took precedence over any responsibilities toward their new families.

These entitled young men frequently tormented employees, particularly targeting those they perceived as more intelligent than themselves. Their behavior was characterized by arrogance, self-indulgence, and breathtaking conceit. Whenever challenged or criticized, they would immediately run to their fathers to report perceived slights or lodge complaints about whoever had dared to question their authority. It was already challenging enough working for their tyrannical fathers, but having to endure additional torture from these spoiled, incompetent young brats made daily life nearly unbearable.

The competition between garment center family businesses extended to their sons, who tried to outdo each other in wasteful spending each year. They showered expensive gifts on friends and girlfriends, threw lavish cocaine-fueled parties in South Beach or New York, and frequently hosted wild gatherings at their fathers' secret penthouses and hidden apartments that were maintained specifically for extramarital activities. These young men were obsessed with celebrities and were regularly spotted at Hollywood parties, parading around with supermodels, becoming obnoxiously drunk, and starting fights that their fathers or trusted family members would inevitably have to resolve through expensive legal intervention.

The Three Types of Women in a "Garmentos" Life

In my day, many wealthy, established "garmentos" maintained multi-million-dollar apartments in Manhattan solely for their "entertainment" purposes, or they would borrow such spaces from major store owners who were financially beholden to them. Their sons used these luxurious apartments frequently for their own entertainment, and on any given night, these spaces would feature open bars and B-list celebrities freeloading at daddy's expense. The fathers consistently turned blind eyes to their sons' destructive behavior, often proudly comparing their offspring's sexual conquests with their business peers, using the "boys will be boys" philosophy to excuse even the most egregious behavior.

Sexual harassment was not only alive and well in the fashion industry but was actively celebrated and never condemned by either the older generation of "garmentos" or their sons. Their sexual exploits were considered badges of honor by most of these men, and their sons faithfully followed their fathers' deplorable examples.

Despite claiming to be deeply religious, many "garmentos" frequently employed prostitutes for themselves and their male relatives. I found this particularly disturbing given how much they publicly preached about "family values" while simultaneously and openly displaying their girlfriends in public settings. There was constant competition to see who could attract the most physically attractive mistress, and generally, the more money a "garmento" possessed, the more beautiful his girlfriend appeared to be.

Let me break down the intricate social hierarchy, as grasping these relationships was essential for me to successfully navigate their environment during my time working for them:

The Wife: The first category of woman in a "garmentos" life was unequivocally of the same religion and usually came from an arranged marriage or was someone selected by the family. These women were known simply as "the wife" and were expected to be ideal homemakers. They married "garmentos" primarily to maintain family values and religious traditions, but most importantly, to reproduce and continue the family lineage. The family selected wives for their sons based primarily on social status and family wealth—while physical attractiveness might be considered, the woman's family's financial standing and social position usually took absolute precedence.

The Employee: The second category was the female employee who worked for the "garmentos" company—women like myself. We were known simply as "the employee," and we devoted virtually every waking moment to generating profits for the family business, working impossibly long hours because we genuinely enjoyed our careers and needed the substantial salaries, despite all the inherent problems of bullying and sexual harassment.

We typically worked for decent compensation and were constantly promised large bonuses if we remained loyal to the family business. These promises were almost never fulfilled, but hope springs eternal in the fashion world.

If you were a single woman working in the garment center, this situation actually benefited the "garmentos" tremendously. Without husbands or children requiring attention, single employees could dedicate significantly more time to the office, which directly translated to higher profits for the companies. Single staff members were viewed as particularly valuable assets by "garmentos" and often found themselves being transferred from one company's divisions to another within the extended family network. When there was urgent need to increase sales at a struggling business, talented designers would be shipped around like valuable livestock to wherever their skills were most desperately needed. Although we always hoped our dedication and hard work would result in promotions, these expectations were seldom met. The harsh reality was that we functioned as highly skilled workhorses, systematically exploited by our employers who viewed us as interchangeable assets rather than human beings.

The Girlfriend: The third woman in a "garmentos" life was "the girlfriend"—essentially arm candy for wealthy, powerful bosses who required attractive companions for clubs, expensive dinners, and exotic vacations far away from their families. These women were kept women in the truest sense, hidden in lavish apartments conveniently located near the office, compensated through designer clothing, expensive furs, cash payments, and substantial diamond jewelry. All their expenses were covered completely as long as they maintained their physical appearance, sexual availability, and absolute discretion about the relationship.

By age twenty-eight, these women were typically replaced by younger models, creating a constant turnover in this peculiar marketplace. Throughout my career, I encountered many such women who essentially functioned as well-compensated escorts, motivated primarily by financial gain rather than emotional connection. Given that the men they associated with were generally older, physically unattractive, and married, this purely transactional approach was entirely understandable.

The Roman Holiday from Hell

It was absolutely essential that the three categories of women in a "garmentos" life remain completely separated from each other. Any accidental mixing of these worlds could jeopardize your employment, and even worse, could potentially lead to expensive divorces that would cost the "garmento" significant money, thereby putting your position on Seventh Avenue at serious risk of permanent blacklisting.

My first European business trip for this new clothing company provided an ideal illustration of all three types of women converging in one absolutely comical scenario. I was genuinely excited to be invited to travel to Italy with my new boss, but I had absolutely no comprehension of the circus I was about to join. The ostensible purpose was for designers to travel to Europe to observe the latest fashion trends before they reached the American market and to purchase competitive samples that we could adapt—or more accurately, knock off—for our domestic brands.

I found myself traveling to Rome with Dave and his large, unattractive wife. Wives rarely accompanied their husbands on business trips unless the primary purpose was shopping for themselves. As we boarded the international flight, the seating arrangement told the entire story: Dave's girlfriend sat directly behind him in business class, while he and his wife occupied first-class seats. The wife typically had no idea that the girlfriend was even on the same aircraft, much less that she existed at all. Naturally, I— the lowly employee—was relegated to the last seat on the plane in coach, physically and symbolically separated from the entire drama unfolding in the premium cabins.

Upon arrival in Rome, Dave and his wife departed to the hotel in a stretch limousine, while the girlfriend was discreetly escorted to a prearranged black sedan that would transport her to the same luxury hotel. I was required to take public transportation—the bus—like any other budget traveler to the hotel.

Despite staying at the same five-star hotel as Dave, his wife, and his girlfriend, I was assigned a small single room while they all occupied magnificent suites on different floors. The girlfriend received strict instructions to remain in her hotel room except when her services were specifically required by Dave, or when she was permitted to shop discretely by herself. Meanwhile, the wife found herself stuck with me as her assigned companion, because entertaining Dave's wife was now part of my official job responsibilities, in addition to my primary duties of shopping the market for fashion trends. Ironically, the girlfriend and I ended up eating all our meals together, usually exploring Rome after dark when the wife and Dave were safely tucked away in their suite.

The Sangria Incident

When Dave desired intimate time with his girlfriend, he would assign me to escort his unsuspecting wife around Rome for several hours, ostensibly to show her the historic sights. I would take her shopping and to lengthy lunches consisting primarily of alcohol, since most Roman restaurants back then were not kosher and she could only consume kosher food. It became a delicate balancing act, trying to keep Dave's extramarital activities concealed while managing his increasingly intoxicated and demanding wife. However, I was so thrilled to be experiencing Rome that I determined to make the best of this impossible situation.

During the summer months, Rome transforms into a sweltering furnace, with humidity levels soaring above one hundred degrees Fahrenheit. I attempted to enjoy leisurely lunches while Dave's wife sat across from me, alternating between voicing bitter complaints about her husband and kids and consuming glass after glass of cold sangria. Beads of perspiration streamed continuously down her flushed face, and I couldn't help but feel genuine sympathy for her predicament. Dave would routinely excuse himself from our company by claiming urgent business meetings, thereby providing himself several hours each day to spend with his girlfriend while abandoning his wife to my care.

On one particularly memorable afternoon, several days into our Roman adventure, Dave's wife was feeling rather ill from consuming too many glasses of sangria combined with the oppressive humidity. While I savored my delicious lunch at an outdoor restaurant near the famous Via del Corso, she continued drinking sangria and snapping irritably at me. It was a blazingly hot July day, and she adamantly refused to continue our planned shopping expedition.

Most "garmentos" wives dressed extremely modestly year-round due to their strict religious beliefs, regardless of weather conditions. Dave's wife was wearing a high-necked, long-sleeved designer blouse, a heavy woolen sweater, and a long-pleated cotton skirt that extended well below her knees, complete with thick polyester stockings and flat Chanel ballet flats. Although every item of her clothing was expensive designer merchandise, the overall effect made her appear dowdy and perpetually miserable. She was not a pleasant woman under the best circumstances, and despite my sincere efforts to engage her in friendly conversation, she remained extremely resentful about being "pawned off on a lowly employee" for entertainment.

On this specific afternoon, she not only requested but absolutely insisted that I escort her back to the hotel immediately and ahead of our planned schedule. She claimed to be on the verge of fainting from the heat and alcohol. I felt my anxiety skyrocket, knowing that barely an hour had passed since we left the hotel and that Dave was undoubtedly in his suite with his girlfriend at this very moment. Desperately, I suggested that she remove her wool sweater and try to relax in the shade, but she became even more agitated at my presumption in offering unsolicited advice.

"I want to return to my hotel immediately!" she demanded with the imperious tone of someone accustomed to instant obedience.

"Of course," I replied, frantically stalling for time. "Let me just finish my lunch and settle the bill, then we can leave," I said while simultaneously pouring her another large glass of sangria. She continued consuming the cold, fruit-filled beverage as if it were water, and I watched with growing alarm as her eyes began rolling back in her head.

Perfect! I thought to myself. At least now I might be able to finish my absolutely delicious pasta dish before dealing with this crisis.

She suddenly declared that she was seeing double images of me, which sent me into complete panic mode. I frantically attempted to reach Dave by calling his hotel room repeatedly from the restaurant's payphone, but only succeeded in reaching the voicemail each time. I was absolutely terrified of taking his wife back to the hotel while he was obviously engaged with his girlfriend. In desperation, I managed to get her to consume three glasses of ice water and relocated her to a shaded table, secretly hoping she might simply pass out and solve my immediate problem.

The Great Hotel Room Shuffle

I rushed back to the payphone and dialed Dave's room number again, pretending to his wife who was watching me that I was calling our office back in New York. Remember, this was long before the era of cell phones, when such communication challenges were simply part of international travel.

Dave's wife was becoming increasingly agitated, visibly drunk, and appeared pale and nauseous from the combination of heat and alcohol. I almost felt genuine sympathy for her suffering, except that she continued calling me a "stupid moron employee" for not immediately helping her return to the hotel.

"Please, just remove your heavy sweater," I pleaded with her, genuinely concerned about heat stroke.

"Absolutely not!" she responded indignantly. "Modesty must come first!" she declared angrily. "But what would someone like you understand, sitting there in that sleazy Versace tank top and a denim mini skirt?" she barked at me with surprising fashion knowledge.

She struggled to stand up, swaying from side to side like a Weeble toy, and leaned her full weight against me as I attempted to catch her before she collapsed. I slowly half-carried, half-dragged her back toward the hotel, which was several blocks away, pretending to be lost and taking wrong turns to buy more time, while she continued her verbal assault, repeatedly calling me a "stupid and an idiot employee."

"I need help getting to my room immediately. I feel violently ill and will vomit on you if you don't get me to my hotel room right now! Where is my husband? Call him this instant!" she slurred repeatedly.

"I've been trying to reach him, but he's in an important business meeting and his voicemail keeps answering," I lied with growing desperation.

"You're simply stalling for time because you know perfectly well that Dave is upstairs having sex with his girlfriend," she suddenly yelled at me, leaning even more heavily against my increasingly aching shoulders. I acted shocked and innocent, but internally I was panicking about the very real possibility of losing another job and an imaginary bonus.

"Please hurry!" she pleaded between slurred words. "I'm going to be sick. How much farther is it to the hotel? I know you're deliberately misleading me!"

"No, absolutely not!" I lied again, feigning complete ignorance. "I have no idea what you're talking about, and I certainly don't know anything about Dave having a girlfriend." The lies were flowing freely now.

"Complete bullshit!" she angrily spat at me. "You're an accomplished liar, but I know that disgusting fat bastard I'm married to is a serial cheater!"

"We're almost there," I lied once more. "Just hang on a little longer," I pleaded while sweat poured down my face as I struggled to prevent her from collapsing entirely. "Just try to stand up and walk on your own. We're almost there."

I was completely fed up with this entire ridiculous situation and desperately wanted to return to my air-conditioned room for a long cold shower. The charade had gone on long enough, and I was reaching my breaking point.

Finally, after what felt like an eternity but was probably only twenty minutes, we reached the hotel lobby. I deposited Dave's wife into a lobby chair and continued frantically calling Dave's room from the house phone. Still no answer.

"Thank God we're finally here!" she exclaimed with obvious relief. "Now get me to my room before I faint completely or, even worse, die!" she screamed loudly enough for other guests to stare.

Oh God, I thought desperately. I'm absolutely going to get fired again! What should I do? The elevator ride would take five minutes, plus another eight minutes to reach the top penthouse floor. That gives me maybe thirteen more minutes before Dave discovers his wife is drunk and fires me on the spot.

I could already envision the headlines: Dave's messy divorce would be plastered across international newspapers, his wife would receive millions in the settlement, and she would undoubtedly force me to testify against him in court, which would undoubtedly get me blacklisted from the garment center.

The Cleaning Cart Solution

I managed to get Dave's wife in the elevator, and absolute panic flooded my mind. I felt faint and terrified about what was about to unfold.

Oh God, please let Dave have received my voicemail messages! Please help me survive this. I promise I'll go to the Vatican tomorrow and light a candle for forgiveness! Please, God, make sure Dave isn't in his suite with his girlfriend right now. Please don't let me get fired again.

Just then, Dave's wife pushed the button for the penthouse and handed me her room keycard with shaking hands.

"Get me to bed immediately. I feel like I'm going to faint," she moaned repeatedly as I supported her weight against the elevator wall. We quickly reached the penthouse floor, and as I inserted the key into Dave's suite door, I had to brace all her weight against the hallway wall to maneuver the keycard properly. Then I knocked softly on the door, praying desperately that Dave wasn't inside with his girlfriend.

Suddenly, there was a loud thud as Dave's wife slid down the wall and collapsed onto the floor in a big heap. She had passed out completely.

Oh no, I thought in desperation. Now I'm really going to get fired. I've actually killed his wife!

I frantically tried to lift her unconscious body, but it was absolutely impossible—like attempting to lift a two-hundred-pound sack of potatoes. Her arms were flopping around uselessly, and although I think she unconsciously tried to help me lift her, I ended up falling on top of her anyway, creating an even more ridiculous scene.

Just then, a hotel bellhop walked by and observed me sprawled on top of this large, sweaty, unconscious woman. He looked absolutely horrified but kept walking, pretending he had seen nothing unusual.

"Scusi!" I called out desperately. "Aiutami!" I cried to the bellhop in my pathetic attempt at Italian. He smiled weakly and continued to scurry down the long hallway, pretending he couldn't understand a single word I was saying.

"Typical Italians!" I whispered under my breath while attempting once more to prop Dave's wife against the wall, but I still had no success whatsoever.

In desperation, I jumped up and began frantically ringing Dave's doorbell while pounding on the door as hard as possible. I was startled when he finally opened the door and stood there completely naked and visibly agitated.

"What the hell are you doing, Katie?" he began yelling at me as I pointed frantically toward his wife's unconscious body on the hallway floor. I shushed him urgently since she was still completely unresponsive.

He grabbed me by the fabric of my tank top. "Are you completely out of your mind, bringing my wife here while I'm screwing my girlfriend?" he whispered angrily.

"Holy shit! Is she actually dead?" he asked with curious amusement while staring at his wife's limp body sprawled across the hallway floor.

"No, I don't think so." I whispered back, "Just extremely drunk and passed out cold."

"You got my wife drunk?" he demanded furiously as his face turned deep crimson.

I insisted it wasn't my fault that she had such an obvious love affair with sangria!

"No, of course not, Dave. She drank all that alcohol completely by herself," I said as innocently as possible while trying not to look directly at his naked, overweight body.

Suddenly, the beautiful girlfriend appeared at the door beside Dave, wearing nothing but an expensive diamond necklace and enormous diamond earrings.

"Honey, what's happening out here?" she asked as Dave motioned for her to remain quiet.

"Hi Katie," she smiled at me while standing there in all her naked glory.

"Katie got my wife drunk," Dave whispered to his girlfriend. "Now she's passed out on the floor." He glared at me with renewed anger.

"No, I absolutely did not—" I started to protest, but he cut me off immediately.

"Actually, this is perfect," he said happily, suddenly realizing his wife was completely unconscious. "This means I have about twenty more minutes of fun." He winked at his girlfriend. "Right, Katie?" he asked with obvious satisfaction.

"Seriously, Dave? Are you actually serious right now?" I whispered in disbelief. "What exactly am I supposed to do with your unconscious wife?"

"Wonderful!" the girlfriend mouthed silently to him with obvious delight.

"Does this mean you'll buy me that extremely expensive diamond bracelet from the hotel gift shop?" she giggled quietly.

"Absolutely," he mouthed back to her. "Just charge it to your room account." He slapped her bare behind and closed the door firmly.

"But what should I do with her?" I whispered desperately, but he had already shut the door completely. I stood there staring at his wife sleeping peacefully on the cold marble floor.

Completely mortified, I knocked on the door again. Dave jerked it open irritably and I nearly fell against his naked body.

"Excuse me, Dave, but your wife is collapsed and drunk in this public hallway. What exactly do you want me to do with her?" I whispered angrily.

"Just put her in your room and tell her the keycard malfunctioned, then I'll call your room in thirty minutes," he whispered back. "Actually, make that forty minutes." He grinned with obvious lust and anticipation.

But you said twenty minutes! I mouthed silently back to him.

"How am I possibly supposed to get her to my room?" I cried quietly.

"Figure something out—or you're fired immediately!" He threatened with a stern glare of disapproval.

He gave me an enthusiastic thumb up and closed the door again, laughing as he called for his girlfriend to come out and play with him some more.

This is insane, I thought to myself. But I genuinely liked my design team, I was earning decent money, and I was in Rome! This situation couldn't really be all that terrible, I rationalized desperately.

While trying to devise another plan as his wife lay snoring on the hallway floor, I looked around and saw my salvation approaching. Perfect! I thought as I noticed the cleaning lady pushing a large housekeeping cart down the hallway directly toward me.

"Scusi," I whispered as I ran over to her, frantically waving a thousand-lira note to get her to notice me.

This immediately got her attention, although she looked completely puzzled about why I might need her assistance.

"Carrello! I need your carrello right now!" I whispered frantically in my absolutely terrible Italian accent.

"You need my cart?" she asked in perfect, unaccented English.

"Oh wonderful, you speak English perfectly," I smiled with enormous relief.

"Listen, I'll give you a thousand lira if you help me get that woman over there onto your cart and help me push her to the elevator."

"Is she dead?" the maid asked, clearly amused by this bizarre situation.

"No, just extremely drunk on too much sangria," I whispered, now laughing at this utterly ridiculous comedy unfolding around me.

I absolutely could not make this up!

"I can't wake her up or I'll lose my job because her husband Dave, who's my boss, is inside having sex with his—"

"I completely understand, honey. Trust me, I've seen absolutely everything working in luxury hotels!" she laughed knowingly.

Together, we managed to lift Dave's unconscious wife onto the housekeeping cart, and the cleaning lady expertly escorted us to the service elevator so no one would notice me pushing a large, sweaty, passed-out woman on a hotel housekeeping cart through the hotel!

"This route is much faster and more discreet," she explained as we quickly wheeled Dave's wife down the service corridor and into the freight elevator.

We successfully transported the unconscious wife to my room, where the cleaning lady helped me carefully roll her inside. Together we managed to lift her off the cart and position her snoring body on my small bed.

"Thank you so very much," I said gratefully as I handed her the promised thousand lire.

"No problem at all, and good luck with whatever this is about," she whispered as she closed my door behind her, laughing uncontrollably.

I sat at the foot of my bed, staring at Dave's completely passed-out wife, and let out a long sigh of relief while waiting for enough time to pass before Dave would call my room.

Nobody would ever believe this absolutely insane story, I thought to myself, laughing quietly.

The Revelation of a Wife

An hour later, Dave's wife finally woke up feeling groggy and disoriented. She looked around my small room with obvious confusion and asked bluntly, "This room is absolutely terrible. Why am I here?"

"Yes, it certainly is," I answered with obvious annoyance, just as my room telephone began ringing and I picked it up.

"It's Dave!" I announced with feigned excitement. "He's wondering where you've been." Now I had to perform the elaborate charade about the malfunctioning keycard for her benefit.

"No worries, Dave, she's perfectly fine. She just had a minor case of heat exhaustion," I said into the phone while she listened.

"I'll bring her up to your suite immediately. Since I couldn't get your keycard to work properly, I brought her to my room to rest." I added this fabricated detail so his wife would overhear and believe my completely fictitious story.

After hanging up, Dave's disheveled wife climbed off my bed and headed toward the door to leave. She turned around and stared directly at me with a knowing smile.

"Don't worry, dear. I'm going to tell that disgusting bastard to give you a substantial raise for this, or I'll castrate him for screwing his girlfriend in my suite," she said with a conspiratorial wink.

Feeling simultaneously relieved, mortified, and completely exhausted, I was finally ready to leave Rome forever. I took a long, cold shower, packed my bags efficiently, and called for the bellhop to collect my luggage. When my doorbell rang, I jumped up excitedly, thinking I was finally going home to end this completely insane international fiasco.

I opened the door wide and found the girlfriend standing there, dressed in her expensive diamonds and wearing a stunning white eyelet Chanel dress with matching Chanel pumps.

"This room really is terrible," she observed bluntly.

"I know, I know," I replied with obvious irritation.

"Here," she said, extending a long, red leather jewelry box toward me.

"What is this?" I asked, completely shocked.

I opened the elegant box to discover the most beautiful, obviously very expensive diamond bracelet that Dave had purchased for her.

"Consider this the bonus Dave owes you," she said with a laugh as she glided gracefully back down the hallway toward the elevator.

"Are you absolutely certain?" I called after her curiously.

"Honey, it's the very least he could do after everything," she smiled and waved.

"Are you returning to New York as well?" I shouted after her.

"Absolutely not! Dave's wife just gave me an enormous check

and told me I can never see her husband again," she laughed with obvious delight.

"I'm so sorry about that!" I said, feeling genuinely puzzled by her cheerful reaction.

"No, sweetie," she smiled brilliantly. "This is actually a dream come true! I don't have to sleep with that disgusting man anymore, and now I can move back to Los Angeles with all her money and finally pursue my acting career seriously. It's a complete win-win situation! Take care of yourself, Katie." She smiled warmly as she disappeared into the elevator.

"You too," I called back sincerely.

The following Monday, I returned to the office feeling happy to be home and reunited with my design team. The CFO immediately informed me that I was receiving a very substantial raise. He also mentioned that I would never again be asked to travel to Europe with Dave and that management felt it was time for me to handle international trips independently.

That arrangement was absolutely fine with me, I smiled to myself, admiring my new bracelet, knowing that the CFO had absolutely no idea why I was so pleased or what had actually transpired in Roma between the wife, the girlfriend, and the employee!

Many years later, I always get a laugh when I see Dave's girlfriend on the big screen, knowing that I was instrumental in her pursuit of her Hollywood dream of becoming a famous actress.

CHAPTER 9:
All American Ronny

A New Beginning with High Hopes

Several years had passed since my previous fashion industry misadventures, and I was doing well, but I found myself presented with what seemed like a golden opportunity. A close friend within the industry, someone who understood my burning ambition to break free from the grimy confines of the garment center, recommended me for a position that appeared too good to be true. After years of dealing with sexual harassers, abusive bosses, and unethical business practices, I was desperate for a fresh start with a reputable company.

At this stage of my career, having reached my mid-thirties, I carried myself with the confidence of someone who believed she had seen it all. The fashion industry had thrown its worst at me—or so I thought. I had survived Belinda's psychological warfare, endured Barney's sexual predation, and navigated Dave's corruption. Surely, I reasoned, there couldn't be much left that could surprise or defeat me. This overconfidence, as I would soon discover, was perhaps my greatest vulnerability.

The opportunity that presented itself was nothing short of a fashion professional's dream. I was offered the position of design director for one of Ronny's licensed divisions—a sleepwear and loungewear brand operated by a brother and sister team named John and Kay. What made this offer particularly enticing was that while they held the license, they operated directly out of Ronny's prestigious corporate headquarters. The prestige associated with Ronny's name was enough to make any designer's heart race with anticipation.

First Impressions and False Security

On that crisp morning of my first day in October, I took extra care with my appearance, selecting a stunning grey wool cashmere Max Mara coat that spoke of sophistication and success. Beneath it, I wore a matching grey cashmere crew neck sweater paired with impeccably tailored grey tweed pants and black alligator pumps. My hair had been freshly styled with subtle highlights that caught the light just right, and I kept my makeup minimal yet polished—the epitome of 1990s professional chic. As I looked at myself in the mirror that morning, I felt like I had finally made it as I grabbed my Birkin bag and ran out the door. I looked the part of a successful fashion executive, and I was ready to claim my place in the industry's upper echelons.

Walking into Ronny's corporate offices for the first time was like stepping into a fantasy world only accessible to the glamorous gods of fashion. The building itself was a monument to success, with gleaming floors, soaring ceilings, impeccable interior design features and an atmosphere that practically hummed with creative energy and financial prosperity. Multiple departments spread across several floors, each one more impressive than the last, with high-end showrooms that showcased the brand's collections like works of art in a museum. After years of working in cramped, sometimes squalid conditions in various garment center buildings, this felt like ascending to heaven's atelier.

John and Kay's initial warmth toward me, was at first welcoming. They were enthusiastic about my background, and seemed genuinely excited to have me join their team. Regretfully, I missed the warning signs that I should have noticed immediately—the overly effusive praise, the promises that seemed too generous, and especially the way they spoke negatively about their previous design directors—were invisible to me in my euphoric state of wanting this opportunity to work at Ronny's brand.

The Legend Behind the Brand – Ronny's Story

Ronny himself was nothing short of a fashion industry legend, though his story began humbly enough. During his college years, he had started selling T-shirts directly from his dorm room—a classic American entrepreneurial tale that resonated with anyone who believed in the power of hard work and determination. After graduation, he made the pilgrimage to New York City that so many aspiring fashion professionals make, starting at the bottom as a design apprentice and learning the business from the ground up.

What set Ronny apart was not just his talent, though he possessed that in abundance, but his resilience in the face of setbacks. When he lost his first job as a design assistant—a devastating blow that might have sent others scurrying back home—he discovered something crucial about himself: he thrived when working independently. This realization became the catalyst for launching his own sportswear line, a decision that would prove to be one of the most prescient moves in fashion history.

The transformation from struggling designer to industry titan didn't happen overnight. Ronny's journey was marked by the kind of persistence and vision that separates the truly successful from those who merely dream of success. When a major financial backer recognized his potential, and decided to invest in his vision, it marked the beginning of what would become one of the largest and most successful clothing companies in the world. By the time I joined his organization, Ronny's brand was synonymous with quality, innovation, and commercial success on a global scale.

The Reality Behind the Glamour

Despite not reporting directly to Ronny himself, simply being in his presence was intoxicating. On the few occasions when our paths crossed in meetings or hallway encounters, his charisma was undeniable. He possessed that rare combination of creative brilliance and business acumen that mark true industry leaders. He was personable without being fake, confident without being arrogant, and his genuine enthusiasm for fashion was infectious. These brief interactions only reinforced my belief that I was exactly where I needed to be in my career.

The licensing structure that brought me to Ronny's company was typical of how major designers expanded their brands. Rather than trying to manage every product category internally, successful designers like Ronny partnered with specialized companies who had expertise in specific areas. John and Kay had built a successful sleepwear business, and licensing Ronny's name allowed them to leverage his brand recognition while he benefited from their specialized knowledge and established manufacturing relationships.

However, the reality of working for John and Kay quickly began to tarnish the golden sheen of my new opportunity. John, despite his thirty years of industry experience, represented everything that was wrong with the old-school garment center mentality that I had encountered for years. He was crude, abusive, and carried himself with the arrogance of someone who believed his longevity in the business gave him license to treat others, especially women, poorly. His verbal abuse was legendary in all the worst ways. Kay, his older sister and business partner, proved to be equally problematic, displaying an arrogance and dismissiveness that made daily interactions challenging at best.

Had I done my due diligence and researched John's career trajectory, I might have discovered that he had spent most of his thirty-year career bouncing between some of the least reputable companies in the garment center. These were the companies that serious fashion professionals avoided—the ones known for cutting corners, treating employees poorly, and operating with questionable ethical standards, yes, the ones that I had also worked for in the past. I was so dazzled by the opportunity to work under Ronny's brand umbrella that I failed to look beneath the surface, and really wanted to give John the benefit of doubt.

The First Challenge: Redemption Through Design

My inaugural assignment was both an opportunity and a test: John and Kay needed me to create a new sleepwear and loungewear collection for a major department store. This wasn't just any collection—it was a redemption project. Their previous attempt had been such a spectacular failure that the department store had limited distribution to only four locations instead of their usual four hundred store rollouts. The failure had been so complete and so public within industry circles that John and Kay's reputation was hanging by a thread.

Understanding the gravity of the situation, I immediately reached out to Rita, a talented designer I had worked with previously and trusted implicitly. Rita's background at the Fashion Institute of Technology had given her solid technical skills, and her natural design sense made her an invaluable collaborator. She was thrilled to be offered the opportunity to work on such a high-profile project, and her enthusiasm matched my own determination to succeed.

Together, Rita and I threw ourselves into the project with the kind of intensive focus that only comes when you know failure isn't an option. Working eighteen-hour days became routine as we conceptualized, designed, and refined what would become a comprehensive sleepwear collection. The timeline was brutal—just eight weeks to create an entire line that would need to compete with the best collections in the market. But we were driven by the knowledge that success here could establish both our careers at a new level.

Journey to Peru: Creating Something Special

The next phase of our project took us to Peru, where John and Kay had arranged for us to work with a factory called "Textile P." The prospect of international travel for work still held glamour for me, despite my extensive experience in global manufacturing. Peru offered the promise of high-quality production capabilities combined with competitive pricing—exactly what we needed to make the collection both beautiful and commercially viable.

The three weeks we spent in Peru were intensive, educational, and ultimately triumphant. Working directly with the factory's skilled artisans, we were able to translate our design concepts into reality with a precision and attention to detail that exceeded our expectations. The factory's capabilities were impressive, and their willingness to work with us on achieving exactly the aesthetic we envisioned made the long days and cultural challenges worthwhile.

When we returned to New York, we carried with us 120 carefully crafted samples that represented some of the best work of my career. The collection featured a striking red, white, and blue theme that perfectly captured the essence of Ronny's all-American brand identity while offering the sophistication and comfort that modern consumers demanded in sleepwear. Each piece had been constructed with meticulous attention to detail, from the quality of the fabrics to the precision of the stitching to the thoughtful placement of design elements.

The Moment of Truth: Presenting to Success

The presentation to the major department store's CEO was one of those career-defining moments that every fashion professional dreams of. As we unveiled the collection, piece by piece, I watched the buyer's expressions shift from skeptical interest to genuine enthusiasm. The contrast between this collection and John and Kay's previous failure was stark and undeniable. Where their earlier work had been confined to four test stores, this new collection had the potential to reach all four hundred locations in the chain.

The validation came not just from the department store team and the CEO, but from Ronny himself. When he flashed me one of his characteristic warm smiles and expressed his genuine pleasure with what we had created, I felt like I had finally arrived as a fashion professional. This was the recognition I had been working toward for years—acknowledgment from one of the industry's most respected figures that my work met his exacting standards.

However, even in that moment of triumph, I noticed the sour expressions on John and Kay's faces. The praise and recognition that should have been a source of pride for our entire team instead seemed to highlight their own previous failures. Rather than celebrating our collective success, they appeared resentful that Rita and I were receiving the credit and recognition that they felt should belong to only them as the license holders.

A Moment of Recognition and Its Consequences

During the meeting to review our collection, a moment arose that perfectly encapsulated both the quality of work Rita and I were producing and the impossible political situation we faced. Ronny turned to John with a question about production issues related to his signature embroidery, and John's complete ignorance of manufacturing processes became embarrassingly apparent. As John stammered and sweated, unable to provide even basic information about his own production, I made the decision to step in with the solution.

My explanation of how I had resolved the embroidery problem, along with my mention of the comprehensive production manual I had created for our division and our factories, clearly impressed Ronny. His face lit up with genuine appreciation as he expressed his confidence in my capabilities and his pleasure at having me on "his" team. For a brief moment, I felt the validation I had been seeking throughout my career—recognition from one of the industry's most respected figures.

But I knew that this moment of triumph would come with consequences. Speaking directly to Ronny, especially in a way that highlighted John's incompetence, was bound to earn me harsh retaliation from John and Kay. The political dynamics of working for a licensee meant that demonstrating superior knowledge or capabilities could be seen as insubordination, even when it benefited the overall brand.

Later that day, as I had predicted, John and Kay called me into their office for what would become one of the most unpleasant confrontations of my career. John's accusation that I was a "fame whore" for speaking knowledgeably to Ronny revealed his fundamental insecurity and his resentment of anyone who might overshadow his claimed expertise. Kay's suggestion that I was an "ass kisser" showed her inability to distinguish between professional competence and political maneuvering.

The Complexity of Multiple Masters

Upon our return from Peru, the organizational structure that governed my work became exponentially more complicated. In addition to reporting to John and Kay, I now found myself answerable to two of Ronny's corporate employees: Joan, the Head of licensing, and Ann, her assistant, whose neurotic attention to detail would soon become the bane of my existence.

Joan represented everything that was simultaneously attractive and frustrating about luxury corporate fashion jobs. She had managed to secure what appeared to be a dream position—arriving at ten in the morning, taking leisurely breakfast breaks, attending back to back meetings, enjoying long lunch hours with other executives in her field, hitting the gym, and then spending time on personal errands like hair and nail appointments. It was the kind of schedule that would make any overworked designer envious, but it came at the cost of actually contributing meaningful work to the organization.

The real work of managing the licensing relationship fell to Ann, Joan's assistant, whose paranoia about maintaining her position created a reign of terror for everyone who had to work with her. Ann's greatest fear was that any mistake or oversight would reflect poorly on Joan, which would then result in Ann losing her coveted position in Ronny's corporate hierarchy. This fear manifested as an obsessive attention to detail that went far beyond reasonable quality control and entered the realm of harassment.

Ann's behavior toward Rita and I seemed particularly hostile, and I couldn't help but suspect that she viewed us as beneath her social standing. In her mind, we were just two women who had gotten lucky enough to work on a prestigious project—a project that should have been handled by someone of her caliber rather than outsiders from the grittier world of freelance design work.

The Impossible Balancing Act

Reporting to four different people with four completely different priorities created an impossible working situation. John and Kay cared about nothing beyond maximizing their profit margins, viewing every decision through the lens of how it would affect their bottom line. Quality, employee satisfaction, and even the long-term success of the brand were secondary considerations compared to their immediate financial gain.

John's cost-cutting obsession led him to constantly pressure Rita and me to find ways to reduce expenses, even when these cuts would compromise the quality that made our collection successful. He pushed for cheaper fabrics, simplified construction techniques, and reduced labor time—all of which would have undermined the premium positioning that made the collection attractive to upscale department stores. When I resisted these changes, explaining how they would damage the brand's reputation, he would become belligerent and accusatory.

Kay's contribution to this toxic dynamic was her constant encouragement of John's penny-pinching approach. Every additional dollar of profit was money she could spend on herself, and she made no attempt to hide her prioritization of personal luxury over product quality or employee welfare. Her attitude toward Rita and I was dismissive at best, and she seemed to take particular pleasure in undermining our professional judgment whenever possible.

Ann's obsession with Ronny's signature embroidery represented the opposite extreme of John and Kay's cost-cutting mentality. While they wanted to spend as little as possible on production details, Ann demanded absolute perfection in the placement and execution of the brand's signature design elements. This perfectionism might have been admirable if it had been reasonable, but Ann's standards were so exacting that they bordered on the pathological.

The Embroidery Nightmare

Ann's fixation on the precise placement of Ronny's signature embroidery created weeks of unnecessary work and stress. If the embroidery was even a sixteenth of an inch off from her predetermined specifications, she would demand that the entire sample be remade—a process that could take three weeks and cost hundreds of dollars per piece. Her refusal to accept any variation, no matter how minor or unnoticeable to anyone but her, created an atmosphere of constant anxiety and frustration. I tried to explain to her that knitted cotton stretched and there could never be a precise measurement, without some leeway.

The scope of Ann's obsessive behavior became clear when I calculated that she had demanded 242 separate adjustments to the embroidered logo placement across our collection in just a few short months. Each of these adjustments required coordination with the factory, additional sampling time, and often complete reconstruction of the affected samples. Rita, already overwhelmed by the workload, eventually refused to continue making these endless revisions, creating more tension within our small team at the worst possible time.

When I approached John for support in dealing with Ann's unreasonable demands, his response revealed the depth of his character flaws. Rather than addressing the legitimate business concern I was raising, he chose to make a racist comment about Rita, referring to her as "that Chiquita of yours needs to fix it" in reference to her Puerto Rican heritage. This casual racism was delivered with the confidence of someone who believed his position gave him license to demean others without consequence.

The Harassment Escalates

John's inappropriate behavior wasn't limited to racist comments about Rita. His treatment of me became increasingly problematic as he became more comfortable asserting his perceived authority. His comments about my appearance, particularly his obsession with making crude references to my breasts, created a hostile work environment that reminded me of the worst aspects of my previous jobs.

The harassment seemed strategic and calculated. John's most inappropriate behavior occurred when Kay was out of the office, often after he had consumed several alcoholic drinks during extended lunch breaks. He would invade my personal space, leaning over my desk while making his lude comments, and would find excuses to make physical contact that I found clearly unwelcome and unprofessional.

His verbal abuse escalated when his sister wasn't present to witness it, as if he understood that even Kay might find some of his behavior excessive. He would make these offensive comments quietly, so that Ronny's corporate employees couldn't overhear him.

I was convinced that this consistent conduct demonstrated that he understood exactly how inappropriate his behavior was, even as he continued to engage in it.

Kay's Cruelty and Control

Kay's contribution to our miserable working conditions took the form of psychological manipulation and cruelty. She would publicly undermine my professional judgment while maintaining a friendly facade when Ronny's staff was present. This two-faced approach was particularly insidious because it made it difficult to document or address her behavior through normal channels.

Her refusal to allow me to hire additional designers despite our overwhelming workload was a clear indication that she prioritized her profit margins over the quality of work or the well-being of her team. Rita and I found ourselves working seven days a week regularly, often staying in the office until ten or eleven at night just to keep up with the demands of the project. The only silver lining was that the late hours meant I could bring my dog to the office daily, providing some emotional comfort during those grueling periods.

Breaking Point in the Hamptons

The Hampton's incident represented Kay's cruelty at its most extreme. Demanding that Rita and I make a three-hour journey to her summer home for what amounted to unnecessary micromanagement over the fourth of July, was bad enough. Putting us up in a substandard motel while treating us as servants by asking us to serve drinks at her weekend soiree was even worse. But her suggestion that I should euthanize my dog rather bring her with me crossed every line of human decency.

The weekend in the Hamptons became a crystallizing moment that revealed the true nature of John and Kay's characters. After forcing Rita and me to work in her home office, with no air conditioning—providing mediocre take-out food, refusing to allow breaks, and maintaining an atmosphere of hostility—they insisted on taking us to dinner at an upscale restaurant on our final night, where they could parade us in front of their friends as examples of the "little people" who worked for them.

The dinner became an exercise in public humiliation as John's alcohol consumption lowered his inhibitions and amplified his worst tendencies. His racist comments toward Rita became louder and more frequent, while his sexual harassment of me became more blatant. Kay's participation in mocking us transformed what should have been a professional dinner into a degrading spectacle that left both Rita and me feeling dehumanized.

John's slurred question about Rita's ethnicity, delivered with deliberate mispronunciation designed to mock her Puerto Rican heritage, represented the kind of casual racism that was still common in certain corners of the fashion industry. Rita's dignified response—affirming her pride in her heritage—only seemed to encourage John's continued abuse. His suggestion that she should be grateful for the opportunity to work for such a "prestigious" company revealed his fundamental inability to see Rita or me as professionals deserving of respect.

When the dinner was finally over, the drive back to New York through a fierce thunderstorm felt like a welcome escape from hell. Rita and I barely spoke during the three-hour journey, both of us processing the humiliation we had just endured and trying to figure out how to continue working for people who clearly had no respect for us as human beings, let alone as professionals.

The Egypt Ultimatum and Hidden Agendas

On one rainy morning John and Kay called Rita and I into a meeting. The conversation quickly moved from personal attacks to a business decision that would have far-reaching consequences. John's announcement that Rita and I would be traveling to Egypt to establish production with a new factory came as a complete shock. We had built a successful relationship with our Peruvian factory, achieving excellent quality and reasonable pricing. The decision to change factories without any apparent business justification seemed both risky and unnecessary.

John's dismissive response to my questions about this decision—"I don't give a shit what you think"—made it clear that he wasn't interested in professional input or careful evaluation of the change. His focus was entirely on the potentially lower costs he believed he could achieve in Egypt, regardless of the risks to quality, timeline, or brand reputation that such a change might entail.

Kay's parting shot about our food expenses during the upcoming trip, suggesting that Rita and I were overweight and could benefit from eating less, was gratuitously cruel and revealed the depth of her disdain for us. Her willingness to make such personal attacks in a professional setting showed how completely she had abandoned any pretense of proper workplace behavior.

Meeting the Players: Mohammad and the Egyptian Connection

That afternoon, the introduction to Mohammad, the Egyptian factory representative, immediately raised red flags that I should have heeded more seriously. His appearance—the greasy ponytail, gaudy jewelry, and unbuttoned shirt revealing his chest hair and fake tan—suggested someone more interested in projecting wealth and power than in running a legitimate manufacturing operation. His resemblance to a stereotypical Middle Eastern crime boss was so pronounced that it seemed almost like a caricature.

Mohammad's conversation style, filled with boastful name-dropping about celebrity connections, vast wealth, multiple properties, and sexual conquests, painted the picture of someone who was either completely delusional or involved in activities that couldn't withstand scrutiny. The fact that someone so obviously repulsive could claim such extensive female conquests should have been an immediate warning sign about his truthfulness in other matters.

Rob, the handsome Canadian VP, who accompanied Mohammad to the meeting, presented a stark contrast in professionalism and demeanor. His calm, well-informed presence suggested that he was the legitimate business face of the operation, while Mohammad served some other role that wasn't immediately apparent. Rob's obvious discomfort with Mohammad's behavior and his seeming reluctance to be associated with him suggested that even he had concerns about the partnership he was facilitating.

Entering the Danger Zone: Egypt and Mounting Concerns

The trip to Egypt began with frightening encounters that should have served as warnings about the dangerous situation Rita and I were entering. The political unrest in Cairo, combined with the racial slurs and riots we witnessed from the crowds outside of our hotel upon arrival, created an atmosphere of hostility and danger that neither of us had anticipated. The hotel Kay had booked for us was substandard and felt unsafe, adding to our sense of vulnerability in an unfamiliar and unstable environment.

Rita's immediate comfort with Mohammad at dinner, demonstrated by her flirtatious behavior that continued at breakfast the following morning, was troubling for several reasons. Her failure to maintain professional boundaries with a factory representative violated basic business protocols that I had tried to instill in her, but more concerning was her apparent willingness to ignore the obvious red flags about Mohammad's character and background. I was eager to speak with her about my observations, but we were escorted to a waiting car after breakfast that drove us to the factory we were to inspect.

The factory visits that day was unlike anything I had experienced in my decades of international manufacturing work. While most factories show signs of active production—fabric scraps on floors, works in progress on tables, the normal sounds of industrial activity—this facility felt more like a movie set than a functioning manufacturing operation. I questioned Abdul, the factory manager who was leading the tour, but he refused to answer me. In most of the factories that I had worked in worldwide, the chatter from the workers was loud and continuous, these workers were silent and looked frightened. The unnaturally clean conditions, the absence of finished products, the pristinely wrapped bolts of fabrics on shelves and the workers' strange behavior all suggested that we were being shown something designed to deceive rather than to inform.

Discovering the Connection: A Terrorist's Factory

My decision to excuse myself from our meeting in the factory's conference room for a bathroom break, was a rouse so that I could snoop in Abdul's office while the others were distracted with our design goals, proved to be one of the most consequential moments of my career. Seeing Osama bin Laden's name on multiple documents and photographs on the walls, confirmed my growing suspicions that this factory was connected to something far more dangerous than simple manufacturing fraud. At the time, bin Laden was already known as a terrorist leader, though the full scope of his organization's capabilities wouldn't become apparent until the September 11th attacks many years later.

Later that day, I confronted Abdul about his relationship to bin Laden, and it provided crucial confirmation of what I had suspected. He proudly admitted that he worked for and was related to bin Laden's family and that the factory belonged to them. This transformed what had seemed like a questionable business situation into a clear moral crisis. His description of bin Laden as "an exceptional man" and his dismissive attitude toward American concerns about terrorism made it clear that we were dealing with people who viewed themselves as enemies of our country.

Abdul's physical intimidation when I pressed him about bin Laden's terrorist activities—grabbing my wrist and threatening me with consequences if I continued asking questions—demonstrated that the danger was real and immediate. The intensity of his stare and the implied threat in his words made it clear that continuing to pursue this line of inquiry could put Rita and me in physical danger. All I wanted to do was to get out of Egypt and return to New York as quickly as possible.

The Betrayal Unfolds: Rita's Deal with the Devil

On the plane home the next day, the revelation of Rita's betrayal came as a devastating blow that recontextualized everything that had happened during our trip to Egypt. Her presentation of a bag full of cash to me, accompanied by her excited explanation of the kickback arrangement she had negotiated with Mohammad, showed how completely she had abandoned any ethical considerations in favor of personal financial gain.

Rita's justification for accepting what amounted to blood money—that she had worked for low wages her entire career and deserved the opportunity to buy her family a house—revealed how the fashion industry's systemic underpayment and discrimination had corrupted someone I had trusted. Her argument that such corruption was common in the garment center and that we shouldn't try to maintain higher ethical standards was perhaps the most disheartening aspect of her betrayal.

Her threat to create false accusations against me if I tried to prevent her from participating in the kickback scheme showed how far she was willing to go to protect her newfound source of income. Her confidence that John and Kay would believe her accusations of her accusing me of being too tough on her, over my denials was based on her understanding that they would prefer to maintain a profitable relationship with the factory rather than address inconvenient ethical concerns between the two of us.

The Final Confrontation and Its Aftermath

The meeting with John and Kay the morning after our return and my confrontation with Rita played out exactly as I had feared. Rita's preemptive strike, providing them with written accusations about my behavior, had effectively positioned me as the problem rather than the person trying to prevent them from doing business with terrorists. Their immediate termination of my employment, without any investigation or consideration of the evidence I could provide, showed how completely they prioritized profit over any ethical considerations.

John's violent reaction to my mention of the factory's terrorist connections—throwing a book at my head and barely missing—demonstrated the lengths to which he was willing to go to protect his profitable arrangement. His shouted declaration that he didn't care if "Hitler himself" manufactured their products revealed the complete absence of moral boundaries in his business practices.

Kay's smug satisfaction at my firing and her frank admission that they had already committed to a fifteen-million-dollar order with the factory showed how thoroughly money had corrupted their decision-making process. Her statement that no one would believe "a nobody" like me demonstrated her confidence that their positions of power would protect them from any consequences of their actions. Rita with thrilled with herself for accomplishing her kickback goals and I was gutted by her complete and total betrayal.

The aftermath of my termination included unsuccessful attempts to find anyone willing to take action against John and Kay's arrangement with the terrorist-owned factory. My corporate lawyer friend's refusal to pursue the matter, despite acknowledging that my concerns were legitimate, showed how the legal system failed to provide recourse for whistleblowers who lacked sufficient power or resources to challenge established business interests.

Consequences and Vindication

The eventual consequences for various players in this drama provided some measure of vindication for my actions, though they came too late to prevent the immediate damage to my career. Rita's termination for cheating on expense reports, after John and Kay discovered she was stealing kickbacks from them as well, showed that her ethical flexibility extended to betraying her new allies as easily as she had betrayed me.

The failure of Kay's attempt to design the fall collection herself, resulting in such poor sales that Ronny terminated their license, demonstrated that my contributions had been more valuable than they had recognized. Their inability to maintain the quality and commercial success that I had achieved proved that their focus on cost-cutting and profit maximization was ultimately self-defeating.

The September 11th attacks and their aftermath gave my warnings about the factory's terrorist connections a tragic vindication that I would never have wished for. The knowledge that I had tried to prevent an American company from doing business with Osama bin Laden's organization, only to be ignored and punished for my efforts, remains one of the most frustrating and haunting aspects of my career.

Lessons Learned and Principles Maintained

This experience reinforced my understanding that maintaining ethical standards in the fashion industry often comes at significant personal cost. The systemic corruption that allows companies to prioritize profit over all other considerations creates an environment where whistleblowers are punished rather than protected, and where those who try to do the right thing often find themselves isolated and unemployed.

However, the experience also confirmed that some principles are worth defending regardless of the personal consequences. My refusal to remain silent about the factory's terrorist connections, even when it cost me my job and damaged my career prospects, represented a line that I was not willing to cross. The knowledge that I had tried to prevent American consumer dollars from flowing to terrorist organizations provided a sense of moral satisfaction that outweighed the professional costs.

The broader implications of this experience extend beyond my personal story to highlight the need for better oversight and accountability in global supply chains. The ease with which John and Kay were able to arrange manufacturing with a terrorist-owned factory, and their confidence that they could do so without consequences, reveals dangerous gaps in the systems that are supposed to prevent such arrangements.

Looking back on this chapter of my career, I can see it as a turning point where the naive optimism that had sustained me through earlier challenges finally gave way to a more realistic understanding of the fashion industry's capacity for corruption and moral compromise. While this loss of innocence was painful, it also prepared me for the even greater challenges that lay ahead in my career, armed with a clearer understanding of the stakes involved in standing up for ethical principles in an industry that often rewards their abandonment.

The story of my time with Ronny's company serves as a cautionary tale about the hidden costs of chasing prestige just because it is presented in a shiny, pretty package and the importance of maintaining moral boundaries even when they conflict with professional advancement. It also demonstrates that sometimes the most important victories are the ones that prevent greater harm, even when they come at significant personal cost and may never receive the recognition they deserve.

CHAPTER 10:
Harry, Rudi and Tyra Banks

Back to the Dark Side

After my disappointing experience with John and Kay, I found myself reluctantly returning to what I had come to think of as the "dark side"—the relentless, cutthroat world of Seventh Avenue's garment center. Harry, a seasoned "garmento" in the industry who had spent decades navigating its treacherous waters, offered me a position at his highly profitable apparel company. The salary he proposed was substantially higher than what most other brands were offering at that particular moment, which should have been my first warning sign.

Harry had built an impressive empire, managing a diverse portfolio of brands that featured collaborations with numerous renowned rappers, all of whom had achieved remarkable commercial success. His company was thriving in the urban fashion market, riding the wave of hip-hop culture's influence on mainstream fashion. I suspected the generous compensation package might come with a catch—Harry was most likely going to be a nightmare to work with. But at this stage of my career, approaching my late thirties, I had bills to pay and a lifestyle to maintain.

The fashion industry had taught me that financial stability was always temporary and elusive. I found myself constantly struggling to keep up with mounting expenses while trying to maintain the polished image that was expected of someone in my position. It was crucial for me to project the image of a successful fashionista, which unfortunately meant racking up charges on my credit cards for designer clothes that I couldn't really afford. Even when hunting for bargains at sample sales and outlet stores, luxury fashion remained expensive. As an established designer who had climbed to a management position, dressing the part had become more important than ever—it was an investment in my professional credibility.

The Odd Couple: Harry and Rudi

Harry and his business partner Rudi reminded me of the classic comedy film "Twins," starring Arnold Schwarzenegger and Danny DeVito—two completely mismatched partners who somehow made their unlikely partnership work. Harry embodied the Arnold Schwarzenegger character: tall, lean, and neurotic, at sixty-three-years-old he had survived decades in the business through a combination of charm and shady business practices. On the surface, he appeared to be charismatic and engaging, the kind of person who could sell ice to Eskimos. However, the moment anyone dared to challenge his old-fashioned views or question his authority, his demeanor would transform completely. In the blink of an eye, he could become ruthlessly cold and calculating, unleashing verbal attacks with the precision and sharpness of a surgeon's scalpel. He was an equal opportunity offender, men, women and relatives, no one was off limits to his merciless insults.

Rudi, on the other hand, was the Danny DeVito of this partnership. Standing at barely four-foot-eight inches tall, he was a chubby, middle-aged man in his mid-forties who sported a comb-over hairstyle that would have made Donald Trump proud. Despite his diminutive stature, Rudi possessed an outsized personality—he was cocky, egotistical, and blessed with an incredibly sharp sense of humor that could cut through the tension in any room. What I immediately appreciated about Rudi was his straightforward, no-nonsense approach to business. He was direct in his communications and surprisingly generous with his employees, a stark contrast to Harry's more manipulative and greedy tendencies.

Both men had brought their sons into the family business, creating an additional layer of complexity and competition within the company. Rudi had two sons, while Harry had one, and all three young men worked under the long shadows cast by their successful fathers. The dynamic was fascinating to observe—each son competed fiercely not only with each other but also for their respective father's attention and approval, creating an undercurrent of rivalry that permeated every business decision.

The Reality Check

When Harry had initially recruited me, he had painted a picture of a spacious, well-equipped design studio where I would have the freedom and resources to create groundbreaking fashion. However, reality hit hard when I arrived on that dreary Monday morning in November. Instead of the promised studio, I discovered that I had been assigned to what could generously be described as a glorified storage closet. This cramped space was already occupied by a disgruntled designer who worked on one of Harry's rapper brands, and his resentment was palpable from the moment I walked through the door. He clearly despised his job and had been trapped in that suffocating environment for far too long, his creative spirit slowly being crushed by the daily grind.

When I approached Harry to express my frustration with the inadequate workspace, his response was both dismissive and telling of what our working relationship would be like. "Shut up and deal with it," he said without even looking up from whatever he was doing. It was clear that the generous salary came with the expectation that I would accept whatever conditions he imposed, no matter how unreasonable they might be.

The Assistant from Hell

The budget constraints meant that I couldn't offer a competitive salary for an assistant position, which significantly limited my options when it came to hiring support staff. After interviewing several underwhelming candidates, I eventually settled on Alice, a young woman whose design portfolio showed promise and potential. During the interview process, Alice had managed to convince me that she was serious about pursuing a career in fashion and was committed to learning and growing within the industry. Unfortunately, this turned out to be an elaborate deception.

Alice's true nature revealed itself on her very first day. She arrived looking pale and unusually quiet, completely lacking the enthusiasm and energy one would expect from someone starting a new job in the exciting world of fashion. Given that it was an exceptionally busy day, her lackluster attitude immediately set my teeth on edge. When I asked her repeatedly what was wrong, she claimed to be suffering from the flu, complete with all the appropriate symptoms and complaints.

Feeling sympathetic toward what I thought was a genuinely sick employee, I prepared some tea for her and was actually considering sending her home to recover properly. However, my compassion quickly turned to fury when I accidentally overheard her phone conversation with a friend. She was actually bragging about her wild night out, describing in detail how she had been partying with her boyfriend until four in the morning, had thrown up in a taxi cab, and was now suffering from a severe hangover. The most infuriating part was listening to her boast about how she had successfully conned me into believing her flu story, and how she planned to cut the day short so she could go home, sleep off her hangover, and gear up for another night of partying.

My anger at being so blatantly deceived and disrespected led me to make a decision that Alice would quickly regret. Instead of sending her home as she expected, I made her stay in the office for the next six hours, working on logo designs and other tedious tasks while feeling absolutely miserable. By the time six o'clock rolled around, she looked genuinely green around the gills and could barely function. As she headed toward the elevator, clearly desperate to escape, I intercepted her and made it crystal clear that if she ever showed up to work in such a condition again, her employment would be terminated immediately. The look of shock and realization on her pale face as the elevator doors closed told me that she finally understood I was not the pushover she had assumed I would be.

Despite this early warning, I had a sinking feeling that Alice was going to become a significant problem for me down the road.

The Tyra Banks Opportunity

The next day brought a complete transformation in Alice's attitude and behavior. She arrived at the office focused, alert, and seemingly ready to tackle whatever challenges the day might bring. It was during the next few weeks that I conceived what I believed could be a game-changing strategy for the company: a lingerie brand collaboration with Tyra Banks, one of the most recognizable and successful supermodels in the world.

When I presented this concept to Harry and Rudi, their reaction was immediate and enthusiastic. Both partners could instantly see the enormous potential in associating their company with Tyra's star power and impeccable reputation. The combination of her status as a Victoria's Secret Angel and her broad appeal across different demographics made her the perfect celebrity partner for a lingerie line. Energized by their positive response, I threw myself into creating impressive concept boards that would effectively communicate my vision to Tyra's management team.

Getting in touch with Benny, Tyra's manager, proved to be a challenge in itself. I spent days persistently calling his assistant, trying to arrange a meeting while being politely but firmly rebuffed at every turn. Benny was known throughout the industry as both incredibly intelligent and notoriously difficult to reach, protecting his time and his client's interests with the ferocity of a guard dog. However, persistence eventually paid off, and his assistant finally relented, agreeing to set up a meeting.

The workspace situation presented its own set of challenges. Designing professional presentation boards in our cramped office felt nearly impossible—there simply wasn't enough room to spread out materials, reference images, and work on multiple concepts simultaneously. However, I was determined to make it work, and somehow managed to pull together a presentation that I felt proud of. When Rudi saw the final result, and realized how beautifully the designs had turned out, he was genuinely impressed. His enthusiasm was infectious, and he immediately convinced Harry to provide us access to a fantastic studio space they owned on the lower floor of the building.

This new workspace was nothing short of spectacular—a breathtaking loft-style design studio on one side, complemented by a showroom featuring floor-to-ceiling windows that flooded the space with natural light. The change in environment was transformative, and I felt a surge of excitement about the possibilities that lay ahead. More practically, it also meant that Harry wouldn't be able to drop by every hour to check on my progress and micromanage every decision I made.

Meeting the Power Player

A few days later, I learned that Benny had arrived in New York for business and was staying at one of the city's most luxurious downtown hotels. Knowing his reputation for being both exceptionally clever and demanding, I felt my nerves building as the meeting approached. This was my opportunity to present my vision directly to one of the most influential managers in the entertainment industry, and I knew I might not get a second chance if I didn't make a strong first impression.

The day of the meeting, I arrived at the hotel with Rudi and Alice in tow, my design boards carefully organized and my presentation mentally rehearsed. As we were escorted into Benny's suite, I was immediately struck by the sheer opulence of the space. The room featured its own private swimming pool, luxurious Hermès blankets casually draped over pristine white couches, and expensive candles that filled the air with exotic fragrances. This was clearly the most extravagant hotel accommodations I had ever encountered, and it spoke volumes about the level of success and influence that Benny had achieved in his career.

Benny's stunningly handsome male assistant efficiently guided me to a chair and helped me set up my presentation materials, while

Alice and Rudi were directed to seats in the living room area. He gestured for silence, indicating that Benny was engaged in what appeared to be a crucial phone conversation that couldn't be interrupted.

For the next two hours, I sat quietly and observed as Benny conducted what seemed to be a high-stakes business negotiation. Even though he was facing away from me and I could only hear his side of the conversation, it was clear that he was engaged in a heated argument with someone on the other end of the line. What impressed me most was his tenacity and strategic thinking—he refused to back down, continued to press his points, and ultimately seemed to get exactly what he wanted from the conversation. It was a masterclass in negotiation tactics, and I found myself both intimidated and inspired by his skill.

When Benny finally turned his attention to me, I could see that he was impeccably dressed and groomed, every detail of his appearance carefully considered despite his relatively small stature. There was an aura of power and confidence about him that was immediately apparent. He asked me directly to show him my design boards, and then proceeded to examine each one with the focused intensity of an art critic evaluating a masterpiece, looking for any flaws or weaknesses that might undermine the overall concept.

Occasionally, he would glance up at me to ask specific questions about color choices, fabric selections, or design elements, and I could tell that he was genuinely engaged with the material I was presenting. After reviewing all the boards multiple times and asking detailed questions about various aspects of the proposed line, he handed them back to me. The silence that followed felt endless, and I held my breath waiting for his verdict.

Finally, he broke into a brilliant white smile and delivered the words I had been hoping to hear: "You are very talented, Katie and I love all of the designs." The relief and excitement I felt in that moment was overwhelming. Rudi, who had been watching anxiously from across the room, immediately leaped up to join me, his smile stretching from ear to ear as he realized that we had successfully captured Benny's interest and approval.

The Respect Factor

As we prepared to leave the hotel, I reflected on how much respect I had developed for Benny during our brief interaction. Here was someone who had built an empire through intelligence, hard work, and an unwavering commitment to excellence. Over the years that followed, I would watch with admiration as he guided Jennifer Lopez's career to even greater heights, helping her transition from music to movies to business and fashion ventures with remarkable success. His ability to spot talent, develop strategies, and execute complex business deals was truly impressive.

What I particularly appreciated about Benny was his lifestyle and the way he had earned every luxury he enjoyed. Unlike many people in the entertainment industry who lived beyond their means or relied on others for their success, Benny had built his wealth through genuine talent and hard work. He was the creative force behind "The Fresh Prince of Bel-Air," one of television's most beloved sitcoms, and had worked tirelessly to break through barriers in an industry that was predominantly controlled by white male executives.

His personality was a fascinating combination of bold humor and straightforward business sense, tempered by genuine compassion and remarkable insight into human nature. During our brief interactions, he had helped me recognize and appreciate my own creative abilities in a way that rarely happened in the fashion industry. While I had always known that I was a skilled designer, receiving genuine compliments and recognition was virtually unheard of in the garment center, where criticism and negativity were the norm.

The Tensions Rise

When we returned to the office, I found Harry anxiously waiting to learn whether our presentation had been successful or if we had failed to capture Benny's interest. As I entered his office to deliver the news, I couldn't help but notice that he and Rudi were engaged in yet another one of their typical heated arguments. This was such a regular occurrence that I had almost become immune to their bickering, but it still made me uncomfortable to witness grown men behaving like children.

The constant arguing between the partners created an unpleasant atmosphere throughout the office, and anyone who dared to intervene or take sides would quickly become the target of their combined hostility and verbal abuse. Despite the tension their fights created, I found myself secretly rooting for Rudi in these confrontations. His quick wit and direct approach often got the better of Harry's more calculating and manipulative style.

"Shut the fuck up!" Rudi yelled at his business partner during one particularly heated exchange.

"You're a spiteful little midget and I have more money than you!" Harry fired back, his voice dripping with contempt.

"You are an old, nasty bastard and everyone hates you!" Rudi shouted in response, his face flushed with anger.

As this argument unfolded, I watched their sons quickly move to position themselves protectively near their respective fathers, ready to defend their family's honor if the situation escalated further. The family dynamics were complex and often uncomfortable to witness.

Rudi's two sons presented an interesting contrast to each other. The younger son was genuinely endearing—diligent in his work, intelligent beyond his years, and eager to learn the business from the ground up. His older brother had inherited his father's quick wit and sharp tongue, but channeled these traits in a more volatile direction. He was unpredictable and seemed driven by a desire for revenge against anyone who dared to cross or disrespect his father.

Harry's son presented his own set of challenges and contradictions. He was notably handsome, tall, and always impeccably dressed in the latest fashion trends but not always focused during business discussions as I thought he could be because he was definitely intimidated by his father.

Harry's treatment of his son was particularly cruel to witness. He would openly mock and humiliate the young man in front of employees, calling him stupid and useless, questioning every decision he made. Then, in a twisted display of manipulation, Harry would suddenly embrace his son with an exaggerated hug, as if the cruel words had never been spoken. It was a toxic cycle of abuse and false affection that clearly took its toll on the young man's self-esteem and confidence. I found myself sympathizing with him, wondering if Harry were my father how I would cope with the stress and criticism.

Rudi's approach to parenting was completely different. He genuinely adored both of his sons and took pride in their accomplishments, no matter how small. Everything he had built— his business, his wealth, his reputation—was motivated by his desire to provide for them and ensure their future success. The contrast between the two fathers' approaches was stark and telling.

The Racist Revelation

When the argument between Harry and Rudi finally subsided and both men turned their attention to me, I seized the moment to share our triumph.

"Well hello!" I announced with barely contained excitement. "Benny loves my designs!"

Harry's response revealed both his ignorance and his prejudice. "Who?" he yelled, clearly having no idea who I was talking about. "Who the hell is Benny?"

Rudi's exasperation with his partner's ignorance was immediately apparent. "Are you fucking kidding me? You moron!" he screamed at Harry. "He's Tyra's manager! Tyra fucking Banks, the Victoria's Secret model!"

What happened next shocked me to my core and revealed the ugly truth about Harry's character. "Don't we have enough *black* brands and people here?" he yelled, his racism displayed openly and without shame.

The comment hit me like a physical blow. In that moment, I realized that I was working for someone whose values were fundamentally opposed to everything I believed in. Rudi's reaction was immediate and telling—he walked out of Harry's office with his sons following behind him, hands flailing in the air in disgust and frustration. His body language made it clear that he was equally appalled by his partner's racist outburst.

"Oh my God! I cannot believe he just said that!" I said, my voice filled with disbelief and anger.

Rudi, clearly embarrassed by his business partner's behavior, simply rolled his eyes and beckoned his sons into his own office, closing the door firmly behind them. The message was clear—he wanted no part of Harry's bigotry and was distancing himself from the comment as much as possible within the constraints of their business partnership.

Finding an Ally

Standing there in Harry's office, feeling deflated and disgusted by what I had just witnessed, I was rescued by Deb, the company's office manager, who grabbed my hand and pulled me down the hallway away from the toxic atmosphere.

"What the hell just happened?" I asked her, still processing the shock of Harry's casual racism.

"Welcome to my world," she replied with a bitter laugh that contained years of accumulated frustration and disappointment.

Despite the unpleasant scene we had just witnessed, Deb managed to maintain her sense of humor and perspective. "Great job on Tyra, by the way!" she said with genuine enthusiasm, holding up two cigarettes and gesturing for me to follow her to the stairwell where the office smokers congregated.

I had always found that smoking a cigarette helped me cope with work stress, particularly after especially challenging or emotionally draining days. But sharing a cigarette with someone I could confide in about the daily circus of working with "the twins" made the experience even more therapeutic. It gave us a chance to decompress and process the constant drama that seemed to surround Harry and Rudi's volatile relationship.

The office smokers had created their own informal support group on the cramped fire escape, where they would gather to exchange stories about Harry and Rudi's latest antics while keeping their voices low to avoid detection. Every employee who worked under Harry's management had developed a healthy hatred for him, and Deb was no exception. She had witnessed his behavior firsthand for years and had no illusions about his character.

Word of our success with Tyra spread quickly through the smoking circle. "Katie just presented a new Tyra Banks lingerie line to her manager, Benny!" Deb announced to the group.

"No shit!" responded Allen, the company's production manager, with genuine excitement. "Great job!"

"That's amazing," whispered Jenny, another member of our informal support network.

The Los Angeles Trip

A week later, the phone call we had been hoping for finally came. Benny reached out to Rudi directly to discuss the possibility of flying me to Los Angeles so that I could review my design boards with both him and Tyra herself. This was exactly the kind of development we had been working toward, and when Rudi discussed the opportunity with Harry, both partners agreed that sending me to the West Coast was the right strategic move for the company.

Throughout that week, Alice and I worked intensively to refine and polish Tyra's proposed lingerie line, making sure every detail was perfect before the crucial Los Angeles presentation. During this period, I grew quite close to Deb, who had started spending more time in our studio to escape Harry's constant bullying and harassment. Her presence was always a source of great entertainment and moral support, and she had a way of lifting everyone's spirits even during the most stressful periods. She also had an incredible flair for fashion, so her input was welcome.

One day, as we were working on the designs, Deb made an observation that revealed another disturbing aspect of Harry's character. "You know Harry's a slumlord?" she said casually, as if discussing the weather.

"What?" I replied, only half-listening as I focused on adjusting one of the design elements.

"Every day, people call his secretary begging for basic repairs," she explained. "Tenants are asking him to fix heating systems, plumbing problems, electrical issues—you know, the things that landlords are legally required to maintain. But he ignores all of their requests and actually seems to find their suffering amusing. He's a sick fuck," she concluded with disgust.

If, this revelation was true, it added another layer to my growing understanding of Harry's character. Here was a man who not only displayed racism and treated his employees poorly, but also took pleasure in the suffering of vulnerable people who depended on him for basic housing needs.

Deb: A Complex Friend

As I spent more time with Deb, I began to understand both her remarkable qualities and her significant struggles. Standing at five feet nine inches tall with an extremely thin frame, she was genuinely stunning and possessed a remarkable sense of style that allowed her to wear virtually anything with confidence and grace. Her fashion choices were always bold and creative, making her appear as though she had just stepped off the runway at a Paris fashion show. With her beautiful light complexion, dark hair, and expressive blue eyes, she embodied a European elegance that was impossible to ignore.

Deb had originally come to the US from Europe, with dreams of pursuing a modeling career in Los Angeles, but she felt that she didn't quite meet the industry's increasingly narrow beauty standards. The rejection and criticism she faced in that competitive environment had driven her to relocate to New York, where she could be closer to her mother and find a different path forward.

Despite the setback to her original dreams, she had managed to channel her aesthetic sense and people skills into her role as office manager.

Her personality was a fascinating combination of sharp intelligence, vibrant humor, and magnetic charisma that drew people to her like a moth to flame. She had an innate ability to captivate everyone around her and could light up any room she entered with her beautiful smile. However, I also think she had poor decision-making skills that sometimes-created chaos for herself and those around her.

Running Harry and Rudi's office required considerable skill, and Deb handled these responsibilities with remarkable efficiency and competence. She always seemed to be plugged into the office gossip network, maintaining detailed knowledge about the activities and personal lives of all her colleagues. This information network made her incredibly valuable to the organization, and also gave her significant power over the business.

What I gradually discovered was that Deb's personal life was a complicated mess of poor choices and self-destructive behavior. She told many of us that she regularly engaged in sexual relationships with several co-workers, typically after hours and right there in the office, often after consuming several shots of tequila, hiding the bottle in her desk drawer. She approached these encounters with complete openness and seemed genuinely indifferent to what others might think about her behavior.

I think most of us in the office were aware of Deb's notorious reputation and late-night activities—most except Harry, who remained blissfully ignorant of what was happening right under his nose. She would often joke with me and others about her sexcapades, even bragging about having sex on Harry's own desk. To her, it was all harmless fun, and even at work, she never hesitated to speak her mind about any topic, no matter how inappropriate.

The Struggle with Addiction

While Deb's irreverent attitude toward office relationships might have been amusing, her battle with alcoholism was anything but funny. Though she was still young, she was clearly struggling with severe alcohol dependency that affected her social life. When she managed to limit herself to one or two drinks, she remained the lively, captivating, and amusing person everyone loved to be around. However, once she crossed the threshold of three drinks, her personality would undergo a dramatic and disturbing transformation.

The fun-loving, charismatic woman would disappear, replaced by someone who was aggressive, cruel, and indiscriminate in her romantic pursuits. In this altered state, she would pursue anyone who showed even a hint of interest in her, regardless of their age, gender, or appropriateness as a partner. She became predatory and unpredictable, making decisions that she would later regret but seemed unable to prevent in the moment.

The impact of her drinking on my own life became increasingly problematic as our friendship deepened. Many nights, I would return home from a long day at work, only to receive frantic phone calls at three or four in the morning. Sometimes it would be her boyfriend wondering where she was, other times it would be complete strangers demanding that I come retrieve her from their apartments because she was refusing to leave and causing a scene.

These rescue missions became a regular part of my routine. I would have to get dressed, travel across the city in the middle of the night, and somehow convince a drunk and belligerent Deb to get in the cab so I could drop her off at her apartment. The next day, she would always appear at work looking absolutely gorgeous and acting as if nothing unusual had happened, while I would show up tired, frazzled, and exhausted from having to deal with her crisis in the early hours of the morning.

Her romantic life was equally troubling. Her boyfriend was a genuinely disturbing individual—a gangster type who seemed to take pleasure in verbally abusing her. She told me he controlled her finances, taking her paychecks and using the money as he saw fit, but he would never leave her permanently because she represented his meal ticket. Deb's mother was wealthy, and he had figured out how to exploit that relationship for his own benefit.

Over the years that I knew her, I made numerous attempts to help Deb break free from this toxic relationship, but my efforts were consistently unsuccessful. She and her boyfriend had developed a codependent dynamic that she seemed unable or unwilling to break. Deb insisted that she couldn't survive without him, even as his manipulation continued to damage her self-esteem and wellbeing.

Periodically, Deb would make genuine efforts to get sober, and during these periods she would stop drinking for a month or two at a time. However, sobriety seemed to make her feel lost and unhappy, as if alcohol had become so central to her identity that she didn't know who she was without it. During these dry spells, she would become increasingly difficult to be around, and I learned to tread carefully to avoid triggering a relapse or losing her friendship entirely.

Despite all of her personal struggles and self-destructive behaviors, there were several reasons why I maintained my friendship with Deb over the years. Many people questioned my loyalty to someone who caused so much chaos and drama, but I always felt there was something special about her that was worth preserving. She possessed an enchanting quality that was hard to define—a combination of vulnerability and strength that reminded me of a lost child trying to find her way home. Her charm and infectious laughter had a way of wrapping around you and making you want to help her, even when logic suggested that she was beyond saving.

I naively believed that I could be the person to rescue her from her demons and help her build a better life. What I failed to recognize at the time was that addiction is a disease that can only be overcome by the person suffering from it—no amount of love, support, or intervention from friends can force someone to get sober if they're not ready to do the work themselves.

What kept me connected to Deb, despite all the chaos she created, was her fierce loyalty when she was sober and her remarkable creative talents. She was one of the most genuinely loyal friends I had ever encountered, and when she wasn't drinking she was an absolute joy to be around. Her eye for fashion and design was extraordinary—she could look at one of my designs, make a few small adjustments, and transform it into something that would become a bestselling item. Her instincts were flawless, and her technical skills were impressive, but her personal demons prevented her from reaching her full potential.

The Incompetent Business Manager

Just before my crucial trip to Los Angeles to meet with Benny and Tyra, Deb delivered some unwelcome news. She informed me that I would be traveling with Steve, the companies newly hired and notably incompetent business manager. Harry had recently brought Steve onto the team with the intention of having him manage Tyra's lingerie division, despite serious questions about his professional ethics and track record.

My reaction to this news was immediate and intense. "What?" I shouted, making no attempt to hide my dismay. "I can't stand that idiot, Steve! I know him from the garment center; he's a washed-up relic who has driven several brands into bankruptcy. He's a complete failure who messes up everything he touches. Why on earth would Harry hire him?"

Deb's response shed some disturbing light on Steve's character and behavior. "I don't know," she said with a laugh, "but he's a pervert!" She went on to explain that Steve had already been fired from several previous jobs for spending his work hours looking at pornographic websites instead of focusing on his professional responsibilities.

"Oh my God," I said, torn between laughter and horror. "How do you know that?"

"Right now, he's sitting directly across from me, and I can see everything on his computer screen—it's pretty disgusting!" she replied with a grin. As if to emphasize the bizarre nature of our workplace, she pulled a tiny bottle of Jack Daniel's from her pocket and took a sip, offering it to me as well.

"Want some?" she asked, holding out the bottle.

"No, I'll pass. It's ten o'clock in the morning," I replied, shaking my head at the absurdity of the situation. "You're crazy!"

"I know," she said with a self-aware chuckle, "but check out these amazing Manolo Blahnik boots I got on sale!" She gestured toward her feet, showing off a pair of bright red designer boots that probably cost more than most people made in a week. Despite everything else that was wrong with the situation, I had to admit they were fabulous.

Seeking Answers

Frustrated by the news about Steve's involvement in the Los Angeles trip, I decided to go directly to Rudi for answers. I found him in his office and asked why Steve would be attending what should have been my presentation to Tyra and her team.

"I know he's an old fool," Rudi replied without looking up from whatever he was working on. "Harry has been friends with him for a long time and thinks highly of him, so there's nothing I can do about it."

"Why?" I asked, genuinely baffled by Harry's decision to trust someone with such a questionable track record.

"I don't know," Rudi said with characteristic bluntness. "Maybe he sucks Harry's dick." The crudeness of his response made me laugh despite my frustration with the situation.

Seeing my disappointment, Rudi offered a compromise that would at least give me some support during the trip. "I'm sorry, Katie," he said with genuine concern. "Take my youngest son with you. He needs to learn the business, and besides, you can handle a moron like Steve, so don't worry about it."

This suggestion actually appealed to me quite a bit. Rudi's younger son was only sixteen years old, but he had already demonstrated that he was intelligent, eager to learn, and willing to work hard—qualities that were notably absent in most of the other owners' children I had encountered in the industry.

"Okay," I agreed. "I could use an ally."

The Disastrous Journey Begins

The next day, I arrived at JFK airport with my carefully prepared design boards, and samples waiting for Alice to join our group for the flight to Los Angeles. When she finally shuffled into the terminal, it was immediately obvious that she was suffering from yet another hangover. She looked like she had vomited in the car during the ride to the airport, and the smell emanating from her ratty sweat shirt and sweat pants suggested that she had indeed been sick on herself.

"Hey," she said with a weak smile, pretending that nothing was wrong and that her appearance was perfectly normal for a business trip.

"Oh my God, we're going to miss our plane and you smell awful!" I yelled at her, making no attempt to hide my frustration and disgust.

Alice had become such an annoying burden, and I was absolutely sick of dealing with her unprofessional antics and poor decision-making. I had already made the decision to fire her immediately after this trip was completed, but I couldn't afford to let her behavior distract me from the important business at hand.

When we finally arrived at the W Hotel in Los Angeles, I discovered that Rudi's son had already checked in and was waiting for us in the lobby, along with Steve. While I was handling the check-in process for our group, I noticed that Alice was swaying slightly on her feet, clearly still feeling the effects of whatever substances she had consumed the night before.

I strongly recommended that she order room service, eat something substantial in her room, shower and get to bed early. We had an incredibly important meeting scheduled for nine o'clock the next morning with Tyra and her entire team, and I was determined to avoid an embarrassing incident caused by Alice's infamous hangovers.

After ensuring that Alice understood the importance of getting rest, I headed to the hotel gym to work off some of my nervous energy, then ordered room service for myself before finally settling down for the night. Despite my exhaustion from travel and stress, I found it difficult to fall asleep as I mentally rehearsed my presentation and worried about all the things that could go wrong during our meeting with one of the world's most successful supermodels and her professional team.

Dressing for Success

The following morning, I woke up early and took extra care in selecting my outfit for this career-defining meeting. I chose a black linen pantsuit by Dolce & Gabbana that featured crisp white piping details, paired with a fitted white Versace t-shirt that would look professional yet stylish. I completed the look with black Manolo Blahnik pumps that added the perfect amount of height and sophistication.

My hair was pulled back into a sleek ponytail that wouldn't distract from my presentation, and I wore a thick gold Versace choker that added a touch of glamour without being excessive. Looking at myself in the hotel mirror, I felt confident and stylish— exactly the image I needed to project when meeting with one of the fashion industry's most successful models.

The Crucial Meeting

I made my way down to the hotel lobby with my samples and portfolio to wait for the rest of our team, mentally preparing for what could be the most important presentation of my career. Rudi's son arrived first, and I was pleased to see that he looked professionally dressed and genuinely excited about the opportunity ahead of us. His enthusiasm was refreshing and reminded me why I enjoyed working with him.

Steve appeared next, and the contrast couldn't have been starker. This man in his late sixties looked disheveled and was sweating profusely despite the air-conditioned lobby. I could see the fear written all over his face—he was absolutely terrified about the prospect of presenting to Tyra Banks and her high-powered team.

Alice arrived last, as usual, and her appearance made me question my decision to bring her along. She was dressed in black fishnet stockings full of holes, a rumpled tulle skirt, combat boots and a rock-and-roll T-shirt that made her look like she had stumbled out of a Madonna concert from the 1980s. There was no time to address her inappropriate outfit, so I quickly ushered everyone into the car I had arranged to take us to the Four Seasons hotel.

When we arrived at our destination, we were escorted into an elegant conference room that spoke to the level of professionalism and success that Tyra had achieved in her career. I carefully arranged my design boards while Alice set up a clothing rack displaying our latest lingerie samples. The presentation setup was crucial—everything needed to look polished and professional.

Steve sat in the corner, muttering to himself while frantically reviewing his note cards. He appeared to be on the verge of a panic attack, which wasn't exactly confidence-inspiring for someone who was supposed to handle the financial aspects of our presentation. Rudi's son, in contrast, remained calm and professional, greeting everyone with genuine warmth while taking careful notes. I had assigned him the note-taking responsibility because I knew Alice would be needed to hold up the lingerie samples for Tyra and her team, while I spoke about the line. I didn't have the confidence that Alice could handle more than one task at a time.

Meeting a Superstar – Tyra Banks

The conference room doors opened, and an impressive entourage entered: Tyra herself, her manager, three assistants, two lawyers, Benny, his assistant, Tyra's mother, and several other members of her professional team. The energy in the room immediately shifted as these powerful individuals took their seats and prepared to evaluate my design boards, samples and our proposal.

Seeing Tyra Banks in person was genuinely awe-inspiring. She wasn't just stunningly beautiful—though she certainly was that—but she radiated intelligence and business acumen. With every interaction, my respect and admiration for her continued to grow. This wasn't just a pretty face who had gotten lucky; this was a sharp businesswoman who understood her brand and her market.

I stood up confidently and introduced myself and my team to the assembled group. Then I launched into my presentation, sharing my vision for "Tyra Banks lingerie and sleepwear" with passion and conviction. I had put countless hours into developing this concept, and I was genuinely proud of what we had created. As I spoke, I could see that both Tyra and her team were responding positively to the designs and the overall brand concept.

Tyra asked several challenging questions about production capabilities, manufacturing timelines, and quality control measures. I was prepared for these inquiries and handled them with confidence, drawing on my years of experience in the industry. However, when the conversation shifted to financial projections and pricing strategies, I knew I was entering territory where Steve was supposed to take the lead.

I looked at Steve, who was dressed in an ill-fitting blue suit that made him look even more uncomfortable than he already was. With what I hoped was an encouraging smile, I told the group that he would handle all financial questions and handed the presentation over to him.

What happened next was nothing short of a disaster. When Steve stood up to speak, he was visibly trembling, his face had turned bright red, and he stumbled over his prepared remarks like someone who had never given a presentation before in his life. His obvious terror was almost comical, especially given how he had bragged about his extensive experience in the garment center and his ability to handle high-pressure business situations.

His eyes kept darting to me, silently pleading for help, and I found myself torn between satisfaction at watching his arrogance crumble and concern that his incompetence would jeopardize everything I had worked to build. It wasn't until I realized that his failure could destroy my presentation that I decided I needed to intervene, even though financial planning wasn't my area of expertise.

Just as I was about to jump in and try to salvage the situation, Rudi's sixteen-year-old son stood up and smoothly took control of the financial discussion. He addressed every question with poise, intelligence, and remarkable insight for someone his age. I was genuinely impressed by his knowledge and grateful for his quick thinking, especially since Steve had just proven himself to be completely incompetent.

Watching this teenager outperform a supposed industry veteran was both inspiring and embarrassing. It confirmed my belief that Rudi's son had tremendous potential and would become an invaluable asset to his father's business as he continued to develop his skills.

The Product Review

After successfully navigating the business discussion, I invited Tyra and her team to examine the 120 lingerie samples that I had brought from our European sample shopping trip for trends and from our manufacturing facility in China. This was the moment of truth—would our designs meet the exacting standards of someone who had worked with Victoria's Secret and understood what made lingerie both beautiful and commercially viable?

Tyra's reaction exceeded my expectations. She was enthusiastic about nearly every piece in the collection, praising the design aesthetic, the quality of construction, and the attention to detail that had gone into each item. Out of 110 samples, she only had reservations about two pieces. "Yellow isn't really my color," she noted diplomatically about one particular set.

The overwhelmingly positive response gave me confidence that we had created something special—a collection that could succeed both commercially and creatively. This was more than just another celebrity endorsement deal; this was an opportunity to launch the first comprehensive lingerie line designed specifically for women of color, with one of the most successful African American models in history as the face of the brand.

The significance of this opportunity wasn't lost on me. Tyra was at the height of her fame as a Victoria's Secret Angel, and everything she wore or endorsed seemed to fly off store shelves. If we could capture even a fraction of her influence and translate it into sales, we would have a massive success on our hands.

As the meeting concluded, we shook hands all around, and I left feeling elated and optimistic about the future. This felt like the breakthrough I had been working toward throughout my entire career—a chance to work with a global superstar on a product line that could make a real impact in the fashion industry.

Celebrating and Planning

As we waited for our car to take us back to the hotel, I called

Deb to share the exciting news. Her reaction was everything I had hoped for—she screamed with excitement and immediately began talking about how we could work together to make this project a success.

During our conversation, I made her a promise that would prove to be significant: I told her that she could work with me on the Tyra Banks project, but only if she would quit drinking. This was my attempt to give her the motivation she needed to get sober and turn her life around, while also ensuring that such an important project wouldn't be derailed by her personal struggles.

In the twenty years, I had been working in fashion, I had never encountered anyone who possessed Deb's unique ability to transform ordinary clothing into extraordinary pieces with just a few strategic cuts and carefully chosen accessories. She had an innate understanding of style and fashion that was both intuitive and sophisticated. Her approach was laid-back yet determined, and she had complete confidence in her aesthetic choices.

I genuinely believed that I could help rescue Deb from her self-destructive patterns, and I had spent years trying to support her through various attempts at sobriety and relationship changes. What I didn't realize at the time was that our friendship would eventually end with a betrayal that would be as sudden and unexpected as our initial connection had been.

The rest of our group was ready to celebrate our success, and Alice suggested we go to In-N-Out Burger, the California chain that had become something of a cultural phenomenon. I was starving after the intense meeting and happy to join the celebration, though I had little interest in anything Alice had to contribute to the conversation.

Rudi's son had to decline the food portion of our outing

because the restaurant wasn't kosher, but he was happy to come along for the company. "I'll just come along for the ride," he said with his characteristic sweet smile.

As we sat around the table eating burgers, fries, and milkshakes, we talked excitedly about the potential for this deal to transform our company and our careers. The atmosphere was celebratory and optimistic.

"Oh shit, we forgot Steve," Rudi's son said suddenly, breaking into laughter.

"Oh well," I replied with a smile. "I'm sure he can find his way back to the hotel."

"Congratulations, Katie!" Rudi's son said warmly. "You really nailed it today."

Trying to be generous despite my frustration with Alice's behavior, I replied, "I had help from you and Alice."

"Yes, I did a great job," Alice said with characteristic smugness, taking credit she hadn't earned.

Rudi's son excused himself to call his father and report on how the meeting had gone. "I'm going to call my dad," he announced. "I'll call Harry too." He gave me a conspiratorial wink as he headed outside to make his calls.

The Aftermath and Betrayal

When we returned to the hotel that evening, we were met by Greg, the Public Relations Director for our company, who had arranged to join us for drinks. Greg was a smooth-talking individual who had mastered the art of exaggeration and self-promotion. He claimed to be well-connected with everyone important in the celebrity world of Los Angeles, though his actual influence was questionable at best.

What wasn't questionable was Greg's talent for spending other people's money. Harry adored him despite—or perhaps because of—Greg's ability to justify enormous expenses on the corporate American Express card. He would purchase designer clothing, expensive shoes, and luxury accessories, all under the guise of "work-related expenses." His argument was always that looking good was essential for his role in public relations, though ironically, no one ever saw him wearing anything other than sweatpants when he wasn't actively spending the company's money.

While Harry was completely taken in by Greg's charm and supposed connections, Rudi was far more skeptical of his value to the company and well aware of his tendency toward fiscal irresponsibility.

Since I had just successfully presented to one of the biggest stars in the world, Greg was suddenly very interested in being my new best friend. The potential for this deal to generate significant publicity and financial returns had captured his attention completely.

I maintained a polite facade and informed Greg that the Tyra deal would most likely move forward. His eyes lit up with dollar signs as he processed this information, and he immediately announced, "Champagne for all to celebrate Katie's success!"

What followed was typical Greg behavior—he invited his freeloading friends to join us at the Hotel bar and proceeded to buy drinks and food for everyone, charging it all to Harry's corporate credit card. The bill was going to be enormous, and none of it served any legitimate business purpose.

Rudi's son leaned over to me and whispered with a knowing smile, "There go all our profits!" We both burst out laughing at the accuracy of his observation.

"Yes, he's a jerk," I agreed as we watched Greg and Alice consume shot after shot of expensive vodka.

"Alice sure likes to party, huh?" Rudi's son observed with the wisdom of someone far beyond his sixteen years.

"Yes, way too much," I replied, making a mental note that her she was becoming more obvious and more problematic.

During our conversation, I noticed that Rudi's son was looking increasingly tired and pale. When I asked if he was feeling alright, his response revealed another layer of complexity to our trip.

"I forgot to pack my kosher food, so I'm really hungry," he said faintly.

"You haven't eaten anything since we arrived?" I asked with growing concern for his wellbeing.

"No, just some fruit." he replied, looking genuinely unwell.

The realization that this young man had been going without food while the rest of us celebrated hit me hard. I immediately got up and hurried into the hotel dining room, where I approached the manager and urgently requested fresh whole fruits for Rudi's son. I also asked him to arrange for kosher food to be delivered to our location as quickly as possible.

When I returned to our table, I discovered that Greg had been pushing alcohol on the hungry teenager, insisting that he drink a shot of liquor. "He's sixteen!" I yelled at Greg. "Get away from him!" But it was too late—Rudi's son had already consumed the alcohol before I could stop him.

The combination of alcohol and an empty stomach could have been dangerous, but fortunately the fruit arrived quickly and I was able to get him to eat something before the liquor had too strong an effect. When the kosher meal was finally delivered, he ate it with the enthusiasm of someone who hadn't had a proper meal in days.

Given the early flight time and his need for rest, I strongly advised Rudi's son to go to bed. He willingly left the increasingly rowdy bar scene, and I felt relieved that Greg would no longer be able to influence him negatively. The last words Rudi had spoken to me before this trip were burned into my memory: "You'd better take care of my son, or I will kill you!"

By this point in the evening, Alice had progressed from drinking heavily to sitting in the lap of one of Greg's friends, clearly intoxicated beyond any reasonable limit. I knew that whatever I said to her at this point would be ignored, so I decided to cut my losses and head to bed.

Steve eventually joined the party, but I was too exhausted from the day's events to deal with any more drama. I left the group to continue their celebration and went to my room to get some rest before our early morning flight.

At six o'clock the next morning, Rudi's son, Steve, Greg, and I boarded our plane back to New York. Alice was nowhere to be found, and frankly, I was beyond caring about her whereabouts or her ability to get home.

The Return and the Power Play

When we arrived back in New York City, I quickly dropped my bags off at my apartment, paid my dog sitter, spent a few precious minutes with my beloved pug, then jumped into a cab to head directly to the office. I was eager to share our success with Rudi and Harry and begin planning the next steps for what could become a transformative business partnership.

Deb was waiting in the lobby of our office building when I arrived, and her enthusiastic greeting resulted in both of us tumbling to the floor in our excitement. "Harry wants to see you and Steve," she informed me with a sigh that suggested she knew something unpleasant was about to happen.

Despite her warning tone, I felt a surge of excitement as I prepared to share the details of our successful presentation. I was already envisioning my future role in spearheading this brand and imagining the promising possibilities that a partnership with Tyra's brand could bring to both the company and my own career. With her widespread appeal and global recognition, I was confident that everyone would be drawn to the new line we were proposing.

However, my optimism was about to receive a crushing blow. As soon as the elevator doors opened on our floor, I could hear Harry screaming for Steve and me to come into his office immediately. His tone suggested that this wasn't going to be the congratulatory meeting I had anticipated.

"So, congratulations!" Harry yelled as he stood up and towered over me, but his attention was focused entirely on Steve. "Steve, you did a great job," he said with a smirk that made my stomach sink.

I stared at him in complete disbelief, unable to process what I was hearing.

"Steve told me he nailed the meeting and got the deal closed," Harry continued, his smugness becoming more apparent with each word.

"Oh really!" I responded, my voice rising with indignation. "Are you serious, Steve?"

"What's your problem?" Harry yelled at me, as if I was the one behaving unreasonably.

Before I could formulate a response, Rudi's son entered the office with his brother and Rudi, providing crucial backup for my version of events. "Her problem is that she nailed the meeting because Steve freaked out and acted like a deaf mute!" the young man interjected with the kind of honesty that only a sixteen-year-old could deliver.

"So, what?" Harry replied dismissively. "The deal is moving forward. I just got a call from Tyra's lawyer confirming everything."

Rudi, clearly fed up with his partner's behavior, pushed past his son and me to confront Harry directly. Despite the significant height difference between them, Rudi's moral authority was unmistakable. "Katie did all of this!" he declared passionately. "She designed the entire line, created beautiful samples, and put this potential hundred-million-dollar deal together for us!"

Harry's response revealed his true character. Looking down at Rudi, he yelled, "Everyone get the hell out of my office now, except Steve!" Then he slammed the door in our faces while Steve remained inside, smirking at me with satisfaction.

The Breaking Point

Standing in the hallway, rejected and humiliated after bringing the company its biggest opportunity ever, I watched Rudi struggle with his own sense of betrayal and frustration.

"I hate that bastard," he said with genuine pain in his voice. "And to think he's been my partner for ten miserable years!" The depth of his regret about their business relationship was evident in every word.

Rudi then gathered his sons and retreated to his own office, leaving me standing with Deb, who was trying to process what she had just witnessed. She grabbed my arm and, laughing with the kind of hysteria that comes from witnessing something truly absurd, said, "You've got to take this call."

"Okay, now what?" I said, grabbing the phone from her.

On the other end, I could hear Alice's voice, whining that she had missed her flight, lost her airline ticket, and had no way to get home from Los Angeles. Without hesitation, I delivered the news she deserved to hear: "You're fired," I told her and hung up the phone.

"Yippee!" Deb laughed with genuine joy. "Finally, that idiot is gone."

A few minutes later, my conscience got the better of me, and I asked Deb to call Alice back and ensure she could get on a plane home. Despite her unprofessional behavior and terrible attitude, I didn't want to be responsible for stranding her across the country.

A New Complication

Now I faced the challenge of explaining the situation to Lisa, my sales manager, who would be expected to handle the sales and marketing aspects of Tyra's upcoming lingerie launch. I had brought Lisa onto the team on a trial basis after knowing her briefly from previous industry connections. At the time, she wasn't working, and I felt sympathetic toward anyone facing unemployment in our challenging industry.

What I quickly discovered was that Lisa, despite being a decade older than me, was possibly the most incompetent salesperson I had ever encountered. Over the years, she had convinced numerous companies to hire her by presenting herself as experienced and capable, always negotiating two-year contracts that guaranteed substantial severance payments when her lack of ability became apparent.

Her strategy was brilliantly cynical: she would get hired, perform poorly, get fired, and then live off the mandatory severance payments for a year or two before repeating the cycle with another unsuspecting company.

I had begun to genuinely dislike her as I recognized her manipulative patterns. The fashion industry seemed to attract people who were willing to throw anyone under the bus to protect their own interests, and Lisa was a master of this particular skill.

I regretted hiring her and hoped that Harry would soon recognize her incompetence and terminate her employment. Given Harry's generally poor judgment about people, I wasn't optimistic about this outcome.

The Continued Manipulation

When I informed Lisa about our success with the Tyra Banks deal, her response revealed her true character and her alignment with the forces working against me.

"I heard Steve got the deal," she said with a malicious smile that told me everything I needed to know about where her loyalties lay.

Deb, never one to hold back her opinions, immediately jumped to my defense. "Fuck you, Lisa!" she said with characteristic bluntness. "You're an old bag. You know Katie got this deal and you're just jealous."

"I know nothing except what Steve told me," Lisa replied with smug satisfaction. "He said he was in charge of the new division for Tyra and that I would be selling the line."

Deb's response was both crude and accurate: "Ha! You couldn't sell crack to addicts!"

Rather than engage in a futile argument with someone who had clearly chosen her side, I decided to walk away before saying something that Lisa could use against me later.

The Ugly Truth Emerges

The meeting that would determine the fate of the Tyra Banks

deal was scheduled for the following Monday morning. Tyra herself was flying to New York to sign what we hoped would be the largest licensing agreement in garment center history. The stakes couldn't have been higher, and I was determined to ensure that everything went perfectly.

I arrived at the office early that morning, having carefully chosen to wear my black Chanel tweed double-breasted suit—an outfit that projected both professionalism and success. I had even brought an umbrella, sensing that a storm might be approaching, though I couldn't have predicted how accurate that intuition would prove to be.

After ensuring that all the presentation materials were properly arranged in the conference room, I waited anxiously for the call informing me that Tyra and her team had arrived. When the moment finally came, I took a quick puff of Deb's cigarette for courage, gave her a thumb up, and walked into the conference room with a confident smile.

The room was packed with more than twenty people: Larry and his son, Rudi and both of his sons, Steve, Lisa, Tyra and her extensive entourage of lawyers, managers, and agents, plus our own legal team. The energy in the room was electric with anticipation.

I delivered what I considered to be an excellent final presentation, covering all the key points we had discussed in Los Angeles and addressing any remaining questions about the proposed partnership. Harry fidgeted nervously throughout my presentation, and when I finished, he quickly moved to the next agenda item: "Now, let's review the licensing agreement."

What happened next revealed the true depth of the betrayal I was facing. Tyra's team had drafted the agreement the previous week and forwarded it to our lawyers for review. As a woman in the company, I had been deliberately excluded from all financial discussions and hadn't been allowed to see the contract terms.

While reviewing the document, Tyra looked directly at Rudi and Harry and asked a question that changed everything: "Where is the percentage for Katie that we included in the agreement?"

Her question surprised me—I had no idea that she and her team had specifically negotiated to give me a small percentage of the brand's profits in recognition of my creative contributions and hard work. Rudi frantically flipped through the pages, clearly confused, and asked Harry, "Where is it? Katie's percentage was in the agreement yesterday!"

When Rudi turned to their lawyer for an explanation, the man simply put his head down and refused to answer.

Harry's response revealed his true character and the depth of his prejudice: "I took it out of the agreement," he said with a cold smirk.

"Can I see you outside?" Rudi asked, his voice tight with controlled anger.

As they left the conference room, the rest of us sat in stunned silence, but not for long. Harry's voice carried clearly through the walls as he yelled his ugly truth for everyone to hear: "I will never give a percentage to a woman!"

Even Steve and Lisa looked shocked by the blatancy of Harry's sexism, though their surprise was probably more about his lack of discretion than his actual beliefs.

What followed was a chaotic physical confrontation between the two partners, complete with loud crashes, shouting, and what appeared to be attempts at violence. Their respective sons jumped up to defend their fathers, creating a scene that would have been comical if it weren't so professionally devastating.

Tyra's team watched this display with a combination of shock and disgust, clearly unable to believe they were witnessing such unprofessional behavior from people they were considering as business partners.

I was deeply moved by the fact that Tyra had valued my work enough to specifically negotiate for me to receive a percentage of the brand's profits. In my entire professional career, no one had ever offered me that kind of recognition or financial participation in a project I had helped create.

The Final Confrontation

When Harry finally returned to the conference room—alone, since Rudi had apparently walked out in disgust—he sat down and faced Tyra's team as if nothing unusual had happened. "Now, where were we?" he asked with casual arrogance.

Tyra's lawyer immediately demanded to know where my percentage had gone and why it had been removed from the agreement.

Harry's response was to pound his fist on the conference room table and declare in a voice that everyone could hear: "There is no percentage for her and there never will be!"

The silence that followed felt eternal as Tyra's team processed what they had just witnessed. After a brief consultation among themselves, Tyra turned to her lawyers and made a statement that would haunt me for the rest of my career: "I don't want to work with a company that doesn't support women."

With that declaration, she stood up and walked out of the conference room, followed by her entire professional team. The hundred-million-dollar deal that I had worked so hard to create had just evaporated because of one man's sexism and greed.

Steve and Lisa remained in their seats as Harry turned to his attorney and made another statement that revealed the depth of his prejudice: "I never want any 'women's' licenses brought to me again!"

The Moment of Truth

I walked out into the hallway with tears streaming down my face, watching as Tyra and her team waited for the elevator. Deb stood beside me in complete shock, trying to process what we had just witnessed. Outside, thunder was rolling and rain was beginning to fall heavily, as if the weather was reflecting the chaos that had just destroyed months of hard work.

As Tyra's team prepared to board the elevator, Tyra held the door open and looked directly at me. "Coming?" she asked with genuine concern in her voice.

I looked at her with confusion, not immediately understanding what she was offering.

"Katie, you cannot work for that awful man!" she said firmly. "You are better than this!"

"I know," I replied through my tears.

"Well, leave with us," she said, making it clear that this was a real invitation, not just a polite gesture.

"I just need to grab my purse and my design boards," I said, suddenly realizing that she was offering me a way out of an impossible situation.

"Okay, I will wait for you downstairs in my car," she replied with a supportive smile.

As I walked back to collect my belongings, I found Alice, Lisa, and Steve huddled in a corner, clearly trying to figure out how this disaster would affect their own positions. When Steve called out to ask where I was going, I didn't bother to respond.

At the elevator, I was surprised to find Deb standing there with her coat on, clearly prepared to leave with me.

"What are you doing?" I asked, touched by her gesture but concerned about the consequences for her future.

"I'm coming with you," she replied with a determined grin.

"But you'll be fired," I protested.

"Well, so will you!" she laughed, pointing out the obvious reality of our situation.

As we got into the elevator together, I reflected on the magnitude of what had just happened. "I cannot believe we just lost a hundred-million-dollar deal that I brought to this company, all because Harry wouldn't give me a small percentage just because I'm a woman!"

Deb put the situation in perspective with her characteristic bluntness: "Look, you did an amazing job and you will do it again, but this time I'll be there to help you! And besides, Harry is a sexist bastard and Rudi is a coward for not standing up for you!"

A New Beginning

When we reached street level, I grabbed Deb's hand and pulled her into Tyra's waiting car. The gesture felt symbolic—we were literally and figuratively leaving behind a toxic work environment to pursue something better.

"I'm proud of you," Tyra said as we settled into the car. "Now, who's this?" she asked, smiling warmly at Deb.

"My new partner," I announced with growing confidence. "We are going to start our own lingerie company!"

"Good for you," Tyra replied enthusiastically. "Now, let's get lunch and talk about this new company. I'm starving."

As we drove away from Seventh Avenue, the sun broke through the storm clouds, and I felt a wave of optimism wash over me.

Looking up at the clearing sky, I knew that the future was going to be bright after all. Deb's loyalty during this difficult time was unwavering, and I was grateful to have her support as we faced this new challenge together.

Reflection and Resolution

This chapter represents a pivotal moment in my career and serves as a powerful reminder of both my capabilities as a professional woman and the deep-rooted sexism that continues to plague the fashion industry like a cancer. The experience of successfully creating a potentially transformative business partnership only to watch it destroyed by one man's prejudice was both heartbreaking and illuminating.

Despite my success in capturing Tyra's interest and securing her team's enthusiasm for the opportunity, I faced significant challenges in finding another company willing to support a brand fronted by a woman of color. Many garment center companies, at the time, were reluctant to invest in what they perceived as a risky demographic, a woman of color.

The loss of this opportunity back then, represented not just a personal setback, but a broader tragedy for the industry and for consumers who would have benefited from innovative, inclusive products. Today, such a collaboration would likely become a multi-million-dollar success story, easily embraced by consumers hungry for authentic representation in fashion as proven by the success of Rihanna's lingerie brand, Savage X Fenty.

Even after all these years, I still have every one of the lingerie design boards from my presentation with Tyra Banks. They serve as a reminder of what could have been, but also as evidence of the quality of work I was capable of producing. I believed then, and still believe now, that I had the skills and deserved the support that Tyra and Benny so generously offered me.

Unfortunately, in the garment center of that era, being a woman held little value in the eyes of men like Harry, and that reality was a difficult pill to swallow. The experience taught me valuable lessons about standing up for my principles, even when the cost was significant, and about the importance of surrounding myself with people who shared my values and respected my contributions.

While the immediate aftermath of that deal collapsing was financially challenging and emotionally difficult, it ultimately led to new opportunities and partnerships that were about to challenge me to my core. Sometimes the most important victories come not from the deals we close, but from the principles we refuse to compromise.

CHAPTER 11:
Jessica Simpson and Mariah Carey

A New Beginning After the Tyra Banks Disaster

The fashion world moves quickly, and bad news travels even faster. When word spread about losing the licensing deal with Tyra Banks, the fallout was immediate and dramatic. Harry and Rudi, who had been business partners for years despite their constant bickering, finally reached their breaking point and decided to dissolve their partnership. The toxic atmosphere that had built up around the failed deal became the catalyst for a complete company restructuring.

In the aftermath, heads rolled. Steve, the incompetent business manager who had frozen during our presentation with Tyra, was fired. Alice, my unreliable assistant who showed up hungover more often than sober, quit. Most satisfying of all, Lisa—the vindictive saleswoman who had sabotaged me at every turn—found herself without a job. While the company was cleaning house, Deb and I suddenly found ourselves free agents in an uncertain market.

Standing in my apartment, surrounded by boxes of design boards and fabric samples, I realized this might actually be a blessing in disguise. Deb and I had talked about striking out on our own, and now circumstances were forcing our hand. We needed to find work quickly—bills don't stop coming just because your career implodes—but we also needed to position ourselves for something bigger.

I spent the weekend organizing my portfolio, carefully selecting the best designs from my years in the garment center. Each piece told a story of late nights, difficult clients, and creative breakthroughs. If we were going to pitch myself to new companies, I needed to showcase not just my talent, but my versatility and professionalism.

The Staten Island Opportunity

Within a week of our unemployment, I discovered a promising lead in an unlikely place. A small catalog company in Staten Island, New York, was looking for designers to create a fresh sleepwear line on a consulting basis. The position offered good pay and complete creative control—exactly what Deb and I needed to rebuild our reputations and bank accounts.

There was just one catch: the daily commute would require a thirty-minute ferry ride from Manhattan to Staten Island. For New Yorkers accustomed to subway trains and taxi cabs, the idea of commuting by boat seemed almost foreign.

"Not a chance," Deb protested when I explained the situation. "I refuse to be seasick every single day. Do you know what salt air does to my hair?"

I understood her reluctance, but we were running out of options. "Look," I pleaded, "the pay is excellent and we desperately need it. I'm nearly forty years old, and jobs in this industry are becoming increasingly limited. We can't afford to be picky right now."

After considerable back-and-forth discussion, Deb finally agreed to give it a try. She made me promise that if the seasickness became unbearable, we would find another solution. The next morning, we prepared for our first day at what we hoped would be a fresh start in our careers.

The Daily Commute and First Impressions

That first summer day was brutally hot and humid—the kind of New York weather that makes you feel like you're swimming through the air. As we made our way to the ferry terminal, the heat rose in waves from the concrete sidewalks, and my carefully chosen outfit began to wilt before we even reached the dock.

I had selected a pink floral slip dress paired with comfortable espadrilles, trying to strike a balance between professional and practical. A pink cashmere sweater was tied around my shoulders in case the office air conditioning was too cold. Fashion industry offices were notorious for being kept at arctic temperatures, and I had learned to always come prepared.

Deb, as usual, looked effortlessly stunning. She wore a flowing turquoise-and-white tie-dye silk caftan over white shorts, with tan leather sandals that probably cost more than our first paycheck. Her golden tan made the bright colors pop, and she moved with the kind of confidence that turned heads wherever she went.

The ferry ride became an immediate source of conflict between us. "Oh my God!" I yelled over the boat's engine noise. "I think I'm going to be sick."

Deb burst into delighted laughter, thoroughly enjoying the irony of the situation. "I love this!" she shouted back. "This is absolutely perfect! I thought I'd be the one getting seasick, but look at you—you're turning green!"

By the time we reached the Staten Island side of the New York harbor, I felt queasy and already dreaded the thought of making this journey twice a day, five days a week for the next few months. Deb, meanwhile, seemed energized by the boat ride and excited to start our new adventure. However, the twenty-minute walk from the pier to the office in the blazing sun quickly dampened both our spirits.

"Just suck it up," Deb said with characteristic bluntness. "Remember, this whole Staten Island thing was your brilliant idea."

"Think of it as three months of consulting money," I replied, trying to stay positive. "We can treat it like an extended summer job."

"More like three months in purgatory," she muttered, but I could tell she was already planning how to make the best of the situation.

Workplace Dynamics and Red Flags

Our introduction to the new workplace immediately revealed potential problems. The moment we walked into the office and met our new boss—the vice president of apparel—Deb began acting out in ways that made me cringe.

"This place is a dump," she whispered, though her voice carried loudly enough for everyone in the vicinity to hear her unflattering assessment.

I quickly realized that managing Deb's mercurial personality was going to be a full-time job in addition to my actual work responsibilities. When Deb wasn't interested in something or felt uncomfortable, she had the attention span of a bored child and the impulse control to match. I would need to keep her entertained and engaged, or risk having her sabotage our professional relationships.

As the weeks progressed, a clear pattern emerged. I genuinely enjoyed the work and found satisfaction in designing sleepwear that was both comfortable and stylish. The small company environment allowed for more creative freedom than I had experienced in years, and I began to feel optimistic about our future prospects.

Deb, however, rarely participated in the day-to-day work and frequently failed to show up altogether. By the end of two months, her attendance had dropped to almost zero, leaving me to scramble with excuses for her absence while trying to maintain the quality of our output.

The situation came to a head when I finally managed to reach Deb's mother, who reluctantly admitted that her daughter was in the middle of an extended drinking binge. While I felt frustrated and betrayed, I couldn't risk losing the job by making waves about my missing partner. I carried on alone, fabricating increasingly creative explanations for Deb's absence while producing enough work for two people.

My boss seemed unconcerned about Deb's disappearance. She had never warmed to Deb's attitude and clearly preferred working with me alone. This should have been a relief, but I couldn't shake the feeling that I was enabling Deb's self-destructive behavior by covering for her.

The Dramatic Exit

On the final day at the Staten Island company, I was scheduled to present my completed sleepwear collection to the president and board of directors. This was my big moment—the chance to showcase months of hard work and potentially secure ongoing contracts with the company.

To my shock and horror, Deb made a grand entrance just as I was preparing for the presentation. She looked absolutely stunning in a designer mini dress and thigh-high gladiator sandals, topped off with a straw fedora and oversized sunglasses. She moved with the confidence of a runway model, completely unbothered by the fact that she had been essentially AWOL for weeks.

As I arranged my design boards and prepared my presentation materials, Deb settled into a conference room chair and began spinning around like a child on a playground. "Wheeeee!" she called out loudly, clearly enjoying herself while I tried to maintain my professional composure.

"Deb, please knock it off," I hissed, aware that company executives would be arriving any minute.

"Oh, screw you!" she replied cheerfully. "Who cares what these people think? It's our last day anyway." I was too angry to engage with her.

When the executive team filed into the conference room, their attention immediately focused on the bizarre spectacle of my fashionably dressed but clearly unhinged business partner. I felt my cheeks burn with embarrassment as I tried to redirect their attention to the work I had produced.

Despite the distraction of Deb's presence, my presentation went very well. The sleepwear designs were well-received, and the executives seemed genuinely pleased with the quality and creativity of the collection. When I finished, they applauded enthusiastically.

Marvin, the company CEO, approached me with a warm handshake and a broad smile. "Excellent work, Katie!" he exclaimed. "We would love to have you continue working with us on a more permanent basis." The offer was clear and appealing—they wanted me to stay, without my unpredictable partner.

At this moment of professional triumph, Deb chose to make her grand finale. She leaped from her chair and addressed the room full of executives in a voice that could probably be heard three floors down.

"You know what? Fuck all of you people!" she announced with dramatic flair. "This place is a complete shithole, and I wouldn't be caught dead working here with you losers anyway!"

The silence that followed was deafening. Every person in the room sat frozen, unsure how to respond to this unprecedented outburst. I stood trembling with a mixture of humiliation and rage, watching months of professional reputation building crumble in real time.

Marvin recovered first, his face darkening with anger. "Are you quite finished with your little tantrum?" he asked coldly.

"Oh yes," Deb replied with satisfaction. "I'm completely done here."

"Good. Then get the hell out of my company right now," He commanded, his voice carrying the authority of someone unaccustomed to being disrespected in his own boardroom.

With theatrical grace, Deb smoothed down her designer dress, tipped her fedora in a mock salute, and sauntered toward the exit. "See you later, losers!" she called over her shoulder as she disappeared through the doorway, loudly popping her gum.

I remained standing in the conference room, offering profuse apologies to everyone present while knowing that any chance of continuing with the company had just evaporated. No matter how much they liked my work, no executive team would risk bringing back the partner of someone who had just publicly humiliated them.

The Ferry Ride Home and Twisted Logic

The walk back to the ferry terminal felt like a death march. I was mortified, professionally wounded, and financially stressed about my uncertain future. Deb, meanwhile, seemed to be in the best mood I had seen from her in months.

I found her at the pier, sitting on a bench like a woman without a care in the world. She was drinking a beer, smoking a cigarette, and snacking on potato chips, completely unbothered by the professional bridge she had just burned to the ground.

"You should thank me," she said as she jumped up to give me a hug.

"Thank you?" I shouted, finally losing my temper. "Are you completely insane? Those were genuinely nice people, and you just destroyed any chance I had of working with them!"

"So, what if they were nice?" she replied with a shrug. "I did you a huge favor. That place was completely beneath your talents, and deep down, you know it."

During the ferry ride back to Manhattan, I sat in sullen silence while Deb entertained herself by tossing potato chips at me. The other passengers gave us a wide berth, clearly wanting no part of whatever drama was unfolding between us.

When we docked in Manhattan, I hailed a taxi and Deb climbed in beside me. "Come on, let's get some Bloody Mary's and celebrate our freedom," she suggested with her characteristic ability to reframe disaster as opportunity.

Despite my anger and frustration, I found myself unable to stay mad at this damaged genius for very long. The truth was, she was probably right about the job not being a good long-term fit for my career aspirations. Her methods were completely unacceptable, but her instincts about my professional needs were usually accurate.

"Fine," I said, finally laughing despite myself. "But you're buying the drinks."

"No problem at all!" she replied with a grin. "Life is good, Katie. Our rent is paid, we're alive and healthy, we're fabulous and talented. We'll find something better that actually deserves our skills."

Her optimism was infectious, even when it came wrapped in chaos and unprofessional behavior. "Deb, you're going to be the death of me someday," I said with a mixture of affection and exasperation.

"I know," she winked. "But I promise to throw you an absolutely spectacular funeral in Nantucket!"

Finding the Jessica Simpson Connection

The next morning, nursing a mild hangover from our impromptu celebration, I decided to take a more proactive approach to our job search. I placed a carefully worded advertisement in Women's Wear Daily, the fashion industry's premier trade publication.

Within days, my phone began ringing with potential opportunities. The most intriguing call came from a man named Carl, who introduced himself as a current licensee for Jessica Simpson's swimwear line. He was looking to expand into lingerie and needed an experienced designer to make it happen.

The mention of Jessica Simpson's name immediately got my attention. Love her or hate her, she was one of the biggest pop culture figures of the moment, and her brand carried significant commercial potential. This could be exactly the kind of high-profile opportunity that would reestablish our credibility in the industry.

Carl's office was located in an impressive Manhattan building that spoke to the success of his existing business ventures. When Deb and I arrived for our initial meeting, I brought along my best design boards and fabric samples, hoping to demonstrate our range and capabilities.

Carl himself was an imposing figure—nearly six and a half feet tall, probably in his early sixties, with the kind of commanding presence that comes from decades of successful business dealings. Unfortunately, he was also somewhat crude and obviously wealthy in the way that some successful "garmentos" displayed their prosperity like a peacock shows its feathers.

His physical appearance was less than appealing: an oversized, bulbous nose dominated his face, and his considerable weight was poorly concealed by expensive but ill-fitting clothing. Despite these shortcomings, the prospect of working with Jessica Simpson's brand was too exciting to pass up.

"You're absolutely breathtaking," said to Deb, his eyes lingering appreciatively on her long, tanned legs. His flirtation was neither subtle nor professional.

"I know," Deb replied with characteristic directness, immediately falling into her familiar pattern of using her looks to advance our business interests.

While I found Carl's manners unseemly, I had heard positive things about Vince, the brand licensor, who controlled Jessica Simpson's overall brand strategy. Vince was known throughout the industry as a class act—someone who had built a multi-million-dollar empire in the shoe business through hard work and ethical practices.

The backstory of Jessica's brand was already the stuff of industry legend. Before partnering with Vince, Jessica had reportedly been involved in an unfavorable licensing deal with another manufacturer that was taking advantage of her inexperience in business matters. Vince had stepped in, rescued her from that situation, and taken over her licensing agreements with the intention of building a legitimate, long-term brand rather than just exploiting her celebrity status for quick profits.

The contrast between Carl and Vince was stark. Carl was clearly an old-school "garmento"—crude, opportunistic, and primarily interested in short-term gains. Based on what I had heard about him,

Vince represented a more sophisticated approach to celebrity licensing, focusing on quality products and sustainable business relationships.

The Deal and Deb's Negotiations

"So, here's what I need from you ladies," Carl explained, leaning back in his executive chair. "I want you to create several lingerie design boards for Jessica's brand and prepare a comprehensive presentation. If you can be ready by next week, I'll arrange a meeting with Vince and his team."

This was exactly the kind of opportunity we had been hoping for. A chance to design for a major celebrity, work with a respected industry leader like Vince, and potentially establish ourselves as go-to designers for high-profile licensing deals.

Deb leaned forward with her most dazzling smile. "I'm going to need at least two weeks to create proper design boards for someone of Jessica's stature," she said with complete confidence.

Carl looked annoyed at the timeline, but I could see that Deb's charm was working on him despite his business instincts.

"Tell you what," he said, his eyes never leaving Deb's face. "If you'll have drinks with me this week, I'll give you the two weeks you're asking for."

I felt like a third wheel watching this negotiation unfold, but I had learned to appreciate Deb's ability to use her natural advantages in business situations. As long as she could maintain some professional boundaries while securing better terms for our work, I was willing to let her take the lead.

After we concluded our meeting with Carl, Deb gave him a playful wink and blew him a kiss as the elevator doors closed between us. Once we were alone, she immediately stuck her finger in her mouth and made a gagging gesture.

"Oh my God, he's absolutely obnoxious," she said with distain.

"Nice work though," I replied with admiration. "You just got us a high-profile job and managed to negotiate better terms in the process."

"What can I say? I'm a rock star at this stuff," she replied with justified pride. "How about we celebrate with wine and cheese at Luca's downtown?"

I agreed to join her for a drink, though I had learned to limit my exposure to Deb's evening activities. Her drinking could escalate quickly, and I had witnessed too many nights where her behavior became increasingly unpredictable and potentially dangerous.

As I hailed a taxi to leave her at the restaurant, I called back one final instruction. "Please be at my apartment first thing tomorrow morning. We have serious work to do if we're going to meet Carl's timeline."

I watched her approach an older gentleman at the bar, completely confident in her ability to charm yet another unsuspecting victim. While I sometimes worried about her safety, I also had to admire her fearless approach to life.

Deb's Complex Background and Our Partnership

Over the years I had known Deb, I had noticed unexplained bruises on her arms and face that she refused to discuss. Whenever I asked about them, she would shut down completely or change the subject. I suspected her black-outs were responsible, but she maintained strict silence about their relationship dynamics.

Despite concerns from mutual friends about her increasingly erratic behavior, I couldn't bring myself to cut ties with Deb completely. She had an invaluable ability to push me toward bigger and better opportunities, and her feedback on my work was always brutally honest—even when it stung.

For example, after I had spent two hours perfecting a nightgown design that I thought was particularly clever, Deb took one look at it and shook her head dismissively.

"That design isn't very good at all," she said matter-of-factly.

"What do you mean it's not good?" I demanded, frustrated by her blunt criticism. "I worked on that for hours."

"Because my grandmother wouldn't be caught dead wearing something that frumpy, and she's basically an old cow," Deb laughed. "Your design makes beautiful women look like they're going to bed in a potato sack."

Before I could respond defensively, she had grabbed a pencil and sketched out a fresh version of my design. In less than five minutes, she had transformed my admittedly pedestrian nightgown into something that looked like it belonged in the pages of Bergdorf Goodman catalog.

"You're absolutely brilliant," I said, genuinely impressed by her ability to see possibilities I had missed.

"Yes, I am," she replied without false modesty. "That's exactly why you pay me the big bucks."

These moments of creative collaboration made all of Deb's personal struggles and professional unpredictability worthwhile. She had an innate understanding of what made clothing both beautiful and commercially viable—a combination that was surprisingly rare in the fashion industry.

Her background helped explain both her talents and her demons. Money meant very little to Deb because she had grown up with nothing. Her childhood had been marked by neglect and abandonment issues that shaped her adult relationships in profound ways.

Deb told me that her mother had left her with an alcoholic father in Europe while she pursued an architectural career in the United States. This abandonment haunted both mother and daughter for decades afterward. When Deb finally came to America in her twenties, her now wealthy, successful mother tried to compensate for years of guilt by showering her with expensive gifts, luxury apartments, and unlimited financial support.

However, the emotional wounds from childhood were too deep to heal with material possessions. Despite her mother's genuine love and remorse, she had essentially lost control over her daughter's life. Deb manipulated both her mother's feelings and her finances, using guilt as a weapon whenever she needed money or wanted to avoid consequences for her actions.

At sixteen, Deb had run away to Los Angeles, where she lived for several years under circumstances she refused to discuss. Whenever I tried to ask about that period of her life, she would become visibly distressed and change the subject immediately. I learned to respect those boundaries and focus on our present work rather than digging into her painful personal history.

The Jessica Simpson Project Begins

The two weeks Carl had given us flew by in a blur of creative activity. Deb and I worked closely together to develop design boards that would showcase our vision for Jessica Simpson's lingerie line, and the collaboration reminded me why our partnership could be so productive when circumstances aligned properly.

Our presentation to Vince and his team exceeded all expectations. The designs were sophisticated, commercially viable, and perfectly suited to Jessica's brand image. More importantly, Vince and his executives were impressed enough to offer us the opportunity to meet with Jessica herself and her team in Los Angeles.

This was the break we had been working toward—a chance to present our ideas directly to one of the biggest pop stars in the world and potentially launch a major new product line. The financial implications were enormous, but the career opportunities were even more significant.

Deb was extremely nervous about the Los Angeles trip and initially tried to back out completely. Her reluctance seemed unusual given her typically adventurous nature, but I insisted that I needed her support and expertise for such an important meeting. After considerable persuasion, she reluctantly agreed to accompany me to California.

We booked a red-eye flight to Los Angeles, bringing with us an extensive collection of lingerie samples and design concepts. The presentation materials represented months of work and our best thinking about how to translate Jessica's public persona into successful commercial products.

The Los Angeles Meeting and Strange Encounters

Upon arriving at the Los Angeles hotel for our presentation to Jessica and her team, I excused myself to use the restroom and immediately encountered something that should have served as a warning about the challenges ahead. As I exited the bathroom stall, I discovered a petite brunette woman hunched over the sink, obviously snorting what appeared to be cocaine.

"Hey, want a hit?" she asked casually, as if she were offering me a piece of gum.

"No thank you," I replied firmly, trying to avoid direct eye contact while processing this unexpected encounter.

I chose not to mention this incident to Deb, knowing that her own struggles with substance abuse might lead her to join this stranger rather than focus on our professional responsibilities. However, I couldn't help but notice that Deb had been acting strangely ever since we landed in Los Angeles, constantly looking over her shoulder as if she expected to encounter someone from her mysterious past.

The presentation with Jessica Simpson and her team proved to be both enlightening and frustrating. Jessica lounged casually on a couch surrounded by her entourage, while her mother maintained a more professional demeanor nearby. As we displayed our carefully crafted designs, Jessica's friends couldn't resist making sarcastic comments that undermined the serious nature of our presentation.

"Wow, I could totally get some action wearing that lingerie set!" one remarked loudly, causing everyone to burst into inappropriate laughter.

When we showed Jessica a particularly elegant bra design, she added, "That would be ripped off me in about five minutes!" Again, her entourage responded with juvenile giggling that made it difficult to maintain the professional atmosphere we had hoped to establish.

Based on Jessica's friend's constant interruptions and disrespectful comments made, I felt that Jessica had little genuine interest in the creative process or the commercial potential of the lingerie line. I could see Deb's anger building throughout the presentation, and I rushed through the remaining designs to avoid a potential confrontation.

Despite Jessica's entourages behavior, her mother expressed appreciation for our work and assured us that Jessica was genuinely enthusiastic about the designs. She promised to communicate with Vince about moving forward with the project. I smiled and thanked her professionally, but privately I couldn't wait to get out of Los Angeles before Deb said something that would destroy our chances completely.

The Airport Wait and Growing Tensions

"Well, that was a complete bust," Deb said angrily as we sat on the floor of LAX, waiting two hours for our red-eye flight back to New York.

"No, I think it actually went quite well," I lied, trying to maintain some optimism about our prospects.

"Are you completely out of your mind?" Deb demanded loudly. "Those women were total bitches to us! Did you see how they treated our work?"

"Yes, but our design boards were gorgeous," I replied weakly. "Sometimes the creative vision matters more than the client's initial reaction."

"Who cares how beautiful our boards were?" Deb continued, downing her fourth beer while nervously scanning the crowds of travelers around us. "They made it clear that they don't respect us or take this project seriously."

Her agitation seemed to go beyond simple frustration with Jessica's behavior. She appeared genuinely anxious about being in Los Angeles, constantly checking the faces of passing travelers as if she expected to recognize someone she preferred to avoid.

The Unexpected Good News

We returned to New York exhausted and emotionally drained from the difficult Los Angeles experience. After two days of anxious waiting, we received an email from Vince's chief financial officer requesting an immediate meeting at their corporate offices.

"Oh great," I said sarcastically. "They're going to reject us in person. How thoughtful of them to waste our time with a face-to-face humiliation."

"I'm not going," Deb announced firmly. "I can't handle another round of corporate politics and fake politeness."

"We have to go," I replied, though I shared her reluctance to face what seemed like inevitable disappointment.

"What should we wear to our funeral where we get professionally rejected?" Deb laughed, trying to inject some humor into our gloomy mood.

"Something in black that looks elegant," I suggested with dark humor.

The next day, we arrived at Vince's impressive corporate headquarters to find six executives waiting for us in their main conference room. I had chosen a simple but professional black Calvin Klein sleeveless dress with low-heeled sling back shoes. Deb, true to form, showed up dressed for a nightclub rather than a business meeting, wearing John Galliano's famous newsprint dress with thigh-high boots and her ever fabulous fedora.

The CFO pulled out my chair while giving Deb's outfit a puzzled look that suggested he had never encountered such creative interpretation of business attire. Deb slumped into her seat looking bored and unimpressed, and I could smell a faint hint of Jack Daniel's on her breath despite the early hour.

"So, what do you people want from us?" Deb asked rudely, making no effort to hide her disdain for corporate formality.

A small, stern woman in an unfortunately ill-fitting suit responded with matching coldness. "We have several questions about your qualifications and experience."

"Fine, shoot away," Deb replied while popping her gum loudly.

For the next hour, I fielded detailed questions about our expertise in lingerie design, our understanding of Jessica's brand positioning, and our interpretation of the design concepts we had presented in Los Angeles. Deb remained silent throughout the interrogation, leaving me to carry the entire conversation while she sat looking like she would rather be anywhere else in the world.

When the questioning finally ended, we were asked to wait in the lobby while the executive team deliberated our fate. As we sat in the elegant reception area, Deb resumed her complaints about the entire process.

"This is complete bullshit," she muttered loudly enough for nearby employees to hear. "Who are these corporate clowns anyway? I thought that dreadful Carl character was supposed to be our boss."

"Please keep your voice down," I whispered urgently. "They can probably hear every word you're saying."

"Honestly, who cares what they think?" she replied with characteristic indifference to social conventions.

After what felt like an eternity, we were summoned back into the conference room for the verdict. I prepared myself for polite rejection and began mentally planning our next career moves.

"Well, congratulations, ladies!" the CFO announced with genuine enthusiasm. "Jessica and her mother absolutely loved your designs!"

"No shit?" Deb exclaimed, looking genuinely shocked by this unexpected turn of events.

"We'll send you the contract tomorrow morning," the CFO continued matter-of-factly.

I asked about Carl's role in the project, and the executive team made it clear that he would not be involved in moving forward. We would report directly to them, which was actually preferable given

Deb's flirtatious behavior towards Carl that could have become problematic.

I reached out to shake hands with everyone in the room, expressing sincere gratitude for the opportunity and assuring them that Deb and I were committed to producing exceptional work for Jessica's brand.

Celebration and New Beginnings

Deb and I practically floated out of the building, shouting with excitement as we entered the elevator. The offices were conveniently located directly across the street from my West 57th Street apartment, which would make our daily commute refreshingly simple after the Staten Island ferry experience.

"We absolutely have to celebrate this!" Deb declared with infectious enthusiasm.

Although it was only eleven in the morning, I suggested lunch at a restaurant near Central Park where we could sit outside and toast our success without attracting too much attention. It was a gorgeous sunny Monday, and we managed to secure a perfect outdoor table for our impromptu celebration.

Deb raised her Bloody Mary glass in a toast. "To us and this incredible opportunity!" she said with genuine excitement. "This is going to be so much fun, and I promise to be on my absolute best behavior throughout the entire project."

"I don't think this is going to be easy," I warned, though I was caught up in her optimism. "Working with celebrity brands brings unique challenges and pressures."

"We can handle anything that comes our way," she replied confidently. "Have some faith in our abilities, Katie. We've overcome bigger obstacles than this."

For the first time in months, I felt genuinely happy and optimistic about our professional future. This could be the breakthrough opportunity that established us as major players in the celebrity licensing market and finally put Tyra's brand debacle behind us.

Setting Up the Operation

The following day brought the signed contracts along with compensation terms that exceeded our expectations. With substantial funding secured, we decided to expand our team by bringing on additional talent to ensure we could meet all of Jessica's brand requirements.

Deb was enthusiastic about hiring a trendy young British designer whose work she admired greatly. While I wasn't entirely convinced this person was the right fit for our team dynamic, I lacked the energy to argue with Deb's choice. I hoped that bringing in fresh perspective might actually benefit our creative process, even if it meant managing another potentially difficult personality.

We established a daily work routine in my apartment, developing what would become a fun, sophisticated, and edgy lingerie collection perfectly suited to what we thought was Jessica's Macy's customer base. The designs balanced commercial appeal with fashion-forward thinking, creating pieces that would stand out in a crowded marketplace.

Deb remained critical of Jessica's public image throughout the design process. "I can't believe we have to let that airheaded blonde represent this amazing collection," she complained regularly. "These designs are far too sophisticated for someone so irritating."

"Please try to focus on the positive aspects," I would respond diplomatically. "This is an incredible opportunity, and we're being paid very well to do work we love."

"Fine, but I still wish we were designing for Beyoncé instead," Deb would mutter, though she always returned to the work with professional dedication.

As our team grew and the project became more complex, my small Manhattan apartment proved inadequate for our needs. With plans to hire a production manager and additional support staff, I realized we needed proper office space that could accommodate our expanding operations.

I approached Vince's CFO about the possibility of using available space in their building, but he explained that they were already at full capacity. He suggested that we look for rental offices in the area and promised to discuss potential financial assistance with Vince directly.

Finding the Perfect Workspace

Deb and I spent a frustrating week touring potential office spaces throughout Manhattan. Everything we saw was either prohibitively expensive or completely unsuitable for our needs—dark, cramped spaces that would stifle creativity rather than inspire it.

"What about looking for a loft space instead of traditional offices?" I suggested during one particularly discouraging day of apartment hunting.

"That could be interesting," Deb replied with renewed enthusiasm.

While shopping for fabric samples one afternoon, we noticed a vacancy sign on a striking two-story loft in Chelsea. The building's contemporary architecture caught our attention immediately, and we arranged to meet with the broker that same day.

The property exceeded our wildest expectations. We entered through an elegant wrought-iron gate and climbed four steps to a grand black door adorned with a brass lion's head knocker. When the door swung open, I felt my heart skip a beat at the sheer beauty of the space.

The interior was sophisticated and contemporary, featuring a magnificent marble kitchen island and backsplash, two working fireplaces, and a stunning twelve-hundred-square-foot outdoor area on the ground floor. The design aesthetic was exactly what I had envisioned for a high-end creative workspace.

"Oh my God!" I screamed as I walked through the expansive main room. "This is absolutely perfect!"

Deb rushed past me toward the outdoor space, and I could hear her excited shouts echoing through the property. "Holy shit! This is literally my dream workspace!" she called back to us.

We stood together in amazed silence, barely hearing the broker's detailed description of the property's features: radiant heated floors, working fireplaces, retractable sliding glass doors that opened to create seamless indoor-outdoor living.

The glass staircase led to a huge open room that would be ideal for our design studio, complete with a Japanese-style bathroom and changing room and massive walk-in closets for sample storage. The upstairs space could easily accommodate six design stations, with the additional room downstairs for client presentations and meetings.

"Let's designate the downstairs as our showroom and use the upstairs for actual design work," I suggested, already envisioning how we would organize our operations.

"Perfect plan," Deb agreed enthusiastically.

We grabbed each other and jumped up and down like excited children, probably convincing the broker that he was dealing with two completely unprofessional clients.

"We'll take it," Deb announced without hesitation.

"I'll need to conduct a credit check and collect a security deposit," the broker explained in his professional manner.

Deb's expression suddenly changed as reality set in. "Oh shit, my credit is absolutely terrible."

"Don't worry, I can handle the financial arrangements," I assured her, though I knew the monthly rent of fifteen thousand dollars would strain our budget significantly.

I called the CFO immediately to arrange a viewing of the space at the end of the day. He graciously agreed to come see the space with us and the broker.

"I love it, it's perfect for your needs." he said. "I will run the numbers and get back to you."

"Okay," I said anxiously, "but it won't last long."

The CFO was an exceptional and compassionate individual whom I greatly admired and respected for transforming Vince's business into its current success. He was so incredibly kind to me throughout my time at Jessica's brand.

The next day, as we were all sitting on the floor of my apartment cutting out fabrics, when the phone rang.

"Okay, Katie, it's yours. I negotiated the price down to 12 thousand dollars a month," the CEO said firmly.

"Thank you," I said, trying to maintain my calm.

I turned to Deb and she looked visibly upset.

"We didn't get it? Did we? Oh shit! Now what?" she said, totally defeated.

I let her rant for a few minutes then said calmly, "Start packing. We are moving in to our new loft space next week!"

We both started screaming and dancing around my apartment while my pug started howling.

The next few weeks were crazy. We had to move in, buy furniture, and then head to China to make samples for Jessica's new line.

I chose to furnish the showroom in white and silver, mirroring Vince's showroom style.

I decorated the design office on the upper floor with glass desks and white chairs. We brought in a carpenter to create a lighted deck outside and to plant beautiful bamboo trees.

Even though the outside area cost $20,000, the CFO believed it was a fantastic idea since it would allow for outdoor meetings with buyers in the summer and future brand events.

The Search for New Opportunities

Deb and I stood back to admire what we had accomplished. The outdoor space had been transformed into a sophisticated extension of our workspace, complete with comfortable seating areas and professional lighting that would allow us to hold client meetings even during evening hours.

"This is absolutely perfect," Deb said, raising a glass of champagne as her mother joined us to celebrate our achievement. The three of us stood in our new outdoor space, surrounded by the carefully planted bamboo and the warm glow of the custom lighting, feeling proud of what we had built together.

Deb's mother began to cry as she looked around at the beautiful new showroom we had created. "Katie, thank you for saving my daughter," she said through her tears. "She was so lost before you came into her life."

"Mom, stop it!" Deb snapped, clearly uncomfortable with her mother's emotional display of gratitude.

"No, she's right," I replied, putting my arm around Deb's shoulders. "But you also saved me from the horrible garment center too. We saved each other."

I looked directly at Deb, my expression becoming more serious. "Now it's time to buckle down and focus. We have enormous responsibilities on our shoulders with this project."

Deb raised her champagne glass in a toast to both her mother and me, and we headed out to dinner to continue our celebration. It felt like we were finally positioned to achieve something truly significant in the fashion industry.

The First Major Mistake: The Production Manager

However, my initial euphoria was short-lived. The real challenges began when I made what would prove to be my first critical error in managing Jessica's line. I hired an overly polished production manager who came with impressive credentials and claimed extensive experience producing lingerie for Victoria's Secret.

During our initial interviews, she spoke confidently about her factory connections and her deep understanding of intimate apparel manufacturing. She presented herself as exactly the kind of experienced professional we needed to ensure that Jessica's line would meet the highest quality standards. Her references seemed solid, and her knowledge appeared comprehensive.

It took me several months of working with her to realize that she actually possessed very little genuine knowledge about lingerie production or the intricate processes involved in creating high-quality intimate apparel. Despite her polished presentation and confident demeanor, she had somehow managed to convince me and Deb that she was an expert in a field where she was essentially a novice.

When it came time to travel to China to work with our manufacturing partners, I made the mistake of bringing her along, believing that her supposed expertise would be invaluable in overseeing production. This decision would prove costly in both time and money, as her inexperience became glaringly obvious once we were working directly with the factories.

The China Trip and Factory Challenges

The trip was supposed to establish our manufacturing relationships and ensure that our designs could be translated into high-quality finished products.

Upon our arrival in China, it immediately became clear that the production manager's claimed factory connections were essentially nonexistent. She had promised access to established manufacturing networks, but when we actually tried to visit these facilities, we discovered that her relationships were superficial at best.

This revelation triggered my anxiety about the entire project, as I realized we were operating without the solid manufacturing foundation that I had believed was in place.

Fortunately, I had a backup plan in the form of a reliable factory owner named Sunny, whom I had worked with successfully on previous projects. Sunny actually did have legitimate connections to Victoria's Secret and other high-end lingerie brands, and he agreed to produce all of our samples for Jessica's initial product launch.

The results from Sunny's factory were outstanding. The samples were not only visually stunning but also featured perfect fit and construction. The attention to detail was exceptional, with genuine shell buttons, beautiful hand-finished stitching, and premium materials including silk and cashmere knits. Every aspect of the production demonstrated the kind of craftsmanship that we needed to establish Jessica's brand as a serious player in the lingerie market.

Both Deb and I were thrilled with the quality of the collection and felt immense pride in what we had accomplished. The designs successfully captured Jessica's brand personality while maintaining the sophisticated aesthetic that we believed would differentiate her line from other celebrity fashion ventures.

Once we returned to the United States, I immediately fired the production manager. Her deceptive claims about her experience and connections had nearly derailed our entire project, and I couldn't risk further complications from someone who had proven to be both dishonest and incompetent. This type of behavior was unfortunately common in the garment center, where individuals often survived by pretending to possess skills and connections they didn't actually have.

The Second Misstep: Misreading the Market

My second significant error involved a fundamental misunderstanding of the market positioning for Jessica's products. Our lingerie line was very fashion-forward and upscale, featuring sophisticated designs that would have been more appropriate for high-end boutiques than for the mid-tier department stores that were Jessica's primary retail partners.

I had assumed that we could create a more unique and daring collection that would break away from the mundane, predictable options that dominated the department store lingerie market at that time. I believed that Jessica's celebrity status would allow us to introduce more innovative and edgy designs that would elevate the entire category.

This assumption proved to be completely wrong. The existing retail strategy for Jessica's other products was carefully calibrated to appeal to a specific demographic and price point, and our sophisticated lingerie designs simply didn't align with that established brand positioning. We had created beautiful, well-made pieces that were too innovative for our intended market.

Despite this mismatch, we did receive some validation for our creative direction prior to presenting the line to Jessica's team and the Macy's buyer. Jake, an influential figure in the lingerie trade publications and someone who had always been supportive of my work throughout my career, reviewed our designs and praised our unique approach to luxury fabrics and cutting-edge styling. He featured our collection in his magazine, recognizing the quality and creativity of what we had produced.

Jake had been a wonderful friend and supporter for many years, consistently featuring my new launches in his publications and serving as one of the few people in the industry who refused to simply follow established trends. His approval meant a great deal to me personally, even though it didn't solve our fundamental market positioning problem.

After a quick trip to Los Angeles where we presented our new collection to Jessica's team, we were thrilled to hear their enthusiastic response to our fresh approach, luxurious materials, and unique styles. Jessica's mother made all the business decisions, so when Jessica was a no-show at the presentation we were not surprised. We also showed Vince's team the new collection and they were equally enthusiastic about our new designs for Jessica Simpson lingerie and sleepwear.

The Third Mistake: Lisa's Return

The third and perhaps most devastating mistake occurred while I was still in China working on production issues. Somehow, Lisa—the vindictive saleswoman who had undermined me during the Tyra Banks project—managed to get her way into an interview with

Vince's vice president of sales and secured a position as my new sales director.

When I returned from China and was introduced to Lisa in my beautiful new office space, I could hardly believe what was happening. This woman had been instrumental in destroying my previous project, and now she was being presented as my new sales director.

"What?" I screamed at Vince's vice president of sales who had brought her to meet with me and Deb. "No! Absolutely not! Get her out of here immediately!"

"What the hell?" Deb shouted, equally shocked by Lisa's appearance. "Why is that incompetent moron here?"

"Wow! You two are really mean girls!" Vince's vice president of sales replied angrily, clearly not understanding the history between us.

"She's terrible at her job, and she used to work for me," I explained frantically. "Please tell me you didn't actually sign a contract with her!"

"Yes, they did," Lisa said with a satisfied smile. "Now, where's my office going to be?"

"Not in our workspace!" Deb yelled back. "You're never sitting upstairs with us!"

"That's fine," Lisa replied calmly, clearly relishing the chaos she was causing. "I'll just work downstairs."

I pulled Vince's vice president of sales aside to demand an explanation. "Why would you hire her without consulting me first?" I asked, my face turning red with anger and disbelief.

"Because she told us that you and she were great friends and had worked together successfully before," Vince's vice president of sales explained matter-of-factly.

"And you never thought to verify this information with me?" I was practically shouting at this point, thinking I might actually faint from the stress.

"She said she had called you while you were in China and that you had given your approval for her hire," she continued, seemingly oblivious to how ridiculous this explanation sounded.

"I would never take a call from that woman!" I cried out in frustration. "I wouldn't speak to her if my life depended on it!"

After Vince's vice president of sales and Lisa left our office, I screamed after them, "Don't you dare show up here tomorrow, Lisa!"

"We're completely finished," Deb said, panic in her voice. "What are we going to do now?"

"The same thing we always do," I replied, though I was still shaking from the confrontation. "We'll find a way to sell this line despite her interference."

We were in no position to make waves with Vince's management team, so I couldn't call the CEO and explain how much I despised Lisa and why her presence could potentially destroy our project. Instead, we would have to find ways to work around her sabotage efforts.

"I'll call the CEO myself," Deb said, reaching for a shot of Jack Daniel's she kept in her desk drawer.

"No," I replied firmly. "We just have to ignore her completely if she shows up, and we need to tell the freelance designers not to engage with her under any circumstances."

The Macy's Disaster

A week later, our fears about Lisa's destructive influence were realized when a notoriously difficult buyer from Macy's arrived to review our new spring collection for Jessica. This buyer was known throughout the industry for her harsh critiques and resistance to new, innovative designs, and she happened to be a personal friend of Lisa's.

"I hate this design; no, I don't like this one either; no one's going to buy these styles," she complained loudly, spending over an hour systematically tearing apart our entire collection. Throughout this devastating critique, Lisa sat silently beside her, smiling and nodding in agreement, never once defending our design choices or the quality of our fabrics and samples.

I tried to argue against the buyer's criticisms and explain the creative vision behind our pieces, but it was completely pointless. It was evident that the buyer had reached a conclusion prior to exploring the collection, and Lisa's presence served only to amplify her conspiratorial negativity.

In the end, I lost the battle completely, and the Macy's buyer rejected our entire spring line. This was catastrophic news, as Macy's was one of Jessica's most important retail partners. Even though several other stores loved the designs and planned on buying the line, without Macy's blessing we were doomed.

The next morning, I received a call from the CEO that confirmed my worst fears.

"Katie, I know that Jessica's team, her mother, and all of us here at the company love your new designs," he said carefully. "But if Macy's doesn't approve of the collection, then we're dead in the water commercially."

"But this buyer is old-fashioned and hates change," I protested. "She has no appreciation for real fashion innovation. Plus, Lisa provided no support whatsoever and actually seemed to side with the buyer against us."

"Isn't supporting the buyer part of her job?" the CEO asked, sounding confused.

"No, absolutely not," I replied emphatically. "Her job is to support us and advocate for our design decisions."

After a long pause, the CEO delivered the devastating news: "Katie, I'm sorry, but you're going to need to redesign the entire collection from scratch-quickly."

"Oh my God!" I said as I hung up on him and immediately called our design team together to deliver this terrible news.

When I explained the situation to our staff, Lisa boldly walked over and plopped down next to Deb with a satisfied smile on her face.

"Get out of this office right now!" both Deb and I shouted at her in unison.

"Nope!" she replied cheerfully. "I want to watch you all try to pull this impossible task off." She was clearly enjoying our distress.

Without warning, Deb grabbed a design pad from the table and hurled it directly at Lisa's head. Lisa ducked just in time to avoid being hit, then stood up and walked calmly out of our office, still smiling.

"God, I hate that disgusting woman," Deb said with pure venom in her voice.

"All right, let's focus on this redesign challenge," I sighed, knowing that we were facing an almost impossible deadline.

The design team was understandably unhappy about having to start over, and I could sense that we were on the verge of a full-scale rebellion. The combination of unrealistic deadlines, constant interference from Lisa, and a lack of support from the buyer was creating an unsustainable work environment.

The State of the Lingerie Market

During this period, the lingerie market was characterized by a troubling lack of innovation, particularly in department stores. The buyers were typically older women who were uninspired and extremely resistant to any kind of change. They adhered rigidly to safe, boring choices that had been dictated to them by even more conservative supervisors.

The primary objective for these buyers was to avoid making any dramatic changes that might attract attention from their superiors. Their strategy was to keep quiet, maintain the status quo by selling the same old designs, and collect their bonuses without rocking the boat. This risk-averse mentality was systematically destroying creativity and innovation throughout the entire industry.

This institutional stagnation ultimately contributed to the broader decline of the department store business model. During the early 2000s, e-commerce was still in its infancy, and websites were relatively new to consumers, so in-store sales were absolutely vital to the success of companies like Vince's. The conservative, backward-looking approach of department store buyers was essentially choking off the innovation that might have kept their businesses relevant and competitive. I was approximately three years premature in anticipating the shift to more innovative designs in the moderate market. This experience seems to define my life; it's as if I possessed a crystal ball for upcoming trends, yet I constantly found myself too far ahead.

A Welcome Distraction: Mariah Carey

While we were struggling with the Jessica Simpson line to be more conservative, redesign and dealing with the toxic atmosphere created by Lisa's interference, I received an unexpected phone call that would provide a welcome distraction from our daily problems.

My friend Seth, a celebrity product manager whom I had worked with previously, called to tell me about a potential opportunity with Mariah Carey. He had been doing business with her team and had suggested the possibility of developing a lingerie concept specifically for her brand. According to Seth, Mariah was intrigued by the idea and was eager to meet with Deb and me to explore the possibilities.

As major fans of Mariah's music and style, we were absolutely over the moon about this opportunity. The chance to work with one of the most iconic singers in the world would be a dream come true, and it offered a much-needed escape from the Jessica Simpson drama that was consuming our daily lives.

We eagerly awaited Seth's call to finalize the meeting details. A week later, while Deb and I were on a conference call in my apartment, discussing design strategies changes with our factory partners in China, Seth called with urgent news.

"Mariah is available to meet with you tonight," he announced without preamble.

"Tonight?" I shouted in disbelief. "But it's already six-thirty in the evening!"

"Well, that's your problem to solve," Seth replied, clearly annoyed by my surprise. "A car will pick you up in one hour, so you better get ready immediately."

I quickly explained to Deb that we would be meeting Mariah at her apartment at eight o'clock that same evening.

"You mean tomorrow night, right?" Deb asked, looking confused.

"No, tonight!" I yelled back. "We have less than an hour to get ready!"

"Oh shit! I have absolutely nothing appropriate to wear," Deb panicked.

"Go look through my closets and find something suitable," I shouted, already rushing toward my bedroom to figure out my own outfit.

By the time we had both gotten dressed, it was already seven-thirty, and we were told by my doorman that the car waiting for us was outside on the street.

"We have to leave right now," I called out, grabbing my portfolio and some fabric samples we had bought during our last shopping trip in Paris.

"I'll be ready in five minutes," Deb smiled as she rummaged through my closet and pulled out my brand-new white eyelet dress by Catherine Malandrino, which I had recently purchased for four hundred dollars and hadn't even had a chance to wear yet.

She quickly pulled the dress over her head and cinched it with a wide leather cowboy belt, then grabbed a pair of strappy sandals from her bag. The transformation was remarkable, and she looked absolutely stunning.

"Why do you always manage to look like a supermodel in just five minutes?" I complained, still struggling with my own outfit selection of all black.

"Good genes," she replied with characteristic confidence.

The Meeting with Mariah

We climbed into the waiting car. When we arrived at Mariah's building, I initially thought we had been brought to some kind of office complex and began to worry that the driver had made a mistake.

However, the doorman immediately guided us to a private elevator, and we rode up to the penthouse level in complete silence, both of us too nervous and excited to speak. At the top floor, a petite blonde woman greeted us at the front door and politely asked us to remove our shoes before entering.

She gestured for us to enter a spacious living room filled with luxurious white furniture and asked us to make ourselves comfortable while we waited. I attempted to settle on the large white satin sofa, but it was so overstuffed with matching decorative pillows that it was nearly impossible to find a stable place to sit.

Meanwhile, Deb wisely decided to sit cross-legged on the floor, watching with amusement as I struggled with the impractical furniture.

Within five seconds of sitting down, I slid completely off the couch and landed on the floor next to Deb with a soft thud.

"Jesus, Katie!" Deb laughed quietly. "Just get back up on the couch and try again!"

I climbed back up and attempted to sit down again, but immediately slid back down to the floor. While I was down there for the second time, I glanced around the room and noticed a stunning white grand piano positioned across from us, elegantly surrounded by red velvet ropes like a museum piece.

"Wow," I whispered to Deb in amazement. "That's where Mariah sits and plays when she's composing her incredible songs."

"That's absolutely right," I heard the blonde assistant say from across the room as I tried once again to get back onto the couch and look presentable.

"Please follow me upstairs," she said with businesslike efficiency.

I grabbed my design portfolio and samples, and we climbed an elegant staircase that led to another beautiful room, which we later learned was called the "Moroccan room" because of its exotic decorative theme.

Five minutes later, while Deb and I were organizing our presentation materials and design boards, we heard footsteps on the stairs. When we looked up, we saw this tall, breathtakingly beautiful woman walking into the room, and we were both immediately mesmerized.

Mariah was wearing a simple but elegant white-and-green print Diane von Furstenberg wrap dress. Her long hair was pulled back into a sleek ponytail that highlighted her gorgeous facial features: flawless skin, pristine white teeth, and sparkling brown eyes that seemed to light up the entire room.

She stood barefoot on her tiptoes in the doorway, and although she was naturally thin, she had soft, feminine curves that gave her an approachable, warm appearance despite her superstar status.

"Hi there," she said with a genuinely warm smile. "Thank you both so much for coming on such short notice. I know this was really last-minute."

"Hi!" Deb and I responded simultaneously, both of us completely starstruck by her presence.

"Would you like some wine?" Mariah asked graciously, then immediately instructed the blonde assistant to bring us a bottle of wine and several glasses.

An Unforgettable Evening

For the next several hours, the three of us sat comfortably on the floor of the Moroccan room, discussing not just lingerie design concepts but also life, music, creativity, and the challenges of building authentic brands in a commercial marketplace. The conversation flowed naturally, and I felt like I was talking with a close friend rather than one of the most famous entertainers in the world.

Deb was animated and engaging, displaying her best social skills and creative insights. It was wonderful to see her in this element, where her natural charisma and design intelligence could shine without the complications that often arose in more structured business environments.

I always tell people to be skeptical of celebrity stories they read in tabloids because the vast majority of them are either completely fabricated or grossly distorted. Based on my personal experience that evening, Mariah was exactly the kind of person you would want to become friends with if she wasn't so famous and wealthy. She was genuinely warm, naturally funny, and remarkably down-to-earth considering her global superstar status.

The more time we spent with her, the more excited I became about the possibility of designing a lingerie line that would truly represent her personal style and artistic vision. This felt like the kind of creative collaboration that could produce something genuinely special and commercially successful.

It was two o'clock in the morning by the time Deb and I finally left Mariah's apartment. We rode in complete silence, both of us feeling like we were still living in a dream. The driver dropped me off at my apartment first, then continued on to take Deb home.

Days passed, then weeks, as we waited to hear back from Seth about the next steps in developing Mariah's lingerie concept. Seth worked tirelessly to secure funding for the new line, but unfortunately, no investors were willing to commit to yet another female celebrity brand. The market had become oversaturated with celebrity fashion ventures, and many of them had failed to deliver the expected returns.

Mariah was so enthusiastic about having her own lingerie line that she even offered to fund the entire project herself, but Seth later told us that her business manager had vetoed that idea, probably concerned about the financial risks involved in launching a new product category.

Despite my heartbreak over this missed opportunity, I realized how crucial it was to refocus our energy on finalizing Jessica's collection. Deb and I redirected our creative efforts toward completely rethinking the designs that had been rejected by the Macy's buyer.

We never spoke about our magical evening with Mariah again, but it will always remain one of my most treasured memories from my entire career in the fashion industry. The experience reminded me why I had originally fallen in love with fashion—the possibility of working with truly creative people to produce something beautiful and meaningful.

The Launch Party Disaster

By the time we had completed the redesigned Jessica Simpson collection, the tension in our office had reached a breaking point. Everyone was stressed, overworked, and at each other's throats. In an attempt to create some positive momentum and generate media interest in the line, Deb and I decided to organize a launch party timed to coincide with Jessica's next scheduled trip to New York.

The planning process consumed weeks of our time and a significant portion of our budget, but we believed that a successful launch event could help overcome the negative response from the Macy's buyer and create buzz that would drive sales through other retail channels.

On the day of the party, we hired professional models to showcase the new designs, and everything seemed to be proceeding smoothly until one of the models revealed a small tattoo on her lower back. This seemingly minor detail created an unexpected crisis when Lisa saw it and became visibly upset.

Fortunately, we had hired a talented makeup artist who was able to cover the tattoo before anyone else noticed, but the incident highlighted the level of micromanagement and control that Lisa expected to have over every aspect of our brand presentation. She was angry that we hadn't consulted with her about our model selections, even though she had never been involved in any of our previous business decisions.

"What a complete bitch," Deb said within earshot of Lisa, who immediately turned around and glared at her with undisguised hostility.

Despite this backstage drama, I was too excited about the event itself to let it dampen my spirits. We had managed to attract an impressive crowd of retail buyers and fashion press, including representatives from Entertainment Tonight, People magazine, and Women's Wear Daily. The media attention was exactly what we needed to establish credibility for Jessica's brand in the competitive lingerie market.

"Where is Jessica?" I asked the CFO anxiously, scanning the crowd for any sign of our celebrity partner.

"She's not coming," he replied quietly, his expression apologetic. "I'm truly sorry, Katie."

"What do you mean she's not coming?" I stared at him in shock. "This is *her* launch party!"

"I know, and I'm really sorry about this," he said with another deep sigh. "It's completely out of my hands."

I stood there in complete disbelief that Jessica would fail to show up for her own product launch. This was supposed to be a celebration of her new redesigned line that finally got the blessing from the Macy's buyer, and her absence sent a terrible message to everyone in attendance.

Deb's reaction was even more extreme than mine. She immediately drank two shots of tequila, grabbed the entire bottle, and spent the rest of the evening getting progressively drunk in a corner of the venue with her boyfriend. Her disappointment and anger were palpable, and I couldn't blame her for wanting to escape the humiliation we were both feeling. I was left to lie to all of the people at the party on why Jessica had not shown up, as Lisa gloated.

Later, the rumor was that Jessica was distraught after apparently receiving an e-mail from her boyfriend breaking off their relationship over his concerns that she was being pursued by another male, which explained her absence from the launch event. This pattern of absence was unfortunately consistent with her approach to most of our presentations and business meetings. Except for that initial meeting in Los Angeles, I rarely encountered Jessica unless Vince held and attended a brand discussion.

The Reality Behind Celebrity Brands

This experience taught me an important lesson about the reality behind celebrity fashion brands. The popular belief that celebrities are deeply involved in designing their own products is not always true. In some cases, they have minimal involvement in the creative process and usually only see the final collection when they're required to wear pieces for media appearances or promotional events.

Jessica Simpson was a perfect example of this phenomenon, in my experience with her. While her name was on the lingerie brand and her image was used in all the marketing materials, she showed little interest in the actual design process, or even the promotional activities that were essential to our brand's success.

Fortunately, Jessica's mother was much more engaged and business-savvy. She understood the importance of brand management and frequently stepped in to make decisions that Jessica seemed uninterested in handling herself. Without her mother's involvement, I believe Jessica's over-all brand would have failed completely within its first year.

The financial success stories that celebrities and their teams share with the media are also significantly exaggerated. After working behind the scenes on these projects, I learned that the actual earnings are usually much lower than the publicized figures. My general rule of thumb became: take whatever earnings number a celebrity claims, cut it in half, then cut it in half again, and you'll probably be closer to the truth.

During the late 1990s and early 2000s, just before the major economic downturn, securing licensing agreements with celebrity brands required enormous upfront investments and extensive contract terms with ridiculous perks and requirements. For example, I was told once by one of colleagues who was working on another celebrity brand, that all his celebrities clothing and handbags were manufactured in high-end Italian factories, while the products sold to consumers were produced in much cheaper Chinese facilities.

The contrast between what celebrities used personally and what they sold to their fans was often dramatic and ethically questionable. This two-tier system allowed celebrities to maintain their luxury lifestyles while profiting from much cheaper products sold to their admirers.

Today, celebrities are fortunate to secure any kind of licensing deals at all, and upfront payments have become almost nonexistent. The risk of a celebrity falling from grace and destroying the reputation of their branded products has proven to be too great for most investors to accept.

The fashion industry is littered with celebrity brand disasters: Kanye West's Pastelle line never fully launched; Sarah Jessica Parker's Bitten was tied to a retailer that went bankrupt; OutKast created a clothing line that they themselves reportedly disliked. The list goes on and on.

Of course, there are still a few well-funded celebrity brands like Rihanna's Savage X Fenty that have achieved success, but these brands work because the celebrity is actively and consistently promoting their products through social media and personal appearances.

Ultimately, investing millions of dollars in a celebrity who won't commit to a morality clause or actively market their products has proven to be far too risky for most investors and business partners.

The China Production Trip

Despite our disappointment with the launch party, Deb and I were scheduled to fly to China two days later to finalize production details for the redesigned collection. I was still upset about Jessica's no-show at her own launch event, but we had commitments to fulfill and deadlines to meet.

As we prepared for the trip, I could already see warning signs that this project was likely to fail. Lisa's deliberate efforts to limit our progress and not bring in any new accounts, and Jessica's apparent disinterest in promoting our line created a perfect storm of problems that would be difficult to overcome.

Deb was utterly defeated and unhappy about the entire situation. Her mood had darkened considerably since the launch party, and I could tell that she was beginning to lose faith in our ability to make the project successful.

We did get many orders from smaller stores because I took over the reins from Lisa and started selling the line myself, but it wasn't enough to reach my initial sales goals. This move angered Lisa and she plotted her revenge.

The Airport Detention

A week after our challenging trip to oversee factory production, Deb and I arrived back at JFK airport from China, both of us exhausted from the intensive and stressful manufacturing process. I proceeded through customs without incident, but as I waited at the baggage claim area, I saw that Deb was being escorted by two armed men into another room.

I waited for over an hour, scanning the crowds of arriving passengers and checking the various exits, but she never appeared. Growing increasingly worried, I decided to step outside and hail a taxi, thinking perhaps she had somehow gotten ahead of me and was waiting outside the terminal.

After waiting another hour with still no sign of Deb, I became genuinely concerned about her and decided to contact her mother to see if she had any information.

"Deb may have been detained by customs officials," I explained nervously during the phone call. "I don't know why this would have happened, but she never made it to the baggage claim area."

"Oh, that's nothing unusual," her mother replied casually, which struck me as an odd response to news that her daughter was potentially being held by federal authorities.

Just as I was beginning to panic about what steps to take next, Deb casually walked up to me on the sidewalk and said simply, "Let's go home."

During the entire taxi ride back to Manhattan, she offered no explanation for her delay or her detention by customs officials. We sat in complete silence, and when I tried to ask what had happened, she deflected my questions and changed the subject.

"I'm completely exhausted," Deb said as she jumped out of the taxi in front of her boyfriend's apartment building. "I'll see you tomorrow morning." She smiled as if nothing unusual had occurred.

I arrived home feeling drained and confused, but I was too tired to press for answers about Deb's mysterious detention. I went to bed assuming that whatever had happened would be explained the following day.

The Background Check Crisis

At six o'clock the next morning, I was awakened by an urgent phone call from Jessica's CFO requesting an immediate meeting at his office with me.

I arrived thirty minutes later, still groggy from the early hour and worried about what kind of crisis could require such an urgent discussion.

"We conducted background checks on both you and Deb while you were away after receiving a call from customs officials about Deb," the CFO stated without preamble.

"Background checks?" I laughed nervously. "We've been working together for over a year. Why would you do background checks now?"

"Lisa made some serious accusations about Deb's drinking problems and emotional instability," he explained. "Given customs concerns about Deb's employment, we felt we needed to investigate these claims."

"Of course, Lisa made accusations," I said angrily. "She's the one who's actually unstable. She's been trying to sabotage our project from day one."

"Your background check came back clean," the CFO continued. "You have nothing to hide, and we're not concerned about your reliability or professionalism."

"Okay, I knew that." I replied. "What about Deb?"

"Deb's situation is considerably more complicated," he said with a heavy sigh.

"What are you talking about?" I asked, though I was beginning to feel a sense of dread about what he was about to tell me.

"Several years ago, Deb was incarcerated," the CFO stated firmly, watching my reaction carefully.

I burst into laughter, assuming this had to be some kind of mistake. "I've known her for years! That's absolutely impossible. She would have told me something that significant."

He then handed me an official report that documented the details of her situation. As I read through the documents, the reality of the situation began to sink in.

"She's my best friend and business partner!" I said, beginning to cry. "Everyone makes mistakes in their past. That doesn't define who they are today."

"I understand your loyalty to her, Katie," he said with genuine sympathy. "But Jessica is a major celebrity, and we absolutely cannot afford to have the press discover anything derogatory about your team.

"So, what are you asking me to do?" I asked, though I already knew what he was going to say.

"You have to fire her immediately," the CFO replied. "Today."

The Painful Truth and Impossible Choices

I arrived at my office, feeling like I was walking to my own execution. The weight of the conversation I knew I had to have with Deb pressed down on my chest, making it difficult to breathe normally. Every step felt heavier than the last, and I found myself hoping against hope that there might be some way to avoid what was about to happen.

When I entered our workspace, I found Deb in her element—animated, engaged, and genuinely excited about showing our design team the new materials and samples we had brought back from our trip to China. Her enthusiasm was infectious as she spread fabric swatches across our conference table, explaining the unique properties of each material and how they would translate into the final garments.

Seeing her like this made what I was about to do infinitely more painful. This was the Deb I had admired as a friend and collaborator—creative, passionate, and completely committed to producing exceptional work. She had thrown herself into this final redesign project with everything she had, working tirelessly to overcome the setbacks we had faced with the Macy's buyer rejection and the disastrous launch party, even though I knew she felt defeated.

The truth was, I genuinely don't think I could have completed this challenging redesign without her incredible talent, unwavering dedication, and creative problem-solving abilities. Even when everything seemed to be falling apart around us, Deb had maintained her focus on the work itself, pushing both of us to create something beautiful despite the chaos swirling around our business relationships.

My eyes were swollen and red from crying, and the moment Deb looked at my face, she immediately understood that something serious had happened. Her expression shifted from excitement to concern in an instant, and I could see her mentally preparing for whatever bad news I was about to deliver.

"Okay, everyone, go upstairs for a while," Deb announced firmly to our design team, her voice carrying the authority of someone who recognized that privacy was essential for whatever conversation was about to unfold. "Katie and I need to have an important business discussion that requires confidentiality."

The team members gathered their materials and headed upstairs to the design studio, leaving Deb and me alone in the showroom. Deb led me out to our beautifully appointed outdoor terrace, the space that provided countless hours of peaceful refuge during stressful periods. The morning sun was filtering through the bamboo plantings, creating patterns of light and shadow on the custom deck we had installed with such hope and optimism just months earlier.

Without saying a word, Deb suddenly stood up and disappeared back into the office for several minutes. When she returned, she carried a bottle of Patrón tequila and two shot glasses, moving with the deliberate purpose of someone who understood that this conversation would require liquid courage. She carefully closed the sliding glass doors behind her, creating a barrier between us and the curious ears of our employees.

She poured two generous shots and raised her glass toward me with a rueful smile that didn't quite reach her eyes. "Well, my friend, this has been one hell of a wild ride, hasn't it?" she said with forced cheerfulness as we both downed the tequila, even though it was barely nine o'clock in the morning.

The burn of the alcohol provided a momentary distraction from the emotional pain I was feeling, but I knew there was no avoiding the conversation we needed to have. Above us, I could see our design team pressed against the windows, their faces reflecting bewilderment and confusion as they tried to understand why their bosses were drinking tequila before breakfast while having what appeared to be a serious crisis meeting.

Taking a shaky breath, I pulled the official background check report from my bag and handed it to Deb with trembling fingers. "I'm completely confused about why you never shared this with me," I said through my tears. "We've been best friends for years. How could you keep something this significant secret from someone who trusted you completely?"

Deb's face went pale as she scanned the document, but she didn't seem surprised by its contents. She had obviously been expecting this moment to arrive eventually, though perhaps not in quite this manner or at quite this time.

"That period represents one of the most difficult and shameful chapters of my entire life," she said quietly, her usual bravado completely absent. "It happened after I made a series of incredibly foolish decisions, and I felt far too embarrassed and ashamed to admit what I had done."

As she began to explain the circumstances that had led to her imprisonment, the pieces of her mysterious behavior finally began to make sense. Her extreme reluctance to travel to Los Angeles, her nervous scanning of crowds in airports, her complete absence from social media—all of these seemingly quirky personality traits suddenly had a much darker explanation.

Years earlier, when Deb had been living in Los Angeles during that period of her life she refused to discuss up until now, she had become involved with a dangerous crowd of people who evidently were entangled in an international drug smuggling operation. Seduced by the promise of intrigue and easy wealth, she naively had agreed to carry drugs into Europe in exchange for what seemed like an enormous sum of money at the time.

She told me that the operation had gone disastrously wrong, and she had been caught by European customs officials almost immediately upon arrival. The subsequent legal proceedings had resulted in several years of imprisonment in a European correctional facility—an experience that had left deep psychological scars and explained many of her ongoing behavioral problems.

When she had eventually returned to the United States, she lived in constant fear that the drug dealers who had recruited her might try to track her down, either to seek revenge for her cooperation with authorities or to force her into additional smuggling operations. This explained her ghost-like existence online and her extreme anxiety whenever she traveled to Los Angeles where she might encounter people from her criminal past.

The detention at the airport upon our return from China now made complete sense. She was obviously flagged in federal databases and any international travel would trigger additional scrutiny from customs officials. The experience of being questioned and detained must have brought back terrible memories of her arrest and imprisonment.

"This explains so many things about your behavior over the years," I said, feeling a mixture of sympathy and betrayal. "But I still don't understand why you couldn't trust me enough to tell me the truth. I've always been loyal to you, even when other people warned me about your problems."

"I was terrified that you would judge me for my past mistakes,"

Deb replied, tears now flowing freely down her cheeks. "You're one of the few people in my life who has ever seen me as something more than just a damaged, self-destructive person. I couldn't bear the thought of losing your friendship and respect."

The Impossible Choice Between Friendship and Success

Looking at Deb sitting across from me on our beautiful terrace, surrounded by the evidence of everything we had built together, I felt my heart breaking in ways I had never experienced before. This woman had been my closest friend, creative partner, and professional confidante for many years. She had supported me through some of the darkest periods of my career and had consistently pushed me to pursue bigger and better opportunities.

But now I was faced with an impossible choice that would define not only my immediate future but also my fundamental character as both a friend and a business professional. The CEO had been crystal clear about his ultimatum: fire Deb immediately, or lose the Jessica Simpson contract.

"Look, we can find another way forward," I said, desperately searching for alternatives to the devastating choice I was being forced to make. "I hate Lisa and the way this entire project has been corrupted by her sabotage efforts. Maybe this is actually a sign that we should pivot to something else entirely. I've been working on designs for my own shapewear line I mentioned—we could pursue that instead."

"Katie, I absolutely cannot ask you to make that kind of sacrifice for me," Deb said, her voice breaking with emotion. "You've worked incredibly hard to get this opportunity with Jessica's brand. This could be the breakthrough that establishes you as a major player in celebrity licensing. I won't let my past mistakes destroy your future."

"You are my best friend!" I replied fiercely. "We're supposed to be ride-or-die business partners who support each other no matter what happens. If I can't stand by you when you need me most, what kind of person does that make me? What kind of friendship have we really had all these years?"

A long moment of silence stretched between us as we both contemplated the magnitude of the decision we were facing. The financial implications were staggering—walking away from the Jessica Simpson project would mean losing hundreds of thousands of dollars in potential revenue and abandoning years of relationship-building with Vince's organization.

But the personal implications felt even more significant. How could I abandon someone who had been such an integral part of my creative and professional development? How could I prioritize business success over personal loyalty to someone who had stood by me through so many of my difficult situations?

"Well, okay then," Deb finally said with a shaky laugh that was part resignation and part relief. "I guess we're going to pursue that shapewear concept after all. Let's show this industry what we can accomplish when we're working for ourselves instead of trying to please other people."

Making the Decision That Would Haunt Me

The next morning, I sat in my apartment staring at the phone for over an hour before finally working up the courage to call the CFO at Jessica Simpson's brand. I knew that what I was about to do would be viewed by most business professionals as professional and financial suicide, but I also knew that I wouldn't be able to live with myself if I abandoned Deb to save my own career prospects.

"I've made my decision about the situation with Deb," I said when the CFO answered his phone. "I'm walking away from the Jessica Simpson project entirely. We're dissolving our partnership with your company effective immediately."

"Are you absolutely certain about this decision, Katie?" he asked, his voice reflecting genuine concern and disbelief. "This is really going to be a terrible mistake from a business perspective. You're walking away from what could have been a multi-million-dollar opportunity."

"If I can't maintain my loyalty to my friend and business partner, what kind of person am I?" I replied, trying to project more confidence than I actually felt. "Some things are more important than money and career advancement."

"I have to tell you honestly, Katie—you're not being very intelligent about this situation," he said bluntly before hanging up the phone.

His words stung because I knew he was probably right from a purely business standpoint. I was making an emotional decision that would likely cost me dearly. But I also knew that I would have to live with whatever choice I made for the rest of my life, and I couldn't imagine abandoning someone who had been such an important part of my life.

I immediately called Deb to deliver the news about my decision and tell her I was on my way to the office.

"Hey Deb, do you want to have the satisfaction of firing Lisa?" I asked, trying to inject some humor into what was otherwise a devastating situation.

"Hell yes!" she laughed with genuine enthusiasm for the first time in days. "I've been waiting for this opportunity for months."

The Dramatic Office Confrontation

I arrived at our office just in time to witness Deb delivering what may have been the most satisfying termination speech of her entire career. She had gathered not only our design team but also Lisa, who had obviously come in to gloat over what she assumed would be my humiliating dismissal from the project.

"Listen up, everyone," Deb announced in a voice that carried throughout our beautiful workspace. "I have an important announcement to make about the future of our operations here."

The room fell silent as everyone waited to hear what she was going to say. Lisa stood near the back of the group with a satisfied smirk on her face, obviously anticipating news about our termination and her increased authority over the project.

"Effective immediately, you're all fired," Deb declared with dramatic flair. "Please pack up your personal belongings and leave the premises as soon as possible. This includes you especially, Lisa."

Everyone in the room stood in stunned silence, trying to process what they had just heard. Most of our design team looked confused and upset, since they had been working hard on the project and had no understanding of the personal and professional conflicts that had led to this moment. I did give everyone a decent severance check to ease the pain, except Lisa.

Lisa, however, understood exactly what was happening and what had motivated this sudden termination of the entire project.

"You're even more stupid than I thought you were," Lisa said with malicious satisfaction as she gathered her things. "You're throwing away a great opportunity because of your misplaced loyalty to someone who doesn't deserve it."

"You created this entire disaster, you vindictive, evil bitch," Deb shouted back as Lisa headed toward the exit. "This is all your fault, and you know it your vengeful bitch!" I shouted at Lisa.

Lisa remained completely unfazed by Deb's and my anger because she understood that her two-year contract with Vince's company would continue to pay her substantial salary even though the project was being terminated. From her perspective, she had successfully sabotaged my project while securing ongoing financial compensation for herself. In many ways, she had achieved exactly what she had set out to accomplish from the beginning.

As the office cleared out and our employees gathered their personal belongings, Deb and I found ourselves alone in the beautiful space we had created with such hope and enthusiasm just months earlier. We settled onto the luxurious silver leather Chesterfield couch that I had special-ordered from London and had waited months to receive.

The workspace that had once been filled with music, creative energy, animated discussions, and frequent laughter was now eerily quiet. The silence felt oppressive as we contemplated the magnitude of what we had just done and what the future might hold for both of us.

"How are we going to manage the rent payments now?" I asked, suddenly confronting the practical realities of our situation. "This space costs twelve thousand dollars a month, and we just eliminated our primary source of income."

"We'll figure something out, Katie," Deb said, pulling me into a tight hug.

"You always manage to find a way forward, no matter how impossible the situation seems. That's one of your greatest strengths as both a friend and a business professional."

"Ride or die, right?" I said, returning her embrace and trying to project optimism I didn't entirely feel.

"Always," she replied with conviction as she cranked up Aretha Franklin's "I will survive" on the turntable.

The Painful Aftermath and Lingering Regrets

Looking back on this decision now, many, many years later, I can honestly say that walking away from the Jessica Simpson project represents one of the choices I most deeply regret in my career. The financial implications were devastating, but the professional opportunities that I forfeited may have been even more significant in the long run.

I had genuinely believed at the time, that choosing personal loyalty over business success represented the morally correct path, and I still believe that my motivations were honorable. But I also can't ignore the reality that this decision could possibly ended any chance I had of establishing myself as a major player in the celebrity licensing market.

The irony is that despite my noble intentions and personal sacrifice, my friendship with Deb didn't survive after my new shapewear line took flight. The stress of my financial situation, combined with her ongoing struggles with alcohol and the psychological trauma from her past, created problems that our relationship ultimately couldn't withstand.

Within a year after trying to start the shapewear business, Deb had essentially disappeared from my life entirely. She stopped returning my phone calls, failed to show up for meetings, and eventually moved away without providing any forwarding address or contact information. The woman I had sacrificed my biggest career opportunity to support simply vanished, leaving me with enormous debt, no income, and a beautiful office space I could no longer afford.

I struggled desperately to manage the rent payments on my own, determined to maintain the workspace and continue pursuing the shapewear concept that was supposed to justify the decision I had made. I sold furniture, personal belongings, and anything else of value I could find, but it wasn't nearly enough to cover the ongoing expenses.

The final insult came when Vince's office contacted me to demand the return of furniture pieces that I had personally purchased for our showroom with my own money. They claimed that these items were now company property since they had been used in a workspace funded by their organization. I was too emotionally and financially exhausted to fight this additional battle, so I simply allowed them to take whatever they wanted.

"I truly apologize for how this situation has developed, Katie," the CFO said with genuine sadness as he supervised the removal of furniture from my office. "You're an incredibly talented designer, and I wish things could have worked out differently."

Left alone in the nearly empty showroom that had once represented all of my hopes and dreams for the future, I found myself crying for hours. The beautiful space that Deb and I had created together with such enthusiasm and optimism now felt like a monument to poor decision-making and misplaced priorities.

When I learned several years later that Vince had passed away, I was filled with sadness about the relationship we might have built and the projects we might have accomplished together if I had made different choices during that critical period.

The experience forced me to question whether I could continue in the fashion industry at all. The combination of financial devastation, professional disappointment, and personal betrayal had left me feeling defeated in ways I had never experienced before. The thought of surrendering and finding a completely different career path became increasingly appealing as I contemplated the wreckage of what had once seemed like such a promising opportunity.

But deep down, I knew that giving up entirely wasn't truly an option for me. I felt a responsibility to both myself and to Deb's memory of our partnership to attempt creating something that we could genuinely call our own.

I had always thought of myself as a Phoenix—a creature that rises from its own ashes, stronger and more determined than before. This devastating setback would simply have to become another chapter in that ongoing story of resurrection and renewal. The question wasn't whether I would recover from this disaster, but rather how long the recovery would take and what form it would ultimately assume.

CHAPTER 12:

Shapewear and the NBA

Finding New Investors After Jessica's Collapse

The collapse of my partnership with Jessica Simpson left me scrambling to find new financial backing for my shapewear concept "Sliminizer." Once I regained my footing after the collapse of Jessica's business, I threw myself into developing what would become—a revolutionary shapewear line that broke new ground by offering products specifically designed for different skin tones. This was unprecedented in the shapewear industry at the time. I believed I was creating something truly innovative, something that would fill a gap in the market that no one else had recognized.

My timing couldn't have been better, or so I thought. But within a year of launching "Sliminizer," I watched in dismay as several established companies began releasing their own versions of my skin-tone shapewear. This pattern of idea theft had become all too familiar during my years in the garment center.

The Reality of Design Theft in Fashion

The fashion industry operates on a brutal principle: steal fast, profit faster. If you have a great idea but lack the resources to bring it to market quickly, someone with deeper pockets will simply take your concept and beat you to the shelves. This isn't an occasional occurrence—it's standard operating procedure.

Years later, this pattern would repeat itself on a bigger scale. In 2017, I pitched a clothing line concept for Kendall and Kylie Jenner's team for the Chinese market. I was told by their Chief Executive Officer that I would be vetted by the Kardashian and Jenner teams to assure a cohesiveness within the brands. I submitted my portfolio of work that included all of my lingerie and shapewear designs along with the rest of my work. The following year, Kim Kardashian launched SKIMS, a shapewear line that bore striking similarities to my "Sliminizer" concept from 2009 that was featured in my portfolio. The difference? Kim had the celebrity status, huge financial backing, and marketing power to make the same idea into a billion-dollar success. Meanwhile, my original concept had died after a sold-out launch, due to lack of investor funding.

This experience taught me a harsh lesson about the fashion world: celebrities and their teams consistently win because they have the resources to execute ideas at scale, regardless of where those ideas originated. The question of creative ownership becomes irrelevant when you have unlimited marketing budgets and global brand recognition.

The brazen nature of design theft in the fashion industry extended into my personal life on yet another occasion. I once held a patent for an innovative bra design, but without an investor to help bring it to market, the patent sat undeveloped. During a routine search for freelance designers on a creative hiring platform, I discovered my own patented bra design featured prominently on a young woman's portfolio website.

The audacity was breathtaking. Not only was she promoting my patented bra design as her own work, but she was also soliciting donations from her church congregation to fund the production and sales of "her" invention. When I located her and confronted her directly, she showed no remorse whatsoever. Her response was essentially that she didn't care about the theft because she needed the money.

I escalated the matter to her church's management and threatened her with legal action if the unauthorized sales continued. The experience left me so disgusted with the entire process and with people's bad intentions.

The Ecosystem of Fashion Copying

The reality is that nearly every piece of apparel that you purchase has its roots in someone else's original design. The fashion industry operates on a complex ecosystem of inspiration, interpretation, and outright theft. European retailers often set trends that are two to three years ahead of American markets. American manufacturers routinely send teams to European fashion weeks and trade shows, and stores, not to appreciate the artistry, but to photograph, purchase and steal ideas that they can reproduce quickly and cheaply.

There's a fine line between drawing inspiration and committing theft, but that line gets crossed constantly and no one seems to care. Original designers—true artists devoted to their craft—are becoming increasingly rare in an industry that prioritizes speed and profit margins over creativity and innovation.

I must admit that even I wasn't immune to this pressure. When faced with impossible deadlines and demanding bosses, I sometimes resorted to adapting existing designs rather than creating entirely original pieces. I always tried to modify the designs significantly, changing fabrics, colors, and construction details, but the foundation of the garment often came from somewhere else. At the end of the day, the only metric that mattered in the apparel industry was how quickly you could get products to market and generate profits.

Connecting with My Investor Through Bill

My search for a new investor for "Sliminizer" eventually led me back to Bill, my accountant who had worked for both me and Harry's company simultaneously—a clear conflict of interest that I had tolerated because I desperately needed his financial expertise. Bill had lied to me from the beginning about his dual employment, but by the time I discovered the truth, I was too dependent on his services to cut ties.

When Bill offered to connect me with a potential investor for "Sliminizer," I accepted despite my reservations about his trustworthiness. I suspected he was motivated more by guilt over his previous deceptions than genuine desire to help, but I was running out of options and couldn't afford to be picky.

Bill's romantic entanglement with Gail, his former assistant whom I had hired after Harry fired her, added another layer of complexity to our professional relationship. Harry's objection to their affair had more to do with workplace relationships than with Bill's various financial schemes that he openly bragged about mastering.

Meeting Stephon Marbury

A week after agreeing to let Bill help me find investors, I found myself sharing a cab with him to a Wall Street fundraiser. He had given me no details about the event or whom I would be meeting, which should have been my first red flag. Deb who was still involved for the time being, had chosen to stay behind to work on our brand packaging and marketing materials, a decision I would later appreciate.

The fundraiser was held in an upscale venue filled with impeccably dressed men, most of whom were African American. The atmosphere was sophisticated and professional, but I felt completely out of place. I grabbed a drink from the bar and turned to Bill with confusion written all over my face.

"What on earth am I doing here?" I asked him directly.

Bill's face lit up with pride as he pointed across the room to a muscular man in an expensive suit. "Let me introduce you to Stephon Marbury—your potentially new investor," he said with obvious satisfaction at having orchestrated this meeting.

The name meant nothing to me. "Who?" I asked, genuinely confused.

Stephon Marbury, he owns "the Starbury brand!" Bill whispered excitedly. "He makes affordable sneakers for kids and plays basketball in the NBA."

I was still baffled by the connection. "Okay," I said slowly, "and that has what to do with shapewear?"

Before Bill could elaborate, Stephon approached us directly. His presence was commanding—he was handsome, athletic, and carried himself with the confidence that comes from years of professional sports. Without ceremony, he took my arm and guided me toward a private conference room, instructing Bill to wait outside.

An Unexpected Business Proposal

Once we were seated privately, I retrieved the portfolio that Bill had instructed me to bring. Stephon flipped through my designs and concept boards with genuine interest, his expression serious and focused. After several minutes of review, he looked up at me with an intensity that made me slightly uncomfortable.

"These designs are excellent," he said without preamble, "but there's something you need to understand about me before we discuss any business partnership."

I braced myself for the typical speech I'd heard from countless male executives in the apparel industry —the one where they establish their authority, let me know that they were in control, explain their unique qualifications, and detail exactly how lucky I should feel to work with them. I had heard variations of this speech so many times that I could practically recite it myself.

"I want you to know something important about how I operate," Stephon continued, leaning forward across the conference table. His tone was completely serious, which made what came next even more surprising.

"I love to smoke marijuana," he stated matter-of-factly. "Will this bother you in a business relationship?"

The directness of his question caught me completely off guard. I had prepared for discussions about profit margins, production timelines, and marketing strategies. I had not prepared for a possible business partner to lead with his recreational drug use.

For a moment, I wanted to laugh at the absurdity of the situation, but his expression remained deadly serious. This was clearly important to him, and he wanted an honest answer.

"No," I replied simply, "it won't bother me." I didn't mention that I had never smoked marijuana in my life—that seemed irrelevant to the question at hand.

"Good," he said, extending his hand for a firm handshake. "Now let me drive you home and we can discuss this opportunity further."

Getting to Know Stephon

Stephon navigated us through the crowd of people waiting to speak with him with practiced ease. A simple wave of his hand parted the sea of admirers and business associates, as we made our way to the elevator, leaving Bill behind in our wake.

In the lobby, I was introduced to Stephon's chauffeur and found myself settling into the luxurious interior of his customized Rolls-Royce Phantom. Stephon was animated and engaging as he explained various features of the vehicle, clearly taking pride in his success and the lifestyle it afforded him.

True to his word, he produced a large joint and offered it to me. "No, thank you," I said with a nervous smile, declining as politely as possible.

Despite—or perhaps because of—this unconventional introduction, I found myself genuinely liking Stephon's honesty. His cologne was expensive and subtle, his clothing was perfectly tailored to his athletic frame, and he projected an aura of power tempered by genuine kindness and curiosity about the world around him.

What impressed me most was his intelligence and his ability to read people accurately. He had clearly developed sophisticated instincts about who could be trusted and who was trying to take advantage of him. Anyone he suspected of playing games was immediately cut from his circle—a policy I desperately needed to adopt in my own professional relationships.

Meeting the Team and Complications

Over the following days, I was introduced to Stephon's business team, a group that included some genuinely unpleasant individuals. His business manager, in particular, seemed to view me with suspicion and hostility. This man was fiercely protective of his access to Stephon and clearly saw me as a developing threat to his income stream.

The team also included Paul, another former NBA player, and not his real name, whom Bill had brought in as an additional investor in my shapewear line. From our first meeting, I Paul's personality grating and his attitude dismissive, but Bill assured me that he would remain a silent partner with minimal involvement in day-to-day operations.

When Stephon and Paul visited my showroom to meet with Deb and me and review our concept, the contrast between the two men became even more apparent. Deb was immediately charmed by Stephon's enthusiasm and charismatic personality. Paul, however, seemed skeptical of the entire venture from the start and Deb was not a fan of him either.

Stephon's Personal Struggles and Innovation

During this period, Stephon was dealing with significant personal challenges. He had recently lost his father, a loss that affected him deeply. As part of his grieving process, he had begun creating very personal video content about his life and started posting 24 hours of video chats on USTREAM.

Looking back now, I can see that Stephon was years ahead of his time. He was essentially the original influencer, sharing intimate details of his life through video content long before social media made this type of personal branding commonplace. His videos represented an early form of reality television featuring a real person navigating genuine struggles, but at the time, many people—including members of the press—dismissed him as crazy or attention-seeking.

Simultaneously, Stephon's sneaker brand was being sold through Steve and Barry's stores, a retail chain that was struggling through bankruptcy proceedings. With his NBA career winding down, I hoped that partnering with my startup would provide him with a new outlet for his considerable creativity and business acumen.

Stephon particularly appreciated the modern aesthetic of my showroom space. He had a talent for entertaining and soon began using my showroom as a venue for hosting parties and gatherings with his friends and business associates.

The Party Arrangement

I didn't mind Stephon using my showroom for his social events, provided he remembered the security code to enter the office. When he forgot the code, and triggered the alarm system at 2:00 in the morning, I would have to rush over to the space to explain to the responding police officers that he was a prospective business partner and friend, not a burglar.

These late-night explanations to law enforcement became a regular occurrence, but I considered them a small price to pay for maintaining a relationship with someone who I genuinely liked and respected.

Building the Brand Infrastructure

To create a professional online presence for "Sliminizer," I hired the husband, a web developer, of an old friend of mine. He was among the first generation of creative web designers, and his innovative approach came with an appropriately high price tag. The website he created was cutting-edge and visually striking, reflecting the groundbreaking nature of our product concept.

In 2008, I was one of the first fashion entrepreneurs to use models representing all skin tones in advertising and marketing materials. Industry veterans told me this approach was commercial suicide, but I believed it was essential to the authenticity of our brand. My friend, the wife of the web developer, who had been part of my life for over two decades, flew in from California to apply the makeup on our models for our first photo shoot. She was an exceptionally talented makeup artist who had worked on numerous successful Hollywood films. She captured the essence of the diverse models with subtle, yet beautiful makeup artistry. The website was well received.

The Challenge of Trust and Friendship

As "Sliminizer" developed, I became increasingly frustrated with people who pretended to be friends while actually seeking to exploit my financial resources and industry connections. I repeatedly found myself believing in individuals whom I was certain were genuine allies, only to discover they were motivated entirely by self-interest.

This pattern of misplaced trust was entirely my fault. I can trace this tendency to my lack of a reliable business mentor—someone who could have guided me through the complexities of this challenging industry and helped me identify the warning signs of people with ulterior motives. Instead, I consistently wanted to see the good in everyone, which led me to repeatedly choose the wrong business partners and advisors.

Production Challenges and Personnel Issues

After completing the "Sliminizer" website, my next priority was hiring a production manager. When building any fashion brand, the initial hire should ideally be a skilled production expert capable of guiding factories through the manufacturing process and ensuring quality control throughout the supply chain.

The first person I employed came with glowing recommendations from his previous employer, but he quickly proved to be completely unsuited for my needs. Rather than exploring various factory options to find the best fit for our product, he only sent samples to factories in Bangladesh where he had established relationships that would generate kickbacks for him personally. This level of corruption was completely unacceptable, and I terminated his employment immediately.

My next hire was a man named Johnny, who turned out to be an even bigger disaster. From day one, he exhibited aggressive behavior and a fundamental lack of honesty in all of his dealings. You might wonder why I made such a poor choice in hiring him—the answer lies in the glowing praise he had received from his former employer.

What I failed to understand at the time was that his previous company was desperate to get rid of him and was willing to say anything to make him someone else's problem. Finding reliable production staff in the fashion industry is notoriously difficult. The field attracts individuals who are comfortable with lying, cheating, and stealing to advance their own interests, making constant vigilance necessary to monitor their activities.

I fired Johnny and decided to manage all production activities myself rather than risk another bad hire.

Later in my career, I once teamed up with a particularly vile production veteran who was remarkably incompetent; he struggled even with basic garment measurements that were required for his job. He managed to deceive everyone by shifting all of his responsibilities onto his subordinates until they threatened to reveal his shortcomings, leading him to dismiss them before they could report him. When I confronted him on a grave mistake that he had made, he told me that "lying" was perfectly justified as long as he received the outcome he needed. He is still employed at his company and after 12 years they have never figured out that he has been taking kickbacks for years.

Investment Complications

Through Bill's persistence, I secured a small financial investment from Paul, the former NBA player. Although Stephon had initially shown enthusiasm for "Sliminizer," and enjoyed hosting parties at my showroom, his interest in the day-to-day business operations began to wane. Eventually, he stopped visiting entirely except for our launch party, until he moved to China to play for the Chinese Basketball Association.

I sensed early on that working with Paul would be problematic. He constantly complained that women wouldn't want to wear "skin tone" shapewear, dismissing the core concept that made "Sliminizer" innovative and potentially profitable. When Bill returned to his full-time position at his original company with Harry, I was left to manage the entire business single-handedly when Deb finally checked out.

Deb's Decline

After several months of operation, Deb began to mentally disengage from the project. It was difficult to determine whether her withdrawal was due to guilt over our departure from Vince's company or a worsening of the emotional struggles that had led her to drink excessively and unpredictably throughout our partnership.

I had grown weary of constantly managing her personal crises, so when she began missing work regularly, I actually felt relieved.

Her contributions had become minimal, and her presence was often more disruptive than helpful.

Another Launch Party Disaster

In a misguided attempt to generate buzz and drive sales for "Sliminizer," I decided to organize an elaborate launch party. Looking back, this was a significant strategic error. I lacked the business experience necessary to run a company alone and effectively; my strengths lay in design and creative vision for innovative products, not in business operations.

For the launch party, I hired models representing diverse skin tones to showcase how our shapewear products were specifically designed for different complexions. This diversity had always been the foundation and unique selling proposition of the "Sliminizer" brand.

The party was certainly successful as a social event for my friends and acquaintances, but it resulted in costing a devastating $40,000 for my already struggling company. Multiple media outlets covered the event, including "Extra" and "Entertainment Tonight." Stephon brought along a group of NBA players and celebrities, including Sway from MTV. I even managed to get "Sliminizer" featured on the Jumbo Tron in Times Square.

Despite all this publicity, the event was a commercial failure because no actual retailers attended the party. Friends had told me that Lisa, my former nemesis, had been spreading rumors throughout the industry that my skin tone shapewear concept would never sell commercially.

Howard's Exit Strategy

Following the launch party, Paul's business manager began

pressuring me daily to liquidate my remaining inventory so Paul could recoup his investment as quickly as possible. Although Paul had attended the launch party with his friends and seemed to enjoy the social aspects of the event, he was now eager to exit the business entirely.

Paul continued to insist that skin tone shapewear would never achieve commercial success and that the entire concept was fundamentally flawed.

I often wonder what Paul's reaction was when Kim Kardashian launched SKIMS in 2019—eleven years after my "Sliminizer" launch—with a concept remarkably the same as mine and she achieved billion-dollar success.

A Potential Lifeline

During the launch party, I met Londell, who had served as Michael Jackson's attorney and was well-known throughout the entertainment industry. I approached him about investing in my company and potentially buying out Paul's stake to resolve the growing tensions.

Londell was handsome, brilliant, and charismatic, and he seemed genuinely intrigued by the "Sliminizer" concept. He expressed willingness to help me navigate the business challenges I was facing, which gave me hope that the brand could still succeed with proper backing.

However, Paul's reaction to Londell's potential involvement was explosive. He showed dislike for Londell immediately, which led to heated arguments that made it impossible to move forward constructively. Paul became more determined than ever to exit my business as quickly as possible.

To make matters worse, Paul hired Lisa—the same horrible

woman who had been undermining my career—to handle the liquidation of my inventory. This decision felt like a deliberate attempt to cause maximum damage to both the brand and my reputation.

Recognition from Oprah

Despite all these setbacks, "Sliminizer" received validation from an unexpected source. Oprah Winfrey's magazine featured my brand prominently, marking the first time Oprah had ever promoted shapewear products in her publication. This endorsement was incredibly meaningful because Oprah's brand carried enormous weight with consumers, particularly women who were interested in body-positive products.

If I had possessed adequate funding and proper business support, this Oprah endorsement could have been the catalyst for major commercial success. Instead, I was forced to watch the opportunity slip away due to lack of resources and investor disinterest.

Early E-commerce Experiments

I launched "Sliminizer's" online sales website during the early days of e-commerce, when most consumers were still hesitant to purchase clothing online. Many nights, I found myself alone in my showroom, staying awake until 2:00 a.m. in the morning to handle customer service calls and chat with dedicated customers who were enthusiastic about the brand.

I often sensed back then, that my concept was several years ahead of the market, and subsequent developments have proven this intuition correct. The direct-to-consumer model that seemed experimental and risky in 2008 became the dominant retail strategy within a few years.

I did sell out of my first initial order and that had covered the expenses of the showroom, marketing, and the party. I shouldn't have placed a second order because this caused me to have too much inventory that I could not sell once the investor stopped funding me.

The Final Betrayal

Londell offered to return Paul's full investment to resolve the partnership dispute, but Paul spitefully rejected this reasonable solution. Instead, he chose to ensure my company's destruction by hiring Lisa to liquidate all inventory at fire-sale prices.

Even after Paul recovered more than his original investment through inventory sales, he refused to return my "Sliminizer" trademark, effectively preventing me from relaunching the brand in the future. With no money remaining and feeling mentally and physically exhausted, I saw no options other than leaving the apparel business entirely.

When Lisa arrived at my showroom to oversee the liquidation, she made no effort to hide her satisfaction at my downfall. The sight of this woman gloating over the destruction of my life's work pushed me beyond my breaking point.

"I absolutely despise you!" I screamed at her as she began cataloging my remaining assets. "Get out of my space! This is my showroom!"

"Paul hired me to handle this liquidation," she replied with obvious pleasure. "You're finished in this business."

I couldn't tolerate being in the same space as this toxic individual any longer, so I left the showroom and went home to try to process what had happened and I never returned to my showroom again.

Discovery of Theft

Within a week, I began to suspect that Lisa was selling off significant portions of my inventory for pennies on the dollar. It looked like she was deceiving Paul about the actual value of what had been liquidated as per her records on my computer she had taken home with her right after I had fired her. Shortly thereafter, Paul disappeared entirely, leaving Lisa to shut down my business permanently.

Once again, I found myself caught in a web of unscrupulous characters, with Lisa serving as the primary architect of my destruction.

Lisa had taken my company laptop—a computer I had purchased with my own money—and she had been careless enough to leave my original password unchanged. When I accessed the computer remotely, I uncovered evidence of her selling off my inventory for less than it was valued at. In retaliation for me confronting her about cheating me and Paul, Lisa had her friend at the NYPD arrest me on false charges of "breaking into my own computer." She took particular pleasure in my arrest, positioning herself outside my apartment building to watch the entire ordeal unfold while taking photographs.

Although I was eventually released without charges, I was forced to spend a night in the notorious Tombs jail in New York—a harrowing experience that continues to cause me PTSD symptoms to this day.

Legal Harassment

Lisa's vindictiveness didn't end with my arrest. She also had her police officer friend help her file a restraining order against me, despite knowing that I had no intention of ever approaching or contacting her again. This allowed her to escape the consequences for her theft while adding another layer of harassment to my ordeal.

According to some reputable industry insiders, Lisa carried the restraining order in her wallet like a trophy as evidence of how effectively she had "destroyed "my career.

I view Lisa as one of the most sick, toxic individuals I had ever encountered during my time in the fashion industry. Her jealousy over my pursuit of creative dreams and my refusal to support her financially had transformed into a pathological desire to see me fail completely.

Moving On

With no choice but to accept defeat, I gave up. The was emotionally devastating, and I felt completely defeated, wanting nothing more than to curl up and weep over the destruction of years of hard work.

Occasionally, I find myself remembering Deb and our wild adventures and laughing at some of the memories we created together. For many years, she had been my closest friend and most trusted collaborator. Years later, I learned that her mother had passed away and that Deb was struggling with serious health issues. I genuinely hope she has found the peace and stability she needs.

Reflection and Resilience

When "Sliminizer" collapsed before it had a real chance to succeed, I found myself completely uncertain about how to proceed with my faltering career. I had maintained a naive belief that each new venture would finally lead to my big breakthrough, yet my track record of choosing problematic colleagues and business partners had consistently led to disappointment.

This pattern of poor judgment in selecting associates had become a significant obstacle to my professional success. Regardless of how discouraged I felt, I never stopped generating fresh ideas and innovative product concepts that I was proud of.

My friends had begun calling me the "Phoenix" because I kept managing to rise from the ashes of my repeated fashion career failures, always ready to try again with renewed optimism and energy.

A New Inspiration of an Eternal Optimist

One afternoon, while walking my dog through Central Park, an idea for a country-themed fashion concept suddenly struck me. It seemed that no one had ever attempted to create a charming country-inspired lingerie collection, and the concept began forming in my mind as we walked.

"Could this be the breakthrough I've been searching for?" I wondered aloud, picking up my pug for a hug. "Absolutely! This could be the one!" I exclaimed with genuine excitement.

"Tomorrow, I'll start designing a country lingerie brand and this time find better investors," I promised myself with renewed enthusiasm.

The alternative was wallowing in self-pity and depression, which wasn't an acceptable option.

"Hang in there," I told myself encouragingly. "You still have creativity and talent left in you."

The Power of Optimism

I believe my persistent blind optimism had sustained me throughout all these challenging years in the fashion industry. Without this fundamental faith in eventual success, I might have given up entirely and faced a much bleaker outcome.

I often felt isolated because most of my friends worked outside the fashion industry and couldn't understand why I remained so determined to succeed in a field that had brought me so much pain and disappointment over the years.

Despite years of therapy, I struggled to find someone who could help me understand and change my pattern of poor choices and business decisions.

The Breaking Point with My Therapist

For ten years, my therapist had played a supportive, almost fatherly role in my life, helping me process the various challenges and setbacks I faced in the fashion industry. However, everything changed when I was forced to shut down "Sliminizer."

During what would be our final session, he angrily confronted me about what he saw as my self-destructive patterns. "You're fooling yourself," he said with obvious frustration. "Your dog will eventually die, and you'll be left completely alone and in despair. You'll probably even take your own life, all because you refused to seek stable employment outside this industry and this horrible city."

His harsh words felt like a betrayal of the trust I had placed in him over nearly a decade of therapy. From that moment forward, I never contacted him again, because I believed that only I could dictate my future path—not him or anyone else.

Looking back, I'm still not sure whether his confrontation represented tough love or simply his own frustration with my life choices. Perhaps the difficult truth he presented was simply too painful for me to accept at the time, so I steered clear of dwelling on his predictions. He's 85, I reminded myself; he'll likely pass away long before I do—consider that a twist of poetic justice!

Reflections on Celebrity Culture

It was never my intention to build a career around celebrity relationships and partnerships. Over the years, I encountered numerous famous individuals from various fields—rappers, rock stars, actors, and television personalities—but the only time I was genuinely star struck was during my regular visits to Studio 54 in the early 1980s, where I met Michael Jackson.

Michael possessed a truly magical presence; his energy was electric and palpable when you stood near him and he was always so kind to everyone. Years after his death, I was honored to design for the retail store at Mandalay Bay's "Michael Jackson Tribute" show produced by Cirque du Soleil, which felt like a meaningful way to honor his memory and artistry.

My perspective on celebrities has always been grounded in reality. I see them as individuals who came from ordinary backgrounds and worked exceptionally hard to develop their talents and achieve success, wealth, and influence. I respect the perseverance required for their journeys because I have also tried to innovate within the fashion industry through dedicated hard work.

In all of my years in fashion, I have rarely encountered anyone with a work ethic comparable to my own. What astonishes me about today's social media landscape is how some individuals manage to achieve tremendous financial success while appearing to put in minimal effort, largely due to the amplifying power of social media platforms. To me, most of todays influencers lack talent, unless shaking your hips is a strength. It truly baffles me!

The Harsh Reality of Effort vs. Results

At the end of the day, I came to realize that no matter how much effort I invested in my projects, it rarely made the difference I hoped it would. There was always someone willing to undercut my position for a lower salary, appropriate my ideas for their own use, or leverage my skills to advance their personal agendas.

Despite these disappointments, I maintained a deep passion for design and fashion. This industry served as my lifeline, especially during periods of unemployment and financial uncertainty. It also motivated me to confront overwhelming feelings of depression, anxiety, and fear during some of the darkest periods of my life.

Determination to Succeed

The pressure in the fashion industry felt enormous, yet I remained determined to carve out my place in this world. No one was going to push me out of the only industry I had ever known or loved.

Some people might label me an eternal optimist about my fashion career prospects, and they would probably be correct. I consistently held onto the belief that the fashion gods had something incredible in store for me—or at least, that's what I always hoped for and continued to work toward, regardless of the setbacks I faced.

The story of "Sliminizer" wasn't about failure, it was about innovation and foreseeing the future of fashion trends when no one else did. It also wasn't the end of my story. There would be more attempts, more innovations, and hopefully, eventually, more success. The Phoenix was ready to rise again.

CHAPTER 13:
Vintage Heartland Had an Angel

Navigating Getting Older

For three solid weeks, I couldn't bring myself to leave the bedroom floor of my apartment, weeping uncontrollably, unable to eat or speak to another human being.

The fear that consumed me after "Sliminizer" wasn't just about financial ruin—it was the terrifying possibility that I might never work again. At my age, starting over in any industry seemed impossible, but starting over in fashion felt like a cruel joke. All I wanted was to disappear from the world entirely, to find some remote island where I could hide from the judgment of everyone who had witnessed my repeated missteps.

The weight of defeat felt crushing. After decades of fighting to establish myself in the fashion industry, after surviving sexual harassment, corrupt business partners, continued verbal abuse and countless betrayals, I had finally reached my breaking point.

Another Eviction Notice

On a particularly gloomy, rainy morning in November, I finally managed to drag myself out of bed. The simple act of dressing myself and lighting a cigarette to suppress my hunger pangs felt like monumental achievements. The cigarette had become my primary source of appetite control—I couldn't afford food, but I could afford tobacco.

Lying on my kitchen counter was my third eviction notice. I had already sold every designer bag, every piece of designer clothing, and every pair of designer shoes I owned just to make rent payments. The beautiful wardrobe I had built over decades in the fashion industry—pieces that had once made me feel confident and successful—had been reduced to cash for basic survival.

The final blow came when I had to sell my mink coat, a beautiful piece I had purchased years earlier when fur was still fashionable and socially acceptable. That coat represented a time when I had money, when I belonged in the fashion world, when my future seemed bright and full of possibility. Watching it leave my apartment along with my prized Hermes handbag I had to sell, felt like saying goodbye to the last vestige of my former life.

Surviving on Scraps

The management company that owned my building was aggressively pursuing my eviction. They knew that my rent-controlled apartment, where I had lived for over two decades, could command three or four times the rent if they could force me out. Every interaction with building management felt hostile and predatory.

I managed to scrape together just enough money to pay my rent, until my unemployment check arrived—a pathetic few hundred dollars that barely covered essentials. The irony was devastating: after contributing substantial taxes to New York State for decades, this meager assistance was all the support I received during my time of greatest need.

The apartment that had once been my sanctuary now felt like a prison. The spacious rooms that had hosted parties, business meetings, and creative collaborations were now empty shells echoing with memories of better times. My three walk-in closets, once filled with designer pieces, stood half full. The terrace where I used to enjoy morning coffee while looking out over Central Park now seemed to mock me with its view of a life I could no longer afford.

A Simple Coffee Becomes a Lifeline

My craving for a decent cup of coffee led me to the Starbucks conveniently located on the ground floor of my building. Counting out spare change, I joined the queue of young professionals and tourists, dreaming of that first sip of dark roast while fantasizing about escaping to some other time where no one would know about my career choices.

I must have looked completely disheveled—my hair messy and in a ponytail, wearing old pajama pants and a t-shirt with a coat thrown over them, my worn-out Ugg boots barely holding together. I felt utterly drained, both physically and emotionally, like a ghost of my former self.

Standing in that coffee shop, surrounded by young, energetic people discussing their jobs and laughing about weekend plans, I had never felt more disconnected from the world around me. These people represented everything I had lost: purpose, income, social connections, hope for my future.

An Angel Enters my Life

By the time I finally got my coffee, my hands were trembling—whether from caffeine withdrawal, hunger, or emotional distress, I couldn't tell. I entered my apartment building and stepped into the elevator alone, finally allowing myself to break down completely. The tears came in waves as I stood there, feeling utterly defeated and alone.

Just as the elevator doors were about to close, someone stopped them from the outside. In walked an elegant blonde woman with a warm smile, accompanied by a distinguished older man with white hair and a young couple—a handsome young man with a lovely brunette woman by his side.

"Hi there!" the blonde woman said to me in a distinctive Texas accent, her voice warm and friendly despite my obvious distress.

I looked up at her through my tears, completely unable to speak. The other passengers were engrossed in their own animated conversation, apparently discussing family matters and celebration plans. But this kind woman noticed my condition immediately and placed a gentle, comforting hand on my shoulder.

When the elevator reached the tenth floor, the men and the young woman exited, chatting excitedly about dinner reservations and evening plans. "Go ahead," the blonde woman told them with a reassuring smile, "I'll catch up with you in just a moment." The doors closed, leaving just the two of us in the elevator.

She turned her full attention to me, her eyes filled with genuine concern and compassion. "Dear," she said in a quiet, gentle voice that somehow conveyed both strength and tenderness, "where do you live?"

Unexpected Kindness from a Stranger

When the elevator reached the twentieth floor, I pointed down the hallway toward my apartment, unable to form words through my tears. To my amazement, this complete stranger followed me down the hall, as if she had been invited or expected.

In all the years, I had lived in that apartment—nearly two decades—I had never once locked my door, not even when traveling for extended periods overseas. The building had always felt safe, and my apartment was the only place in the world that truly felt like home. The thought of being forced to leave it was breaking my heart.

Years later, when I made the decision to leave this apartment for Nashville, I would deeply regret giving up this sanctuary. Even now, I wish I could return permanently. I miss everything about that space: the memories of my beloved pug, the happiest moments of my life, the laughter and tears shared with friends, my three spacious walk-in closets, the sun-drenched terrace, and the sun filled rooms that overlooked Central Park with their ever-changing views of the seasons.

Meeting My Guardian Angel

This remarkable woman introduced herself as Gerry. She was tall—nearly six feet—with striking blonde hair and penetrating blue eyes. Her elegant designer clothing and impeccable grooming suggested both wealth and refined taste, but what struck me most was the maternal warmth she radiated. Although we appeared to be roughly the same age, I felt like a lost child in her presence.

Throughout our friendship, which would span many years, I would consistently think of Gerry as my "angel." She possessed a magnetic charm that drew people to her effortlessly, like bees to honey, but her appeal went far beyond surface charisma. She had a gift for making people feel seen, heard, and valued.

Gerry followed me into my apartment as if she had been there countless times before. Without asking permission or waiting for direction, she headed straight for my kitchen. "I'm going to make us a cup of tea," she announced with a warm, confident smile.

I simply nodded, pointed toward the kitchen cabinets while I continued to cry, then I waited for this "angel" to return with whatever comfort she could provide.

Sharing My Story with a Compassionate Listener

For the next two hours, I poured out my entire life story to this stranger who had shown me more kindness in five minutes than I had received from anyone in years. I cried as I recounted my decades in the apparel industry, the sexual harassment, the corrupt business partners, the stolen designs, the fizzled ventures, and the repeated betrayals that had led me to this moment of hopelessness.

Gerry sat beside me throughout my emotional outpouring, listening intently without judgment or interruption. She would occasionally nod knowingly, reach over to touch my hand reassuringly, or make soft sounds of understanding and sympathy. Never once did she seem shocked, appalled, or eager to end our conversation.

I was certain that my litany of precarious choices and professional mishaps would terrify this elegant, successful woman. Instead, she seemed genuinely engaged with my story, even asking to see my design portfolio and the sample garments I pulled from my closet to illustrate various points in my narrative.

A New Creative Vision

During our conversation, I shared with Gerry my latest creative inspiration: a lingerie brand with a country theme that I wanted to call "Vintage Heartland." The concept had been percolating in my mind during my weeks of solitude, and I was excited to have someone to discuss it with. Designing had kept me sane, even if it was just for my eyes only. The thought of doing nothing was what scared me the most.

Gerry's eyes lit up when I described the brand concept. She absolutely loved the idea of combining feminine lingerie with country-western aesthetics, seeing it as a unique market opportunity that could appeal to women who felt underserved by existing intimate apparel brands. After all she was a Texan!

Her enthusiasm for "Vintage Heartland" was the first positive feedback I had received about any of my ideas in months. Having someone believe in my creative vision, especially someone who seemed as sophisticated and business-savvy as Gerry, gave me the first glimmer of hope I had felt since my shapewear business collapsed.

An Unexpected Departure

As our conversation was winding down, Gerry suddenly looked at her watch and jumped up with surprise. "Oh, my goodness, time has absolutely flown by," she said with genuine regret. "I need to leave for my dinner reservation. I'm so sorry!"

She gave me a warm, lingering hug that felt like a mother embracing a child. As she prepared to leave, she explained that she and her husband Marvin were staying in the building for the weekend to celebrate their son's engagement to his girlfriend. The entire family was gathering for a special dinner to mark the occasion.

I hugged her back, already feeling a profound sense of loss at her departure. "Thank you so much for listening," I managed to say through my tears. "You have no idea how much this means to me."

As she walked toward my door, I felt overwhelming gratitude mixed with the certainty that I would never see this wonderful woman again. Still, her unexpected kindness had provided exactly what I needed most: the feeling that someone in the world cared about my wellbeing and believed in my potential for recovery.

Divine Intervention

After Gerry left, I felt an incredible sense of relief and peace that I hadn't experienced in months. This complete stranger had listened to my entire story without once questioning my choices, criticizing my decisions, or suggesting that I had brought these troubles upon myself. Her non-judgmental compassion felt like a gift from God—exactly what I needed to begin healing.

Although I never expected to see Gerry again, I felt certain that God had sent her to me at precisely the moment when I needed her most. Her presence had reminded me that kindness still existed in the world and that my life still had some value, even when I couldn't see it myself.

Exhausted from the emotional intensity of our conversation, I made my way to my bedroom around 5:00 p.m., and fell into the deepest, most peaceful sleep I had experienced in weeks. For the first time since my business collapsed, I slept without crushing anxiety.

A Miraculous Gift

At 9:00 p.m., I was awakened by my buzzer's insistent ringing—letting me know that my doorman was trying to contact me, but I figured it was bad news so I didn't answer it. I stumbled to the kitchen, still groggy from my deep sleep, when my doorbell rang then unexpectedly.

Opening the door, I found my building's doorman standing in the hallway with a puzzled expression. "Yes?" I asked nervously, immediately assuming he was bringing me another eviction notice.

Instead, he handed me a small, elegant envelope. "This was left at the front desk for you," he explained. "The lady said it was important that you receive it tonight."

After getting a cigarette and settling back onto my couch, I carefully opened the envelope. Inside was a beautiful white card embossed with the initials "GM" in gold lettering. The message, written in elegant handwriting, read:

> *Dear Katie,*
>
> *When I told my husband Marvin your incredible story and how talented you are, he insisted that we help you. Consider this an investment in your future fashion line.*
>
> *Love,*
>
> *Gerry and Marvin*

As I unfolded the card, a large check fell into my lap. The amount was more than enough to solve my immediate financial problems and provide a foundation for starting over. I stared at it in complete disbelief, overwhelmed by the generosity of these virtual strangers.

I began literally screamed with joy, caught up in the excitement of this miraculous turn of events. It was impossible to comprehend that people I had just met would extend such extraordinary generosity to someone in my desperate situation.

Gratitude and New Beginnings

My heartfelt thanks will forever go to Gerry, Marvin, and God for their intervention during one of the darkest period of my life. Their kindness not only solved my immediate financial crisis but also restored my faith in human goodness.

From that day forward, Gerry and I developed a close, lasting friendship. She became one of the most extraordinary people I have ever had the privilege of knowing—someone whose generosity of spirit extended far beyond financial assistance to include emotional support, creative encouragement, and unwavering belief in my potential.

Creating "Vintage Heartland"

The creation of my country-themed lingerie line "Vintage Heartland" became a year-long labor of love. This project represented more than just another business venture—it was my pathway back to creative fulfillment and professional confidence after the collapse of my shapewear company.

The brand development process was comprehensive and ambitious. In addition to designing the lingerie collection itself, I produced a full-color catalog showcasing the complete line and directed four music videos that captured the spirit and aesthetic of the brand. These videos were filmed at a picturesque sustainable farm in upstate New York, creating authentic country backdrops that perfectly complemented the lingerie designs.

This creative period was filled with new collaborations and friendships that reignited my passion for the fashion industry. My talented photographer and his exceptional crew brought my vision to life with stunning imagery. My assistant designer also proved invaluable, contributing both creative ideas and practical support throughout the development process. Our beautiful models embodied the confident, authentic femininity that "Vintage Heartland" was meant to represent.

International Recognition

The success of "Vintage Heartland" exceeded my most optimistic expectations. My Chinese factory owner, recognizing the brand's potential, persuaded me to introduce the collection at the Shenzhen Lingerie Show in China—one of the most important trade shows in the intimate apparel industry.

I traveled to China with my six-foot blonde model Diana and my assistant designer, all of us flying coach to keep expenses manageable. Upon arrival, I was amazed to discover that my factory had assembled a team of over thirty people to assist with setting up our booth and creating an elaborate display for the lingerie line.

Our booth became the centerpiece of the entire trade show. We constructed a miniature barn as our backdrop and showcased our music videos on multiple screens while our models wore the latest "Vintage Heartland" designs. The combination of authentic country aesthetics with sophisticated lingerie created a unique presentation that captured everyone's attention.

My Assistant Designer's Dedication

Throughout this challenging but exciting period, my assistant designer's enthusiasm and dedication never wavered, even when I felt overwhelmed by the scope of what we were trying to accomplish. Her commitment went far beyond her job description—she helped set up the show booth, personally dressed the models, and even pitched the line to potential retail buyers when I was too exhausted to continue.

Her unwavering support reminded me of the power of having the right team members who believe in your vision and are willing to go above and beyond to make it successful. Her positive attitude and strong work ethic became essential elements in whatever success we achieved.

Media Attention and Industry Recognition

The response to "Vintage Heartland" at the Shenzhen show was overwhelming. More than 15,000 attendees, including international press representatives, came specifically to see my lingerie line and innovative booth presentation. The international fashion media was particularly intrigued by our unique approach to combining country themes with intimate apparel.

CCTV, China's largest television station, invited me to showcase the "Vintage Heartland" collection on a live broadcast—making it the first lingerie brand ever featured on Chinese television. This historic moment represented not only recognition for our brand but also a breakthrough in how intimate apparel could be presented to mainstream audiences.

The attention we received created some tension with other lingerie brands exhibiting at the show, who felt that "Vintage Heartland" was monopolizing media coverage and visitor interest. While this competitive friction was uncomfortable, it also confirmed that we had created something truly distinctive and noteworthy.

Struggling for American Investment

Despite achieving significant recognition in China and receiving positive coverage in American publications like the Huffington Post, I continued to struggle with finding investors in the United States beyond Gerry's generous support. American investors seemed skeptical about the commercial viability of country-themed lingerie, viewing it as too niche or potentially limiting in terms of market appeal. I also knew that Lisa was still spreading disparaging comments about me and my capabilities.

The lack of domestic investment support forced me to rely heavily on my Chinese factory partner to promote and develop the brand in Asian markets. While this partnership provided manufacturing capabilities and local market expertise, it also created dependencies that would later prove problematic.

Betrayal and Theft of Intellectual Property

My reliance on Chinese manufacturing partners led to a devastating betrayal that has become all too common in international fashion business. Without my knowledge or consent, my manufacturer appropriated all of my "Vintage Heartland" designs and launched their own store using my exact brand name in Shenzhen, capitalizing on my success at the Shenzhen show.

This type of intellectual property theft represents one of the most frustrating aspects of working with overseas manufacturers. Many Chinese factories view foreign designers' concepts as free resources to be exploited rather than protected. They assume that American designers lack the resources or knowledge to pursue legal remedies in Chinese courts.

When I discovered what had happened, I confronted the factory owner directly and threatened legal action. After months of challenging negotiations and legal maneuvering in China, I managed to recover a good settlement that helped me survive financially for a while.

Personal Pride in Creative Achievement

Despite the commercial challenges and ultimate betrayal by my manufacturing partner, "Vintage Heartland" remains my favorite among all the brands I have created throughout my career. The collection represented a perfect synthesis of my creative vision, technical skills, and understanding of an underserved market segment.

I remain grateful to everyone who assisted in the launch of "Vintage Heartland" and continue to believe that the apparel industry would benefit from being more open-minded about supporting innovative new brand concepts. Too often, established players in fashion resist ideas that don't fit conventional market categories, missing opportunities to serve consumers in new and meaningful ways.

Personal Loss and Continued Friendship

During the year following the "Vintage Heartland" launch, I experienced profound personal loss when Marvin, Gerry's husband, succumbed to cancer. The grief I felt at his passing was unlike anything I had ever experienced—he had become not just a generous benefactor but a trusted friend and father figure.

With both Marvin and my own father now gone, I found comfort in believing that they were together in heaven, watching over me and continuing to provide guidance from the heavens. The impact of their belief in me and support during my hardest times cannot be overstated.

Finding the Strength to Continue

Despite the paralyzing fear that often urged me to abandon the fashion industry entirely, I found the strength to persevere through the darkest periods of my career. Climbing out of severe depression and re-entering the professional world was incredibly challenging, yet I felt compelled to discover what possibilities still lay ahead.

I spent countless hours wondering what my next chapter might hold—it remained one of the greatest mysteries of my life at that time. The uncertainty was both terrifying and exciting, representing either the end of my career or the beginning of an entirely new phase.

Seeking Guidance and Support

All I wanted was a clear path forward and some sign that my efforts had not been in vain. I called upon whatever fashion gods might be listening and my undying faith in God, for guidance, love, and a reminder that I still possessed creative spark and professional value.

To cope with the ongoing uncertainty, I began accepting consulting projects that would help reignite my creativity while providing modest income. These shorter-term engagements allowed me to stay connected to the industry while exploring new possibilities for more substantial opportunities and heal from all the trauma I had endured.

Throughout this difficult period, I always felt supported by Gerry's friendship. She was consistently available to listen to my concerns, offer advice when asked, and provide the emotional stability I needed to keep moving forward.

A Final Farewell

Tragically, my dear friend Gerry passed away unexpectedly in 2023, altering my life in ways I'm still processing. Her loss represents the end of one of the most important friendships of my lifetime—a relationship that quite literally saved my life during a tough time.

I miss Gerry every single day, but I find solace in imagining her happily reunited with Marvin, the love of her life and now my dear pug who passed away after 21 years with me. Gerry's and Marvin's generosity, kindness, and belief in my potential provided the foundation for everything positive that followed in my career. Their legacy continues to inspire me to treat others with the same compassion they showed me, and to never underestimate the power of helping someone when they need it most.

The story of how these two-remarkable people entered my life serves as a reminder that "angels" sometimes appear in the most unexpected forms, at the most crucial moments, offering exactly what we need to survive and eventually thrive again. Gerry and Marvin will forever remain my proof that genuine goodness exists in the world, even when everything else seems to have failed.

CHAPTER 14:
Harvey and Jail

When Desperation Meets the Devil

As major companies downsized and cut their workforce, survival became the name of the game. I found myself needing employment to continue to keep afloat financially. The irony wasn't lost on me that the only well-paying positions available were back in the garment center—the very place I'd been trying to escape.

One of my only options was to endure a grueling interview process for the vice president of merchandising position at Harvey's lingerie company. For several hours, I faced interrogation from three people: Harvey, his wife, and the company president. Each question felt like a test of my expertise versus my dignity.

Harvey was considered a "legend" in the lingerie industry, though few people understood exactly why he'd earned this dubious distinction. Most whispered about claims of sexual harassment, allegations I would soon discover were not only true but significantly understated.

At seventy years old, Harvey cut an imposing yet repulsive figure. His portly frame carried a noticeable paunch that strained against his ill-fitting suits. With a bad come-over, his most striking feature was a pair of piercing blue eyes that seemed to undress every woman they encountered. When he smiled—which he did often and inappropriately—his crooked, yellowed teeth created an expression that sent chills down your spine. Among all the unsavory characters I'd encountered on Seventh Avenue, Harvey stood out as one of the worst.

I accepted the position out of pure financial necessity. A few of my consulting projects had started to dry up, forcing me back into what I'd come to call "garmento hell." The prospect was unnerving, but my bills wouldn't pay themselves.

The Mysterious Mrs. Harvey

Harvey was married to his fourth wife, a woman whose intelligence and compassion made her choice in husbands utterly baffling. She possessed both business acumen and genuine kindness—qualities that seemed wasted on someone like Harvey. Her husband had a well-established reputation for offending anyone within earshot, hurling vicious insults indiscriminately at everyone, including her.

She had once worked as Harvey's personal assistant. When he offered to elevate her from assistant to wife, promising a better life, she'd jumped at the chance—but not without securing a significant stake in his company first. Her intelligence served her well; she'd essentially learned to run the entire operation while Harvey took credit for her work, though he'd never admit her crucial role.

A Day in Hell

Working for Harvey meant enduring a daily barrage of offensive behavior. Throughout each workday, he unleashed streams of inappropriate comments about a women's body parts and he also made unwelcome physical advances—groping me while I tried to fend him off—and sexually harassing most of the female employees. For him, reducing women to tears seemed like entertainment, a twisted game he never tired of playing.

Harvey's disregard for his own health was as legendary as his cruelty. He consumed Viagra like candy, drank alcohol constantly, and ate with the abandon of a man who'd already survived four strokes. Despite his failing heart, he boasted to everyone that he'd outlive us all. His gambling addiction kept him at the crap tables at least three days a week, and his unsavory friends from the casino regularly visited the office, particularly during fashion week when they could gawk at the lingerie models.

When Harvey's wife retreated to their Hamptons house, prostitutes became regular office visitors. He'd have them model lingerie and parade around the showroom for his friends' entertainment. His wife turned a blind eye to these activities, perhaps grateful that it meant she didn't have to fulfill certain wifely duties with the "legend."

Frustrated by his wife's maternal focus on their young son, Harvey retaliated by increasing his visits to prostitutes, spending more time at the track, and taking frequent trips to Miami.

The Daily Humiliation Ritual

Harvey's company employed sixteen people, fifteen of them women—a detail that wasn't coincidental. Whenever he arrived at the office, he demanded that each female employee stand in line and kiss him on the lips. Despite their obvious disgust, they complied, terrified of his explosive temper or losing their jobs in an uncertain economy.

When he reached me—the new girl—I drew my line in the sand. "I don't want you touching me," I said firmly after he aggressively grabbed my arm. "I won't be kissing you, and neither should anyone else."

He laughed at my defiance but moved on to his next victim, though not before giving my bottom an unwelcome pat. Despite his delusions of grandeur, thinking himself both handsome and beloved by his employees, the reality was quite different. Everyone despised him, myself included.

The office atmosphere depended entirely on Harvey's presence. When he was away, we worked productively and even enjoyed ourselves. When he was there, chaos reigned. He showed no hesitation in calling me—or any woman—a "cunt," "bitch," or "loser," his verbal abuse as constant as his physical harassment.

His wife repeatedly begged him to reform his behavior, even enlisting their personal lawyer to frighten him into compliance. Harvey merely laughed off these interventions and continued his degrading treatment of the staff.

The Telephone Torture

When absent from the office, Harvey conducted phone harassment, calling twenty to thirty times daily. His deteriorating memory meant he'd repeat the same questions he'd asked an hour earlier.

"What are you doing right now?" he'd yell through the phone to whichever unlucky woman answered.

"The same thing I was doing ten minutes ago," I'd reply, struggling to keep the annoyance from my voice.

"Can I speak with Susan?" he'd demand, then systematically work through conversations with every female employee.

He'd interrogate each person about their activities, questioning their motivations and decision-making processes. Then he'd criticize everything, claiming we were incompetent and should be grateful to work for him at all.

This constant harassment devastated company morale. Harvey understood that the struggling job market had these women trapped, so he vindictively cut everyone's salary by twenty percent that summer. His cruelty effectively silenced any potential complaints— no one dared protest for fear of losing their position entirely.

The Corrupt Buyer

One of Harvey's most profitable accounts was a major store chain, managed by a buyer named Betty who was secretly on his payroll. Betty provided him with substantial orders in exchange for lavish kickbacks, but she treated our office staff terribly, making outrageous demands that created delays and turmoil throughout the company.

With his business dependent on Betty's orders, Harvey insisted that the office women tolerate her impossible behavior and meet her every demand. He arranged a summer Hamptons rental for Betty and her family, provided her with cash and a luxury car, and even paid for her children's private education and summer camp expenses.

Betty ensured the orders kept flowing while keeping her "Baby Harvey "—as she called him—content and profitable.

The Computer Illiterate Tyrant

Despite living in the digital age, Harvey was completely "computer ignorant." He owned a computer but never turned it on, never read emails, and never responded to manufacturers or suppliers in a timely manner. When problems arose, he'd accuse you of lying until you physically showed him a printed copy of the email you'd sent explaining the issue hours earlier.

He never apologized for his mistakes, instead screaming, "Get the hell out of my office!"

When he needed to send emails, he'd dictate his responses to his seventy-year-old secretary, who could barely type, then demand she send them immediately.

Meeting with the Monster

We all learned to anticipate Harvey's explosive outbursts, though our efforts to prevent them proved futile. During meetings, we'd cram into his tiny office while he chatted on the phone, devoured his forty-dollar pastrami sandwich from his favorite deli, and hurled insults at each of us.

"Barbara! You're a moron. I've fired you three times, and I don't know why you're still here!" he'd scream at the receptionist, who stood frozen as these daily humiliations had become routine.

"Susan, think with your brains, not your ass!" he'd bark.

"Lena, why the hell did I marry you? You're an ignorant whore," he'd say to his own wife.

"Katie, you're a moron and a loser!" he'd yell while everyone else bowed their heads in fear.

One day, I'd had enough. " Harvey, we made you four million dollars this month in sales. Is it necessary to yell at us and call us horrible names?"

"Shut your mouth! Your dumb bitch!" he replied, his face turning red as if he would explode.

" Harvey, she's doing a great job!" his production manager said, trying to defend me.

"You know what? I hate you most of all, Patty! Kiss my ass!" Harvey screamed at her.

Then he'd dismiss us all with profanity-laden commands to

leave his office. We'd each endure about twenty minutes of this abuse before filing out one by one, leaving him alone with his sandwich and his rage.

The Favorite

Harvey's newest obsession was Amelia, a young designer who'd quickly become his favorite. Pretty but only mildly talented, she acted as if she was heavily medicated most of the time and dressed provocatively. She worked minimal hours—arriving at nine and leaving at four—spending most of her day on Instagram while the rest of us worked ourselves to exhaustion.

The staff resented Amelia's special treatment, but no one dared upset the "legend" by complaining. Harvey would massage her shoulders, promise her gifts for designing "something pretty," coax her into running personal errands, and take her on impromptu shopping trips.

He was completely at her beck and call. Whenever I called her out for missing deadlines, she'd burst into tears and threaten to tell Harvey I was being mean to her.

"Go ahead," I'd laugh. "Then I won't have to take abuse from him or you every day."

The Discovery

Working late one evening, I discovered the true nature of Harvey's relationship with Amelia. His office door stood open, and I could see her bending over his desk. Knowing she never wore a bra, it was obvious what kind of "show" he was enjoying.

"Nice tits, baby!" Harvey cooed, offering her a plastic cup of cheap box wine he kept in his desk drawer.

"Oh, Harvey! Are you trying to get me drunk?" she flirted back.

"Yes, baby. Then I'll take you to Victoria's Secret so you can model some lingerie for me."

Disgusted by this display, I called Harvey's wife immediately. She rushed back from her pedicure appointment and fired Amelia on the spot.

"Who's fired now?" I shouted at Amelia as she gathered her things, the confrontation between Harvey and his wife escalating behind us.

"You bastard!" his wife yelled. "You're a filthy pig!"

"Well, if you'd sleep with me, I wouldn't have to look at her tits," he replied with a laugh.

His wife stormed past me, practically knocking me down while hurling objects from her desk at him.

"Are you okay, Katie?" she asked me calmly amid the chaos.

"How do you do this every day?" I asked. "He's disgusting."

"Money," she laughed. "He pays me handsomely, and I'm just waiting for that jerk to die."

The New Victim

We welcomed Chrissy as our newest sales associate—a delightful woman with an athletic six-foot frame, blonde hair, bronzed tan, and prominently augmented breasts. Harvey immediately insisted she model his lingerie so he could "tailor" pieces to fit her body, claiming this was essential for her to understand the collection.

I could sense her discomfort, but as this was her first garment center job, she remained silent. Harvey clearly didn't care whether she made sales; he'd hired her primarily for her appearance. Despite Chrissy's hard work, she struggled under Harvey's inappropriate management.

During her first week, Harvey invited her to Miami to visit a new store account. The travel arrangements revealed his true intentions: he flew first class with his prostitute Monique while Chrissy sat in coach. Upon arrival, he booked a luxury oceanfront suite with two bedrooms and an adjoining living room.

While Chrissy unpacked in one bedroom, Harvey and Monique disappeared into the other, slamming the door behind them—but not before Harvey shouted, "Chrissy, feel free to join us!"

Chrissy called me that night, hysterical and terrified about her situation.

"Just lock your door," I advised sympathetically. I was fed up with witnessing yet another sexual predator in the fashion industry, but I couldn't help her from New York.

The next day, after their business meeting, Chrissy flew home while Harvey and Monique enjoyed a weekend in Miami. Chrissy confided that Harvey had threatened to fire her if she mentioned the prostitute to anyone.

She quit the next day without explanation. No one blamed her for the abrupt departure, and I hoped she'd find a career path outside the apparel industry, where she wouldn't have to deal with men like Harvey.

The Celebrity Encounter

The following week brought a bizarre meeting with Raquel, Harvey's 1960's dream girl. Most aging celebrities rely on agents to pursue clothing endorsements, but a few handle initial negotiations themselves to save on commission fees.

Generally, there's little industry interest in faded stars, except from passionate "garmentos" like Harvey seeking photo opportunities and credibility.

When Raquel entered our showroom, her unimpressed demeanor and chilly attitude made her disdain obvious. Even in her seventies, she retained her attractiveness, but her unwelcoming behavior toward what she clearly considered an inferior crowd—especially an old, overweight "garmento" infatuated with her—was unmistakable.

"Baby!" Harvey addressed her. "I can make you millions."

"I want millions!" she replied, excited by the financial prospect.

We all understood she probably needed the money; otherwise, she wouldn't be hustling licensing deals at her age. After Harvey and I presented our lingerie line, he suddenly exploded.

"Katie, get out now! I want to be alone with Raquel!" He pushed my chair so violently that I flew out of the conference room into the hallway.

"Fine," I said, "but he can't create your line without me," I told her as I returned to my desk.

Frustrated and mortified by this amateur display, Raquel quickly rose and headed for the exit, recognizing Harvey's proposition as pure fantasy.

"Wait, wait!" Harvey called after her. "Someone get a camera! I need a picture with Raquel!"

Annoyed, she stood rigid as he wrapped his fat fingers around her waist. Without even a hint of a smile, she posed stiffly then walked out.

"Look! I got a picture of the bitch!" he squealed like an excited pig. "Laminate it now!" he ordered the receptionist.

Taking Action

"This is disgusting," I announced, having endured enough of Harvey's abuse that year. "I'm going to stop this bastard from harassing us!"

While everyone cheered me on privately, I was secretly terrified to confront him. Harvey constantly bragged about his mob connections and friends in the NYPD, making his threats seem credible.

Nevertheless, I was finished with his abuse and the humiliation he inflicted on these women daily. I decided to hit him where it would hurt most—his wallet. Despite his wealth, Harvey hated losing money and would eviscerate even his accountant over the smallest financial errors.

The next day, I quit my job, called Betty's company, and reported her kickback arrangement with Harvey. I also detailed his blatant sexual harassment of office staff and Betty's own abusive behavior toward employees.

The company immediately fired Betty and severed all business ties with Harvey. In this gossip-driven industry, word spread quickly, and his other small accounts—which had only stayed because of his big discounts—walked away as well.

Unfortunately, the fourteen remaining women in his company would continue suffering his daily wrath. That was their choice to make, not mine.

The Consequences Begin

I naively thought I was free of Harvey after quitting. With a year having passed since the economic downturn, I hoped to find better employment elsewhere. I dreamed of an ideal position where I could design lingerie and clothing without enduring sexual harassment.

I was foolish to believe Harvey would let me leave without retaliation. Some might argue I was asking for trouble, but I didn't care. I refused to tolerate men like him in the fashion industry any longer. As I grew older, my patience for such behavior had completely disappeared.

A week later, on the Friday morning before Fourth of July weekend, a knock came at my apartment door at 9:00 a.m. I was about to receive the shock of my life.

Two intimidating NYPD detectives asked to enter my apartment and informed me I was under arrest.

"Why?" I laughed, knowing this had to be Harvey's doing. "I didn't do anything wrong."

The menacing officers claimed Harvey had accused me of stealing all his company files from his office computer.

"I did no such thing," I said defensively. "I quit my horrible job because of that pig—that's all. Besides, he can't even turn on a computer, so how would he know what files I had?"

"It doesn't matter," one detective said gruffly as he handcuffed me.

After all these years of living peacefully in my apartment, I found myself in handcuffs, being led to jail for the second time! The entire humiliating scene unfolded as neighbors watched me get escorted through the lobby in restraints and placed in a police car.

I was almost surprised Lisa wasn't standing outside taking photographs.

Life in "The Tombs"

New York City jail is a truly horrific experience. After being booked, fingerprinted, and interrogated for several hours, I could tell the detectives were mocking the entire situation. I heard their laughter outside the interrogation room, and it became clear they knew Harvey had fabricated this story for revenge—and that they were his friends. I was told I would be going to the "tombs."

The "tombs" is a grim underground facility in New York city, where people incarcerated, face appalling conditions. I shared a cell with twelve other women, and my anxiety became so overwhelming

I could barely breathe. The repulsive stench of human waste filled the air, making me physically ill.

Reflecting on my past experiences, I realized I'd endured worse situations. Drawing on inner strength and survival mode, I leaned toward the toughest-looking woman beside me and introduced myself.

"Hi, I'm Katie. What brought you here today?" I managed to smile.

"Shut the hell up, bitch," she glared at me.

"We're all here together. Maybe talking about it will help you feel better," I persisted, still smiling despite the hostility.

"What are you, a therapist?" she asked angrily.

A few moments later, another young woman spoke up.

"I stole a credit card," she admitted matter-of-factly. "I couldn't feed my family and needed to buy diapers and food." She burst into tears as I put my arm around all three hundred pounds of her, offering what comfort I could.

My years in the apparel industry had taught me to navigate any situation through effective communication. I'd learned to defuse tense encounters by simply talking and reasoning with people, and I applied those skills here to prevent these women from turning against each other.

Stories of Desperation

One by one, the other women in our cell began sharing their stories, seeking connection and comfort. Their tales were heartbreaking. One woman had worked as a maid for six years, only to be wrongly accused of stealing her employer's lost diamond ring.

Another woman described how her boyfriend had assaulted her child, prompting her to defend her child by fighting back. When she called the police on him, she was the one who got arrested.

Another young girl had turned to prostitution to pay for her mother's medical expenses—a path she'd never imagined taking.

I'd long observed that New York's justice system seemed particularly harsh and biased against women. Our treatment in jail reinforced this perception. We received dirty water in paper cups, two pieces of stale white bread with one slice of processed cheese, moldy bologna, and rotten apples. We had one steel toilet to share, open for all to see.

I couldn't believe that New York City—one of the world's wealthiest cities—treated these women and me like animals.

Justice Delayed

Due to the holiday weekend, we waited three days to appear before a judge. I was the last to be called to criminal court at 11:00 p.m.

My public defender successfully got the charges dismissed for lack of evidence. The judge seemed baffled about why I'd been arrested in the first place.

I knew, however, that Harvey was delighted about keeping me imprisoned over the entire Fourth of July weekend.

Upon release, I stepped outside the courthouse and immediately vomited on the sidewalk. I took the subway home, double-bolted my apartment door, stripped off my clothes, took a scalding shower, and curled up in a fetal position for the next few hours.

The Campaign of Destruction

My hatred for Harvey intensified, though I knew the universe would eventually make him pay. Unfortunately, his vengeance against me was far from over.

The evil Lisa learned about my employment with Harvey and immediately saw an opportunity to gain another ally in her campaign to destroy me. She rushed to his office with her restraining order, and together they launched a coordinated attack on my reputation.

Harvey hired Lisa as a salesperson, hoping for her loyalty, but the arrangement lasted only a few months before he realized she couldn't sell anything except herself. He was stuck paying out her contract.

I was told by one of the designer's there that before Harvey fired Lisa, they had systematically called every company they thought might hire me, including trade magazines, spreading lies to damage my reputation further. Harvey even had me followed by one of the detectives who'd arrested me—clearly someone on his payroll. Whenever I spotted this surveillance, I'd scream "Pickpocket!" until he scurried away.

Harvey then took me to court, trying to stop my only source of income—a $400-per-week unemployment check.

Survival Mode

Determined not to surrender, I took various low paying jobs, surviving on coffee and fruit, just to pay my rent. I lost twenty pounds and became too anxious to leave my apartment except for work. For four months, I sent résumés to out-of-state companies, hoping they might not have heard about my situation.

My efforts yielded no callbacks. Finding even an interview, let alone employment, in New York seemed impossible. The extent of Harvey and Lisa's vindictiveness infuriated me, and I prayed nightly for divine retribution against both of them.

I fully understood that my actions had triggered Harvey's fury.

Destroying his most important account was hasty and perhaps foolish, but I always stood by my decisions, regardless of consequences.

Rock Bottom

One particularly difficult evening after returning from an interview for a job unrelated to the fashion industry, overwhelmed by reflections on my career mistakes and feeling utterly hopeless, I called a suicide prevention hotline.

"Hello," I cried. "I'm thinking about killing myself."

"Can you hold, please?" the counselor asked.

"No, I can't," I sobbed. "I'm suicidal!"

"Okay," she said calmly. "Why?"

I began explaining my situation when she abruptly interrupted.

"Look, I'm the only one here answering phones, and there are other callers. You seem fine," she said, clearly bored.

"Are you insane?" I yelled. "I want to kill myself!"

"Can you hold on? I need to take this other call," she said matter-of-factly, then put me on hold.

I sat there stunned, listening to elevator music. Really? I thought. Is this person seriously putting a suicidal person on hold?

When she returned, she said, "Okay, continue, but honestly, if you were serious about suicide, you would have already done it."

"Continue? Continue this!" I slammed the phone down.

I couldn't even get help from a suicide hotline! The absurdity made me laugh despite everything.

I poured myself a glass of wine, took two Xanax, and went to sleep, praying for a better tomorrow and praying God would come to my aid once again.

Justice at Last

When my court date arrived regarding Harvey's attempt to deny my unemployment benefits, I went alone to face him. He'd brought his entire staff to intimidate and humiliate me, though notably, his wife was absent—I suspected she was secretly supporting me.

After hearing my account, the judge awarded me the unemployment benefits and severely reprimanded Harvey for unjustly denying them. His fury was explosive as he cursed both me and the judge. I felt relief when the judge called Harvey "despicable" and had him removed from her courtroom.

Divine Retribution

Several months later, through no action of my own, Harvey's business came under government investigation for fraud and corruption. Authorities shut down his business due to several violations. Finally, he had to answer for his truly wicked actions. Unfortunately, I knew he would just reopen his company under another name—which he did a week later.

Shortly after the reopening, a friend from the garment center called me with news: Harvey had suffered a massive heart attack.

He died that same night.

I wondered if Harvey had finally ended up exactly where he belonged—in "garmento hell." Now, if only Lisa would only follow him there!

CHAPTER 15:
Child Labor

A Hidden Horror in Plain Sight

While this narrative might seem like a departure from my fashion industry memoir, it represents just one of numerous child labor scenarios I encountered throughout my three-decade career, from the 1980s through today in 2026. This particular experience stands as one of the most morally challenging situations I've ever faced—one that fundamentally changed how I view the true cost of the clothes we wear.

The Assignment That Changed Everything

In the early 2000s, I secured what seemed like a straightforward consulting role with a small apparel firm located outside of New York City. The family-operated business appeared legitimate and successful, and I approached the opportunity with genuine enthusiasm, eager to help expand their operations and revamp their product lines.

My primary responsibility involved overseeing production for their largest retail client. Having developed extensive expertise in international production and traveled to factories across the globe, I felt confident about tackling their production challenges in China. What I didn't realize was that I was about to uncover one of the most disturbing situations of my career.

The company owner had maintained business relationships with his Chinese factories for years, yet he had never conducted a single audit. More shocking still, he had never even set foot in China. In an industry increasingly scrutinized for labor violations, this negligence was not only unheard of but frankly dangerous.

Recent negative press about child labor in overseas factories had prompted major retailers to demand factory audits from all their suppliers. Without these compliance reports, they would sever business relationships immediately. The owner hired me specifically because his retail accounts now required comprehensive factory audits, and millions of dollars in orders hung in the balance.

Understanding Factory Audits

Factory auditing is standard procedure in the apparel industry—or it should be. These comprehensive assessments evaluate facilities on multiple criteria: quality control, safety protocols, ethical labor practices, and operational efficiency. Any reputable apparel company conducts these audits before establishing manufacturing relationships, making this particular owner's oversight particularly alarming.

I assumed this would be routine work. Given the owner's long-standing relationships with these factories, I expected to find well-established, compliant facilities. I couldn't have been more wrong.

I immediately contacted a seasoned production professional in China whom I had worked with for over ten years. His integrity and thoroughness were unquestionable, and I trusted him to conduct honest, fair evaluations of the facilities in question.

The Calm Before the Storm

While my auditor colleague began his work in China, I remained in New York handling daily fittings and cost analysis for the brand.

The first factory audit came back clean—operations were running smoothly, and production could proceed without concerns.

My new boss fit the typical garment center executive profile. Even though he had relocated his company out of state purely for tax advantages, his management style remained unchanged. Office meetings were exercises in ego rather than productivity. He routinely belittled staff with shouting and profanity, reducing employees to cowering with his harsh criticism. Despite years of building emotional armor against such behavior, his insults still stung.

I worked ten to fifteen-hour days, determined to excel in this role. The commission structure he'd offered was essential to my financial survival, and I harbored dreams of eventually earning enough to buy a house far from the toxic environment of New York's apparel industry.

Then came the call that shattered my assumptions about this "routine" assignment.

The Horrifying Discovery

My auditor friend's voice was tense when he reported that the second factory I had asked him to audit, had failed inspection catastrophically. Child labor wasn't just present—it was pervasive throughout the facility.

Upon hearing this news, my boss panicked. This factory handled the majority of his production orders, representing millions in revenue. Rather than immediately addressing the human rights violations, his primary concern was protecting his business relationships. He decided to send me to China immediately, along with the company president, to assess the situation firsthand.

I tried reassuring him that I could move the factory's production, but he demanded immediate solutions that wouldn't jeopardize his orders. His priorities were crystal clear, and they had nothing to do with the welfare of children.

My boss also admitted he didn't trust my auditor friend's assessment—he needed to see evidence himself. Despite my growing suspicions about what we might find, I sensed that production would continue regardless of what we discovered.

Journey into Darkness

The company president and I arrived in China during a particularly hot and humid June. The oppressive heat, combined with exhaustion from our long journey, made everything more challenging.

As a first-time visitor to China, the president was overwhelmed by culture shock, poverty levels she'd never witnessed, and the stark conditions we encountered. The factory was located in one of China's most desolate regions, where hotels lacked air conditioning, served no Western food, and provided only basic bedding.

I shared my emergency stash of ramen noodles with the president and urged her to rest. She was visibly shaken and frightened by what she'd already seen, and I knew the next day would be far worse.

Entering Hell

The factory owner collected us at 8:30 a.m. for the hour-long drive to his factory. Upon arrival, we encountered the typical scene: gates, guards, and curious workers gathering to observe foreign visitors. What wasn't typical was what I noticed immediately upon stepping from our vehicle.

The workers were children—ranging in age from around five to fifteen years old. They were filthy, dressed in tattered clothing, many without shoes. These children were clearly malnourished, frightened, and desperate. They tugged at my clothes, whispering in a language I barely understood, but their message was unmistakable: they were pleading for help.

The factory owners—a man and woman—shouted shrilly at the children, driving them away with harsh commands that pierced through me like daggers.

We were rushed upstairs to an air-conditioned office that reeked of opium smoke. Many Chinese factory owners I'd encountered over the years used opium regularly, and the distinctive, repulsive smell was immediately recognizable.

Despite the early hour—barely 10:00 a.m.—the factory owners insisted on taking us to lunch immediately. I refused, demanding to inspect our products on the factory floor first. Their anxiety was palpable; they clearly feared what a knowledgeable observer might discover about their operation.

Descent into Horror

Some Chinese factories typically span four to ten floors, most without elevators. I insisted we start at the bottom and work our way up, thoroughly examining each level.

The conditions I encountered in this factory were beyond horrific. A pungent stench of urine and feces permeated every floor. I watched as filthy, malnourished children and teens struggled to operate sewing machines older than I was. Some of the equipment had broken needles, making it nearly impossible for their small hands to work safely or effectively.

I sat down at one machine to test its tension and workmanship. The operator was a young man, perhaps sixteen, whose fingers were punctured and bruised from repeatedly working with dull, broken needles. Under everyone's watchful gaze, I instructed the factory manager to replace every needle on every machine. Though clearly displeased, he complied with my demand.

The other workers—mostly children—stood in complete silence, their faces lifeless and bodies emaciated.

My inspection revealed holes in walls, dead rats littering the floors, filthy bathrooms, no kitchen facilities, and dormitories that would be condemned as unfit for animals in any developed country.

The Chain Room

As we prepared to break for lunch—the president appeared ready to collapse from heat and shock—she rushed downstairs with the factory manager while I lingered, conducting one final inspection of each workspace.

On the fourth floor, I stopped abruptly at the sound of crying. Following the sound to the back of the factory, I discovered several small children sewing in a dark, cramped corner.

That's when I saw them: chains attached to the legs of sewing machines.

These chains served a dual purpose—intimidation, by placing the chains around the legs of their work station to incite fear in the worker or by actually restraining the person with the chains. Children were forced to work around the clock, and those who resisted or tried to escape were intimidated or threatened with restraints. Filthy mattresses on the floor revealed where these children slept during their captivity.

My Chinese auditor later explained that in the worst child labor situations, children endure threats of violence, receive inadequate food and rest, and are forced to sleep in isolation at their workplaces.

Breaking Point

Gasping for air, I dropped to my knees and attempted to communicate with these terrified children. I tried desperately to remove the menacing chains from the legs of the chairs, but my efforts were futile. The children's crying only strengthened my resolve, even as my hands became bloodied from struggling with the chains, I could not remove them. Although at the time the children were not chained physically to the work stations, the presence of the chains was intimidating enough.

As I finally stood up, I felt small hands helping to steady me— these children, despite having so little strength left, were trying to help *me*. Tears streamed down my face, as I smiled at them, desperately hoping to convey that I would somehow find a way to help them.

I rushed to a bathroom where the horror of what I'd just witnessed overwhelmed me. I became sick. Before rejoining the others for lunch, I struggled to compose myself, knowing I had to report these conditions to my company's president.

The Broader Crisis

The child labor crisis in Chinese factories represents a serious human rights violation that demands immediate attention and sustained efforts to ensure ethical labor practices throughout global supply chains. Many children are trafficked from rural areas to work in these facilities, often recruited through deceptive promises of education or better opportunities.

This issue is frequently ignored by apparel industry production managers, particularly those working for fast fashion companies that prioritize low costs above human welfare. Throughout my career, I've witnessed too many American production personnel turn a blind eye to such atrocities. Some are even on factory payrolls, receiving kickbacks in exchange for overlooking child labor violations.

Documenting the Evidence

After lunch—which I barely touched—the president and I toured a different factory, unrelated to this one. This second facility was clean, well-organized, and staffed by cheerful adult employees. The contrast was stark, and I made sure the president understood the significant difference in working conditions and employee morale.

Rather than confront the bad factory owners directly—which would have been pointless—I waited until we returned to the hotel to share my findings with the president. I immediately contacted my auditor friend, asking him to arrange for an independent auditing company to conduct a second comprehensive evaluation of the facility. Professional documentation with photographs and detailed reports would be essential for any meaningful action.

Corporate Callousness

Back at the hotel, I shared my horrific discoveries with the president. She was visibly disturbed and insisted we contact our boss immediately. During the phone call to him, I explained that I could no longer work with the bad factory and that all production needed to be moved elsewhere immediately.

My boss's response was both shocking and sadly predictable. He cursed at both of us, declaring that he didn't care about forced child labor or poor working conditions. He actually found the situation amusing, joking that perhaps those children should come work for him since they'd be cheaper than adult employees.

He threatened to fire me if I didn't ship products from this child labor factory. The president instructed me to proceed with production regardless of conditions. He pressured me to bribe my auditor friend to approve the factory despite its violations.

After I hung up on him, the president wanted to fly home immediately. Despite being well-compensated for her role, she decided that whatever "happened in China should stay in China." She declared it was no longer her problem and that I needed to "fix" the audit and ship products at any cost.

Standing Alone

In China, it's unfortunately possible to bribe auditing firms for as little as twenty dollars to ensure favorable reports. I refused to participate in such corruption, regardless of the personal consequences. I instructed my auditor to proceed with the second official audit.

The next day, we returned to the United States, and in the following days, I awaited the official audit report. Back home, I couldn't stop thinking about those children. I felt emotionally devastated and had difficulty sleeping, haunted by images of their desperate faces. I knew that helping them was a moral responsibility I couldn't ignore.

The official audit report confirmed everything I'd witnessed. The detailed photos and written evaluation clearly documented the factory's dangerous conditions and extensive child labor violations.

When auditing companies in China fail a factory, they face serious consequences from factory owners who often have significant local influence. My auditor had never encountered such horrific conditions in any facility he'd inspected. He risked personal and professional retaliation by writing an up an honest report.

The Cover-Up

I presented the audit report to my boss, who literally threw it in my face and ordered me to "get the hell out of his office and back to work, or be fired if I did not fix the problem."

Faced with another crucial moral decision in my career, I decided to notify the large retail store we were supplying about the failed audit and documented child labor violations. I forwarded the complete report, hoping they would act ethically and demand that my boss severs ties with this factory.

Their compliance manager seemed like a decent person, but he had never traveled internationally and had no understanding of how deplorable factory conditions could be overseas. His inexperience made him unsuitable for such a critical role. After reviewing my report and photographs, he immediately informed his supervisor, who forwarded everything to the buyer responsible for the account.

The buyer was a personal friend of my boss—and likely receiving kickbacks from him. She dismissed the report entirely, authorizing shipment of products from the child labor factory. Her callousness was particularly despicable considering she had children the same age as those factory workers.

The Final Confrontation

I confronted my boss and the president one final time, arguing passionately about the injustice of shipping products manufactured by enslaved children. My boss's response was to laugh at my concerns, fire me immediately, and threaten to ensure I never worked in the apparel industry again if I spoke to anyone else about the situation.

Having heard such threats countless times throughout my career, I simply replied, "I don't care what you do," and walked out of his office forever.

Systemic Failure

The following day, I contacted the retail store's security and compliance department, as well as the president of their apparel division. They were superficially concerned and assured me the situation would be handled immediately. They even flew to New York to meet with me and discuss the situation. They expressed anger that their buyer had authorized shipments despite the violations and provided false hope that they would handle this situation-ethically.

It was the last communication I ever received from them.

A month later, I discovered that all the products manufactured in the child labor factory were shipped and in their stores. Obviously, their concern had been entirely performative.

The American public remained unaware of these products' origins. Had they known, I believe they would have been as disgusted and outraged as I was. However, the fashion industry's complex supply chains deliberately obscure such information.

Fighting the System

I made it my mission to ensure this factory could never ship products to the United States again. Over the following months, I contacted numerous government agencies and child labor organizations, hoping to find allies in this fight.

The responses I received were shocking in their indifference: "I don't know what we can do," and "That's not our problem" were typical replies. Even a website backed by a major celebrity claimed to be "too busy" to help, despite their supposed focus on rescuing children from exactly these situations.

Taking Direct Action

For months, I was haunted by memories of those children's desperate eyes pleading for help. Finally, I decided to use my accumulated frequent flyer miles to return to China and take direct action.

Through my auditor colleague, I connected with a Chinese organization dedicated to rescuing children from factory situations like this one. After careful planning, we conducted a nighttime raid on the facility, successfully rescuing eight children and placing them in safe environments.

As I waited outside the factory during the operation, I made sure every child was accounted for and gave each one a hug. The tears of joy in their eyes confirmed that once again, I had risked my career to do what was morally right.

The thought of abandoning these children—despite being thousands of miles from New York—was never an option for me. Losing another job in the fashion industry was a small price to pay for their freedom.

In the end, the Chinese government took notice of our actions and permanently closed the factory.

Lasting Impact

I pray that those children have been given opportunities for the kind of life that so many of us take for granted. This experience taught me never to overlook the small things that truly matter: acts of kindness and caring, nourishing meals, safe homes, and the freedom we enjoy in America.

While there are committed individuals working to address injustices in global apparel production, too many garment center companies dismiss these critical problems. As child labor still remains an issue in 2025, it's essential for American retailers to strengthen their compliance protocols significantly.

This is why I advocate for "Made in America" manufacturing, where such practices face rigorous scrutiny and legal consequences. We need to bring manufacturing back to the USA.

Gratitude for Freedom

Whenever I travel internationally, I'm always grateful to return home to America. Our freedom represents the most invaluable treasure we possess, though many people take it for granted. Unfortunately, countless individuals worldwide don't enjoy these basic human rights, and that reality is truly heartbreaking.

The children I encountered in that bad Chinese factory reminded me that behind every piece of clothing we purchase lies a human story. As consumers, we have the power to demand ethical manufacturing practices and support companies that prioritize human welfare over profit margins.

Their faces will forever remind me why that power—and responsibility—matters so much and change needs to be made by us.

CHAPTER 16:

Nash-Evil & Taylor Swift

A Journey of Ambition, Betrayal, and Hard-Learned Lessons

My experience working with Taylor Swift's brand in Nashville represents one of the most complex and ultimately devastating final chapters of my career. What began as an exciting opportunity to pioneer celebrity branding in China became a cautionary tale about trust, ambition, and the ruthless nature of business partnerships. To truly understand how such a promising venture collapsed so spectacularly, I need to tell you the complete story—every detail that led to what should have been a remarkable success turning into one of my most challenging professional disappointments of my life.

Leaving New York: The End of an Era

By 2015, I had reached my breaking point with New York. The fashion industry there had worn me down through years of battles, betrayals, and broken promises. Like the mythical Phoenix that rises from its own ashes, I knew it was time to completely reinvent myself and my career. This unexpected move to Nashville, Tennessee, would provide the perfect launching pad for an ambitious new project: connecting American celebrities and brands with China's massive e-commerce marketplace.

The timing seemed perfect. Chinese consumers had developed an insatiable appetite for American designed products and celebrities. Country and Western music held a special place in Chinese culture—along with American films, these were among the few genres that had been widely accessible on Chinese television for decades due to the country's strict censorship policies. This cultural affinity presented an enormous untapped market opportunity.

The Connection That Changed Everything

My introduction to this new world came through Angela, a business acquaintance who lived in Nashville and who connected me by phone with Max, a major Nashville investor. I had visited Nashville several times over the years and always enjoyed the city's energy and hospitality. When Max called me from his multi-million-dollar beach house in Florida, I could hear the confidence in his voice as he described sitting on the sand, gazing out at the Gulf of Mexico after arriving on his private jet for a weekend getaway.

Our initial conversation lasted four hours. During this time, I honestly, opened up about the numerous challenges and disappointments I had faced throughout my career in the apparel industry. Rather than being discouraged by my tumultuous history, Max seemed intrigued. He suggested I fly to Nashville, where his business operations were headquartered, to explore new opportunities together.

Meeting Max in person proved equally encouraging. He possessed a charismatic personality and immediately impressed me with his business acumen. More importantly, he offered me a competitive salary plus moving expenses to Nashville, as we brainstormed potential business ventures that would leverage both China's growing market and Nashville's entertainment industry connections. This positive first impression heavily influenced my decision to make such a dramatic life change. Did I hastily rush into a move to Nashville, Tennessee? Obviously yes, I was eager to start over once again.

The Painful Goodbye to Home

Leaving my New York apartment felt like abandoning my soul. For over two decades, that rent-stabilized sanctuary had been my anchor, my safe haven through every storm in my tumultuous career. The apartment represented more than just a place to live—it was my stability, my identity, my proof that I belonged in the fashion capital of the world.

My landlord had been trying to evict long-term tenants like me for years, eager to charge market rates to new renters. Unlike other situations where I might have been able to sublet and maintain some connection to my former life, this time there was no safety net. If I could have kept the apartment as a backup plan, the move to Nashville would have felt less permanent and terrifying. My landlord's attorneys were persistent in their attempts to evict me, and I had run out of the will to fight.

Loading my belongings into a rental car for the fourteen-hour drive to Tennessee was one of the most emotional experiences of my life. Tears streamed down my face as I drove away from the only place I had ever truly called home. The journey felt endless, giving me too much time to question whether I was making the biggest mistake of my career.

Nashville: A Beautiful Prison

I found a charming ranch-style house in Nashville, on Craig's List and signed a lease for $2,500 per month, a steal considering the size of the 2500 square foot four-bedroom home. Max had promised that once our two-year partnership contract proved successful, he would purchase the house for me as part of his investment in our future together. At the time, his promise seemed genuine and realistic given his obvious wealth and business success. The house was listed for two-hundred and twenty-five thousand dollars.

However, Nashville's social dynamics proved far more challenging than I had anticipated. Despite the city's reputation for hospitality, many locals treated me with suspicion and outright hostility once they learned I was from New York. Ironically, a significant portion of Nashville's population consisted of transplants from other cities, yet they seemed determined to maintain an us-versus-them mentality toward newcomers, particularly those from the Northeast.

The unkindness I encountered was both shocking and hurtful. At a gas station where I was simply adding air to my tires, an elderly woman approached me specifically to complain about my New York license plates. She shouted, "Get the hell out of my town!" with such venom that I was genuinely shaken. I left immediately, my hands trembling as I drove away.

A similar incident occurred at a local deli when the clerk noticed my license plates through the window. After confirming I was from New York, she refused to serve me and demanded I leave her store immediately, warning me never to return. These experiences were so unsettling that I quickly obtained a Tennessee driver's license and changed my car's license plates, hoping to blend in better.

Despite these efforts, I never felt accepted in Nashville's social circles. The realization that I would always be an outsider filled me with regret about leaving New York. I desperately wanted to return home, but I had already committed to this new venture and couldn't afford to move again. Drawing strength from my friend Gerry's wise counsel, I decided to focus entirely on my work responsibilities, knowing I had no other viable options.

Building the Business: E-commerce Dreams

Max was eager to launch our new venture, and I quickly finalized my plan to sell celebrity merchandise in China through major e-commerce platforms like Tmall and JD.com. These platforms represented the gateway to China's massive online shopping market, and Max immediately approved of my strategic vision.

Despite my years of experience working with Chinese manufacturing, I had never attempted to launch a brand directly in the Chinese consumer market, except for Vintage Heartland, my lingerie brand. The challenges ahead would be numerous and complex, involving cultural differences, regulatory requirements, and fierce competition from well-established Chinese brands.

I knew the road would be difficult, marked by inevitable setbacks and learning curves as I attempted to understand Chinese consumer preferences and shopping behaviors. Determined not to disappoint Max, I threw myself into the work with characteristic intensity, even converting a large recreational room in my rented house into a dedicated office space. After witnessing my commitment and work ethic for several months, Max offered me a full partnership in the project, which filled me with excitement and gratitude. And our new company, "Heritage 66" was born.

Understanding Max: Power, Privilege, and Personality

Max was an imposing figure who commanded attention wherever he went. Standing well over six feet tall with a commanding presence, he had a reputation for lavish parties, bawdy humor, and a sharp wit that could be either entertaining or cutting, depending on his mood. He held significant political and social power, which he wielded without hesitation.

Part of his financial success centered around a large company that developed shopping centers across the United States.

I rarely interacted with Max's wife, I felt like I was definitely out of her league. She maintained her distance from me throughout my time in Nashville, treating me politely, but without warmth.

A Shocking Introduction to Nashville Society

My first exposure to Nashville's elite social scene occurred at a lavish party hosted by an entertainment industry executive I had met through mutual acquaintances. Arriving alone at his palatial mansion, I felt completely out of place among the so-called celebrities and business leaders in attendance. I obtained a glass of wine from the bartender and attempted to mingle, feeling increasingly uncomfortable as conversations swirled around me.

My discomfort intensified when a pretty, well-dressed young woman approached me, eager to discuss my business relationship with Max. In a small town like Nashville, news traveled fast, especially regarding newcomers with connections to prominent figures like Max.

Although she was supposedly a celebrity in her own right, I didn't recognize her. She appeared polished and sophisticated, but her conversation quickly took a disturbing turn that revealed the ugly underbelly of Nashville's social elite.

"Oh, I heard you and Max are starting an exciting new venture in China," she said with a bright smile. "How are you settling into your new home? Have you hired a "colored" yet?"

Confused by her terminology, I asked, "What did you say? A colorist for my hair?"

She repeated her question with unmistakable clarity: "A colored girl, honey. We all have them here to clean for us, and you will definitely need one. I can recommend a few if you'd like."

I was completely shocked by her casual racism. "Isn't that just a bit racist?" I replied, unable to hide my disgust.

Rather than being embarrassed by her comment, she looked at me with condescending amusement. "Oh, darling, you've got to get over yourself. You have a lot to learn about this town if you plan on living here. Don't be so naïve."

"I am not naïve!" I said loudly, my voice carrying across the nearby conversations. "I just think that comment is incredibly rude!"

She abruptly walked away from me and started talking to an older man, pretending I no longer existed. Within moments, the man I didn't recognize, appeared beside me, gripping my arm firmly and informing me it was time to leave. As he escorted me from the party, he instructed the valet to bring my car immediately.

That moment crystallized my understanding that my time in Nashville would be limited. I had violated their unspoken social codes by refusing to accept their racist attitudes, and I would never be welcomed back into their circles. True to my prediction, I was never invited to another Nashville social event.

The Work Ethic That Defined Me

Despite the social rejection, I maintained my complete dedication to the business venture I had come to Nashville to pursue. Max consistently praised my work ethic, calling me an "animal" in what he considered a complimentary manner. While the comparison was somewhat insulting, I understood he meant to acknowledge my relentless commitment to our project's success.

Throughout my time in Nashville, I never felt comfortable in Max's world of private jets, sprawling mansions, and casual displays of extreme wealth. I came to terms with the reality that I would never truly belong in his social stratum, but I remained focused on proving my professional value.

Initially uncertain about my feelings toward Max, I gradually began to witness the darker aspects of his personality. As time passed, I understood why he inspired fear throughout Nashville's business community. People who knew Max told me that he could destroy careers and lives without a second thought if someone threatened his reputation or interests.

The Taylor Swift Opportunity

Max endorsed my concept for a China-focused e-commerce platform that would promote American country music and celebrity merchandise. Using his extensive network of entertainment industry contacts, he arranged meetings with several high-profile celebrity agents to present my business proposal. Meanwhile, I worked diligently to establish our Chinese business entity, which would enable us to sell products on major e-commerce platforms like Tmall (owned by Jack Ma) and JD.com (chairman Richard Liu), the two largest and most lucrative online marketplaces in China.

Few foreign companies had successfully penetrated these platforms due to their complex regulatory requirements and cultural barriers. My next challenge involved convincing country music stars and celebrities to explore the Chinese market opportunity. With over one billion potential customers and 95 percent of Chinese consumers shopping online, China represented an enormous untapped revenue source for American brands and entertainers.

When I reached out to Nashville stars through Max's connections, they showed genuine interest in the potential for significant sales in China. However, they were hesitant to pioneer this new market independently, preferring to wait until a major celebrity validated the concept. I realized that I needed to secure a big-name star to make the venture credible for everyone else.

My breakthrough came when I connected with John, who served as Taylor Swift's president, lawyer, and primary gatekeeper. John was also a close personal friend of Max's, which provided crucial access to Taylor's inner circle.

John had been considering strategies to enter the Chinese e-commerce market for Taylor Swift for some time. However, he was deeply concerned about the rampant piracy affecting Taylor's products and music on platforms like Tmall and JD.com. Before taking any steps into China's market, he knew that addressing the piracy issue would be essential to protecting Taylor's brand and revenue streams.

Understanding the Piracy Problem

Piracy represented one of the most significant challenges facing international brands in China. The term refers to the unauthorized copying or duplication of someone else's creative work, where shady individuals or companies illegally use someone's intellectual property to market their products for their own profit. This practice completely disregards the rights of original creators and can have devastating economic consequences.

The impact of piracy on a brand extends far beyond immediate financial losses. It erodes consumer trust, damages brand reputation, and makes it nearly impossible for legitimate products to compete in the marketplace. For a global superstar like Taylor Swift, piracy represented millions of dollars in lost revenue and the dilution of her carefully crafted brand image.

This challenge had never been successfully addressed on the scale that would be required for Taylor's brand, and I was unsure on how to approach such a complex problem. However, the potential rewards for solving the piracy problems were enormous, both financially and in terms of establishing our company as a pioneer in celebrity e-commerce.

John: The Gatekeeper of Taylor Swift

John was an imposing figure, with the kind of commanding presence that immediately conveyed his importance in Taylor's organization. He was both handsome and articulate, greeting me warmly during our initial discussions while listening attentively to my proposals.

He appeared genuinely curious about my innovative strategies for combating Taylor's piracy problem and my vision for launching a clothing line that would appeal to her international fan base. Over the next several weeks, we continued our discussions while I worked frantically to develop comprehensive plans for both Taylor's potential brand launch and a solution to her massive piracy issue.

During our final planning meeting, John made me an offer that would change the trajectory of my entire career. He told me that if I could successfully eliminate a good amount of Taylor's brand piracy in the United States and on Chinese e-commerce platforms, then I would be granted a licensing agreement to launch her clothing line in China.

Building the Anti-Piracy Solution

I was excited about this unprecedented opportunity, and so was Max, whose enthusiasm motivated me to tackle the piracy challenge head-on despite my uncertainty about how to proceed. I began intensive research and reached out to contacts in China for their perspectives and advice.

One of my most valuable contacts was Marco, a British businessman who managed a successful licensing and marketing firm in China. Despite being a foreigner, his two decades of experience in the Chinese market had earned him a stellar reputation, and I respected his judgment greatly. Marco provided honest assessments of the challenges involved in fighting piracy on Chinese e-commerce platforms while offering to assist through his connections with China's largest intellectual property law firm.

As my research progressed, I developed an ambitious plan and sought assistance from a security firm contracted by the United States government. This company's mission involved protecting critical information—both classified and non-classified—that could be used against American interests, focusing on preventing adversaries from accessing sensitive data that might compromise national security operations. I believed no organization was better equipped to help me tackle piracy for Taylor Swift and other celebrities than these cybersecurity experts.

Although they were initially uncertain about the feasibility of my proposal, I succeeded in persuading the firm's president to implement my anti-piracy strategy with his team of specialists. This represented a significant investment of both time and resources, but the potential impact made it worthwhile.

The Anti-Piracy Success

After many weeks of intensive collaboration, we created a revolutionary global anti-piracy tracking system capable of monitoring and eliminating infringing activities across multiple platforms simultaneously. Their team committed to working twelve-hour shifts every day to combat piracy related to Taylor Swift's brand and music along with Keith Urban's brand, who I was introduced to by a colleague who had heard about my ambitious quest to reduce piracy for celebrities.

When my first comprehensive anti-piracy report was completed the following month, I was thrilled to report to John and Max that we had successfully removed fifty million dollars' worth of Taylor's piracy from JD.com and Tmall combined. I also greatly reduced Keith's piracy in China also. While John was both shocked and pleased with these results, I could sense he had doubted my ability to deliver on such ambitious promises.

The effectiveness of our anti-piracy tracking system amazed even me. Over the course of the first year, we achieved a total reduction of over $200 million in piracy linked to Taylor's brand across all Chinese platforms. This accomplishment was truly remarkable, as no one had ever achieved anything comparable for any brand in the entertainment or apparel industries.

The Licensing Agreement: A Setup for Failure

As promised, John granted us the opportunity to launch a Taylor Swift clothing line specifically designed for the Chinese market. The platform would also invite other music celebrities, like Keith to join it and as soon as Taylor was on board, the phones wouldn't stop ringing from other big stars wanting to venture onto our Chinese platform. However, I wasn't aware at the time—since Max handled all contract negotiations—that the agreement with Taylor was only valid for one year. When I eventually learned about this crucial limitation, it became clear that a single year was far too short to successfully launch a celebrity clothing brand in China, particularly when working essentially alone.

Max seemed completely oblivious to the fact that he had essentially guaranteed my failure by accepting such restrictive terms. The complexity of establishing a business in China, combined with the challenges of designing, producing, and marketing a celebrity fashion line, required far more time than twelve months.

The Impossible Timeline

When Max finally informed me about the one-year contract limitation, I was devastated and I was already 6 months into the process of my 2-year contract with him. "Max! We can never launch successfully in China in just one year!" I said, feeling panic rise in my chest. "It will take six months just to obtain our Chinese business license, and another six to eight months to build the website and design the brand collection."

"No worries," Max replied with his characteristic overconfidence. "John is a great friend of mine, and he'll provide us with all the time we need." I didn't believe him for a second.

At that moment, I realized that trusting Max had been a significant mistake. Facing such tight deadlines while managing the delicate nature of a celebrity brand partnership, I went to bed that night feeling anxious and overwhelmed, fully aware that I could lose everything once again.

My desire for professional success stemmed from many factors, but the primary motivation was my deep respect for Taylor Swift as an artist and a business leader. I was absolutely determined not to let her down, regardless of the obstacles I would face.

Building an Inadequate Team

I hired Jen as my assistant, a decision I would quickly come to regret, but Nashville was limited on people with retail experience. She was young and ambitious but plagued by insecurities that made her emotional state unpredictable from day to day. It seemed to me that she had little desire for the job itself, but the allure of working with celebrities was too tempting for her to refuse.

Nashville's Limited Talent

Next, I needed to hire a freelance designer. Nashville's limited pool of graphic design talent forced me to work with an unconventional married couple, Kirby and his wife. From our first meeting, the wife made collaboration difficult. She was often complaining about everything I did or requested.

Her hostility baffled me, especially considering I had given them the opportunity to create graphics for two of the world's biggest celebrities. Kirby tended to tolerate her mistreatment even when he was the target of her insults.

Like Jen, she would quit every couple of weeks, disrupting my progress and complicating my work schedules. On those days, Kirby had to calm his wife down while I found myself apologizing for things I hadn't done just to get her back to work. Despite these personality issues, they were incredibly talented, and their work was exceptional quality.

The Factory Partnership

When I left New York, my only remaining manufacturing option was Albert, who owned a factory in China. He had previously produced goods for other brands I had worked on, and his facility was properly certified and efficient. Albert jumped at the opportunity to work on a celebrity brand, promising to do everything in his power to ensure our success.

While I was initially grateful for Albert's enthusiasm, I knew that greed could easily override good intentions when Chinese factory owners saw potential for huge profits. Chinese manufacturers had a reputation for cutting corners and substituting cheaper materials when they thought they could get away with it. I never fully trusted Albert or any Chinese factory owner, despite our previous working relationship.

The Health Crisis: Lyme Disease

Several months into my Nashville residency, I began experiencing severe physical symptoms that indicated something was seriously wrong with my health. After visiting over ten doctors and undergoing countless tests, I was finally diagnosed with Lyme disease, which is transmitted through tick bites.

Because New York City has no deer population, I had no experience with tick-borne illnesses. In Nashville, I enjoyed feeding the deer that frequently visited my backyard, completely unaware that I was exposing myself to dangerous health risks.

The disease caused severe fatigue and excruciating pain in my legs and joints. Because I had been misdiagnosed initially, the antibiotics prescribed by earlier doctors had been ineffective, allowing the disease to progress to a more serious stage. The pain became so unbearable that I could rarely sleep for more than three hours at a time, even with pain-relieving patches that I had to reapply every hour when they stopped working.

My doctor prescribed stronger pain medications, but I refused to take them regularly, fearing they would make me drowsy and unable to maintain the high level of performance my work demanded. One evening, desperate from the intensity of my pain and exhausted from overwork, I took two of the prescribed pain pills. As a result, I fell asleep on my front lawn and was awakened by police officers who rushed me to the hospital for evaluation.

I was deeply embarrassed when Jen told Max about my illness, but he seemed unfazed and simply told me to push through the pain. As my condition worsened and I became nearly crippled, I never took another pain pill. Instead, I stayed home and worked, sometimes not leaving my house for weeks at a time. I became expert at hiding my condition from Max and Jen, determined not to show any weakness that might jeopardize my position.

The Chinese Website Development

At this stage of the project, Marco's company in China was responsible for creating our celebrity website and managing all branding efforts. Despite their lack of experience with celebrity brands, they created an impressive website and demonstrated remarkable loyalty to our project. No American celebrity brand had ever launched directly in China before, so I was pioneering completely uncharted territory and I was so proud of this and my reduction efforts of piracy.

While Jen often complained about working too hard, I labored diligently to obtain the necessary business licenses, finalize the Chinese website, and design products for Taylor debut collection, which would feature stunning graphic t-shirts. The time zone differences often kept me awake until 2 a.m. resolving issues with my team in China. Although taking on this project seemed overwhelming and perhaps foolish, I remained completely committed to achieving success.

Taylor's Team: Obstruction and Indifference

From the project's inception, Taylor's team appeared to obstruct my efforts. I desperately needed promotional photographs of Taylor for the website and marketing materials, but they provided only eight images—far too few to create any meaningful impact on our e-commerce platform. Despite my repeated requests for additional images they failed to send more.

Taylor's team frequently ignored my calls and emails and when they did respond, they refused to offer any meaningful assistance or support. After I submitted carefully crafted designs and graphics to Taylor's team for approval, weeks would pass without any feedback whatsoever.

Most of Kirby and his wife's excellent graphics were rejected without explanation, which frustrated them enormously and added significant complications to my relationship with them and my time-line. It felt as though Taylor's team was actively working against my efforts to establish this brand, particularly since I believed our designs were superior to their existing merchandise offerings.

When the situation became untenable, Max finally got involved and told me that Taylor's team was simply uninterested in my China clothing launch. I was devastated by this news but powerless to change their attitude.

The Andrea Swift Meeting: A Glimmer of Hope

I encouraged Max to contact John about Taylor's team's lack of support, but he only did so after we had already missed several important deadlines. I think Max's growing frustration with my repeated requests for his help led him to avoid speaking to me for days at a time. Even though John acknowledged my struggles, he preferred not to bring any of my concerns to Taylor's team or her mother, Andrea who oversaw all of Taylor's interests. Max claimed that John was intimidated by Andrea Swift's strong personality and influence over Taylor's business decisions.

Eventually, I managed to arrange a direct meeting with Andrea to review our designs and graphics. Based on her reputation and the fear she seemed to inspire in the men around Taylor, I expected to encounter an overbearing and difficult woman. Instead, Andrea turned out to be pleasant, intelligent, kind and genuinely concerned about protecting her daughter's brand image. I really liked her!

She assured me that she would help secure approvals for my designs and graphics, expressing appreciation for my hard work and dedication I had brought to the project. Throughout our interaction, she remained consistently kind and supportive toward me.

The Chinese Business License Nightmare

Establishing a legitimate business presence in China required obtaining a Chinese business license before launching any commercial operations. This license, known as a WFOE (Wholly Foreign Owned Enterprise), represents a limited liability business structure completely owned by a foreign investor—in this case, me.

WFOEs were initially created by the Chinese government to encourage export-driven manufacturing and facilitate the transfer of advanced technologies from foreign companies. The process of obtaining my WFOE license stretched nearly a year, filled with overwhelming paperwork, bureaucratic hurdles, and regulatory obstacles that almost caused me to abandon the effort entirely.

We settled on calling our company with Taylor, "Heritage 66." The name pays tribute to Route 66 while capturing the nostalgic essence we aimed to reflect, staying true to our origins.

However, I recognized that conducting legitimate business in China was impossible without proper licensing. I also needed approval from the Tennessee state government before I could apply for my business license at the Chinese consulate in Washington, D.C. Once all documents were submitted, I entered a prolonged period of uncertainty, anxiously waiting to learn whether Chinese authorities would approve my application.

For months, I felt like I was walking on eggshells, constantly anticipating either approval or rejection from Chinese bureaucrats. To help manage the overwhelming documentation requirements, I brought Marco onto the team, leveraging his government connections to facilitate the process and expedite approval procedures.

The Investment Mystery

When Max informed me that Taylor's company was planning to invest directly in our business, I was taken completely by surprise. It seemed to me that John was primarily focused on getting me to solve Taylor's piracy problem, with the licensing agreement serving mainly to appease Max rather than representing genuine support from Taylor's team.

Given her team's prior obvious lack of enthusiasm for the project, I was skeptical when Max claimed John was providing a financial investment. Since I never had access to any bank accounts or financial statements, I had only Max's word for this supposed investment and a copy of our operating agreement that stated this also.

My inexperience with the treacherous Chinese business landscape that awaited me left me completely unprepared for what was coming. I never anticipated that running a business as a woman in China would involve such significant risks and overwhelming complexities. The extent of corruption and bureaucratic obstacles I encountered far exceeded anything I had experienced during my thirty years of working with Chinese manufacturers in the apparel production sector.

The E-commerce Platform Battles

My ongoing struggle against the pirating of Taylor's merchandise on Tmall and JD.com was complicated by the complete indifference of Chinese executives who operated these e-commerce platforms. Unfortunately, China showed little interest in assisting American businesses, particularly when it came to intellectual property protection.

American companies were unaware that Tmall and JD.com profited from every store on their platforms, taking at least a ten percent commission regardless of whether the products being sold were pirated or legitimate. This financial structure significantly diminished their motivation to enforce anti-piracy regulations, since removing counterfeit products actually reduced their revenue stream.

After extensive pleading and negotiation, Josh, the senior director of communications for JD.com, finally agreed to help remove Taylor and Keith's pirated products from their platform. Josh worked closely with his IT department and my security team to eliminate all of Taylor and Keith's counterfeit goods within a few months. In return for this cooperation, Josh requested that we establish an official JD.com store to sell Taylor's legitimate merchandise, which John approved for us. This would significantly boost our revenue, but it would also double my workload, and I was already feeling overwhelmed. However, when Max recognized the financial benefits, he urged me to do it, I agreed, albeit reluctantly. Josh at the JD.com and his team were a pleasure to work with, and their corporate and warehouse operations far exceeded Tmall in professionalism and technology.

Alibaba, which operates Tmall, presented an entirely different set of challenges. After receiving no responses to my calls and emails for weeks at a time, I flew to Shanghai to meet directly with Kane, a senior executive at Tmall. My interaction with Kane revealed the ugly reality of sexism in Chinese business culture.

I couldn't tolerate Kane because he openly refused to work with me as a woman on Taylor's account. His behavior was consistently combative, and his sexist attitudes were unmistakably evident in every interaction. Working with him became a constant struggle due to his arrogance and disrespect.

At one point, he made the outrageous demand that Taylor Swift personally fly to China and present her passport to him at his Hangzhou office to prove her identity. In his twisted quest to control the world's biggest pop star, he systematically sabotaged anyone who stood in his way.

After enduring countless lengthy, painful meetings, phone calls, and email exchanges with Kane, he eventually coordinated with his IT team to eliminate Taylor's pirated product from Tmall. However, it was an agonizingly slow and difficult process that my security team and I handled with the utmost discretion. We eventually succeeded in removing hundreds of millions of dollars in piracy for Taylor Swift and Keith Urban across all of JD.com and Alibaba's e-commerce platforms, including AliExpress and Taobao.

The Corruption and Bureaucracy

Every step of setting up the e-commerce infrastructure for Taylor's brand was painfully time-consuming and frustrating because Tmall employed thousands of people who seemed incapable of making any decisions. It often took me days just to communicate a single concept to Chinese staff members, and they frequently failed to implement changes correctly. Progress felt like taking two steps forward and three steps back, with overwhelming red tape and bureaucratic obstacles at every turn.

Kane deliberately hindered my progress at every stage of development. In contrast, I witnessed how the JD.com team excelled in intelligence, organization, and effectiveness compared to the chaotic situation at Tmall. During my interview with Tmall's USA president, he openly admitted that the company had overextended itself by taking on too many brands and was completely unprepared to handle foreign companies effectively.

He acknowledged that Tmall had acquired an excessive number of brands purely to enhance their corporate image, which proved to be misleading marketing similar to their efforts to promote Tmall Global to American companies. These strategies appeared designed primarily to inflate their stock value rather than provide genuine value to international partners.

Tmall Global had been presented to American companies as a quick and easy entry point into the Chinese e-commerce market. However, it failed to resonate with Chinese consumers, with only four percent of shoppers engaging with the platform. Reports from brands and marketing consultants monitoring online shopping trends indicated that Tmall Global, which had promised foreign companies rapid entry into China, fell dramatically short of expectations within ten months of its launch.

American marketing firms capitalized on this false promise by convincing brands to adopt the Tmall Global business model. In exchange for significant fees, they guaranteed substantial success through website development and marketing strategies. However, for most brands, Tmall Global failed to deliver results, causing considerable financial losses for companies that weren't directly managing their presence on Chinese e-commerce platforms.

I chose a more challenging path by launching directly on Chinese platforms rather than using Tmall Global as an intermediary.

The Shanghai Concert and Media Manipulation

In November 2015, Taylor Swift held a major concert in Shanghai, which represented the only occasion when Tmall actively promoted our new e-commerce website. However, their promotion was motivated primarily by their desire to enhance the prospects of Alibaba's upcoming IPO rather than genuine support for our brand.

Simultaneously, Alibaba was negotiating a significant deal with Taylor's team that would allow her music to be sold legally in China for the first time. This created additional leverage for Kane to make increasingly outrageous demands and requests.

Kane began pressuring me for complimentary concert tickets to distribute to his friends, along with meet-and-greet opportunities with Taylor herself. His requests became increasingly difficult to manage, and at one point, he asked Taylor to record a personalized song on her phone for Chinese fans, promising to give it away as a promotional prize.

This demand was completely ridiculous and obviously would never happen, but Kane continued pressuring John about it anyway. All of these efforts represented failed attempts by Kane to seize control of our business operations and marginalize my role in the company I had created.

My contract required me to present any ideas or requests to Taylor's team for consideration, and they often found Kane's submissions laughable and inappropriate and they scoffed at me. As difficulties with Kane mounted, I repeatedly went to John,

Taylor's team, and Max to explain that I couldn't continue working with him effectively, but it seemed to me that no one intervened on my behalf.

As a result of my ongoing disagreements with Kane, he went directly to Max in an attempt to have me removed from my own company. He engaged in unethical tactics, including forging analyses that supported his positions and writing directly to Max and John while excluding me from communications entirely.

It infuriated me that neither Max nor John could see through Kane's obvious power grab, but they were unfamiliar with the dirty tactics that Chinese business men could play. The following week, I found myself completely excluded from any future marketing discussions regarding Taylor's e-commerce brand in China. This not only jeopardized my project timelines but also undermined my credibility and authority as the company's founder.

Even the president of Tmall USA was afraid of Kane and refused to intervene on my behalf, despite knowing that his behavior was inappropriate and counterproductive.

The Humiliation of Sexism

As a woman, I found Kane's treatment deeply humiliating, and being repeatedly bullied by this Tmall executive while receiving no support from my male partners in the USA was devastating. John insisted on meeting with Kane in China, where he was going to discuss other business opportunities with Tmall executives, including a major deal he was negotiating for Taylor.

During a crucial meeting with Max and John, I explicitly asked John to avoid Kane or I would lose what little control I still maintained over our brand operations. At our recent overview meeting, Andrea agreed with my request and told John to stay out of my relationship with Kane. However, John completely ignored both of our requests and met with Kane anyway, making it virtually impossible for me to work with Tmall moving forward.

The situation felt like an impossible uphill battle because neither Max nor John supported my position against Kane. Kane had successfully isolated me from future communications and decision-making processes. My job became completely untenable without constantly involving Max for assistance, which only forced him to consult with John and increased his frustration with me.

Max eventually advised me not to contact John or Tmall directly anymore, stating, "The issue is now handled by the men; we'll take care of everything except design." This statement perfectly encapsulated the sexist attitudes that had plagued my entire work experience.

Product Quality Crisis

To make matters even more complicated, we were preparing to launch an initial website featuring only Taylor Swift graphic t-shirts, but when I received approval samples, the quality of products from my factory failed to meet my original standards. Later on, Albert told me that he had allegedly discussed the fabric change with Max to use less expensive fabrics to increase their profit margins, and he completely disregarded my quality requirements and brand standards.

I completely rejected all of the t-shirts due to their poor quality, which meant I needed to completely revamp the entire t-shirt line within two weeks and create new samples within three weeks. With the project launch rapidly approaching, I made the difficult decision to travel back to China personally to ensure my factory wouldn't secretly substitute inferior materials again. This task seemed nearly impossible to accomplish alone, but I somehow managed to succeed, even with the pain of my Lyme disease effecting my every move.

The "1989" Controversy and Media Sabotage

A few days before Taylor's major concert in Shanghai, Kane contacted John and Max with an outrageous request for Taylor to perform at a Tmall promotional event in a shopping mall just hours before her scheduled concert. When Taylor's team rightfully dismissed this idea as completely unfeasible and ridiculous, Kane quickly withdrew his request but immediately retaliated by leaking a fabricated story to the media about Taylor.

Kane orchestrated a controversy regarding Taylor's album title "1989," suggesting to journalists that it referenced the year of the Tiananmen Square protests—an extremely sensitive and tragic episode in Chinese history. Due to strict government censorship regarding any mention of "1989," discussions about Tiananmen Square were completely prohibited on Chinese social media.

USA and European Media outlets began reporting that "Tmall officials were canceling Taylor Swift's e-commerce site," which I believe was Kane's deliberate attempt at intimidation following his rejected request. Both Chinese and American press coverage escalated dramatically, with reporters claiming Taylor had deliberately chosen a politically provocative album title.

The reality was much simpler: Taylor Swift was born in "1989," which is why her album carried that title. It had absolutely no connection to the political protests. However, the media frenzy Kane had instigated created serious problems for our launch.

Taylor's team directed me to eliminate any promotional items or t-shirts featuring "1989" graphics, despite this being her current album's title and primary branding. Later, I discovered that the

Chinese government had actually approved Taylor's "1989" album a full year prior to our launch, and Kane was completely aware of this approval, yet he misled everyone on this in order to sabotage the launch.

Because Kane's malicious actions led to the removal of all "1989" graphic designs from our website, our first merchandise launch in China was now restricted to just four basic t-shirt designs—far too limited to generate meaningful sales or excitement among Chinese fans. I was devastated and felt defeated.

The Final Power Play

Kane made one final attempt to infiltrate our business by demanding that I close our store on JD.com, threatening that Tmall would provide no marketing support if I maintained relationships with their competitor. I was furious because Tmall had barely supported us from the beginning, and now Kane wanted me to eliminate part of our revenue stream.

I desperately needed JD.com's sales to keep our business viable, and I stressed to both Max and John that closing this partnership with JD.com would be harmful, especially after Josh had provided so much assistance in removing Taylor's piracy. Ultimately it was John's call and he sided with Kane and told me to close our JD.com store. Kane's ultimatum represented clear blackmail and demonstrated the petty rivalry between China's major e-commerce platforms.

When we finally launched on Tmall, Kane's insufficient marketing support for our platform led Chinese consumers to believe our website and all of our products were counterfeit. Without proper promotion and Tmall authentication, legitimate products often appear suspicious to Chinese shoppers who are accustomed to widespread counterfeiting.

After our initial t-shirt release completely failed, so I was resolved to recreate a more fashion-forward clothing line within one month, knowing I risked losing my Taylor Swift license altogether if this final attempt didn't succeed. With only a few months remaining on our contract with Taylor, the situation felt like a hopeless battle, but I refused to give up.

Kane continued attempting to undermine my new fashion line to seize complete control of the business, but I was determined not to back down. In one last, desperate effort to salvage the project, I returned to China again, with Jen to focus entirely on developing a completely new fashion collection.

The Production Marathon

I spent over a month, seven days a week, working inside my Chinese factory alongside Jen, where we developed an entirely new clothing line for Taylor's brand. My responsibilities included not only designing each piece but also fitting them on models, creating technical patterns, selecting all fabrics and trims, and crafting the quality of the labels, packaging, and hangtags, along with very high-tech security tags that were placed on every garment.

I endured grueling sixteen-hour workdays while Jen sat nearby complaining constantly and expressing her desire to return home and quit. She was ill-prepared to handle the pressures of the position.

After this exhausting period in China, I returned to the United States feeling completely worn out and physically ill from the stress, my Lyme disease and overwork.

When I presented our beautiful new samples to John, Max, and Taylor's mother Andrea, their reactions were genuinely enthusiastic for the new direction that I had gone in. John took the samples to Los Angeles to show Taylor and her team directly.

According to John, Taylor approved everything except for one pair of bell-bottom pants.

With this approval, we finally had a fantastic new fashion line, and I felt excited about our launch prospects for the first time in months.

However, I felt profound disappointment that Taylor herself never reached out to meet with me or discuss the new line I had worked so hard to create. Given the enormous effort this project had required, her lack of personal involvement was disheartening.

I recognized that our brand would likely struggle without Taylor's active endorsement and promotion. While I may have been overly optimistic, I genuinely wanted her to feel the same enthusiasm for the brand that I felt after investing so much of myself in its creation.

The Marketing Maze

By mid-July, I needed to photograph our new collection for Tmall and JD.com on models, upload images to the website, design a comprehensive catalog for the Chinese market, and hire the promotional agency that Tmall's policies required. Each of these tasks presented significant challenges and expenses.

One of the most problematic aspects of selling on Tmall involves their requirement that all sellers hire marketing agencies from their approved list before being permitted to sell anything on their platform. Prior to discovering this policy, I had contracted with an excellent marketing company, to handle our brand promotion.

Unfortunately, Tmall's mandatory policy forced me to abandon them and spend over $6,000 monthly on Tmall-approved marketing services, plus an additional five percent of all sales revenue. Combined with Tmall's own five percent commission, the marketing company's five percent fee, Alipay's two percent processing fee (similar to PayPal), Taylor's substantial licensing fees, and the requirement to offer free shipping throughout China, generating any substantial profit became virtually impossible.

To maximize his own profits, Max insisted that I avoid hiring additional staff, leaving me to handle an impossible workload essentially alone.

Further investigation revealed that my original marketing company had been blacklisted because they refused to pay kickbacks to Tmall executives—a common form of corruption in Chinese business practices. After reviewing Tmall's approved marketing firms, I discovered that one offered no English-language support, two were directly owned by Tmall and charged $10,000 monthly, one was personally connected to Tmall's president, and another started with a $6,000 fee that shockingly escalated to $30,000 within a week because of Taylor's celebrity status.

The hours I spent navigating Tmall's deliberately convoluted bureaucracy felt endless, and it clearly represented a systematic scheme designed to extract maximum fees from foreign businesses attempting to enter the Chinese market.

The Endless Delays and Frustration

It took an additional few weeks for Taylor's team to finally approve our new graphics and web designs for the relaunch, despite the urgent deadlines we faced. Their responses to my emails remained infrequent and dismissive, consistently throwing my carefully planned timelines into complete disarray.

No matter how desperately I wanted to voice my frustrations directly to Max, he remained determined not to upset John or jeopardize their personal friendship. Out of misplaced loyalty to John, Max consistently dismissed my legitimate business concerns whenever they were together, treating my professional expertise as irrelevant complaints.

The constant delays pushed our new spring line launch so far back that by October, temperatures in China had already turned quite cold, making my spring clothing launch seem completely out of season. Since the spring collection had already entered production, my ability to make weather-appropriate adjustments was extremely limited.

Without meaningful support from Tmall, Taylor's team, or John, and operating under our company name "Heritage 66" rather than Taylor's name on our website, the situation quickly devolved into chaos. Taylor's team mandated that we use our business name instead of "Taylor Swift" on the website, leaving Chinese customers completely puzzled about the connection between our products and their favorite artist.

Many potential customers assumed our merchandise was counterfeit rather than authentic Taylor Swift products. E-commerce success in China depends heavily on brand authenticity and clear celebrity endorsement, and without Taylor Swift's name prominently displayed as the company name, we ended up only selling a handful of products. Even though I had invested in expensive anti-piracy hangtags that could be validated on the website, we were still viewed as counterfeit.

The Descent into Desperation

I realized that achieving any success for this brand required a completely new strategy, but with impossible deadlines looming, I found myself as the sole person attempting to establish a fashion brand for the world's biggest pop star. Max's pressure on me escalated dramatically; he contacted me during nights and weekends as if to ensure I never stopped working.

Max's behavior became unpredictable—one moment offering encouragement, and the next he would belittle me.

A sense of impending failure weighed heavily on my mind, leading me into a depression, especially as a woman trying to build this complex business essentially alone while battling a serious illness. Adding to these challenges, I was told by Taylor's team that she would not be discussing or promoting our new brand on her social media platforms, despite this being the most effective way to reach Chinese fans and showing that we were legitimate.

In a desperate attempt to generate interest, I asked our marketing firm in China to maximize press coverage by showcasing our new designs to international media outlets. While the fashion press published thousands of positive reviews about our collection, these efforts felt completely futile without Taylor's personal endorsement and social media support.

John finally agreed to rename our store "Taylor Swift" as our contract deadline approached, but this change came far too late to salvage our launch. At one point, Taylor wore our signature baseball dress while exiting her plane at LAX terminal, causing a media frenzy among photographers and fans.

Tragically, I didn't receive approval from Taylor's team to use these photographs for marketing and social media promotion until weeks later, when the news cycle had moved on. It felt as though Taylor's team was continuously undermining our efforts, ensuring that no one in China knew she had worn our signature design until the opportunity had completely passed.

Hong Kong Fashion Week: The Last Stand

In one final attempt to salvage the brand, I decided to show the line during Hong Kong Fashion Week, one of Asia's most prestigious fashion events. My goal was extremely ambitious considering my limited resources and deteriorating health, but I had to attempt one last effort to achieve success for Taylor's brand.

By this point, I was receiving eight steroid injections each week to manage the excruciating pain from Lyme disease, and I could barely walk without assistance. My health was deteriorating rapidly, and I felt utterly defeated and exhausted, but I refused to give up.

Albert, my factory owner in China, secured an exhibition booth for me at Hong Kong Fashion Week. Over the following two weeks, I redesigned some of our collection to accommodate colder weather looks while Taylor's team reviewed every aspect of my new approach, from visual presentations to clothing modifications.

We needed approval for our booth design and had to immediately order construction materials. Once I completed the updated collection designs, I sent detailed specifications to Albert's factory with strict instructions to follow my directions exactly.

I made it absolutely clear that if Albert deviated from my specifications in any way, there would be serious consequences when I arrived in China the following week. Albert was responsible for producing revised samples for the fashion show I was planning, and he understood my perfectionist standards—I expected nothing less than a flawless execution.

However, Taylor's team surprised me by demanding that the word "**fashion**" be completely eliminated from our new website, marketing materials, signage, packaging, hangtags, press and design descriptions. With only one week remaining before my trip to China, I was forced to redo everything once again.

John emphasized that Taylor's line must never be referenced as a "**fashion**" collection at Hong Kong Fashion Week. Initially, I thought he was joking when he explained that the term "**fashion**" was reserved exclusively for designers like Dior and Oscar de la Renta.

According to John, Taylor—who was co-chairing the Met Gala that year—aimed to prevent any mix-up between her commercial items in China and authentic high-fashion lines from well-established couture brands that might provide her with complimentary products.

The "Merch" Miscommunication

To emphasize our brand's authenticity, I believed a promotional video from Taylor would provide an exciting way to introduce her new product line to Chinese fans. Taylor's team filmed a simple six-second clip where Taylor greeted her Chinese fans and encouraged them to purchase her "**merch**." Unfortunately, this video fell completely flat because few Chinese consumers understood what "**merch**" meant.

Despite this odd request from John to call our line "**merch**," I conducted around twenty interviews with various newspapers and magazines and stores during Hong Kong Fashion Week without ever using the word "**fashion**" to describe our products. When interviewers asked what inspired Taylor to create this "**fashion**" line, I would smile diplomatically and explain that the "**merch**" represented a combination of Taylor's unique style preferences and her favorite clothing pieces.

What I desperately wanted to say was: "It **IS** a fashion line!" I stayed awake nights and weekends for two years designing and redesigning it, and every store buyer, and trade publication also recognized it as a **"fashion"** collection. **"Fashion"** can be sold at Target's or Bergdorf Goodman-it's not exclusive to a price point or a brand.

The Fashion Week Success

Eighteen thousand international buyers attended Hong Kong Fashion Week, representing the largest concentration of fashion industry professionals in Asia. Jen and I arrived in China, once again, to review Taylor's final remade samples and prepare for what would become either my greatest triumph or final failure.

By this time, I had developed serious issues with Albert, my production manager, but I had no choice but to continue working with him due to our impossible time constraints. Under my direction, Albert's team assembled a fantastic exhibition booth, complete with a life-size cutout of Taylor near the entrance since she wouldn't be attending the event personally.

The cutout became an unexpected highlight of the entire fashion week, drawing crowds of buyers and media representatives eager to take photographs with Taylor's image. While I maintained active supervision over Albert's factory operations, he had never previously disappointed me with product quality before this project, so it was extremely disheartening that he was taking this route.

However, as Taylor's celebrity brand gained international attention and potential profitability, Albert began exhibiting the greed that I had always feared. He attempted to reduce costs and increase his own profits by substituting the higher-quality fabrics I had chosen with cheaper alternatives, believing I wouldn't notice the difference during my brief visits to oversee production.

While our designs remained visually appealing, the fabric quality, once again, fell significantly short of my approved standards.

Knowing I wouldn't tolerate the use of mediocre materials, Albert sought approval for these inferior samples directly from Max without informing me of the changes.

I warned Max that I would resign immediately if he didn't insist on using my originally specified fabrics, but he dismissed my concerns and laughed off my threats. At that moment, I realized that Max and Albert were already collaborating to maximize their profits at the expense of my reputation.

The Production Standards Crisis

Even though our fashion show was scheduled for broadcast on Chinese television, I was completely dissatisfied with samples Albert had produced because they clearly deviated from my strict quality guidelines. Since it was too late to withdraw from the event entirely, I decided to reduce the number of samples we would show and returned to the factory that night to make necessary corrections personally.

After three days of working and sleeping at Albert's factory, the samples finally met my standards and looked appropriately professional for the show. Generally, designing a complete clothing line requires approximately six months, with an additional three to six months needed for sample creation and refinement.

Yet here I was, attempting to complete my third complete collection for Taylor's brand in less than seven months—an absolutely unprecedented timeline in the fashion industry. Producing a professional clothing line typically requires specialized team members, including lead designers, production coordinators, technical designers, fabric experts, pattern makers, trim specialists, fit consultants, and packaging designers.

Fabric selections require approval from both the designer and the client, and fit sessions must be completed and perfected before moving into production phases. Often, it's necessary to adjust fit and proportions two or three times to achieve ideal results. Every detail of construction and all decorative elements must be approved and tested before authorizing production.

For Taylor Swift's Chinese fashion line, I had only Jen, two difficult graphic designers, plus business partners and a factory owner who actively worked against my efforts to establish and meet my high product standards. This was definitely not the dream team I had envisioned when I started this ambitious project.

Despite the chaotic circumstances and inadequate support, I managed to complete Taylor's line for the show and felt genuine pride in what we had accomplished under such difficult conditions.

The Hong Kong Fashion Week event proved incredibly demanding. I spent at least ten hours each day at our exhibition booth with Jen, promoting our brand and presenting the collection to international media representatives, potential retail customers, and major department stores.

By each day's end, I was completely exhausted. My legs throbbed from standing all day in professional shoes, and every night I returned to my hotel room crying from pain and stress, soaking my swollen feet in ice water to reduce inflammation enough to sleep.

Max and Ray's Arrival: The Betrayal Revealed

The evening before our Hong Kong Fashion Week presentation and fashion show, Max surprised me by arriving in China with Ray, one of our supposed investors and a high-ranking executive from a major American mattress retail chain. Max had maintained a long-standing business relationship with Ray's company.

I still harbored concerns about Albert's sample quality because he had failed to follow my production directions, so I immediately brought these issues to Max's attention while he was in China. After our fashion show concluded, I expressed my firm belief that Albert needed to be terminated immediately to protect Taylor's brand reputation.

However, Max admitted that he had been communicating with Albert about an entirely different business venture and had no intention of firing him. He told me I needed to find a way to work with Albert despite his questionable practices.

I was furious that Max had been conducting business behind my back with Albert, clearly betraying our partnership. I realized that Albert was deliberately trying to ingratiate himself with Max, recognizing his wealth and financial potential while attempting to marginalize my oversite role.

At dinner that evening, Max revealed his primary goal: getting Taylor's brand into as many international stores as possible to recoup his investment as quickly as possible. Both Max and his investors were eager to recover their money from Taylor's project immediately, regardless of long-term brand building or reputation management.

The Mattress Store Conspiracy

The day after Max's arrival, he informed me that Albert would immediately begin searching for mattress store locations throughout China for both him and Ray. I was confused and asked why Albert was qualified to scout retail locations for a completely different industry.

Max revealed that he, Ray, and Ray's supervisor had formed a secret partnership to open mattress retail stores in China, directly competing with American mattress company's. Max, Ray, and

Albert had spent the previous evening drinking and enjoying karaoke while discussing their plans for this new Chinese business venture.

In a catastrophic mistake, Max accidentally sent me emails intended for Albert, revealing his urgent need to sell off Taylor's inventory regardless of quality issues. His priority was raising funds quickly for their upcoming mattress project in China, and Taylor's brand had now become nothing more than a cash source to fund their new venture.

Max's late-night emails to Albert and our investors, indicated that Max, Ray and his boss were engaged in questionable activities that violated their employment agreements with their American mattress company employer. I felt deeply uncomfortable with this unethical behavior, but I stayed silent.

The emails also revealed that Albert was attempting to blame all production problems on me while positioning himself as Max's preferred partner along with Ray. Max informed Albert that if I continued investigating quality issues with Taylor's merchandise, he would replace me with Ray, who had no experience in apparel manufacturing and was still employed by the mattress company.

This revelation broke me completely. I had dedicated eighteen-hour days to building Taylor's brand in China, but it seemed Max was no longer interested in my efforts because he had discovered far greater financial opportunities with Albert, Ray and Ray's boss in the mattress business.

The Final Quality Battle

After the Hong Kong event concluded, my immediate priority was assessing production quality at Albert's factory, so I ordered a comprehensive audit of all completed merchandise. I also insisted that no products be shipped to any retailers until I could verify the quality, as I was deeply worried about potential damage to Taylor's brand reputation.

When I opened several production boxes for inspection, I immediately discovered that Albert had substituted cheap fabrics for the beautiful materials I had approved. The patterns hadn't been followed correctly, and there were burn marks, white streaks, and poor dyeing throughout the production run.

To disguise the inferior quality, clothing had been hastily stuffed into bags and covered with old tissue paper instead of our custom packaging. We had invested $50,000 in beautiful packaging materials, hang tags, labels, signature tissue paper, and encrypted security tags, but none of these materials had been used in production.

I immediately contacted Max and told him that Taylor's brand reputation was too important to risk by shipping substandard merchandise. Although Max promised to handle the situation with Albert, I later learned through Albert that they had arranged to sell the inferior products to a major Korean retail chain regardless of quality issues.

I was absolutely furious when Albert attempted to silence my objections by offering me a cash bribe to approve the terrible production quality. "There's no way these products will be sold!" I shouted during a conference call with Albert and Max. "I demand that everything be destroyed immediately!"

I felt it was my moral obligation to contact the Korean retailer directly and warn them about the poor quality of our products, informing them that we would not be shipping anything to their stores. When Max learned that I had canceled this deal, he exploded with rage, and I realized I was about to lose my job once again.

The British Success That Never Mattered

At Hong Kong Fashion Week, Taylor's brand received an overwhelmingly positive reception from international buyers and media representatives. A major British retailer with approximately 8,000 stores worldwide expressed serious interest in acquiring our line for distribution throughout Europe and Asia.

I successfully negotiated an order with a large British clothing chain for graphic t-shirts and dresses based on my beautiful quality fabric's, totaling 3 million pounds, which would have provided substantial profits and established Taylor's brand in international markets. The British chain also signed a guarantee for 15 million pounds in sales for the first year. Despite the enormous financial opportunity this represented, Max claimed he wasn't interested in the deal, and told me to cancel it.

I suspected he had already informed John about his intention to fire me for canceling the Korean order, making all future business opportunities irrelevant to his plans. Taylor's brand had attracted numerous other major retailers and e-commerce platforms eager to carry the line, and hundreds of positive reviews appeared in international fashion publications, including a featured article on the cover of Women's Wear Daily!

Given our collection's popularity and media attention, I remained optimistic that the brand could succeed if we transferred production to a different factory and addressed the quality concerns that Albert had created. Unfortunately, by this point, the decision was completely out of my hands.

Jen had completely disengaged from the project and effectively quit, expressing her hatred of being in China and her complete exhaustion from our demanding schedule. I understood her frustration since she was had never expected the grueling pace and high-pressure deadlines we faced daily.

Ultimately, I deeply regretted my partnership with Max, and I felt utterly devastated by how the situation had developed despite my best efforts and complete dedication to Taylor's brand.

The Breaking Point

Consumed by despair and overwhelming anguish over the failure of everything I had worked toward, I fell into a deep depression and I desperately needed to escape the pain and disappointment I was feeling over this failed partnership and Taylor's brand.

Fortunately, my dear friend Gerry flew to Nashville immediately to help me through this crisis. She encouraged me to let go of "Nash-evil," as we had begun calling the city, and move forward from what had become a completely pointless and destructive situation.

The Aftermath

I reached out to Max via email. As his partner, I felt a strong moral and fiduciary obligation to keep Taylor's team informed about everything going on between us. I had planned to move production within a few weeks to address the ongoing issues but I feared I would not be allowed to since he planned on firing me. Additionally, I pleaded my case to keep the brand going and told Max that the recent order from the UK retailer would help us maintain our momentum.

In response, Max declared that I was "dead" to him, fired me, and insisted I leave "his town" Immediately.

"That's fantastic!" Gerry remarked. "Let's get you packed and out of here."

Gerry advised me to notify John and Andrea in an email to

explain my situation to them. She believed that if John was a person of integrity, he'd reach out to me to discuss a resolution. However, John never made an effort to contact me after I sent him a detailed letter about my experiences in China with Albert, Max and Ray.

I forwarded the same email I sent to John and Andrea to Taylor's attorneys in Los Angeles. Sadly, I never received a response from them either, and I'm unsure who even read it.

This is the letter I sent to Taylor's attorney's a decade ago.

Attention: Taylor Swift's team,

Since I am unable to reach Andrea Swift directly and John has not returned my calls, I am writing to request that you, Andrea's lawyers, forward this email to her as soon as possible, considering the urgency of this matter.

I assured Andrea, when I first started the Taylor Swift Brand in China, that I would always safeguard Taylor's reputation and uphold integrity in my business practices for her. As the individual responsible for building Taylor's brand, all my efforts were focused on maintaining the highest quality of products for her, something I know John recognized and appreciated.

Unfortunately, the brand is at significant risk, as it has been ripped out of my control and now in the hands of my partners, Max and Ray, both unqualified in the apparel industry. Max had taken over my production with our factory while I was in China and approved lesser quality fabrics in order to increase his profit margin. Against my partners' intentions, I halted a large shipment of Taylor Swift subpar apparel intended to be sold to a major Korean retailer.

I confronted my partners' unconscionable decision to ship these products, but they ignored my concerns and tried to move forward with the delivery to the store chain anyway. I took matters into my own hands and contacted the Korean store to cancel the order-which they did and they were grateful for my honesty.

Taylor's collection received an enthusiastic response at Hong Kong Fashion Week, with thousands of stores globally expressing interest. At the show, I secured a $3 million order for graphic-approved T-shirts and dresses from a large reputable store chain in London, and other stores were keen to buy the brand once I changed factories and remade higher quality products, just like I had originally intended.

Taylor's line garnered numerous positive press mentions and was featured on the cover of "Women's Wear Daily" due to the favorable brand image I had developed for her in China.

Building this brand alone with just the help of an assistant, proved unfeasible for one woman due to the lack of support and the presence of some unscrupulous individuals who I had no control over. Taylor's team also provided minimal assistance in my efforts to establish the brand and it was an impossible task without their support.

Furthermore, I successfully reduced Taylor's piracy on Chinese e-commerce platforms by more than $200 million (John can share the reports with you), a feat unparalleled in either the China or the American apparel sector. Additionally, I was able to reclaim several of her trademarks that had been pilfered by individuals in China.

I feel Max has no interest in selling Taylor's brand to anyone except to dump the inferior quality products and recoup his minimal investment-then move on to his new venture in China.

On another note: Max and Ray and his boss, our investors, aims to launch a mattress store business in China to mitigate their *financial investment they incurred with Taylor's brand.*

I would appreciate the opportunity to discuss this with Andrea, as I have more documented evidence that supports my actions and exposes the potential corruption. The brand could be profitable with my new factory-which I have already lined up-and a seasoned team that I could put in place, if given the chance. My commitment to both the brand and Taylor should have demonstrated my loyalty and it never wavered. All I ask is that I have a fair chance to move forward with the brand that I so lovingly built.

Sincerely, Katie Liegey

The Truth About the Mattress Company Investors Scheme

After I sent this letter to Andrea's lawyers, Max's attorney—who was also supposed to be representing me—made an unexpected move by issuing me a legal notice that ended my partnership with Max. Ray, our investor, was appointed to fill my role, but soon after, both he and his boss were abruptly dismissed from their mattress company jobs. They had allegedly violated their code of conduct policy by working with Max on several projects and investing alongside us in Taylor Swift. When Max learned about their termination, he blamed me for their demise. What Max, Ray and his boss didn't realize was that they had been openly discussing their plans for Taylor's brand, including their idea to open mattress stores in China, using their company email accounts and telephones—an incredibly reckless move on their part. The mattress company's attorneys contacted me, demanding that I provide all emails exchanged between Max, Ray, and his boss regarding the China store project. I consulted a new lawyer who warned me about the seriousness of the situation, suggesting I might be drawn into their misconduct. According to the attorney's, Max, Ray, and his boss had already been under scrutiny from the mattress company's compliance team long before I had ever crossed paths with them. Max, Ray and his boss were being monitored closely for years before their termination from their company.

Allegations indicated that Ray and his boss approved inflated pricing for the mattress store projects and were purportedly receiving kickbacks from Max. I only became aware of their intentions to open stores in China during Hong Kong Fashion Week, where Max and Ray first shared their plans with me.

As soon as I discovered Max's scheme, I told a senior member of Taylor's team who I trusted, but it was too late since Max had already notified everyone that he was firing me and Ray would be taking my place.

When I started packing for my move out of Nash-evil, my health had deteriorated to the point where I feared I might not survive. The week prior to my move, Max showed up at my house unexpectedly and expressed regret for having trusted Albert. When he inquired if I would consider collaborating with him and Ray again, I firmly declined. He then mentioned a possibility of securing an extended license from John for Taylor's brand, but I had no faith in that claim, so I told him I was finished and would never work with him again. I think at this point he did not know about the mattress company firing him and his friends and he needed to secure my silence—but it was too late.

During this confrontation, Max's anger became palpable, which in turn frightened me. He insulted me, as he stormed out of my house with threats of ending my career. I was left shaken, fully aware of his vindictive nature and the power that he held.

Later that day, Max returned with Ray and demanded I hand

over my company stock to him so he could give it to Ray. When I refused, Max lunged at me until Ray intervened. Max threatened to "destroy me," and having experienced his temper before, I told him to leave my house immediately. He departed with a visibly upset Ray. To make matters worse, Max flatly refused to reimburse me for my forty thousand dollars in expenses from Hong Kong Fashion Week, including Jen's accommodation and our flights. I asked a lawyer friend of mine to pursue the money owed to me, believing that my attorney's skills could rival Max's ruthless legal tactics, unfortunately Max refused to pay me more than twenty thousand dollars for my expenses, causing me further financial harm.

After dedicating so much of my time to build Taylor's brand and combat her piracy, I found myself devastated by Max, Ray and John's actions. Then out of left field, Max wrongfully accused me of theft from bank accounts I never had access to, along with stealing files his lawyer already possessed. Those same files were also in Jen, my assistant's possession, yet she refused to acknowledge this, fearing Max's wrath. Max was trying to protect himself in the eyes of John, making it seem as though I was the one being dishonest. Ultimately, Max shut down the company and I was told he left all of the companies' debts unpaid.

The week before I departed from Nash-evil, I experienced two potential break-ins at my home, my car sustained damage, and a black SUV crept by my house each night, pausing in my driveway to unnerve me. Overwhelmed with fear, I gave away most of my furniture to a friend, to expedite my exit from Nashville. I made the decision to relocate as far away as possible. Gerry remained by my side until I boarded my flight to out of town and she stayed and waited for the truck that would gather my car and personal belongings.

The Truth Finally Came Out

Several years after I moved out of Nashville, I ironically received a set of articles from a friend of mine who still lived there. Max had been locked in a legal dispute with the mattress company for several years. At last, the truth about him emerged, validating my previous concerns. He was allegedly accused of providing substantial kickbacks and bribes to executives at the mattress company, which involved a shared purchase with Ray and his boss of a lavish four-bedroom, 2,766-square-foot waterfront house in Florida for $1.6 million, along with co-investing in a $110 thousand-dollar fishing vessel.

Here are some of the article titles sent to me:

Forbes Magazine Probe: Mattress Company Fraud Defendant Claims Retailer Has 'Unclean Hands' In Real Estate Conspiracy.

Nashville Business Journal: Mattress company accuses Nashville developer of bribery scheme, including jet trips and the Taylor Swift brand.

Since late 2017, the mattress company has been caught up in legal disputes with multiple defendants in the real estate industry, alleging a broad scheme of fraud, bribery, and kickbacks that spanned several years. Fresh from Chapter 11 bankruptcy, the major mattress retailer was focusing on resolving parts of its extensive lawsuit.

After negotiating a settlement, the company dropped its case against Max.

If only people had recognized my real struggle when I raised my concerns to Taylor's team, but once again my voice was ignored.

I felt that Nash-evil was driven by wealth, influence, and recognition, often at the expense of others. My blind faith in Max and my ambition to work with the biggest superstar in the world led to what should have been a remarkable experience, but unfortunately it was some of my darkest times in my life and career.

Although Taylor is often celebrated as a defender of women, I sadly did not see myself as one of her beneficiaries. Maybe if she had been more personally involved when I first created the clothing line for her, things would have ended differently. If I could convey one final message to Taylor, it would be to emphasize that I never compromised my values in the two years that I dedicated to her brand.

Reflecting on the past, I recognize that I lacked the necessary support and personnel to effectively handle Taylor's brand on my own, making that two year-long contracts with Max, impractical. Working for Taylor Swift was a true privilege, even though I dealt with considerable hurdles created by certain questionable individuals throughout this journey.

Successfully being the only individual to counteract the piracy efforts of Taylor and Keith in China is an accomplishment I look back on with immense pride. I feel a deep sense of satisfaction in the collections I created for her, along with the impressive graphics developed by my team.

CHAPTER 17:
The End of the Road?

A Moment of Self-Reflection

I can see what you're thinking by now: you believe I'm not very intelligent and I've faced a run of bad luck that surpasses anyone you know. You might also think that I've created much of the chaos swirling around me. This assessment holds some truth, and I frequently reflect on my earlier actions, wishing I had paused before acting without thinking. Had I done that, I might have forged a financially successful career for myself.

The reality is, throughout my journey in the fashion industry, I've been my own worst enemy at times. My inability to keep my mouth shut when I witnessed injustice has cost me dearly. Every time I saw sexual harassment, bullying, unethical business practices, or exploitation of workers' wages, something inside me compelled me to speak up. This compulsion has led to numerous job losses, legal battles, and professional setbacks that could have been avoided if I had simply looked the other way.

But here's the thing—if I had chosen to stay quiet, I probably wouldn't have had the opportunity to address the systemic problems in the garment center or voice my concerns about unethical business practices that plague the industry. My silence might have preserved my career, but it would have betrayed my conscience and potentially allowed others to suffer the same abuses I witnessed.

The Quest for Moral Clarity

My journey has been motivated by a relentless quest to explore the moral dilemmas of right and wrong in my professional life. In an industry where cutting corners and turning a blind eye to harassment are often considered normal business practices, I've made a conscious effort to align my actions with my own principles, even when it hurt me professionally.

This moral compass has been both my greatest strength and my most significant weakness. It gave me the courage to stand up to powerful men and women in the fashion industry and it also gave me the strength to walk away from potentially lucrative deals when they involved child labor or other unethical practices.

I have learned to accept my difficulties and imperfections, recognizing that they have shaped my evolution into a strong woman who chose to participate in an industry that is often inequitable to many. The scars from my battles—both the victories and defeats—have made me resilient in ways I never imagined possible when I first walked into Macy's training program as a naive young woman.

I take solace in the discomfort I caused to numerous individuals in this industry. Perhaps my small acts of defiance positively impacted a few people along the way. Maybe some of those colleagues I worked with found the courage to speak up because they saw me do it first. Maybe some of those factories improved their working conditions because they knew someone was watching. I'll never know for certain, but I choose to believe that my struggles weren't entirely in vain.

Why I Couldn't Walk Away

You might think I should have left the fashion industry long ago. The thought of abandoning the only profession I've ever known seemed unimaginable, though. Fashion wasn't just my career—it was my identity, my passion, and my creative outlet.

Despite the challenges, I derived genuine happiness from the design process. The opportunity to travel the world, meeting new people from different cultures and learning about their craftsmanship, enriched my life in ways no other career could have. When you've dedicated forty years to mastering a craft, walking away feels like abandoning a piece of your soul.

The Exhaustion of Constant Battle: So, is my career in fashion really over?

So, is my career in fashion really over?

I am exhausted from the constant struggles against deceivers, fraudsters, and the malevolent aspects of the fashion industry. Fighting the same battles over and over—takes a toll on your spirit. There's only so many times you can pick yourself up before you start to wonder if the fight is worth it.

Although I've always had faith in God's plan for my life, the aftermath of all my experiences has left me questioning what He truly wanted from me. Was I supposed to be a crusader for justice in an unjust industry? Or was I simply stubborn and naive, tilting at windmills when I should have been building a stable career?

The Cost of Integrity

My career has cost me dearly. The financial cost has been enormous—lost jobs, legal fees, missed opportunities, and the constant struggle to make ends meet because I refused to compromise my principles. The emotional cost has been even higher. The betrayals by people I trusted, like Lisa, Deb, and Rita, cut deep. The loneliness that comes from being the person who speaks up when everyone else stays silent has been overwhelming.

I'm frustrated because I know I possess talent and have so much more to contribute. I've created innovative designs, solved complex production problems, and built brands from the ground up. Yet, I've come to understand that I no longer fit in the industry, and perhaps I never truly did. The fashion industry rewards conformity, silence, and the ability to look the other way when convenient. These have never been my strengths.

A Message to Future Fashion Dreamers

I wrote this book for the aspiring fashion enthusiasts who believe that the fashion world is all about fun, glamour, and excitement. The reality is far more complex. The apparel industry can be ruthless, and it's flawed in fundamental ways that need to change. But despite all this, it can still be magical. There's nothing quite like the rush of seeing your designs in a store, or holding a garment you created and knowing that someone will feel beautiful wearing it.

My story lays bare the darker side of the apparel industry, and I truly hope it shields others from going through what I faced. But I don't want to discourage people who have a genuine passion for fashion from pursuing their dreams. Instead, I want to arm them with knowledge and realistic expectations.

Practical Advice

My suggestion to anyone entering the fashion industry:
Secure a reliable lawyer to draft and read your contracts

before you sign anything. The fashion industry is notorious for exploitative contracts. Don't trust handshake agreements or fake promises.

Always document your experiences, both good and bad. Keep copies of emails, take photos of working conditions, maintain detailed records of your contributions. This documentation will serve as a safeguard if you encounter wrongdoing.

Build a network of allies, but be careful about who you trust completely. Some of my greatest betrayals came from people I considered friends. Look for mentors who share your values, not just your ambitions.

Don't compromise your core values for career advancement. Yes, it may cost you opportunities in the short term, but maintaining your integrity is worth more than any job.

The Story Continues

Each time I believe my book is complete, another wild anecdote pops into my mind.

Did I tell you about the time I was the only white person at an all-Asian apparel company in New York City where my boss insisted that his employees learn to shoot AK-47's during our mandatory summer retreat? I courteously declined to participate in the bizarre weekend at a shooting range in upstate New York, where the plan involved managing automatic firearms while chatting about fall fashion styles.

Or the celebrity who demanded I redesign an entire collection because the shade of blue she had originally decided on, now reminded her of her ex-boyfriend's eye color?

Or the factory owner who tried to bribe me with a real diamond Rolex watch to approve substandard working conditions?

Or at 3 a.m., when a famous rapper reached out to me to fetch purple threads from a rug he liked at a downtown New York strip club for his upcoming fashion brand. He then attempted to give me $50,000 in cash as a reward, which I politely and groggily declined?

Oh, and one boss withheld my paycheck until I mediated his divorce agreement with his wife, because he thought I would side with him. I successfully negotiated the terms, leaving her delighted. He fired me.

In the garment center, there are attorneys who will advocate for you against clothing companies for their wrongdoings. However, many are unaware that these lawyers (often relatives) are frequently compensated by these exact clothing companies you are going after, so it's likely your case will be dismissed or never initiated at all.

The fashion industry is filled with characters so outrageous that fiction writers couldn't invent them. There's always another story to share. Each day in this industry brings new drama, new challenges, and new opportunities to witness the extremes of human behavior.

Final Reflections

As I conclude my story—and perhaps this phase of my life—I'm reminded that every ending is also a beginning. The fashion industry shaped me, challenged me, and ultimately revealed who I truly am beneath all the designer clothes and professional facades.

I am a fighter. I am someone who believes that doing the right thing matters more than doing the profitable thing. I am a woman who refused to be silenced, even when silence would have been easier. Whether these qualities make me a hero or a cautionary tale, I'll leave for others to decide.

What I know for certain is this: I have no regrets about speaking up, even when it cost me everything. The fashion industry may be done with me, but I'm not done with my story. Whatever comes next, I'll face it with the same determination that got me through four decades of garment center battles. Every failed venture, from my shapewear line to the Taylor Swift debacle, reinforced my understanding that success without integrity is hollow victory indeed.

The road may be ending, but the journey continues. And who knows? Maybe the best chapters are yet to be written.

CONCLUSION

Hope for Future Generations

Most importantly, I want to leave this industry better than I found it. The young people entering fashion today are more socially conscious, more globally aware, and more willing to demand ethical practices than my generation ever was. They have tools—social media, instant communication, global connectivity—that make it harder for abusers to operate in shadows and easier for victims to find support and solidarity.

The fashion industry needs these young idealists. It needs people who believe that beautiful clothes can be made without exploiting workers or damaging our planet, that creative vision doesn't require silencing dissent, that success can be achieved without sacrificing basic human decency. They will face the same temptations I faced—the pressure to conform, to stay quiet, to prioritize personal advancement over collective good. But they'll also have advantages I never had: awareness of these issues, legal protections that didn't exist in my early career, and a generation of allies who understand that business ethics and profitability are not mutually exclusive.

The Phoenix's Final Flight

My friends called me the Phoenix because I kept rising from the ashes of my repeated failures and missteps. But perhaps the metaphor was incomplete. The Phoenix doesn't just rise—it transforms. Each resurrection brings wisdom, strength, and a clearer understanding of purpose. The woman writing these final words is not the same person who began this journey forty years ago. She is scarred but not broken, disappointed but not defeated, financially poorer but spiritually richer.

I may never know if my battles were worth fighting or if my sacrifices achieved their intended purpose. What I do know is that I can sleep at night without the weight of compromised principles. I am prepared to meet whatever follows, confident in the knowledge that I have been tested under difficult circumstances and have proven my strength and resilience has only made me stronger.

As this chapter of my life closes, I'm grateful for the experiences. They made me who I am: a woman who knows the difference between right and wrong, who understands the true cost of speaking out, who refuses to be silenced by those who would prefer a more compliant world.

To those still fighting the good fight in fashion, I offer this encouragement: your voice matters, your conscience is not a liability, and your refusal to accept the unacceptable is not naive idealism— it's the foundation upon which a better apparel industry will be built.

The Phoenix has learned to fly. The question now is not where she's been, but where she's going next.

MY WORK THROUGHOUT THE YEARS

Launched and designed *Avon Style*, one of the largest contributors to Avon's bottom line

Launched and designed Nicole Miller Lingerie

Trading Places

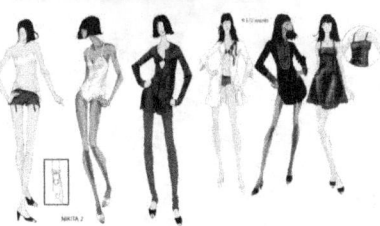

Designed the lingerie for Usher's *Trading Places* video

Future 50 Top Designers

MY DESIGN SHOWROOM

THE FRONT ROW
My Own Brand

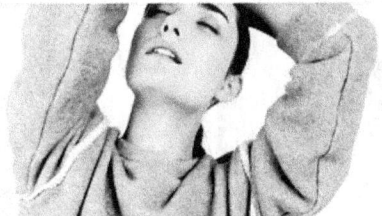

The Front Row

PICK YOUR COLOR & SHOP

IVORY   GREY   TAUPE   BLACK

DESIGNED TO FLATTER EVERY FIGURE,
FOLLOWING THE NATURAL CURVE OF A WOMAN'S BODY.

THE FRONT ROW
My Own Brand

THE FRONT ROW
Mongolian Natural Cashmere

ECO CASHMERE LUXE
SWEATER COAT
100% CASHMERE
TFR3001

COST : $146
MSRP : $250

ECO CASHMERE LUXE
DOLMAN SWEATER
100% CASHMERE
TFR1036

COST : $180
MSRP : $270

ECO CASHMERE LUXE
TURTLENECK
100% CASHMERE
TFR1035

COST : $210
MSRP : $400

ECO CASHMERE
LUXE SURPLUS
100% CASHMERE
TFR1034

COST : $180
MSRP : $280

JESSICA SIMPSON
LAUNCH

JESSICA SIMPSON INTIMATES & SLEEPWEAR
S/S 2009 COLLECTION
2 / 25 DELIVERY

LABELS AND HANGTAGS:

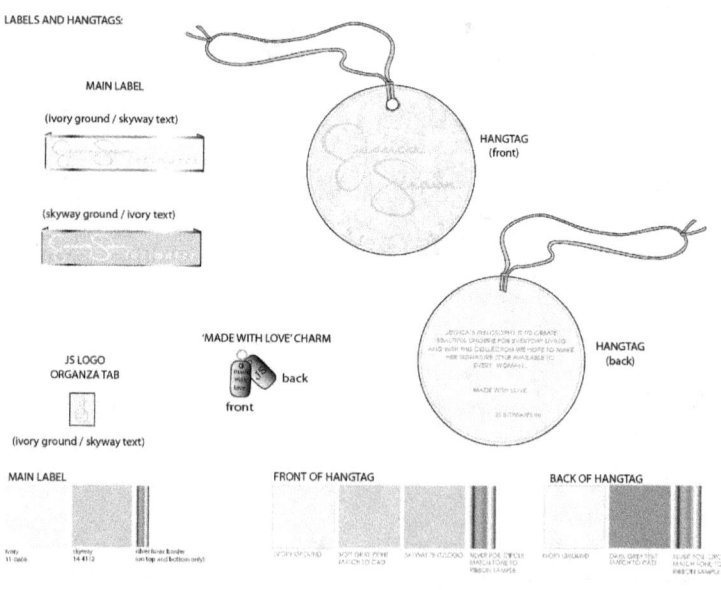

MAIN LABEL

(ivory ground / skyway text)

(skyway ground / ivory text)

HANGTAG
(front)

JS LOGO
ORGANZA TAB

'MADE WITH LOVE' CHARM

front

back

HANGTAG
(back)

(ivory ground / skyway text)

MAIN LABEL

FRONT OF HANGTAG

BACK OF HANGTAG

JESSICA SIMPSON
LAUNCH

MY SHAPEWEAR

MY SHAPEWEAR DESIGNS

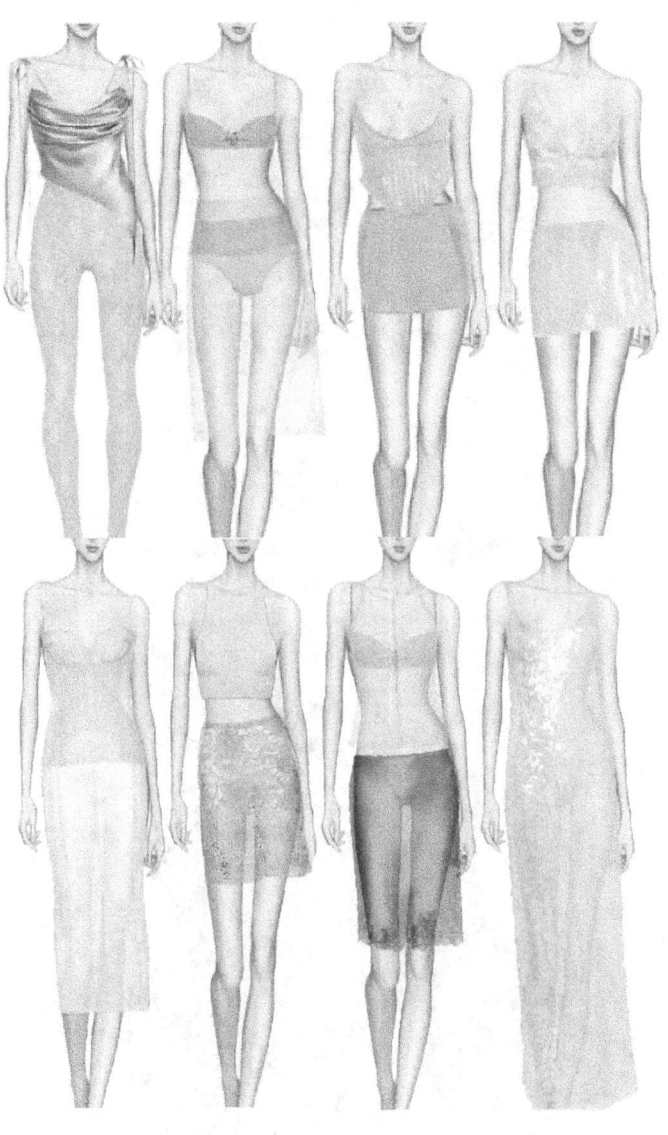

RALPH LAUREN
LINGERIE LAUNCH
*I was the first to put men's waistbands on
women's underwear*

SLIMINIZER
My Shapewear Brand
2009

FEATURED IN OPRAH

THE OPRAH MAGAZINE, July 2009 Issue
Adam Glassman Style Report

SLIMINIZER
My Shapewear Brand
2009

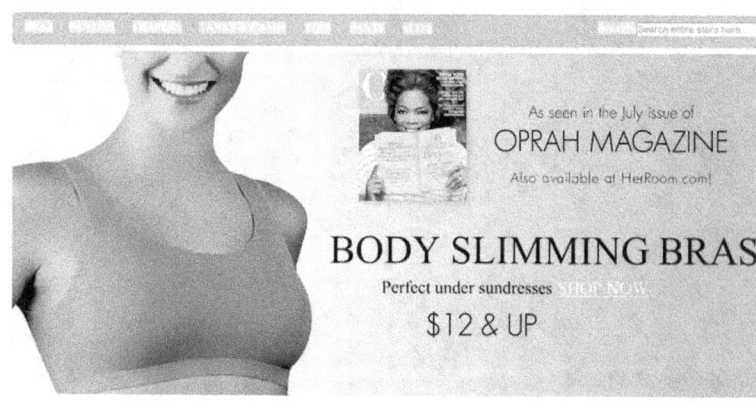

As seen in the July issue of
OPRAH MAGAZINE
Also available at HerRoom.com!

BODY SLIMMING BRAS
Perfect under sundresses SHOP NOW
$12 & UP

Extra TV

Get Sexy with Sliminizer

SLIMINIZER
on the Jumbotron

My shapewear company Sliminizer Jumbotron Time...

TYRA BANKS
Showroom Idea

TYRA BANKS
Lingerie

Back View

Back View

Koi Lace Print

Back View

Back View

Back View

LACES OUT

CAMI
Style # 11105

BODY SUIT
Style # 15105

SLIP
Style # 16105

PANTY
Style # 12105   HEAVY CONTROL,
WAIST CINCHED

LAVENDER

TOMMY HILFIGER
Designed the Launch of Tommy Hilfiger
Sleep & Loungewear

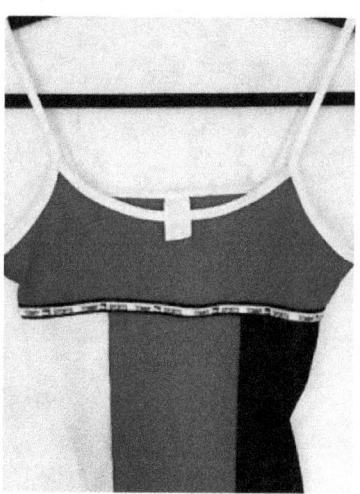

TOMMY ☰ HILFIGER

introducing women's robes and sleepwear

merchandising update • holiday • pre spring

MY ACTIVEWEAR DESIGNS

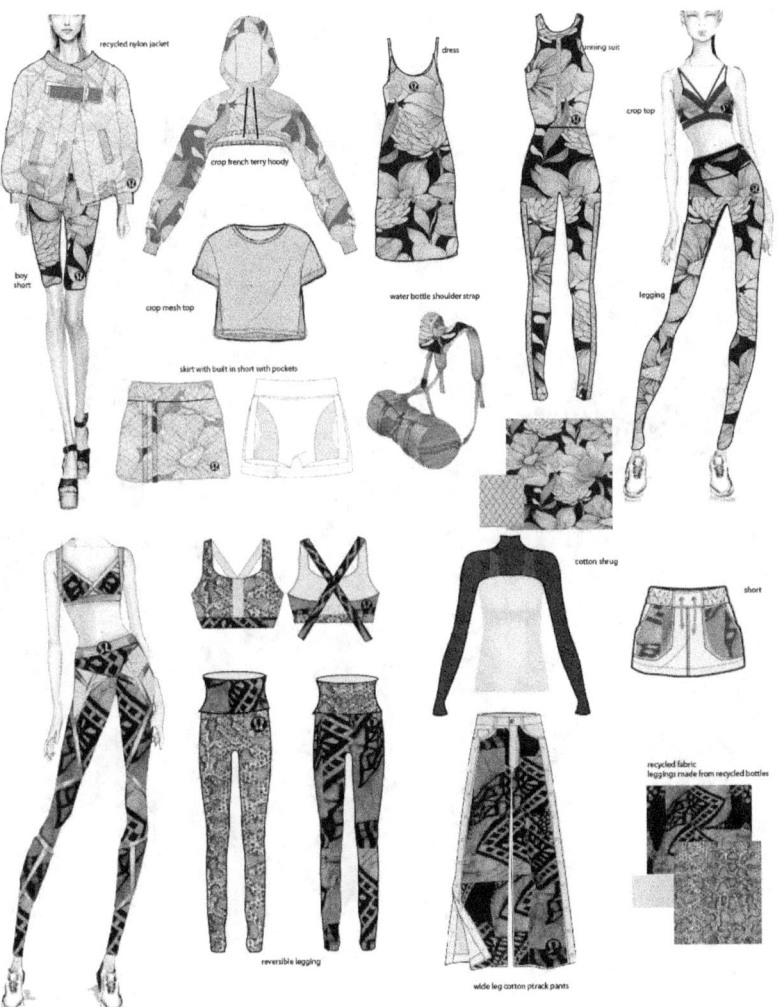

VINTAGE HEARTLAND
Sustainable Packaging

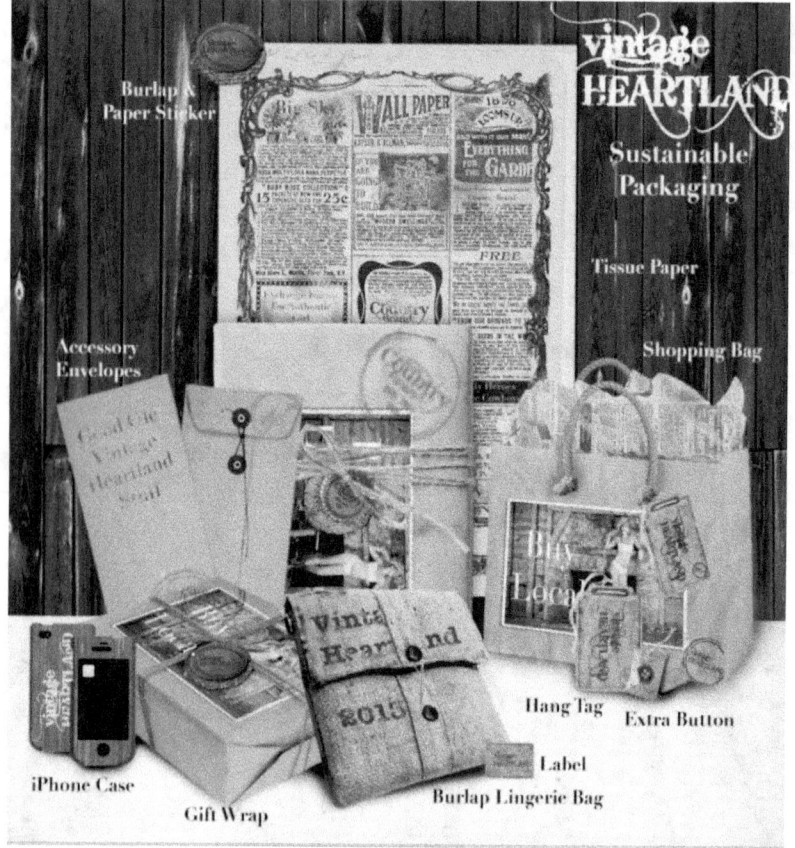

VINTAGE HEARTLAND
Catalog

Designed Vintage Heartland's Lingerie & Sleepwear Launch
At the Shenzen Fair – 30,000 people showed up

Designed Vintage Heartland's Lingerie & Sleepwear Launch
The only lingerie ever launched on CCTV

KEITH URBAN
China Launch

TAYLOR SWIFT
Hong Kong Fashion Week Launch

TAYLOR SWIFT
Hand Sketches

TAYLOR SWIFT
China Press

Taylor Swift Line Shows in Hong Kong

Taylor Swift's newly launched clothing line for the Chinese market staged a small runway show amid the booths of garment manufacturers.

By AMANDA KAISER [+]   JANUARY 18, 2016, 7:07AM

Taylor Swift's clothing line launches in Hong Kong

TAYLOR SWIFT
China Launch

Daily Mail

TAYLOR SWIFT
China Launch

PRESS
Nashville Business Journal

Kate Liegey, left, showing her Vintage Heartland lingerie line in China
VINTAGE HEARTLAND

THE WALL STREET JOURNAL.

	$70		$142

KING The Trump administration will provide Ukraine with intelligence for long-range missile strikes on Russia's energy ir

BUSINESS

Taylor Swift Counters Knockoffs in China

In an effort to thwart counterfeiters, singer to sell branded clothing with JD.com, Alibaba

By Laurie Burkitt [Follow] *and Alyssa Abkowitz* [Follow]
Updated July 21, 2015 7:32 pm ET

⌲ Share   A A Resize   💬 31

CELEBRATING 115 YEARS OF WOMEN'S WEAR DAILY

FASHION / FASHION SCOOPS

Taylor Swift Line Shows in Hong Kong

Taylor Swift's newly launched clothing line for the Chinese market staged a small runway show amid the booths of garment manufacturers.

By AMANDA KAISER   JANUARY 18, 2016, 7:07AM

HUFFPOST

Hot Damn! Lingerie Goes Country

I don't know about you, but the idea of attending a fashion show much less Fashion Week in NYC, makes me start to look for a rafter from which I can hang myself. This would be my worst case scenario:

 By Relentless Bill Robinson, Contributor

... well then, like most guys, I think I'd be most agreeable to attend.

Kate Liegey is the founder of Vintage Heartland, a country-oriented lingerie company built by Liegey to be green, sustainable and worker-friendly.

And, of course being lingerie, inherently ... sexy.

≡ Inside⦿etail

NEWS / MARKETS

Fashion range fights Taylor Swift fakes

As a countermeasure to fake Taylor Swift branded products being sold in Asia, the singer's new fashion range was launched for the Chinese market during <u>Hong Kong Fashion Week</u>. Fashion insiders see the move as a bid to have stores in the international market, and particularly in Mainland China, pick up the collections first released by <u>Heritage66</u> exclusively on eCommerce outlets <u>Tmall</u> (Alibaba) and <u>JD.com</u>, according to <u>Women's Wear Daily</u>.

For Nov. 2013: Vintage Heartland lingerie line ›

Lovely lingerie is always welcome in a woman's wardrobe.

Renee Minus White

The showcased items of clothing were pulled from both the spring and fall merchandise collections and the pieces included styles like cropped T-shirts, form-fitting mini-dresses and tight pants emblazoned with the singer's name or initials.

Sources tell Women's Wear Daily the apparel had "a sporty feel to it", and one stand-out dress appeared to be inspired by American high school varsity jackets.

Taylor's partnership with Heritage66 began last year after the company started selling her clothing on JD.com and Alibaba's Tmall platforms. Heritage66 executives have very distinct objectives with the merchandise collections - they want to capitalize on Taylor's popularity in China while trying to keep pirated and fake items off the market there.

There are a number of products selling overseas with Taylor's likeness printed on them. Kate Liegey, chief operating officer of Heritage66, informed WWD she was prompted to host the runway show at Hong Kong Fashion Week because Taylor's merchandise has reached a "phenomenal" level of sales success since it debuted on Tmall and JD.com.

"We realized that the demand was just incredible for the store business and we decided to do this show," Liegey said.

"Everybody wants the product line."

CHILD LABOR

Child Labor Factory China

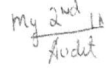

my 2nd Audit

that Failed!

Do To bough condition

Delivering Confidence Worldwide

COMPLIANCE MONITORING VISIT RECAP

Client: I		
Vendor Name: I	Underwear Co., Ltd.	Name of Vendor Rep. Present: No information
Factory Name:	Underwear Co., Ltd.	Name of Factory Rep. Present: I
Factory Address: B		, Guangdong, China
Report#: SZSCH090025		
Audit Date: May 10-11, 2010		Auditor: Jack

Compliance Summary

	Yes		No		Yes		No
Wages & Hours	Yes	X	No	First Aid & Medical Services	Yes	X	No
Benefits	Yes	X	No	Electrical Safety & Protective Equipment	Yes	X	No
Child Labor	X	Yes		No	Canteen	X	Yes		No
Legal Issues & Licenses	X	Yes		No	Boiler Operation		N/A	
Ventilation & Sanitation	X	Yes		No	Dormitories	Yes	X	No
Fire Safety Practices		Yes	X	No	Environment	X	Yes		No
Labor Practices (Freedom of association, force labor, disciplinary & discrimination)					Yes	X	No

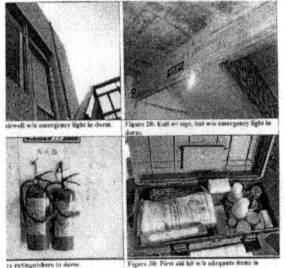

stirwell w/o emergency light in dorm.   Figure 28: Exit w/ sign, but w/o emergency light in dorm.

re extinguishers in dorm.   Figure 30: First aid kit w/o adequate items in dorm.

Violations comments:

1. Found some workers' wages did not meet the legal minimum wage standard of local area on Feb. & Mar. 2010. Factory paid overtime compensations less than the legal requirement.
2. Payroll register did not include regular working hours, overtime hours, regular wages and overtime wages.
3. Workers did not have at least one day off in seven in Feb. & Mar. 2010.
4. Workers did not have time for rest periods other than meals.
5. Employees did not sign their time records.
6. Found workers' total working hours exceeded 60 hours per week in Feb. & Mar. 2010.
7. Found workers' overtime hours exceeded 3 hours per day, and 36 hours per month, but without government's overtime permit.
8. Statutory holidays were not paid to piece rate workers as legal requirement.
9. Factory did not provide social insurances to all employees, and also without government's certificate to prove the factory had bought right rate of social insurances.
10. Rmb50 or Rmb100 meal fee would be deducted from wages per month.
11. No transportation was provided to workers.
12. Found minor workers performed overtime works from 9:30pm to 11:00pm.
13. Found some employees' I.D. card copies were expired.
14. Found some personnel files were without experience and education.
15. Employees were deducted Rmb100 to Rmb500 as deposit via review the payroll of Mar. 2010.
16. Found money deduction rules were posted in the factory, and money deductions were happened via review the payroll of Mar. 2010.
17. No hand soap, towels or dryers and toilet paper were provided in toilets.
18. Drinking water was not tested annually.
19. Found the inspection room with semi-finished products on the 6th floor was without fire extinguisher equipped.
20. No records to show that employees were trained at regular intervals in fire safety, emergency evacuation, and the use of fire extinguisher.
21. Found some fire extinguishers were without outside qualified organization's annual inspection.
22. Found some fire extinguishers were out of pressure.
23. No fire sprinkler system was available.
24. Found some exits and stairwells were without emergency lights equipped.
25. Found some doors that were not exits without labeled such "Not-An-Exit".
26. No records to show that evacuation drills were conducted twice per year in the factory.
27. Found pictures of drills were without dates indicated.
28. No evacuation plan was posted at the 1st floor of production building.
29. Found some evacuation plans were with wrong direction, and without "you are here" mark, location of extinguishers and hydrants.
30. Factory did not have a system in place to address severe injuries (such as an agreement with the local hospital, transportation arrangements, etc.)

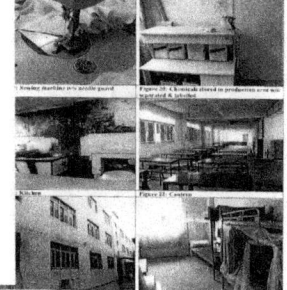

Sewing machine w/o needle guard   Figure 29: Chemicals stored in production area w/o segregated & labeled.

Kitchen   Figure 25: Canteen

Figure 27: Restroom   Figure 36: Bedroom

CHILD LABOR

From:
Date: Fri, 30 Apr 2010 09:09:35 -0400
To: Kate Liegey <katel@

Cc:
Subject: FW: Alert Notification of Child Labor in the audit of
         -JCSZ10A20317-I
27,April,2010

Please be advised that a Child Labor was found at the above
mentioned Facility. Please be advised that the factory will be
deactivated and I need to know what process the May and June
orders are in pertaining to fabric, because these orders will have
to be moved to another approved facility. Attached is a PO
Report for Reference.

Please advise.

International Customs Compliance Coordinator

EMAILS

Seth

> ----- Original Message -----
> From: kate liegey
> To:
> Sent: Wed Oct 03 10:38:57 2007
> Subject: Re: Fw: Mariah Carey
>
> Kate, not only was Mariah impressed with your boards and product, but she
> doesn't want anyone else to do her line! you are one talented girl!
> thanks for making me look good
> seth

 Londell

From:
To:

Wed, Nov 25, 2009 at 5:42 AM ☆

Hi Kate:
I always believed in you and wanted to support your dream. My law practice and media business
has me consumed. I did not want to prevent Howard, Gus, Stephon or anyone from maximizing
their investment in you therefore I pulled back but my heart and my support for you will not waiver.
Moreover, I adore you so let's keep in touch regularly. I am here for you and we remain friends!!!

Happy Thanksgiving!!!

Xoxo
Londell

EMAILS
Jessica Simpson CFO

Jeff
From
To: ki

Sat, Jul 12, 2008 at 12:50 AM ☆

Thanks for the nice note Kate. You guys have been exceptional partners inspite of the challenges we put in front of you (. etc. etc.). It sounds horrible that I didn't call you very much, but its not for lack of interest. You and   earned our trust right from the start, with the first beautiful samples and boards you presented. I not only think you are extremely talented, but you and   are extremely nice people to work with together. I knew by staying out of your hair it was the right thing to do. Get some well deserved rest and don't hesitate to let me know if you need anything. I wish you the most sucessful launch of any imtimates company ever, and I hope you will soon see the fruits of your hard work very soon.

All my best,
Jeff

--- On **Mon, 2/27/12, Ted**   Industry Insider

From: Ted
Subject: Re: [BODY]   -- 2/20/12
To: "Kate"
Date: Monday, February 27, 2012, 4:46 PM

I am glad life introduced us.

On Mon, Feb 27, 2012 at 4:40 PM, Kate <   wrote:
 :) u made my day

 Sent from my iPhone

 On 27 Feb 2012, at 04:14 p.m., Ted `   vrote:

      Your already rich. Your one talented lady.

      Sincerely,

      Ted

EMAILS
Oprah Picked Sliminizer
for her Magazine

--- On **Tue, 6/16/09, Jen**

From: Jenny
Subject: Re: Thank you for helping me bring my dream to life!!
To: "kate liegey"
Date: Tuesday, June 16, 2009, 9:04 AM

So glad it all worked out Oprah and Gail loved it!
Xo
Jenny

On 6/15/09 5:32 PM, "kate liegey" wrote:

Jenny, Thank you so much for picking Sliminizer for the July issue. I cannot tell you how it feels to finally see it in print. I started this company with $650.00 and a wing & a prayer!
I truly believe that if you have passion, hard work and alot of faith ʻu can achieve anything!
take a peek at the website
www.sliminizer.com <http://www.sliminizer.com>

again, Thank you from the bottom of my heart!

Kate Liegey

Sliminizer.com <htto://www.Sliminizer.com>

EMAILS
Tyra Banks

Subject: RE: Tyra
Date: Mon, 26 Jun 2006 12:36:59 -0700
From: ;@handprintent.com>
To: "kate liegey" ·

Kate,

 forgive the lag on response as we are not trying to hold up
the process,

I DO want to let you know that all other deals we are
exploring include you in our
minds. Tyra really feels comfortable and confidant in your
abilities, as do Benny and I, and we want to ensure that you
know that what we have found in you we don't want to loose,
but we understand that our process is not as fast and
seamless as we would like it to be. I will see what I can do to
push things along.

Thanks Kate,

Jean

www.ingramcontent.com/pod-product-compliance
Lightning Source LLC
Chambersburg PA
CBHW070902130626
46555CB00001B/7